Ninth Edition

Drugs in Perspective:

Causes, assessment, family, prevention, intervention, and treatment

Richard Fields, Ph.D.

Owner/Director, FACES Conferences, Inc.
(www.facesconferences.com)

McGraw Hill Education

DRUGS IN PERSPECTIVE: CAUSES, ASSESSMENT, FAMILY, PREVENTION, INTERVENTION, AND TREATMENT, NINTH EDITION

Published by McGraw-Hill Education, 2 Penn Plaza, New York, NY 10121. Copyright © 2017 by McGraw-Hill Education. All rights reserved. Printed in the United States of America. Previous editions © 2013, 2010, and 2007. No part of this publication may be reproduced or distributed in any form or by any means, or stored in a database or retrieval system, without the prior written consent of McGraw-Hill Education, including, but not limited to, in any network or other electronic storage or transmission, or broadcast for distance learning.

Some ancillaries, including electronic and print components, may not be available to customers outside the United States.

This book is printed on acid-free paper.

2 3 4 5 6 7 8 9 LCR 21 20 19 18 17

ISBN 978-0-07-802865-6
MHID 0-07-802865-5

Chief Product Officer, SVP Products & Markets: *G. Scott Virkler*	Director, Content Design & Delivery: *Terri Schiesl*
Vice President, General Manager, Products & Markets: *Marty Lange*	Program Manager: *Jennifer Shekleton*
	Content Project Managers: *Jane Mohr, Katie Klochan, and Sandra Schnee*
Vice President, Content Design & Delivery: *Kimberly Meriwether David*	Buyer: *Laura M. Fuller*
Managing Director: *Gina Boedecker*	Design: *Studio Montage, St. Louis, MO*
Brand Manager: *Penina Braffman*	Content Licensing Specialist: *Melisa Seegmiller*
Director, Product Development: *Meghan Campbell*	Cover Image: *Getty Images/Tim Teebken*
Product Developer: *Anthony McHugh*	Compositor: *SPi Global*
Marketing Manager: *Meredith Leo*	Printer: *LSC Communications*

All credits appearing on page or at the end of the book are considered to be an extension of the copyright page. pg. xvii: © Hero Images/Getty Images; pg. xviii: © Getty Images/iStockphoto

Library of Congress Cataloging-in-Publication Data

Names: Fields, Richard, author.
Title: Drugs in perspective : causes, assessment, family, prevention,
  intervention, and treatment / Richard Fields, Ph.D., Owner/Director, FACES
  Conferences, Inc. (www.facesconferences.comm).
Description: Ninth Edition. | Dubuque : McGraw-Hill Education, 2016. |
  Revised edition of the author's Drugs in perspective, 2013.
Identifiers: LCCN 2016012992 | ISBN 9780078028656 (alk. paper)
Subjects: LCSH: Drug abuse. | Alcoholism. | Drug abuse—Prevention. |
  Alcoholism—Prevention. | Drug abuse—Treatment. | Alcoholism—Treatment.
Classification: LCC HV5801 .F42 2016 | DDC 362.29/17—dc23 LC record available
at https://lccn.loc.gov/2016012992

The Internet addresses listed in the text were accurate at the time of publication. The inclusion of a website does not indicate an endorsement by the authors or McGraw-Hill Education, and McGraw-Hill Education does not guarantee the accuracy of the information presented at these sites.

mheducation.com/highered

I dedicate this book to my son, Matthew Fields.

Brief Contents

SECTION I   Understanding Substance Abuse 1

CHAPTER 1   Putting Drugs in Perspective 2

CHAPTER 2   Why People Use and Abuse Drugs and Alcohol 23

CHAPTER 3   Drug-Specific Information 58

CHAPTER 4   Assessment of Substance Abuse, Dependence,
and Addiction 121

SECTION II   Family 137

CHAPTER 5   Substance Abuse and Family Systems 138

CHAPTER 6   Parents and Family: At-Risk Factors for Substance
Abuse 158

CHAPTER 7   Growing Up in an Alcoholic Family System 180

SECTION III   Motivation, Intervention, Co-occurring Disorders,
Prevention, Recovery, and Relapse Prevention 205

CHAPTER 8   Motivation and Change 206

CHAPTER 9   Intervention 223

CHAPTER 10   Prevention of Substance Abuse Problems 240

CHAPTER 11   Disorders Co-occurring with Substance Abuse 264

CHAPTER 12   Alcohol/Drug Recovery, Co-Occurring Disorders, Suicide,
and Alcohol/Drugs 293

CHAPTER 13   The Problem of Relapse: Relapse Prevention (RP) 317

Index I-1

Contents

Preface xvi

SECTION I   Understanding Substance Abuse 1

CHAPTER 1   *Putting Drugs in Perspective* 2

Outline of Chapter 1 2

Objectives 2

Introduction 3

THE LACK OF UNDERSTANDING OF ALCOHOL/DRUG ABUSE 3

Failed Approaches to Alcohol/Drug Abuse: "Scare Tactic" 3

Supply Side Approach—Neglect of the Demand Side 4

The Myth of the "Simple," Magical Solution 5

Alcohol: The Most "Problematic" Drug 5

ALCOHOL-RELATED PROBLEMS: "BINGE DRINKING" ON COLLEGE CAMPUSES 6

Binge Drinking and Other Age Groups 7

Sexual Assault and Rape on College Campuses—The Role of Alcohol 8

Drinking and Driving among Young Drivers 8

Alcohol and Violence among the General Population 10

Intimate Partner Violence 10

Alcohol-Related Injuries and Deaths 10

Systemic Problems of Drugs 10

The U.S. Federal Government's Role in the Drug Problem 11

Racist Approaches to the Drug Problem 11

Socioeconomic Inequities that Undermine the American Dream 13

Academic Failure and the Role of the U.S. Educational System 14

Denial and Minimization of Alcohol/Drug Problem in the Family 15

EMERGING ISSUES AND TRENDS IN DRUG USE—HIGH SCHOOL STUDENTS—THE 2014 MONITORING THE FUTURE HIGH SCHOOL SURVEY 15

Medical Marijuana 16

Research on Medical Marijuana Is Limited 17

THE MAJOR PERSPECTIVES ON ALCOHOL/DRUG USE 18

The Moral-Legal Perspective 18

The Medical-Health Perspective 18

The Psychosocial Perspective 18

The Social-Cultural Perspective 19

The Fifth Perspective—Your Perspective Questionnaire 19

Moral-Legal Perspective 19

Medical-Health Perspective 19

Psychosocial Perspective 20

Personal Perspective 20

A Perspective of Hope 20

In Review 21

Discussion Questions 21

References 22

CHAPTER 2   *Why People Use and Abuse Drugs and Alcohol: A Better Understanding of Models, Theories, and Contributing Factors 23*

Outline of Chapter 2 23

Objectives 23

Introduction 24

OUR INNATE DRIVE TO ALTER CONSCIOUSNESS 24

MODELS, THEORIES, AND CONTRIBUTING FACTORS OF SUBSTANCE USE AND ABUSE 24

Tension and Stress Reduction 25

Trauma and Substance Use Disorders (SUDs) 26

The Disease Model of Alcoholism 27

Genetic Model of Alcoholism—Adoption and Twin Studies 31
  Adoption Studies 31
  Twin Studies 31

Personality Traits and Personality Disorders 31
  Addictive Personality 31
  Personality Disorders 32

Attachment and Substance Abuse 32

Self-Medication Motive 34

Depression, Anxiety, and Affective (Feeling) Disorders 34
  Mood and Affect Disorders 34

Family Model 35

Adolescence 36

Poor Self-Concept 36

OTHER FACTORS THAT CONTRIBUTE TO SUBSTANCE ABUSE 39

Boredom and Altered States 39

Impulsivity and Disinhibition 41

Social Learning Theory 41

Sociocultural Models 43

Psychoanalytic Models—Psychoanalytic Meaning 43
  Alcohol/Drugs as Power 44
  Alcohol/Drugs as Self-Destruction 45
  Alcohol/Drugs in Seduction and Sexuality 46

Existential Issues 46

Poor Future Orientation and Hope 47

Hopelessness 47

Pessimism and Optimism 49

APPENDIX 50

Other Theories and Models 50

In Review 52

Discussion Questions 53

References 54

Case Study 2.1 Trauma and Addiction 28

Case Study 2.2 Sexual Violation and Addiction 29

Case Study 2.3 Borderline and Narcissistic Personality Disorders with Substance Use Disorders 33

Case Study 2.4 Adolescents and Alcohol/Drugs 37

Case Study 2.5 Debra 38

Case Study 2.6 Lyn: Marijuana and Seduction 46

Case Study 2.7 Poor Future Orientation 48

CHAPTER 3   *Drug-Specific Information: Drugs on the Street Where You Live 58*

Outline of Chapter 3 58

Objectives 58

DRUGS IN OUR SOCIETY 59

A New Era for Marijuana: Its Medical Usage 60
  Financial and Future Implications for Medical Marijuana 61

Lollipops to Vaporizing Marijuana 61

Resurgence of Marijuana Use by the Young and Old 61

Energy Drinks 61

Crystal Methamphetamine 62

Populations Using Methamphetamine 62

Methamphetamine Use by Adolescents 63

You Can Identify Methamphetamine Users by . . . 63

MDMA (Ecstasy) 64

OxyContin Abuse 64

Heroin 66

Inhalants 67

DEFINITIONS OF TERMS 67

Physical Dependence 67

Withdrawal 67

Psychological Dependence (Formerly, Habituation) 67

Tolerance 68

Cross-Tolerance 68

Synergism 68

Antagonism 68

Routes of Administration 69

Set and Setting 69

DEFINITION OF ADDICTION 70

Drug Absorption, Distribution, and Elimination 71

CLASSIFICATION OF DRUGS 73

Narcotic Analgesics 73

Heroin 74

Brief History of the Narcotic Analgesics 74

Routes of Administration 75

Major Effects 75

Hazards 76

Tolerance 76

Withdrawal 76

Opiates and Pregnancy 77

Central Nervous System Depressants 77

Alcohol 77

Brief History of Alcohol 77

Estimates of Alcoholism 79

Major Effects 79

Sobering Up 80

Tolerance 80

Stage 1 Withdrawal Symptoms 80

Stage 2 Withdrawal Symptoms 81

Related Illnesses 81

Fetal Alcohol Syndrome 81

Antabuse 81

Barbiturates 82

Medical Uses 82

Estimates of Use and Addiction 83

Routes of Administration 83

Major Effects 83

Barbiturates and Sleep 83

Barbiturates and Pregnancy 83

Tolerance 83

Withdrawal 84

Overdose Signs and Symptoms 84

Barbiturates Used with Other Drugs 85

Methaqualone 85

Tranquilizers 86

Medical Uses 87

Estimates of Use 87

Routes of Administration 87

Major Effects 88

Tolerance 88

Dependence and Withdrawal 88

Addiction Potential with Alcoholics/Addicts 88

Central Nervous System Stimulants 89

Amphetamines 89

Overview 89

Street Names for Amphetamines 89

Estimates of Use 90

Routes of Administration 90

Major Effects 90

Adverse Effects 90

Dependence and Withdrawal 91

Bootlegged Amphetamines 91

Cocaine 91

Brief History of Cocaine 91

Street Names for Cocaine 92

Estimates of Use 92

Routes of Administration 92

Major Effects 93

Adverse Effects 93

Tolerance and Withdrawal 94

Cocaine Additives 95

Tobacco 95

Diseases Related to Smoking Tobacco 95

Health Consequences 95

Hallucinogens 95

Definition 95

LSD 96

Brief History of LSD and Other Hallucinogens 97

Estimates of Use 98

Routes of Administration 98

Major Effects 98

Adverse Effects 98

Tolerance and Dependence 99

Cannabis Sativa 99

Street Names 99

Brief History of Marijuana 99

Estimates of Use 101

Medical Uses 101

Routes of Administration 101

Major Effects 101

Increased Potency of Marijuana 102

Adverse Effects 103

Damage to the Respiratory System 103

Immune System Effects 103

Reproductive System Effects 104

Brain System Effects 104

Impairment of Maturation Process 104

Marijuana and Driving 104

Inhalants 104

Brief History 105

Route of Administration 105

Available Forms of Inhalants 106

Major Effects 106

Tolerance and Dependence 106

Acute Adverse Effects 107

Long-Term Effects 107

Phencyclidine 107

Street Names for PCP 108

Estimates of Use 108

Routes of Administration 108

Major Effects 108

Adverse Effects 109

Accidents 109

Violence 109

Tolerance and Dependence 110

ATHLETES AND DRUGS 110

Steroids 110

Brief History 110

Terminology 111

Major Effects 111

Adverse Effects 112

Amphetamines 112

Chewing Tobacco 113

Other Drugs/Alcohol in Sports 114

In Review 115

Discussion Questions 118

References 119

CHAPTER 4   *Assessment of Substance Abuse, Dependence, and Addiction 121*

Outline of Chapter 4   121

Objectives 121

Introduction 122

DIAGNOSTIC CATEGORIES 122

A Behavioral Definition of Addiction 122

ASSESSMENT STAGES OF ALCOHOL AND DRUG USE 123

SET AND SETTING 123

Alcohol/Drug Use—A Progressive Disease 124

Addiction 124

VULNERABILITY TO RELAPSE 126

ASSESSMENT FOR RELAPSE 126

Denial—A Problem in Accurate Assessment 126

IDENTIFICATION OF ADOLESCENT ALCOHOL/
    DRUG PROBLEMS 127

ALCOHOL/DRUG ASSESSMENT 129

CONSEQUENCES OF ALCOHOL/
    DRUG USE 131

ALCOHOL/DRUGS AND SUICIDE 131

In Review 135

Discussion Questions 136

References 136

Case Study 4.1 The Marijuana Search 130

Case Study 4.2 Alcohol, Depression, and Suicide 134

SECTION II   Family 137

CHAPTER 5   *Substance Abuse and Family
                Systems* 138

Outline of Chapter 5 138

Objectives 138

Introduction 139

FAMILIES AS SYSTEMS 139

FAMILY RULES 141

IMBALANCED VERSUS *DYSFUNCTIONAL* 141

Rigid Family Systems 142

Ambiguous Family Systems 142

Overextended Family Systems 142

Distorted Family Systems 142

Entitled Family Systems 143

SATIR'S FAMILY PATTERNS OF
    COMMUNICATION 143

FAMILY SYSTEM ROLES 144

Wegscheider-Cruse's Alcoholic/Addict Family
    System Survival Roles 144

Family Roles Played Out at the Dinner Table 147

Five Styles of Managing Anxiety 147

Enabling Behavior 147

STAGES IN FAMILY RECOVERY FROM
    SUBSTANCE-ABUSE PROBLEMS 149

Denial 151

   *Denial Transaction Between Mary and Her
      Sister-in-Law, Maureen 152*

Anger 152

Bargaining 153

Feeling 155

Acceptance 155

In Review 155

Discussion Questions 156

References 156

Case Study 5.1 The Lost Child 146

Case Study 5.2 Enabling Behavior 149

Case Study 5.3 A Bargain That Doesn't Work 153

CHAPTER 6   *Parents and Family: At-Risk Factors
                for Substance Abuse* 158

Outline of Chapter 6 158

Objectives 158

Introduction 159

EARLY ATTACHMENT WITH PARENTS 159

Abandonment Depression 161

Impact of Early Abandonment on Adult
    Interpersonal Relationships 161

TRAITS AND TEMPERAMENT: AT-RISK FACTORS
    FOR SUBSTANCE ABUSE 162

Adoptees: At-Risk for Substance Abuse 163

PARENTAL SUPPORT AND CONTROL 163

SHAME AND IMBALANCED PARENTING 164

Shame and Feelings 168

Adolescent Sexual Identity and Shame 168

Sexual Violation and Shame 169

Drugs, Sex, and Shame 169

PARENTAL IMBALANCE AND BOUNDARY
    SETTING 169

Boundary Inadequacy 171

Boundary Ambiguity 171

Triangulation—Another Boundary Issue 172

PARENTS' USE/ABUSE OF ALCOHOL AND
    DRUGS 173

Criticism, Anger, and Blame 173

FAMILY COHESION, FLEXIBILITY,
    AND COMMUNICATION
    CLARITY 174

Other Obstacles to Reaching Parents
    and Family 174

Parents' Shame 175

COMPASSION, SELF-COMPASSION,
    AND MINDFULNESS 175

In Review 176

Discussion Questions 177

References 177

CHAPTER 7   *Growing Up in an Alcoholic*
                Family System 180

Outline of Chapter 7 180

Objectives 180

Introduction 181

THE ADULT CHILDREN OF ALCOHOLICS
    MOVEMENT 181

CHARACTERISTICS OF ADULT CHILDREN
    OF ALCOHOLICS 182

GROWING UP IN AN ALCOHOLIC HOME AS
    POST TRAUMATIC STRESS
    DISORDER 183

CHILDHOOD IN AN ALCOHOLIC HOME 186

IDENTIFICATION OF CHILDREN OF
    ALCOHOLIC FAMILIES 186

DENIAL OF FEELINGS IN AN ALCOHOLIC
    FAMILY 187

PERSPECTIVE OF THE CHILD
    IN AN ALCOHOLIC FAMILY 187

FAMILY DISEASE MODEL 188

ALCOHOLISM/DRUG ADDICTION—IMPACT ON
    MARRIAGE 189

ACA IN RELATIONSHIPS 189

ACA Define Self Through Others 189

The Disengaged ACA 190

Atypical Depression 190

Codependency 190

Boundary Inadequacy 191

Overattachment and Overseparation 191

Codependent Dances 193

RECOVERY FOR ADULT CHILDREN OF
    ALCOHOLICS 193

Inherited Family Belief Systems 193

Overview of ACA Recovery 193

Powerlessness in the Alcoholic Family System 194

Feeling Awareness 194

Identifying Feelings for ACA 194

Grief Work 197

Group Psychotherapy 199

In Review 201

Discussion Questions 203

References 204

Case Study 7.1 The ACA and Post traumatic Stress Disorder 184

Case Study 7.2 Rejection Sensitivity 195

Case Study 7.3 Difficulty in Making Decisions 196

Case Study 7.4 Letter to Parents from a Recovering Alcoholic and ACA about the Parents' Alcoholism 198

Case Study 7.5 Interpersonal Relationships 200

SECTION III Motivation, Intervention, Co-occurring Disorders, Prevention, Recovery, and Relapse Prevention 205

CHAPTER 8 *Motivation and Change* 206

Outline of Chapter 8 206

Objectives 206

Introduction 206

CHANGE 207

  Common Defense Components of Resistance to Change 208

  Denial and Delusion: Blocks to Seeing the Need for Change 209

  Change—"Mindful Acceptance" 209

  Procrastination 209

  Exertion: An Essential Element of Change 209

CHOICE MAKING—FAMILY OF ORIGIN 210

MOTIVATIONAL INTERVIEWING 211

Client-Centered Motivational Interviewing 213

Effective Motivational Strategies 214

Active Ingredients of Effective Brief Counseling 214

In Review 220

Discussion Questions 221

References 221

Case Study 8.1 Contemplative and Action Stages 215

CHAPTER 9 *Intervention* 223

Outline of Chapter 9 223

Objectives 223

INTERVENTION 223

Interventions at Various Stages of the Alcohol/Drug Use Continuum 223

  Stage 1—Nonuse Interventions 224

  Stage 2—Initial Contact Interventions 224

  Stage 3—Experimentation Interventions 225

  Stage 4—Interventions at the Integrated Stage 225

  Stages 5 and 6—Interventions at the Excessive Use and Addiction Stages 226

Obstacles to Interventions 226

Intervention Services 226

Intervention Approaches 229

Professional Intervention Assistance 229

Intervention as a Caring Response 229

Goals of Intervention 230

Family Interventions 230

Candidates for Intervention 230

Stages of Formal Intervention 231

  Assessment 231

  Preintervention 232

  Intervention 235

  Postintervention 239

In Review 239

Discussion Questions 239

Reference 239

Case Study 9.1 Intervention Without Proper Assessment 232

CHAPTER 10 *Prevention of Substance Abuse Problems* 240

Outline of Chapter 10 240

Objectives 241

Introduction 241

EARLY PREVENTION APPROACHES 241

ALTERNATIVE ACTIVITIES AS A PREVENTION
APPROACH 243

Alternatives Are Actively Pursued by the
Individual 244

Alternatives Are Acceptable, Attractive, and
Attainable 244

Alternatives Use Mentors and Role Models 244

Alternatives Integrate Self-Concepts 244

PREVENTION APPROACHES OF THE
1980s 245

SCHOOL-BASED PREVENTION CURRICULA 246

Empowerment 247

Goal Setting 247

Capability Development 247

KEY COMPONENTS OF A PREVENTION
PROGRAM 248

Address Community Needs 248

Include Youth in Prevention Planning 248

Promote Proactivity 248

Develop a Long-Term Perspective 248

PROGRAMS AIMED AT AT-RISK YOUTH 249

RISK FACTORS FOR SUBSTANCE ABUSE 251

RESILIENCY 252

EMOTIONAL INTELLIGENCE 255

DOMAINS OF PREVENTION 255

PREVENTION PROGRAMS AND PREVENTION
EMPHASIS 256

Developmental Assets Model 256

HIGH-RISK YOUTH AND CSAPs 257

PREVENTION AND SPECIAL POPULATIONS 257

People of Color and Other Minorities 257

College Students 258

Older Adults 258

Prevention and the Family 259

In Review 259

Discussion Questions 263

References 263

CHAPTER 11　　*Disorders Co-occurring with
Substance Abuse* 264

Outline of Chapter 11 264

Objectives 264

Introduction 265

DEFINITION OF A CO-OCCURRING
DISORDER 265

SERIOUS MENTAL ILLNESS (SMI) AND
SUBSTANCE ABUSE 266

AFFECTIVE (FEELING) DISORDERS
AND SUBSTANCE USE DISORDERS 268

The Difference Between a Depressive Mood
and a Depressive Disorder 268

Denial and Depression 269

Categories of Mood Disorders 270
　Major Depression 271
　Persistent Depressive Disorder (Dysthymia) 272
　Atypical Depression 272
　Organic Depression 273
　Bipolar Disorder 274
　Mood-Cycling Disorder 276

AFFECTIVE DISORDERS AND SUICIDE 277

PERSONALITY DISORDERS AND SUBSTANCE
USE DISORDERS 277

Personality Traits versus Personality Disorder 277

Personality Disorder and Chemical Dependency
Disorder 278

Antisocial Personality Disorder 279
　*Antisocial Personality Disorder and Chemical
　Dependency 279*

Childhood Precursors of Antisocial Personality Disorder 280

Denial, Alcohol/Drugs, and Antisocial Personality Disorder 280

Borderline Personality Disorder and Chemical Dependency 283

Narcissistic Personality Disorder 285

Trauma and Substance Abuse Disorder (SUD) in Adolescents 286

TREATMENT OF DISORDERS CO-OCCURRING WITH SUBSTANCE ABUSE 288

Adolescent Co-occurring Disorders Complicates Treatment 289

In Review 290

Discussion Questions 291

References 291

Case Study 11.1 Major Depression and Addiction 270

Case Study 11.2 Eeyore Syndrome 271

Case Study 11.3 Persistent Depressive Disorder (Dysthymia) 272

Case Study 11.4 Atypical Depression 273

Case Study 11.5 Bipolar Disorder 275

Case Study 11.6 Depression and Withdrawal Symptoms 280

Case Study 11.7 Alcoholism 281

Case Study 11.8 Antisocial Personality Traits 283

Case Study 11.9 Borderline Personality Disorder 286

Case Study 11.10 Narcissism and Cocaine 287

CHAPTER 12 *Alcohol/Drug Recovery, Co-Occurring Disorders, Suicide and Alcohol/Drugs 293*

Outline of Chapter 12 293

Objectives 293

Introduction 294

NEED FOR SUPPORT 294

Self-Help Meetings/Alcoholics Anonymous 294

Advantages of AA as a Recovery Model 295

Resistance to Attending AA and Other Self-Help Groups 295

Social Support Empowers Recovery—Voluntary Mutual Help Association 296

Online Social Support Networks (OSSN) 296

Rational Recovery 296

STAGES OF ALCOHOL/DRUG RECOVERY 297

Withdrawal Stage (0–15 days) 298

Honeymoon Stage (15–45 days) 298

The Wall Stage (45–120 days) 298

Adjustment Stage (120–180 days) 298

Resolution Stage (180–360 days) 298

COUNSELING AND CHEMICAL DEPENDENCY 299

Early Phases: Safety and Stabilization 299

Breaking Through Denial 299

Common Denial Defenses 299

Affect (Feeling), Recognition, and Modulation 300

Group Therapy 301

Family Treatment 301

An Effective Alcohol/Drug Recovery Strategy 302

Boundaries with Difficult Patients 304

TREATMENT OF CO-OCCURRING DISORDERS 305

Counseling for Co-occurring Disorders 305

Breaking Denial—Educating and Empowering Patients 305

Developing Skills in Patients Who Have Co-occuring Disorders 306

Feelings and Emotional Buildup 306

Cognitive-Behavioral Approaches 306

Treatment Compliance—Medications 307

Suboxone (Buprenorphine and Naltrexone) to Reduce Opioid Cravings 308

The Family of the Client Who Has Co-occurring Disorders 308

SUICIDE AND ALCOHOL/DRUGS 309

Clues to Suicidal Intentions 311

In Review 314

Discussion Questions 315

References 315

CHAPTER 13   *The Problem of Relapse: Relapse Prevention (RP) 317*

Outline of Chapter 13 317

Objectives 317

Introduction 317

CAUSES OF RELAPSE 318

  Stress 320

  Interpersonal Conflict 320

  Reactivity 320

  Physiological Causes 320

  Cognitive Causes 320

  Behavioral Causes 320

  Affective Causes 321

  Psychological Causes 321

  Environmental Causes 321

  Spiritual Causes 321

  Treatment-Related Causes 322

Treatment Causes 322

DEFINITION OF RELAPSE 322

  High Relapse rate 323

DEFINITION OF RELAPSE PREVENTION (RP) 323

RECOGNIZING THE SIGNS OF RELAPSE— RELAPSE PRONE AND RECOVERY PRONE BEHAVIORS 323

VULNERABILITY TO RELAPSE 324

Applying HALTS 324

  Hungry 325

    Addressing Hunger 325

  Angry 325

    Would You Rather Be Right or Happy? 325

    Addressing Anger 326

  Lonely 326

    Cool Loneliness 326

    Addressing Loneliness 326

  Tired 326

    Addressing Tiredness 326

  Sick 326

    Addressing Being Sick 327

Cravings and Urges 327

  Time 327

  Place 327

  Things 328

  People 328

RELAPSE PREVENTION STRATEGIES 328

  Interpersonal and Social Recovery Support System 328

  Health and Physical Well-Being 328

  Cognitive, Emotional, and Spiritual Self 328

AA Serenity Prayer as a Relapse-Prevention Technique 329

MINDFULNESS: A TOOL FOR RELAPSE PREVENTION 330

Addiction: "Land of the Hungry Ghosts" 330

Definitions of Mindfulness 331

Mindfulness-Based Behavioral Relapse Prevention (MBRP) 333

Mindfulness and Relapse Prevention— Shifting from Reacting to Skillful Responding 333

In Review 334

Discussion Questions 335

References 335

Index I-1

Preface

This text provides a co-ordinated integration of information to help you better understand drugs (which includes alcohol), and drug use, abuse, and addiction. My more than 30 years experience in clinical work with substance abusers, addicts/alcoholics, and, more important, their families frame this textbook.

This text is designed for use in college-level courses in health and human services and health science courses, such as substance prevention education; chemical dependency; substance abuse; alcohol, tobacco, and other drug education and prevention; and addictive and compulsive behavior. The material in this book meets the needs of students with its clear and concise style, while also being a valuable resource to professionals who continue their education in health and counseling.

✷ New to This Edition

The major change to this edition is the creation of a new and separate chapter (Chapter 13), which puts a major focus on relapse, relapse prevention, and mindfulness. For this edition, we have also added chapter overviews at the beginning of each chapter.

McGraw-Hill create

✷ McGraw-Hill Create™

Craft your teaching resources to match the way you teach! With McGraw-Hill Create, create.mheducation.com, you can easily rearrange chapters, combine material from other content sources, and quickly upload content you have written like your course syllabus or teaching notes. Find the content you need in Create by searching through thousands of leading McGraw-Hill textbooks. Arrange your book to fit your teaching style. Create even allows you to personalize your book's appearance by selecting the cover and adding your name, school, and course information. Order a Create book and you'll receive a complimentary print review copy in 3 to 5 business days or a complimentary electronic review copy (eComp) via email in minutes. Go to www.mcgrawhillcreate.com today and register to experience how McGraw-Hill Create empowers you to teach your students your way.

Required=Results

McGraw-Hill Connect®
Learn Without Limits

Connect is a teaching and learning platform that is proven to deliver better results for students and instructors.

Connect empowers students by continually adapting to deliver precisely what they need, when they need it and how they need it, so your class time is more engaging and effective.

Course outcomes improve with Connect.

Exam Scores	80.4% / 74.7%
Pass Rates	83.7% / 72.9%
Attendance Rates	92.5% / 74.5%
Retention Rates	87.5% / 71.1%

■ With Connect ■ Without Connect

88% of instructors who use **Connect** require it; instructor satisfaction **increases** by 38% when **Connect** is required.

Using **Connect** improves passing rates by **10.8%** and retention by **16.4%**.

Analytics

Connect helps students achieve better grades

	A	B	C	D	F
With Connect	36%	29.5%	22%	4.3%	8.2%
Without Connect	22.2%	22.3%	25.6%	9.8%	20%

Based on McGraw-Hill Education Connect Effectiveness Study 2013

Connect Insight®

Connect Insight is Connect's new one-of-a-kind visual analytics dashboard—now available for both instructors and students—that provides at-a-glance information regarding student performance, which is immediately actionable. By presenting assignment, assessment, and topical performance results together with a time metric that is easily visible for aggregate or individual results, Connect Insight gives the user the ability to take a just-in-time approach to teaching and learning, which was never before available. Connect Insight presents data that empowers students and helps instructors improve class performance in a way that is efficient and effective.

Students can view their results for any **Connect** course.

Mobile

Connect's new, intuitive mobile interface gives students and instructors flexible and convenient, anytime–anywhere access to all components of the Connect platform.

Adaptive

THE FIRST AND ONLY ADAPTIVE READING EXPERIENCE DESIGNED TO TRANSFORM THE WAY STUDENTS READ

More students earn **A's** and **B's** when they use McGraw-Hill Education **Adaptive** products.

SmartBook®

Proven to help students improve grades and study more efficiently, SmartBook contains the same content within the print book, but actively tailors that content to the needs of the individual. SmartBook's adaptive technology provides precise, personalized instruction on what the student should do next, guiding the student to master and remember key concepts, targeting gaps in knowledge and offering customized feedback, and driving the student toward comprehension and retention of the subject matter. Available on smartphones and tablets, SmartBook puts learning at the student's fingertips—anywhere, anytime.

Over **4 billion questions** have been answered, making McGraw-Hill Education products more intelligent, reliable, & precise.

STUDENTS WANT

SMARTBOOK®

95% of students reported **SmartBook** to be a more effective way of reading material

100% of students want to use the Practice Quiz feature available within **SmartBook** to help them study

100% of students reported having reliable access to off-campus wifi

90% of students say they would purchase **SmartBook** over print alone

95% reported that **SmartBook** would impact their study skills in a positive way

Mc Graw Hill Education

*Findings based on a 2015 focus group survey at Pellissippi State Community College administered by McGraw-Hill Education

⚹ Electronic Textbook Option

This text is offered through VitalSource for both instructors and students. Vital-Source is an online resource where students can purchase the complete text online at almost half the cost of a traditional text. Purchasing the eTextbook allows students to take advantage of VitalSource's web tools for learning, which include full text search, notes and highlighting, and email tools for sharing notes between classmates. To learn more about VitalSource options, contact your sales representative or visit www.vitalsource.com.

⚹ Acknowledgments

I would like to thank the instructors who reviewed the previous edition and helped lay the groundwork for the improvement and changes in the ninth edition. A special thanks goes to the development editors, Reshmi Rajeesh, Keerthana Panneer, and Erin Guendelsberger, McGraw-Hill, and all other book team members who helped this revision come to fruition.

Nelson Louis Henning
Cedarville University

Tiffany Lee
Western Michigan University

David A. O'Donnell
Governors State University

Kathleen Wikman
Walla Walla University

Victor Aeby
East Carolina University

Carrie Canales
West Los Angeles College

Sandra Croswaite
Pierce College

Mitchell Earleywine
University of Albany

Cathy Follett
Bluffton University

Renee Bobbie Jaeger
Northern Virginia Community College

Darrell Kniss
Stephen F. Austin State University

Kenneth R. Kubicek
Lindenwood University—Belleville Campus

Roland Lamarine
California State University, Chico

Char Perryman
Pierce College

Richard Fields

Understanding Substance Abuse

❖ **Chapter 1:**

Putting Drugs in Perspective

❖ **Chapter 2:**

Why People Use and Abuse Drugs and Alcohol

❖ **Chapter 3:**

Drug-Specific Information

❖ **Chapter 4:**

Assessment of Substance Abuse, Dependence, and Addiction

Putting Drugs in Perspective

Outline of Chapter 1

Introduction

The Lack of Understanding of Alcohol/Drug Abuse
  Failed Approaches to Alcohol/Drug Abuse: "Scare Tactic"
  Supply Side Approach—Neglect of the Demand Side
  Alcohol: The Most "Problematic" Drug

Alcohol-Related Problems: "Binge Drinking" on College Campuses
  Alcohol and Violence among the General Population
  Systemic Problems of Drugs

Emerging Issues and Trends in Drug Use—High School Students—The 2014 Monitoring the Future High School Survey
  Medical Marijuana

The Major Perspectives on Alcohol/Drug Use
  The Moral-Legal Perspective
  The Medical-Health Perspective
  The Psychosocial Perspective
  The Social-Cultural Perspective
  The Fifth Perspective—Your Perspective Questionnaire
  A Perspective of Hope

Objectives

1. Describe the impact of "scare tactics" and other failed approaches to alcohol/drug abuse.
2. Explain the lack of understanding of alcohol/drug abuse.
3. Discuss alcohol-related problems on college campuses.
4. Explain systemic problems of alcohol/drug use in the United States.
5. Highlight the most recent trends in drug use by high school students.
6. Identify the possible dimensions of medical marijuana use, the impact of the usage, and the areas that require research.
7. Name, describe, and give an example of each of the four major perspectives on alcohol/drug use.

❧ Introduction

This textbook is designed to help you identify, clarify, and comprehend the many confounding variables that influence substance use, abuse, and dependence. Chapter 1 emphasizes the problems in perception that have misdirected efforts toward an effective approach to alcohol/drug prevention, intervention, and treatment efforts. The chapter is designed to stimulate both classroom discussion and the exploration of your own biases, viewpoints, experiences, and personal opinions—to help you put **"drugs in perspective."**

I recommend keeping notes and answering the questions at the end of this chapter (Fifth Perspective) to help you understand your personal perspective. I also suggest keeping a journal after each chapter listing information, ideas, and thoughts and anything of special interest to you. When you finish reading the chapter, note any changes in your perspective.

❧ The Lack of Understanding of Alcohol/Drug Abuse

Historically, we have failed in our responses to the alcohol/drug problem in the United States. Alcohol, in particular, has become integrated into the fabric of the mainstream American lifestyle, causing many people to minimize its impact and its cost to our society. It has been estimated that business and industry lose more than $136 billion each year for alcohol-related reasons: reduced productivity; time lost at work because of absenteeism, illness, and/or personal problems; and increased health care costs. The following section identifies major problems related to alcohol and drug abuse, alcoholism, and drug addiction.

Failed Approaches to Alcohol/Drug Abuse: "Scare Tactic"

From the 1930s to the 1960s, public and private responses to alcohol/drug abuse caused tremendous damage, which we are still trying to overcome. These approaches were riddled with personal emotional reactions and political biases, which denied the real dimensions of the problem. Scare tactics—a politically biased approach that alienated young people—began in 1937 and continue to this day, in a variety of forms. For example, the following marijuana scare story appeared in the July 1937 issue of *American* magazine:

> An entire family was murdered by a youthful marijuana addict in Florida. When officers arrived at the home, they found the youth staggering about in a human slaughterhouse. He had ax murdered his father, mother, two brothers, and a sister. He seemed to be in a daze. He had no recollections of having committed the multiple murders. The officers knew him ordinarily as a sane, rather quiet young man; now he was pitifully crazed. They sought the reason. The boy said he had been in the habit of smoking something with youthful friends called "muggles," a childish name for marijuana.

The co-author of this article was Henry J. Anslinger, then commissioner of the Federal Bureau of Narcotics and Dangerous Drugs. After reviewing this single case and a study of the paranoid schizophrenic reactions of heavy hashish smokers in India, Anslinger expounded on the evils of marijuana. He described marijuana as a drug that would consistently result in violent, aggressive, and paranoid behavior, as evidenced in the Florida case.

Another scare tactic example is the 1936 movie *Reefer Madness*. This movie's serious intent to discourage marijuana use backfired because the situations were so absurd that audiences viewed it as a humorous farce.

Those using scare tactics assumed that if young people were frightened by adverse reactions to drug use, they would be too frightened to use the drug. For the young people who perceived drug use as incongruent with their values, goals, and lifestyle, scare tactics were effective. For most young people, however, scare tactics proved to be an ineffective approach because much of the information was exaggerated, overgeneralized, or sensationalized. As a result, young people did not perceive the source of such information as credible. What young people heard did not bear any resemblance to what most users experienced. All in all, scare tactics alienated young people, heightened their curiosity, and increased rather than decreased their experimentation with drugs.

In the late 1960s and early 1970s, President Richard Nixon declared his famous war on drugs. Even though an all-out warlike effort was needed and money was readily available to fight drug addiction, no one knew how to tactically fight this war on drugs. Drug use had spread to epidemic proportions. Also, President Nixon was not the ideal general for this war, having already alienated young people during another war, in Vietnam.

During this same time period, the government was also duped by treatment programs that mismanaged funds for treatment. There were few experts and little, if any, clear direction to the battle. The failure of Nixon's war on drugs left a bitter taste in the mouths of government funding sources. Money for treatment programs was cut each year thereafter, and the focus shifted to prevention. Realizing that the war was being lost, the government developed a new, more positive approach: If we can reach the kids before they become dependent on drugs, we will prevent a future generation of drug casualties.

These early prevention efforts emphasized drug-specific information. The assumption was that if young people were to receive credible drug-specific information, they would then wisely decide not to use drugs. Unfortunately, the reverse held true. Drug-specific approaches heightened curiosity and alleviated the fears associated with drug use, resulting in increases of drug use by young people.

Supply Side Approach—Neglect of the Demand Side

Throughout the ensuing years, U.S. administrations continued to fail to develop a comprehensive and cohesive drug policy. Most of the administrations put a major emphasis on the supply side of the drug problem and significantly neglected the demand side. Emotional and political biases of these administrations caused them to be blind to the many causes of drug dependence and resulted in an adherence to "a simple, magical solution" that was politically advantageous. Administration after administration adhered to a strong supply-side approach, without addressing the reasons for the demand that perpetuated the problem. The Clinton administration repeated this cycle, and the George W. Bush administration was distracted by international issues. All these administrations have focused on the politically expedient supply-side approach of trying to stop drug trafficking, with little effort toward the demand side of the problem.

The Myth of the "Simple," Magical Solution

During the Reagan administration, First Lady Nancy Reagan was influential in shaping the U.S. approach to the "drug problem." Although her intentions were noble and well intended, the "Just Say No" approach illustrates a simplistic view to a complicated problem. Suggesting that adolescents and young adults can overcome the drive to alter consciousness, peer influence, the disease of alcoholism/addiction, and the many factors that influence alcohol/drug abuse by "just saying no" minimizes the obstacles to be overcome.

Often a complicated, emotionally laden problem elicits a simple solution. A simple solution is easily understood and immediately reduces anxiety, shame, and emotional discomfort. However, a simple solution will not resolve the insidious, multifaceted problems of substance abuse and addiction. Drug use, abuse, and dependence are not easily understood. Mrs. Reagan made the same mistake that many people make. Too often, people search for that simple solution to an epidemic problem. Philosopher H. L. Mencken remarked that "any solution to a complex problem, that is simple, is usually wrong."

Having spent more than 25 years working with individuals and their families, I still struggle case by case to try to find some common patterns and new insights into what works in treatment. I am constantly questioning what may have caused alcohol/drug problems and how best to engage, motivate, and approach clients with drug abuse and dependence. For some, the solution is abstinence and strong involvement in self-help groups; for others, it is a different path. For many, it is the acceptance of the "disease," while others label their alcohol/drug use as an "allergy" or a problem with tolerance. Some individuals can stay sober for a month or two and then experience a "binge relapse," while others can abstain for several years. Many, through the help of Alcoholics Anonymous, Narcotics Anonymous, a sponsor, and a recovery support group, can maintain sobriety as a life choice.

Alcohol: The Most "Problematic" Drug

Alcohol abuse and alcoholism are major problems that are often minimized or overlooked as not being a part of the "war on drugs." Administrations have been distracted, focusing on drugs, often forgetting to include alcohol as a drug.

> Excessive alcohol consumption is the third leading preventable cause of death in the United States and is associated with multiple adverse health consequences, including liver cirrhosis, various cancers, unintentional injuries, and violence. (Centers for Disease Control 2004)

Alcohol is the most problematic drug we know of today in terms of the sheer numbers of people it affects. Estimates indicate that there are more than 12 million alcoholics in the United States and that a significant number of other people meet the criteria for alcohol abuse and alcohol dependence. (See Chapter 4 for diagnostic criteria for substance abuse and substance dependence.)

⋈ Alcohol-Related Problems: "Binge Drinking" on College Campuses

This section continues to highlight some of the many problems that are often influenced by alcohol consumption. For instance, binge drinking on college campuses often spirals into other high-risk behaviors and the end results cause damage to the individual and others. Some alcohol-related problems on college campuses include the following:

- Academic difficulties
- Problems in attending class and completing assignments
- Property damage
- Accidents and injuries
- Anger, fights, violence, and road rage
- Interpersonal and social problems
- Psychological issues and problems (e.g., depression)
- Other high-risk behaviors (e.g., drinking and driving)

According to the Centers for Disease Control and Prevention: Morbidity and Mortality Weekly Report, excessive alcohol use is the third leading preventable cause of death in the United States and more than half of alcohol consumed by adults in the United States is in the form of binge drinks. Such studies and statistics continue to prove the same point, as evidenced in the 2009 National Survey on Drug Use and Abuse. The survey found that for those aged 18–30, this group ranked highest in binge use and heavy alcohol use with the 21- to 25-year-olds as the highest binge drinkers and heavy alcohol users. (See Figure 1.1.)

> Binge drinking is at once the most important public health problem on our campuses and a critical challenge to institutional mission. (Keeling 2002)

Binge drinking is a significant problem on college campuses. Research indicates that 40 to 45 percent of college students binge drink. At least half of the sexual assaults on college campuses involve alcohol consumption by the perpetrator, the victim, or both.

Alcohol use on college campuses was first reported to be a problem over a half century ago (Straus and Bacon 1953). Today, studies clarify the extent of the problems of binge alcohol use on college campuses. The Harvard School of Public Health's College Alcohol Study (CAS) found that 40 to 45 percent of college students binge drink. They also found an alarming increase in the prevalence of frequent binge drinking among women—from 5.3 percent in 1993 to 11.9 percent in 2001 for women enrolled in all-women colleges, with a smaller increase in co-ed colleges. More underage students on college campuses reported having been drunk on three or more occasions in the past 30 days.

In his article "The Time to Purge Binge Drinking Is Now" (2005), Dwayne Proctor, Ph.D., highlights some personal cases of binge drinking on college campuses.

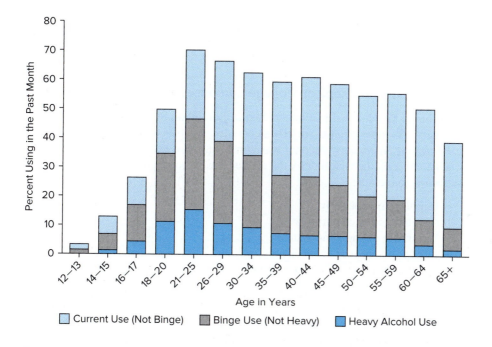

FIGURE 1.1 *Current, Binge, and Heavy Alcohol Use among Persons Aged 12 or Older, by Age: 2009*
SOURCE: National Survey on Drug Use and Health 2010.

> At Colorado State University, 19-year-old Samantha Spady died after downing
> between 30 and 40 drinks. At nearby University of Colorado, 18-year-old
> freshman Lynn Gordon Bailey died in what was reported to be a hazing incident
> involving alcohol. And at the University of Oklahoma, 19-year-old Blake
> Hammontree was found dead with a blood alcohol level more than five times
> the state's legal driving limit.

The first 6 weeks of the school year are certainly "party time" as the freshman class
is inaugurated into the ritual of fraternity and sorority life, which often involve binge
alcohol abuse. Many parents send their children off to college proud of this important rite of passage but fearful of how their 18-year-old daughters and sons will cope
with the freedom, the peer influence, the availability of alcohol and drugs, the party
atmosphere, and sexuality, let alone the classes and schoolwork.

> The first 6 weeks of the school year have been cited as the most dangerous with
> respect to drinking behavior due to the increased stress levels associated with a
> new environment and the pressure to be accepted by a peer group. (Bonnie and
> O'Connell 2004)

Binge Drinking and Other Age Groups

Unfortunately binge drinking problems, although very pervasive in college age students, is not limited to this age group category. According to the Center of Disease
Control (2012) survey, six Americans die each day from "alcohol poisoning" due to
binge drinking. It is reported that 76 percent of those deaths are aged 35 to 64, and a
majority of them are men.

Surprisingly the report also indicated that people over the age of 65 binge drink more often than the other age groups. However, the middle age group consumes more alcohol than any other group.

Sexual Assault and Rape on College Campuses—The Role of Alcohol

According to the National Institute of Justice Survey on Sexual Assault on Campus (2010) and a number of other studies, alcohol use is most commonly associated with sexual assault on campus. Alcohol was consumed in at least half of college sexual assaults, either by the victim or by the perpetrator, or both. The survey outlines other risk factors to include:

- Sorority membership
- Numerous sexual partners
- Freshman or sophomore status
- Higher occurrence on weekends
- Increased risk at off-campus parties

Male college students who are intoxicated at high levels exhibit impaired sexual function but have increased physical aggression. Female college student (victim) intoxication increases vulnerability to penetration but does not reduce odds of injury (Testa et al. 2004). This stresses how intoxication by male and/or female college students increases vulnerability to rape, physical aggression, and/or sexual assault.

The frequencies with which women reported getting drunk since entering college increase the odds of being incapacitated sexual assault victims and are positively associated with being a victim of both physically forced and incapacitated assault. However, voluntary use of other illicit drugs (other than marijuana) was not associated with experiencing incapacitated sexual assault since entering college.

Another factor, the frequency with which women attended fraternity parties since entering college, was positively associated with being a victim of incapacitated sexual assault. At least half of the sexual assaults on college campuses involve alcohol consumption by the perpetrator, the victim, or both (Abbey 2002). (See Table 1.1 for further examination of the consequences of drinking.)

Sexual assault is defined as any act that includes forced touching or kissing, verbally coerced intercourse, or physically forced vaginal, oral, or anal penetration. Rape is any behavior that involves some type of vaginal, oral, or anal penetration due to force or threat of force, a lack of consent, or an inability to give consent due to age, intoxication, or mental status (Abbey 2002).

A Harvard School of Public Health Alcohol Survey of randomly selected women in 119 colleges found that approximately 1 in 20 (4.7 percent) women reported being raped. Even more astounding is that almost three-quarters of these women (72 percent) were intoxicated at the time of the rape.

Drinking and Driving among Young Drivers

Drinking alcohol and driving continues to be a major problem as evidenced by the many traffic fatalities while people are under the influence of alcohol. The relative

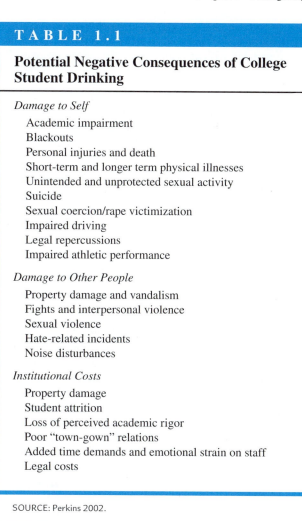

T A B L E   1 . 1

Potential Negative Consequences of College Student Drinking

Damage to Self

    Academic impairment

    Blackouts

    Personal injuries and death

    Short-term and longer term physical illnesses

    Unintended and unprotected sexual activity

    Suicide

    Sexual coercion/rape victimization

    Impaired driving

    Legal repercussions

    Impaired athletic performance

Damage to Other People

    Property damage and vandalism

    Fights and interpersonal violence

    Sexual violence

    Hate-related incidents

    Noise disturbances

Institutional Costs

    Property damage

    Student attrition

    Loss of perceived academic rigor

    Poor "town-gown" relations

    Added time demands and emotional strain on staff

    Legal costs

SOURCE: Perkins 2002.

risk of a fatal single-vehicle crash with blood alcohol (BAC) levels of 0.08 to 0.10 percent varies from 11 percent (for drivers aged 35 and older) to 52 percent (for male drivers aged 16 to 20). The highest driver fatality rates where alcohol is involved are found among the youngest drivers.

Factors contributing to young drivers' greater crash risk include the following:

- A lack of driving experience
- Overconfidence
- The presence of other teenagers in the car (encouraging risky driving)

As a result, many states are instituting stricter guidelines for younger drivers—such as not allowing other young people in the car for the first year of driving, issuing provisional licenses that are suspended with any traffic violation, and increasing the age at which young people can get a driver's license.

Alcohol and Violence among the General Population

Many problems associated with alcohol use involve violence (see Figure 1.2).

Intimate Partner Violence

It is estimated that alcohol is involved in 25 to 50 percent of cases of intimate partner violence (IPV). The psychophysiological effects of alcohol use can lead directly or indirectly to IPV. Alcohol consumption can result in impaired judgment, cognitive impairment, loosened inhibitions, and numerous physical effects that can lead to violence. Alcohol abuse can also lead to exacerbation of already dysfunctional marital or partner relationships and have negative effects on family life, which increases the probability of violence.

Many women entering substance-abuse treatment have a history of physical violence with a family member or significant other.

Alcohol-Related Injuries and Deaths

Accidental injury is the leading cause of death among older adolescents and young adults, and binge drinking is involved in many of these accidents. For young people under the age of 21, intentional deaths include many homicides and suicides that are alcohol related. However, many deaths are not related to drinking and driving. Approximately 55 percent of unintentional alcohol-related deaths of youths under the age of 21 were traffic deaths, but a significant number were from other causes—drowning, burns, and falls.

Systemic Problems of Drugs

A large proportion of the federal money available to fight the drug problem is being spent on programs and agencies that focus on reducing the supply of drugs in the United

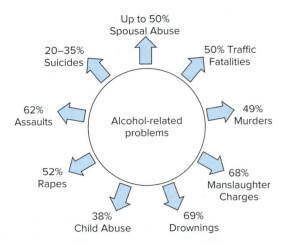

FIGURE 1.2 *Americans Have a Big Problem with Alcohol, the Number-One Drug of Abuse*
SOURCE: Office for Substance Abuse Prevention, modified. Data derived from the National Institute on Alcohol Abuse and Alcoholism, In Carroll, Charles R, *Drugs in Modern Society*. Copyright © 1993 The McGraw-Hill Companies.

States. Despite these efforts, there appears to be no real reduction in the availability of drugs. The lucrative profits are such a strong incentive at every level of the illegal drug trade that government efforts to decrease drug trafficking have not been successful.

The U.S. Federal Government's Role in the Drug Problem

The strong emphasis on the supply-side funding has been neglected for demand-side programs of drug prevention, intervention, and treatment. The problem has escalated to such levels that respected government officials and other prominent individuals are considering the legalization of illicit drugs. Even considering legalizing drugs clearly points to the frustration of a segment of the American society with the lack of progress being made by the supply-side approach.

Most publicly funded agencies are seeing their funding base diminishing, caseloads increasing, and severity of their patients' needs increasing. Publicly financed programs often have long waiting lists for both inpatient and outpatient treatment services. The average waiting time for publicly funded outpatient alcohol/drug treatment can be a month. The average waiting time for publicly funded inpatient alcohol/drug treatment was 45 days. Nationally, more than 65,000 people are waiting to enter public alcohol/drug treatment programs. Once the alcoholic/addict is ready for treatment and breaks through denial, there is such a long waiting list that relapse is inevitable. This costs taxpayers additional money in increased crime and public health care costs.

Money alone cannot necessarily solve the problem. However, it can alleviate delays in providing treatment for those desperately seeking and needing treatment.

Funding for innovative programs addressing the needs of the inner-city crack addict and programs for the prevention of addiction in pregnant women are high priorities. Funding is also needed for alcohol/drug prevention programs for high-risk youth in their communities, with a special early focus on kindergarten to sixth grade. To make a major impact, longitudinal prevention projects with funding for several years are needed. **Innovative** with realistic methods of funding are also necessary to attract the support of big business.

Racist Approaches to the Drug Problem

Historically, there has been prejudice and oppression of people of color, a scapegoating of minorities, and a neglect of substance-abuse problems in the inner city. Legislation on drug policy was often based more on racial scapegoating prejudices than on a concern for the harmful impact of drugs on people. "People's attitudes toward a specific drug became inseparable from their feelings about that group of people with which the drug's use was associated". This is evidenced throughout history to the present day. For instance, in 1875, the goal of suppressing opium smoking and opium dens had little to do with the control of opium but more to do with the fear of interracial contact and a fear of interracial mixing of the Chinese with American women and the white working class. The Chinese question dominated California politics in the 1870s. The tremendous racial and class conflicts resulted in many race riots, the lynching and killing of Chinese, and the burning of their dwellings in numerous West Coast cities. The California Working Man's Party was organized under the cry "The Chinese must go!"

The association between opium and the Chinese into the 1900s was part of the national legislation to prohibit opium smoking and opium dens, even though, at the time, opium was a primary ingredient in most over-the-counter medications and elixirs for physical ailments.

The noted scholar Edward M. Brecher, in his classic book *Licit and Illicit Drugs* (1992), articulately describes various examples of government policies that were driven more by personal agendas and biases and political reasons, than by the true dimensions of the problem.

Brecher accurately describes the United States of America during the nineteenth century as "a dope-fiend's paradise." That might be a rather strong description, but it is quite realistic. Opium was inexpensive, legal, and conveniently sold in not only the local drugstore but even the local grocery store. Physicians were quick to dispense opiate to their patients. Patent medicines, elixirs, and tonics that contained opium or morphine were marketed and sold as the rage for many ailments and conditions.

Brecher points out how drug ordinances were more about rascist fears than the drugs themselves. The most notable early examples were the ordinances adopted by the City of San Francisco in 1875 that prohibited the smoking of opium in smoking houses, or "dens." This was in contrast with the widespread use of opiates in other forms and venues described above.

> "The roots of this ordinance were racist rather than health-oriented. . . ."

The San Francisco authorities, Brecher says, learned upon investigation that "many women and young girls, as well as young men of respectable family, were being induced to visit the (Chinese opium-smoking) dens, where they were ruined morally and otherwise." The Chinese were also a cheap, industrious, and large source of labor and were taking jobs away from the less competitive white population. The Chinese were hated by the white workers and labeled the "yellow peril."

The same held true for the association between cocaine and African Americans during the late 1800s and early 1900s. Hamilton Wright, a State Department official considered by many as the father of American narcotics laws, went before Congress.

> It has been authoritatively stated that cocaine is often the direct incentive to the crime of rape by the Negroes of the South and other sections of the country.
>
> Once the Negro has reached the stage of being a "dope taker" [dope here referring to cocaine] . . . he is a constant menace to his community until he is eliminated. . . . Sexual desires are increased and perverted, peaceful Negroes become quarrelsome, and timid Negroes develop a degree of "Dutch courage." . . . Many of these officers in the South have increased the caliber of their guns for the express purpose of stopping the cocaine fiend when he runs amuck. (Williams 1914/1976)

These racial associations with drugs were documented in a *New York Times* article that reflected anti-Semitic feelings of the time: "There is little doubt that every Jew Peddler in the South carries the stuff [cocaine]."

This historical association of drugs with minority groups includes the following:

- Opium with the Chinese
- Cocaine with African Americans

- Alcohol with urban Catholic immigrants
- Heroin with urban immigrants, African Americans
- Marijuana and PCP with Latinos

The underlying assumption was that minorities were not able to control or tolerate the use of alcohol and drugs because they were inherently lazy and physically, emotionally, and morally/ethically weak. Of course, it was thought, most self-respecting white men could control their alcohol/drug use. This prejudice and association of drugs with minority subgroups caused politicians and others to stir up negative emotions to gain support for antidrug legislation.

Unfortunately, as long as drugs were confined to minority populations, funding and treatment resources were limited. It wasn't until the 1960s, when white middle- and upper-class young adults and college students were using marijuana, hallucinogens, and other drugs, that the modern drug war began.

Until we resolve the more dramatic issues of socioeconomic inequities, racial prejudice and the oppression of minorities, inequities in pay and occupational opportunities, and other related issues, the inner city will continue to be a breeding ground for the abuse of alcohol/drugs.

Socioeconomic Inequities that Undermine the American Dream

The inequities in socioeconomic opportunities have created bitterness, racial conflict, and a general rebelliousness and hopelessness, which fuel the desire to use alcohol/drugs. The American Dream is a nightmare for those who are unable to develop feelings of competency and pride in their lives.

The reality is that hard work and dedication can be rewarded with the attainment of each person's American Dream. Many successful people have refused to be limited by the prejudice of others to the color of their skin, their sex, their religious or ethnic background, or their lack of membership in the inner circles of our society. Many individuals positively strive to reach their full potential by overcoming the prejudices of others and work to correct these inequities when they have an opportunity to change them. Other individuals become so embittered by socioeconomic injustices that they give up, become alienated from society, and lack a personal commitment to strive in life. They use alcohol/drugs to numb and shut down these feelings of embitterment, anger, and pain. Instead of working through these issues and resolving the conflict, they give in to a bitter hopelessness that makes their lives feel meaningless.

Lizbeth Schorr, in her book *Within Our Reach: Breaking the Cycle of Disadvantage* (1988), identifies poverty as the greatest risk factor for chemical dependency and other destructive behaviors. Violent crime, school-age childbearing, and school failure are outcomes that need "early interventions to prevent rotten outcomes," and "high-risk families need high-intensity services." Changes in economic policy, health care reform, and welfare reform can help in "breaking the cycle of disadvantage."

American society needs to acknowledge and address these issues of disparity in opportunity. Other factors contributing to the alcohol/drug problem are the breakdown of the neighborhood, changes in the traditional nuclear and extended family system, limited support systems, stress, and trauma.

Academic Failure and the Role of the U.S. Educational System

In 1959, the launching of the first manned spacecraft by the U.S.S.R. (now Russia) caught the United States by surprise. As a result, the United States took up the challenge for space by rededicating energy and resources to the study of science and math as well as the general education of our young people. Perhaps the current failure of the U.S. educational system and the high incidence of alcohol/drug use by young people will be the impetus to implement reform and innovation in school systems, much like that of the 1960s.

The U.S. educational system has become so neglected that the rates of academic failure and dropout are continually rising. The academic standards for students who do graduate are inferior. The ripple effect of this lowering of academic standards is also seen in colleges and education in general. Illiteracy has increased, and the quest for knowledge and general personal and intellectual improvement is not emphasized or valued by the average American citizen. This complacency in education affects standards in American business and industry. The worker who has no motivation for personal improvement also is not motivated to do high-quality, productive work on the job. The quality and pride in American workmanship are also decreased, resulting in inferior goods and services and a general public attitude that accepts these standards. The industries that employ individuals with good educational backgrounds and positive self-motivating attitudes tend to experience fewer of these problems.

The current failure of the U.S. educational system results from a variety of problems. The biggest problems are poor administration, teacher burnout, lack of adequate funding, and a bureaucratic system that promotes complacency.

The factor that contributes the most to teacher burnout is lack of support from the principal and school board. Innovation is threatening to some school administrations, and the fear of parents' complaints and litigation often results in a political administration that is more concerned with how parents and the school board may respond than the effective development and education of the child.

Another factor is the lack of incentives—other than the genuine desire to work with young people—for teachers to invest themselves in their profession. The teacher who repeats the same lesson plan over and over without making any investment in the job receives the same salary as the teacher who is attentive, is involved, and spends time and energy in educating students.

The combination of inadequate pay, lack of support from the administration, and no financial incentives or other motivations has resulted in dedicated and talented teachers leaving the educational system. This puts students in the hands of teachers who lack the talent or motivation to help them overcome academic failure and a poor sense of self.

Reforms such as site-based management, parent involvement, shared decision making, accountability, and alternative schools have been successful in turning school systems around. We need to apply these principles in educational reform to provide children with the opportunity for academic and personal success. The development of our children as a natural resource is essential in developing a future generation strong enough not to become dependent on or addicted to alcohol/drugs.

Denial and Minimization of Alcohol/Drug Problem in the Family

Denial is jokingly referred to as a river in Egypt (de-Nile), or denial can stand for I **D**on't **E**ven k**N**ow **I A**m **L**ying. Despite these jokes, denial is a problem that leads to the worsening of consequences over time, not only for the substance abuser and addict/alcoholic but also for family members and friends. The longer a family denies and enables the alcohol/drug problems, the more vulnerable the family members become to experiencing the destructive consequences of substance abuse and addiction.

Parental substance abuse, addiction, and alcoholism make the children in that family four to eight times more likely to develop problems with alcohol/drugs. Children who grow up in alcoholic, drug-dependent families exhibit far more problems than children from families who don't abuse alcohol/drugs. Emotional and physical abuse, sexual violation, and other traumas are at a greater risk of occurring when parents abuse alcohol and drugs.

Families and family members, including the addict/alcoholic, often resist admitting that they have a problem. They often feel so ashamed that they maintain their addiction and continue the negative consequences in a cascading, vicious cycle. Asking for help is often difficult for adult family members, for children of the addict/alcoholic, and for the addict/alcoholic.

Early assessment of alcohol/drug problems, related dysfunctional behaviors, and negative consequences of drinking/drugging may prevent a problem from getting out of control. Destigmatizing the dimensions of addiction that emphasize the "disease" and decrease shame while restoring dignity can help facilitate people admitting they have a problem, breaking through denial and helping them to "ask for help."

Public media can address the importance of asking for help and also bring to awareness the impact on the entire family.

✷ Emerging Issues and Trends in Drug Use—High School Students—The 2014 Monitoring the Future High School Survey

The 2014 Monitoring the Future Survey, Overview of Findings, December, 2014, reported some good news and areas of concern.

Some of the good news include the following:

Use of the opioid pain reliever, Vicodin

Nonmedical Use—Past Year

2014 4.8 percent of 12th graders

2009 9.7 percent of 12th graders

Cigarette smoking has decreased dramatically, almost 50 percent over the past 5 years for students. However, the use of electronic cigarettes (e-cigarettes) is high among teens—8.7 percent of 8th graders, 16.2 percent of 10th graders, and 17.1 percent of 12th graders.

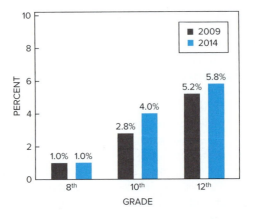

FIGURE 1.3   *Five-Year Increase in Daily Marijuana Use among 10th Graders*
SOURCE: University of Michigan, 2014 Monitoring the Future Study

Marijuana use did not increase despite students seeing it as less harmful. Interestingly 40 percent of 12th graders in medical marijuana states consume edible forms of marijuana in the past year. Might that be related to the fact that only 26 percent of 12th graders reported using edible marijuana in the past year in nonmedical marijuana states. Yet, there was no significant difference in the rates of marijuana use among high school seniors in medical marijuana states compared to nonmedical marijuana states.

Daily marijuana use (smoking) decreased to 1.4 percent by 8th graders, compared to 2.7 percent 5 years ago. However, daily marijuana use (smoking) by 10th graders showed a significant increase (see Figure 1.3):

- Daily use of marijuana (smoking) by seniors was 5.8 percent and 81 percent of seniors reported it is easy to get marijuana.

Use of stimulants Adderall and Ritalin are stable.

- Abuse of prescription drugs and over-the-counter drugs continue to decline.
- Use of illicit drugs has generally declined over the past decades.
- Significant decrease in alcohol use among all grades.
- Significant drop in "binge drinking."
- Use of inhalants is at it's lowest level in the history of the survey.

Medical Marijuana

There are 23 states and the District of Columbia that have legalized medical marijuana. Four of those states (Colorado, Washington, Oregon, and Alaska) and the District of Columbia have legalized recreational marijuana use (see Figure 1.4). Medical conditions that medical marijuana is approved for are cancer, chronic pain, severe pain, epilepsy, and disorders characterized by muscle spasms and/or nausea. Other medical conditions approved by some states are anorexia, arthritis, cachexia or wasting

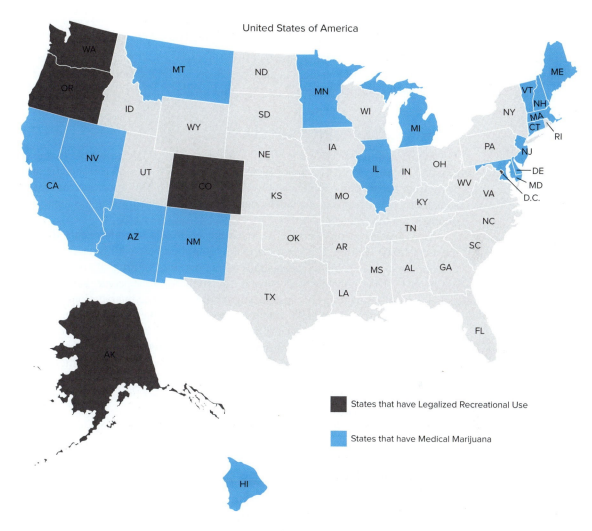

FIGURE 1.4 *States with Medical Marijuana & States Considering Medical Marijuana Laws*

disease, migraines, hepatitis C, Crohn's disease, agitation of Alzheimer's disease, post traumatic stress disorder, gout, and use by hospice patients.

Research on Medical Marijuana Is Limited

Ironically, most of our impressions about marijuana are based on anecdotal information. We now have three generations of marijuana users. Yet, we have very limited clinical research on marijuana use. There is also limited research on medical marijuana. The Harvard Mental Health Letter reports that in Canada, where medical marijuana is legal, there were only 31 studies. A review by the American Medical Association (AMA) agreed that the research was too sparse.

❧ The Major Perspectives on Alcohol/Drug Use

In *Drugs Demystified,* Helen Nowlis (1975) described four major perspectives on drug use: moral-legal, medical-health, psychosocial, and social-cultural. The fifth perspective is your perspective.

The Moral-Legal Perspective

The moral-legal perspective is primarily the viewpoint of law enforcement and the criminal justice system. The major focus of this perspective is to keep specific drugs away from people and people away from specific drugs. This approach reduces the availability of drugs and uses punishment as a deterrent in addressing the supply side of drugs, not the demand side.

The agencies in this perspective have not been able to significantly diminish the availability of drugs. Although they are doing their best with limited resources, these agencies are unable to substantially affect the price of drugs by reducing their availability. The criminal justice system is a deterrent for some people, but few people stop using or dealing drugs because they fear criminal-justice interventions. The anti-social personality of the people caught by the system makes rehabilitation difficult. The weak rehabilitative components of the criminal-justice system have resulted in minimal changes in the attitudes of those convicted or caught by the system.

The moral-legal perspective is the one emphasized by most politicians, yet this perspective alone cannot be effective. Unless we address the demand side, the moral-legal perspective is ineffective. With so many buyers in the marketplace, sellers are motivated to deal, despite the risks.

The moral-legal perspective also encodes specific value judgments about drugs and alcohol. These are often expressed in the licit-versus-illicit debate, personal biases about punishment for illegal use, and moral/ethical views regarding the use of alcohol and other drugs.

The Medical-Health Perspective

The medical-health perspective is held by physicians, nurses, and the medical and health treatment fields. In this perspective, alcohol and drug use is a public health problem. Treatment focuses on the physical damage related to alcohol/drug use, abuse, and dependence.

The medical-health perspective assumes that people seek good health. The perspective is also based on the assumption that health information influences attitudes and behaviors. However, information alone does not change attitudes about the use of alcohol/drugs.

The Psychosocial Perspective

The psychosocial perspective is a common viewpoint shared by a variety of agencies that specialize in addressing the demand side of alcohol/drugs. The services these agencies provide include the following:

- Recovery from substance dependence
- Intervention and treatment services
- Early intervention approaches with adolescents
- Prevention services for young children, adolescents, adults, and seniors

The goals of this perspective are to prevent, intervene in, and treat alcohol/drug problems. Inadequate funding for chemical dependency treatment programs and alcohol/drug prevention programs has made it difficult for many alcohol/drug users to obtain treatment services and for agencies to maintain prevention programs long enough to see conclusive results. (See Chapter 10.)

The Social-Cultural Perspective

The social-cultural perspective is held by most social agencies and institutions. The basic goal of this perspective is to adapt the environment to meet the individual's needs. The underlying assumption of this perspective is that alcohol/drug use is due to the frustration and hopelessness of people's lives. If users had any hope that they could attain the American Dream, they would be motivated to achieve and establish a constructive place in society.

Unfortunately, most social agencies are impersonal, bureaucratic, and rigid in dealing with their clients' needs. Such agencies are poorly funded and therefore poorly staffed; their employees are overworked, underappreciated, and underpaid. As a result, the agencies are reluctant to change, change too slowly, or may even lack a mechanism to change.

Edward Brecher (1992) believes we should "stop viewing the drug problem as primarily a national problem to be solved on a national scale. In fact, . . . the drug problem is a collection of local problems." By supporting neighborhood and community efforts, we could provide an environment that could prevent the development of alcohol/drug problems.

The Fifth Perspective—Your Perspective Questionnaire

What is your perspective on alcohol/drugs? Complete the following Fifth Perspective Worksheet to clarify your perspective on alcohol/drugs.

Moral-Legal Perspective

1. Should drugs be legalized? Explain.
2. Is the supply-side approach to the drug problem effective? Explain.
3. Is alcoholism/drug addiction a defense for irresponsible or criminal behavior? Explain.

Medical-Health Perspective

1. Is alcoholism/drug addiction a disease? Explain.
2. Describe the physician's role in making a patient aware of problems with alcohol/drugs.

3. Do people need more information about the health risks of alcohol/drug use? Does this information change attitudes? Explain.

Psychosocial Perspective

1. What role does parenting play in the development of alcohol/drug problems?
2. Is it important for the entire family system to be involved in alcohol/drug treatment? Explain.
3. How can alcohol/drug treatment be more effective?

Personal Perspective

Circle *true* or *false* and explain the reasoning supporting your answer to each question.

1. Alcohol is a drug with great potential for abuse.
    True
    False
2. My family history does not make me at risk for developing problems with alcohol/drugs.
    True
    False
3. Persons with alcohol/drug problems have to break through their own denial.
    True
    False
4. Alcoholism and drug addiction are family diseases.
    True
    False
5. Parent modeling of alcohol/drug use is an important influence on a child's use of alcohol/drugs.
    True
    False
    Other personal views

A Perspective of Hope

Perhaps the problems that spawn alcohol/drug abuse and addiction seem too difficult to overcome. The negative impact of these problems frequently gives rise to feelings of hopelessness that we can never adequately resolve these issues. However, there has been positive and dramatic success: Millions of Americans are in recovery from alcoholism and drug addiction. Family members are changing their own codependent and enabling behavior in relationships. Adult children of alcoholics are overcoming the trauma of their childhoods. Most important, families are successfully developing more functional and healthy systems for the next generation of youngsters. Their children will be less vulnerable to the familial problems of alcohol/drug dependence and addiction.

There is something to be said for thinking small. Initially, this might sound like strange advice. We each must think about our own small contribution to solving problems that seem large and insurmountable. Each of us needs to first think about our own behavior and our own family and address growth and positive development in those areas. Then, we can begin to address these issues in our neighborhoods, communities, workplaces, and other interpersonal interactions. My hope is that we can each, in our own small ways, address the issue of alcohol/drug dependence and other issues in our society by focusing on our own and our children's functional growth and development.

❊ In Review

- Historically, we have failed dramatically in our responses to the alcohol/drug problems in the United States. These approaches were riddled with emotional, moral, and political biases and agendas, which distracted from the truth. Scare tactics—and political biases, which denied the real dimensions of the problem—began in 1937 with marijuana and have continued with marijuana and other drugs to the present day.
- There are no "simple, magical solutions" (e.g., "Just Say No") to a complex problem such as alcohol/drug abuse and dependence.
- Binge alcohol drinking on college campuses leads to significant problems.
- At least half of the sexual assaults on college campuses involve alcohol consumption by the perpetrator and by the victim.
- Alcohol is often involved in intentional and accidental deaths, driving accidents, and high-risk behaviors.
- Medical marijuana has been legalized in many states, and the impact is expected to result in more widespread use.
- The four major perspectives to view alcohol/drug use include the moral-legal perspective, the medical-health perspective, the psychosocial perspective, and the social-cultural perspective.

❊ Discussion Questions

1. Make a list of problems related to binge drinking. Which one is the worst and why? Discuss your answers in class.
2. Should medical marijuana be legal? Organize a debate of this question.
3. Does alcohol or marijuana cause more problems? Organize a debate, and support your position. Use information found in this textbook and make page references.
4. Consider the four perspectives—moral-legal, medical-health, psychosocial, and socio-cultural—rank them in order of the perspective that you prefer or are more aligned with. Discuss this in class.

�留 References

Abbey, Antonia. 2002. Alcohol-related sexual assault: A common problem among college students. *Journal of Studies on Alcohol* 14: 118–27.

Bonnie, Richard J., and Mary Ellen O'Connell, eds. 2004. *Reducing underage drinking: A collective responsibility.* Washington, D.C.: National Academy Press.

Brecher, Edward M. 1992. *Licit and illicit drugs.* Boston: Little, Brown.

Carroll, Charles R. 1993. *Drugs in Modern Society.* Brown and Benchmark. Center for Disease Control and Prevention Morbidity and Mortality Weekly–Binge Drinking, 2009 Supplement, January 14, 2011/60(01), 101–4.

Perkins, H. Wesley. 2002. Surveying the damage: A review of research on consequences of alcohol misuse in college populations. *Journal of Studies on Alcohol* Supplement (14): 91–100.

Proctor, Dwayne. 2005. The time to purge binge drinking is now. *Washington FOCUS* 14(4) (Winter): 5.

Straus, R., and S. D. Bacon. 1953. *Drinking in college.* New Haven, Conn.: Yale University Press.

Testa, Maria, et al. 2004. The role of victim and perpetrator intoxication on sexual assault outcomes. *Journal of Studies on Alcohol* 65: 320–29.

Why People Use and Abuse Drugs and Alcohol

A Better Understanding of Models, Theories, and Contributing Factors

Outline of Chapter 2

Introduction

Our Innate Drive to Alter Consciousness

Models, Theories, and Contributing Factors of Substance Use and Abuse
> Tension and Stress Reduction
> Trauma and Substance Use Disorders (SUDs)
> The Disease Model of Alcoholism
> Genetic Model of Alcoholism—Adoption and Twin Studies
> Personality Traits and Personality Disorders
> Attachment and Substance Abuse
> Self-Medication Motive
> Depression, Anxiety, and Affective (Feeling) Disorders
> Family Models
> Adolescence
> Poor Self-Concept

Other Factors that Contribute to Substance Abuse
> Boredom and Altered States
> Impulsivity and Disinhibition
> Social Learning Theory
> Sociocultural Models
> Psychoanalytic Models—Psychoanalytic Meaning
> Existential Issues
> Poor Future Orientation and Hope
> Hopelessness
> Pessimism and Optimism

Appendix
> Other Theories and Models

Objectives

1. Explain the relationship between "the drive to alter consciousness" and alcohol/drug abuse.
2. Explain alcoholism as a "disease."
3. Describe the key elements of the following models and theories of substance abuse disorders:
   - Tension reduction models
   - Trauma and SUD

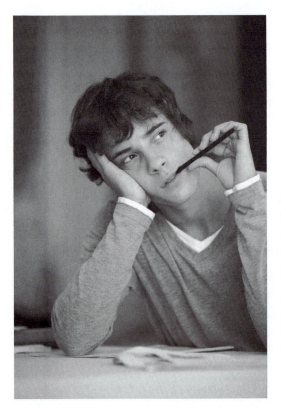

All people consciously or subconsciously alter their states of consciousness. Some common ways children achieve this are through daydreaming, rolling downhill, tumbling, and spinning.

© Alto/Alix Minde/Getty Images

- Disease model of alcoholism
- Personality theories
- Personality disorders
- Depression, anxiety, and feelings
- Family models
- Self-medication motive for drug use
- Boredom
- Social learning theory
- Sociocultural models
- Psychoanalytic models and meanings
- Existential issues

❧ Introduction

This chapter explores the various models, theories, and contributing factors of substance use and abuse. The models provide a framework for understanding substance abuse. The contributing factors help in the treatment strategies that may be implemented. This chapter lays the foundation for later chapters that focus on assessment, prevention, intervention, recovery, and relapse prevention.

I recommend that you complete the worksheet at the end of this chapter to help you explore your own model and theoretical orientation to substance abuse.

❧ Our Innate Drive to Alter Consciousness

There are four primary drives: hunger, thirst, sex (for procreation), and our desire to alter our consciousness. Drugs have been used throughout history to alter consciousness and will continue to be used in this way in the future.

Drugs open avenues to unconscious issues, conflicts, and possibly an awareness or perception new to the user's life. On the downside, drugs can easily become traps that keep us from using our minds in positive ways. Drug use becomes unrealistic and neurotic when it becomes an addiction.

❧ Models, Theories, and Contributing Factors of Substance Use and Abuse

We cannot isolate one specific cause of alcoholism and other drug addictions. There are often multiple, confounding reasons for addiction. Many theories and models of causality exist. Early models of alcoholism labeled alcoholics as inherently weak or unable to control their consumption of alcohol. One test of manliness was the ability to "hold your liquor." Other early models focused on individual psychopathology, arguing that alcoholics used alcohol in a pathological manner to block out memories of unpleasant, traumatic personal experiences that brought with them unmanageable feelings. Over time, a physiological model of alcoholism developed as scientists searched for a biochemical link to, or a genetic marker of, alcoholism.

Today, those of us in the alcohol/drug field generally accept the fact that alcoholism and drug addiction have multiple causes, or etiologies. Clearly, a matrix of genetic, social, psychological, and environmental factors can cause an individual to develop problems with alcohol and drugs. "Evidence has accumulated to indicate that alcoholism is a heterogenous entity arising from multiple etiologies" (Tabakoff and Hoffman 1988).

The models described in this chapter present an overview of prevailing theories, research, and clinical observations in the field of alcohol and drug use and abuse. The models are intended to help you attain a better understanding of substance abuse.

I encourage you to study and explore all of these models. In the classroom, discuss the application and validity of these models.

Unfortunately, no one model explains all substance abuse or fits all users' reasons for using. In the spirit of the old adage "If you are a hammer, everything else is a nail," many people want to find a single variable, approach, or model that will predict all cases of substance abuse—when the reality is that there are many confounding variables. Clients/patients are all different, with different coping skills, family histories, physical traits, affective temperaments, personality traits, and developmental histories. Studying the models will make you aware that factors that play a major role in one individual's substance abuse might play no role at all in another person's drug problems—one size does not fit all.

We might someday have medical tests that accurately predict substance abuse—a simple blood test, or a test for patterns of neurotransmitter activity that correlate with risk. Or maybe one of the models you're going to study in this book will prove to be more correct than the others. For now, our best resource is to study the available models and understand how each can be used to prevent, intervene in, and treat substance abuse.

Tension and Stress Reduction

> It's stress. . . . I just drink to calm down. . . . I need to relax. . . . I'm so tense. . . . It lets me worry less. . . . I can avoid the conflicts. . . . It makes decisions easier. . . . I can do the tedious work easier. . . . I can summon energy. . . . It reduces the tension. . . . It allows me not to think so much. . . . It makes me feel better. . . . It is pleasurable.

These are common reasons people give for using drugs—whether with an alcoholic drink at the end of a busy workday, or marijuana, or another drug.

The *tension-reduction theory (TRT)* is one of the most widely researched theories of drug use. Early research focused on tension reduction and relief from stress as a primary reason for alcohol and drug use. Today, the tension-reduction theory is considered one aspect of drug use. Individuals consume drugs for a variety of reasons, including the sheer pleasurable feelings that accompany drug use.

The tension-reduction model involves the concept of *homeostasis,* or balance. The individual will use alcohol/drugs to counteract (or balance out) stress, anxiety, emotional tension, and conflict—any aversive emotional state. Alcohol/drugs are therefore used as tension reducers.

Tension has been defined as any state that is an aversive source of motivation, causing feelings of fear, anxiety (vague fear), conflict, and frustration due to blocked goals. Stress is just a modern version of tension. Here is one definition of stress, from *Merriam-Webster's Collegiate Dictionary* (11th edition, 2003)*: "a physical, chemical, or emotional factor that causes bodily or mental tension and may be a factor in disease causation." The tension-reduction theory of alcohol use has two major assumptions: alcohol reduces tension, and individuals drink alcohol for its tension-reducing properties (Blane and Leonard 1988). Genetically predisposed individuals may find that alcohol or other drugs have effects that buffer, or reduce, stress for them.

Noted authority on alcohol and drugs, Stanley Gitlow, emphasizes an etiological model that focuses on discomfort and tolerance to stress as a major factor in the decision to use alcohol/drugs. Gitlow believes that we have biological variations in our levels of tolerance to stress and stimulation. "The initiating stimulus could well be perceived by one individual as minimally inconvenient, while another individual would perceive that same stimulus as agonizingly urgent. The overriding determinant and major variable of appetite regulation is most likely the intensity of the individual's perception of need for relief" (Gitlow 1985). Petrie (1960) identified three basic classifications in dealing with stimuli: (1) *stimulus reducers* perceive and react to a stimulus as if that stimulus were less than it is; (2) *stimulus moderators* perceive and react to the stimulus as it is; and (3) *stimulus augmenters* perceive and react as if that stimulus were more than it is. "A perceptual characteristic, such as stimulus augmenting, leading to an overly sensitive need for relief from any discomfort, appeared to be a possible and intriguing genetically determined CNS factor" (Gitlow 1985). In 1984, Lynne Hennecke reported a significantly higher incidence of stimulus augmenters in the sons of alcoholic fathers than in the sons of nonalcoholic fathers. Hennecke suggests that, in stimulus augmenters, alcohol is used to shut down the stimulation overload from the environment.

Gitlow (1972) describes alcoholism as a biochemical defect. The individual possessing this defect is easily agitated by stimuli, becomes uncomfortable, and uses alcohol for its sedating effect. Unfortunately, withdrawal from alcohol creates an agitating effect, and the individual must drink again to relieve this discomfort. Stress, tension, and situations, positive and negative, that involve high levels of stress/tension, are often major contributors to substance abuse.

The stress/tension of crises, change, interpersonal conflict, financial setbacks, and obligations, work and family changes, can all be cited as factors that cause "reactive" overreactions and behaviors that contribute to relapse from sobriety.

Trauma and Substance Use Disorders (SUDs)

The American Psychological Association defines "trauma" as directly experiencing or witnessing an event that "involves actual or threatened death, or serious injury, or

---

*By permission. From Merriam-Webster's Collegiate® Dictionary, 11th Edition ©2016 by Merriam-Webster, Inc. (www.Merriam-Webster.com).

other threat to physical integrity, or learning that a family member or close associate has experienced such events, and has a response that involves intense fear, helplessness, or horror."

Traumatic stressors that fit this definition include disasters, motor vehicle accidents, emergency worker exposed to trauma, war, rape and sexual assault, intimate partner violence (IPV), stalking, torture, prostitution and sex-trafficking, life threatening illness, and child abuse.

There are two major hypotheses regarding *trauma and substance use disorders (SUDs)*. The existing research tends to support the first theory: Substance use and abuse is an attempt by the individual to assuage feelings related to traumatic experiences. The individual self-medicates by trying to "numb out," soothe, or escape the overwhelming feelings of pain, hopelessness, and shame associated with trauma.

The second theory is that substance use and abuse contribute to the development of *post traumatic stress disorder (PTSD)*. The use and misuse of alcohol/drugs can affect the individual in a number of ways making them more susceptible and "in harms way" for trauma.

Chronic substance abuse can change neurochemistry, making the individual more susceptible to PTSD. The lifestyle of substance abuse and alcoholism/addiction puts the individual in situations that are traumatic (e.g., intimate partner violence). The risk behaviors that are associated with substance abuse put the individual in situations that have significant and traumatic negative consequences (e.g., driving under the influence, drug dealing, violence, stealing, medical problems, problems in judgment, criminal and civil issues resulting from financial, interpersonal, work/school problems).

The research tends to view the self-medication theory of trauma and substance use disorders as more likely than the high-risk hypothesis. It is important to realize that the risks of substance use disorders confound the problems of trauma. In addition, these individuals often experience strong feelings of "shame" and self-deprecation that further escalate negative feelings about self.

Individuals who have both trauma and substance use disorders often do better in inpatient/residential treatment programs that specialize in the treatment of both trauma and substance use disorders, as well as the feelings of shame and self-doubt. Treatment programs that do not have this sensitivity or expertise will often result in the client having multiple relapses and further shame. Upon treatment intake, traumatized youth report higher substance frequency and substance problems than nontraumatized youth. Even though youth with high traumatic stress (HTS) respond to treatment, on average, they have higher substance use frequency and problems over time. This suggests that HTS youth may struggle more with substance recovery than nontraumatized youth, and require additional support and more specialized treatment (Williams et al. 2008). (See Case Study 2.1 and 2.2.)

The Disease Model of Alcoholism

In 1957, the American Medical Association declared *alcoholism* a disease on the basis of three criteria: (1) Alcoholism has a known etiology (cause), (2) the symptoms get worse over time, and (3) alcoholism has known outcomes. The outcomes of

Case Study 2.1
Trauma and Addiction

Daniel was traumatized throughout his life. As a young child he could do very little to help his mother escape beatings from his father. He hated his father, not only for beating him and his mother, but also because his father sexually violated him. His father had a negative attitude about everyone. He frequently blamed others for his own misfortune. He then had an excuse to hit the bottle. His father would create conflicts at home so he could leave the house, hit the bars, and get drunk.

At an early age, Daniel learned to be hypervigilant (i.e., watching every move his father made when he was at home) to avoid being the object of his father's wrath.

As an adolescent Daniel was jumping off a cliff with some friends into a swimming hole, when one of the boys drowned. While Daniel was always an outsider with his peer group, when the accident occurred, it pushed him further from his peers. This perpetuated Daniel's feelings of isolation and depression.

Many years later Daniel had a back injury and was introduced to morphine following surgery. He described it (morphine) as the first time he felt good in his life. The morphine not only numbed the physical pain but also quieted the pain of the trauma, the shame, and blotted out the world. It did not take very long before Daniel was in a cycle of heroin addiction that lasted several years.

Attempts at recovery were difficult. Daniel could stay sober for 5 to 6 days, and then would lapse back to heroin use. His back problems combined with emotional and interpersonal issues, plus the unresolved trauma, continued to push Daniel back to regular heroin use.

Despite inpatient/residential alcohol/drug treatment, Daniel continued to relapse. After several years of intensive outpatient treatment (i.e., individual and group treatment). Daniel was able to maintain sobriety. He became very active studying Buddhism and found the teachings both intellectually stimulating and spiritually fulfilling. The combination of a strong therapeutic program, a solid relationship with his partner, and a spiritual and intellectual foundation in Buddhist teachings all helped him maintain recovery, sobriety, and a solid sense of self.

Discussion Questions

1. Explain the confounding problems of trauma and addiction as they relate to this case study.
2. Explain why traditional alcohol/drug treatment was not effective with Daniel.
3. Do you think Daniel would have embraced Alcoholics Anonymous or Narcotics Anonymous? Explain.
4. What role did Buddhist teachings and mindfulness play in Daniel's recovery?

alcoholism are dependence, physical symptoms, and eventual death. For more than 30 years, research has indicated an increasingly strong case for a genetic component of alcoholism; this validates the disease model.

The disease model is the foundation of Alcoholics Anonymous and many other self-help programs.

Case Study 2.2
Sexual Violation and Addiction

Regina was repeatedly sexually violated by her uncle when she was 5 to 8 years old. Her parents divorced when Regina was 10, because of her father's physical abuse of her mother and Regina. Her mother, an alcoholic with periods of sobriety, had a succession of boyfriends, and one of those boyfriends raped Regina when she was 12.

Regina left her mother and lived with her aunt after the rape. Her mother stayed with the boyfriend and claimed Regina was lying about the rape. When Regina was 18, she left her aunt and lived with an older man (32-year-old). Although they lived together, she rarely had sex with him. It was a few years later that Regina began dancing at strip clubs. She said she enjoyed the attention. She also was prostituting. This coincided with her increased use of alcohol and marijuana, which then led to cocaine and cocaine freebase.

For several years, Regina was still living with her same boyfriend (a drug dealer) and dancing and prostituting. Her cocaine use had escalated to the point where she was frequently on the street, smoking crack, and doing whatever it took to get it.

Regina was found dead in an alley in a drug dealing section of the city.

Discussion Questions

1. What do you think could have been done to stop this tragic story?
2. Can you explain the relationship between sexual violation and drugs?

The 12-step approach (see Table 2.1) is based on the disease model. It has been described as an informal biopsychosocial spiritual model. The disease model assumes alcoholics/addicts were predisposed to addiction by genetically transmitted biological risk factors.

Another model is the genetic influence disease model. This model does not emphasize genes or specific disorders but instead assumes that multiple biological risk factors interact with psychosocial environmental factors. It also assumes that addiction is influenced by interpersonal relationships, including family, community, and culture.

> In effect, neither genetic nor environmental operating alone is sufficient to produce alcoholism or drug addiction; alcoholism and drug addiction require the joint presence of both biological and psychosocial environmental factors. (Tarter and Edwards 1985)

The 12-step program helps the addict/alcoholic overcome the terrible sense of isolation and aloneness that occurs as a result of the many negative consequences of use.

> . . . for many people, heavy drinking and drug use culminate in intense feelings of alienation, apartness, emptiness, meaninglessness, and lack of purpose in living. Moral values may have been compromised in the erratic acting out of intoxicated behaviors, urges, cognitions and motivations. (Rotgers et al. 2003)

T A B L E   2 . 1

The Twelve Steps of Alcoholics Anonymous

1. We admitted we were powerless over alcohol—that our lives had become unmanageable.
2. Came to believe that a Power greater than ourselves could restore us to sanity.
3. Made a decision to turn our will and our lives over to the care of God as we understood Him.
4. Made a searching and fearless moral inventory of ourselves.
5. Admitted to God, to ourselves, and to another human being the exact nature of our wrongs.
6. Were entirely ready to have God remove all these defects of character.
7. Humbly asked Him to remove our shortcomings.
8. Made a list of all persons we had harmed and became willing to make amends to them.
9. Made direct amends to such people wherever possible, except when to do so would injure them or others.
10. Continued to take personal inventory and, when we were wrong, promptly admitted to it.
11. Sought through prayer and meditation to improve our conscious contact with God as we understand Him, praying only for knowledge of His will for us and the power to carry that out.
12. Having had a spiritual awakening as the result of these steps, we tried to carry this message to alcoholics and practice these principles in all our affairs.

SOURCE: The Twelve Steps are reprinted with permission of Alcoholics Anonymous World Services, Inc. ("AAWS") Permission to reprint the Twelve Steps does not mean that AAWS has reviewed or approved the contents of this publication, or that AAWS necessarily agrees with the views expressed herein. A.A. is a program of recovery from alcoholism only. Use of the Twelve Steps in connection with programs and activities which are patterned after A.A., but which address other problems, or in any other non-A.A. context, does not imply otherwise.

The shame-based stigma of addiction, along with the guilt, negative feelings, and spiritual bancruptcy, makes the 12-step approach of Alcoholics Anonymous an effective recovery tool for alcoholics.

In recent years the validity of the "disease model" has been questioned by clients, researchers, and clinicians.

Challenges have been made as to whether alcoholism/addiction is truly a disease. There is agreement that AA and NA have helped many alcoholics/addicts to both have and maintain sobriety. As mentioned previously, the disease model takes away the shame and stigma of addiction (which is a good thing). However is it truly a disease. The 1957 AMA definition of a disease was rather broad and could fit many conditions that we would not consider a disease today.

One could also argue that there are diseases caused by something out of the person's control and there are diseases that are caused by the individual themselves.

Genetic Model of Alcoholism—Adoption and Twin Studies

Devor (1994) describes a developmental-genetic model of alcoholism. He proposes that "alcoholism must no longer be thought of as a single disease with a cause that is either genetic or environmental but as a group of illnesses in which the influences of genes and the environment ebb and flow over the course of the at-risk lifetime." The logical conclusion is that treatment for alcoholism would be individually designed and fine-tuned to consider both pharmacological and behavioral therapies.

Adoption Studies

Donald W. Goodwin (1971) conducted a series of adoption studies in Denmark, indicating that sons of alcoholics are four times more likely to become alcoholics than are sons of nonalcoholics. In the study, the results held true whether the sons were raised by nonalcoholic foster parents or their own biological parents, thus supporting the genetic component of alcoholism. Cloninger, Bohman, and Sigvardsson (1981) conducted detailed and extensive adoption studies that confirmed the earlier work of Goodwin in demonstrating the following:

1. Adopted sons of alcoholic biological parents are four times more likely to become alcoholics than adoptees whose biological parents are not alcoholics.
2. Sons of alcoholic biological parents are more likely to be classified as alcoholics at an earlier age than their peers.
3. Daughters of alcoholic fathers, although not demonstrating a greater incidence of alcoholism, exhibit a high incidence of somatic anxiety and frequent physical complaints.

Twin Studies

Studies of identical (monozygotic or MZ) and fraternal (dizygotic or DZ) twins have supported a genetic factor. Because identical twins are genetically identical but fraternal twins have no more genes in common than nontwin siblings, research should show a higher rate of alcoholism in MZ twins than in DZ twins. Kaij (1960) examined 174 sets of twins and demonstrated that, indeed, the MZ twins had a 71 percent concordance rate, and the DZ twins had only a 32 percent concordance rate. In 1981, Hrubec and Omenn again demonstrated a higher concordance rate in MZ twins (26 percent) than in DZ twins (12 percent). A 1984 study by Gurling and associates, however, did not support the previous studies' results.

Currently, no significant genetic research is exploring drug abuse due to the many research design problems with illicit drugs. The assumption is that the genetic factors for drug addiction are comparable with the genetic research findings on alcoholism.

Personality Traits and Personality Disorders

Addictive Personality

The concept of an **addictive personality** is a simplistic approach that makes the mistake of labeling all alcoholics and other addicts as possessing a particular personality that leads to addictive and compulsive behavior. It is more accurate to recognize that many personality traits can make an individual vulnerable to alcoholism and drug addiction. It is more accurate to say that such individuals have **psychological vulnerability:** personality traits that make a pattern of substance dependence more likely to develop (Jellinek 1960).

It is difficult to identify the relationship of alcoholism and drug addiction to particular dimensions of personality, because many personality traits overlap. Cloninger's (1987) three-dimensional model of personality has been applied to the research literature on alcohol-use disorders. Cloninger identifies three temperament constructs that correlate with alcohol-use disorders:

1. Harm avoidant—cautious, apprehensive, fatigable, and inhibited
2. Reward dependent—ambitious, sympathetic, warm, industrious, sentimental, persistent, and moody
3. Novelty seeking—impulsive, excitable, exploratory, quick-tempered, fickle, and extravagant

A more recent study (Hosier and Cox 2011) of college students who drink excessively has found that novelty seeking and maladaptive motivational structure predict alcohol-related problems, beyond those predicted by their alcohol consumption alone.

Maladaptive motivational structure is described as being unable to maintain motivation to achieve goals. Hosier and Cox found that college students who are strongly influenced by novelty seeking or maladaptive motivational behaviors were twice as likely as other students to experience alcohol-related problems.

Personality Disorders

> I'm angry and drugs quiet me. . . . It's hard for me to get close to others without drugs. . . . I feel anxious and fearful, so drugs relax me. . . . I am bored and isolated, so drugs soothe that. . . .

Of all the personality disorders, the one with the strongest relationship to substance abuse is narcissism. The personality disorder with the second highest correlation to substance abuse is borderline personality disorder (for more information on these disorders, see Chapter 11). (See Case Study 2.3.)

Attachment and Substance Abuse

Attachment plays a key role in being vulnerable to problems with alcohol and drugs. The bond between parent and child is a pivotal foundation in feeling safe, nurtured, and connected. "The inability to establish long-lasting gratifying relationships is directly related to the quality of early attachment styles.

Disruptions in attachment create problems in connection. Alcohol and drugs are used to compensate for this disconnection and to alleviate feelings of shame, unworthiness, inadequacy, loneliness, emptiness, boredom, anxiety, and depression. Trauma, sexual, physical and emotional violation confound the problem, and alcohol/drugs are sought out to alleviate the pain and suffering.

Edward Khantzian, clinical professor of Psychiatry at Harvard Medical school in his forward to Phillip Floes book, Addiction and Attachment (2012), describes addiction as a disorder in self-regulation (reactivity) with emotions, self-care,

Case Study 2.3
Borderline and Narcissistic Personality Disorders with Substance Use Disorders

Diane, an extremely attractive 39-year-old woman, has been in residential treatment twice for alcoholism. Upon returning home, she relapsed within 2 weeks.

The pattern of relapse is related to escalated conflicts with her boyfriend. Despite strong suggestions from the treatment program and her outpatient therapist, Diane continues to battle over issues with her boyfriend. She exhibits a jealous rage and escalated conflicts that get physical. There is a pattern of extreme closeness that they engage in, followed by strong conflicts when she gets disgusted with the way he treats her. This back and forth, in and out of the relationship, high drama is enervating and distracts them from working on their own issues.

Rusty, Diane's 42-year-old boyfriend, is a wealthy accountant and has started dating a very attractive 27-year-old attorney. This occurred after Diane and Rusty's last big conflict. When Diane found out about the dating, she relapsed and showed up at Rusty's house drunk. Rusty apologized and told her that he loved her (Diane), and they reconnected.

Rusty has been diagnosed as narcissistic with a mood cycling disorder. A few weeks after he and Diane reunited, he went on a cocaine binge and told Diane that he was still dating the young attorney. This started another cycle of escalated conflicts. They disengaged, and a few weeks later, Rusty called her and told her the relationship with the young female attorney was over.

Discussion Questions

1. Can you explain this dramatic and chaotic cycle in terms of their personality traits and their substance abuse disorder?
2. What treatment recommendations would you make for Diane? And for Rusty?

self-esteem, and difficulty in making connection in relationships. Difficulty in interpersonal bonds disrupts self-compassion and compassion for others. This difficulty in making connection and reactivity further fuels substance abuse problems and is potentiated or fueled further by the sense of isolation.

"The worst fate, however, is not the suffering, the worst fate is suffering alone."

These dysfunctional attachment styles are described by Flores (2012) as interfering with the ability to both derive satisfaction in relationships and the inability in maintain prolonged satisfaction in relationship.

The individual then uses alcohol/drugs to compensate for this dissatisfaction and to alleviate the pain, further pushing others away, while experiencing deep feelings of isolation. (i.e., "The dragon in the corner, eating your own tail.")

The result is disconnection from spouses/partners, family members, and friends, as alcohol/drugs become the primary relationship. As Flores points out "The vulnerable individual's attachment to chemicals serves both as an obstacle and as a substitute or interpersonal relationships."

"We don't have relationships, we take hostages." Alcoholics Anonymous

Self-Medication Motive

Edward Khantzian (1985) makes the case that drug use is not a random phenomenon. Instead, he says, it is a purposeful attempt by the user to assuage painful affective states and manage psychological problems and disorders:

> Rather than simply seeking escape, euphoria, or self-destruction, addicts are attempting to medicate themselves for a range of psychiatric problems and painful emotional states. Although most such efforts at self-treatment are eventually doomed, given the hazards and complications of long-term, unstable drug use patterns.

Khantzian observed more than 200 narcotics addicts with lifelong problems of rage and violent behavior and concluded that these addicts used opiates primarily for the drugs' anti aggression and anti rage action. In his work with cocaine addicts, he found that these addicts tended to take cocaine to medicate themselves against chronic depression, hyperactivity, restless syndrome, attention deficit hyperactivity disorder (ADHD), and two mood (affective) disorders—cyclothymic disorder and bipolar disorder (see definitions of these disorders in Chapter 11).

Clearly, the importance in exploring the self-medication motive is to help users identify why they are taking drugs and then learn how to better cope with the affective states and psychological problems they find so unbearable. The ability to identify and label emotional states, and then to "work through" these feelings, is a foundation of drug prevention with young people and of treatment for those who are experiencing drug abuse, dependence, and addiction.

An example of the self-medication motive for marijuana is listed in Table 2.2. These adult daily users had a variety of reasons for using marijuana. The table highlights the many self-medication reasons for smoking marijuana.

Depression, Anxiety, and Affective (Feeling) Disorders

> Drugs quiet the pain of my depression. . . . Drugs are catalysts to my mania.

Disturbances in affect, mood, and depression are common causes of substance abuse and addiction to medical and nonmedical psychoactive substances, especially in women (Whitlock et al. 1967).

Mood and Affect Disorders

Individuals who are experiencing problems in regulating their affect and mood may self-medicate with alcohol/drugs. Alcohol/drugs may be used to alleviate and self-medicate feelings of anxiety or panic, as well as other negative emotional states, including melancholia, depression, and even mania. Major depression, dysthymic disorder, cyclothymic disorder, atypical depression, and bipolar disorder (manic-depressive illness) are the primary affective, or feeling, disorders associated with self-medicating with alcohol/drugs (for more information on these disorders, see Chapter 11).

Major depression and dysthymia occur one and a half to two times more commonly in alcoholics (Helzer and Pryzbeck 1988). Female alcoholics have a tenfold increased incidence of mania, and male alcoholics have a threefold increased incidence of mania (Hesselbrock, Meyer, and Keener 1985).

TABLE 2.2
Reasons for Using Marijuana

- Stimulation of thought
- To relieve boredom
- To enhance senses and sensation
- To relieve anxiety and dysphoria
- To stimulate creativity and artistry
- To increase enjoyment of sex, food, music, etc.
- To complete mundane tasks
- To stimulate interest, for a different perspective, for improving self-confidence and decreasing pessimistic views
- To quiet anger
- To connect with people
- To enhance conversations and social interaction
- For fun and stimulation and enhancement of enjoyable activities
- To enjoy nature more
- To enjoy movies and entertainment

SOURCE: Herbert Hendin et al., *Living High: Daily Marijuana Use by Adults*, copyright © 1987 Human Sciences Press.

Patients with major depression who experience intermittent or chronic dysphoria may come to value the powerful, though brief, euphorigenic effects of opioids or cocaine. Patients with bipolar or cyclothymic disorder who use cocaine may discover that the drug not only can bring them out of their depressive episodes but also can enhance their endogenously produced highs (Marin and Weiss 1986). *Seasonal affective disorder (SAD)* is another form of depression that leads to increased alcohol/drug use, especially during the "sunless" winter months in certain environments.

The person who starts taking alcohol or other drugs to assuage the negative effects of a mood or affect disorder can be led by those drugs into a spiraling pattern of isolation and interpersonal distancing. This isolation exacerbates the affective disorder. The pattern can lead to social phobia and paranoid ideations.

Family Model

I drink/drug because I come from a "dysfunctional family.". . . My mom drank a lot. . . . I felt neglected. . . . I was abandoned. . . . I was abused. . . . I was shamed, violated, and traumatized.

The family model is the model most emphasized throughout this book; it includes all aspects of family life. Factors contributing to alcohol/drug use in the family include the following:

- Imbalance in parenting
- Marital discord

- Alcoholic/addict behavior
- Imbalanced and dysfunctional family interaction
- Significant trauma and stress in the family
- Physical, emotional, sexual, and psychological violation
- Inappropriate boundaries
- Shame, abandonment, and rejection

The family model of chemical dependency is developed in more detail throughout this book. According to the family model of alcohol/drug use, alcohol and drug addiction and dependence are **family diseases.** The genetic predisposition to alcoholism is well documented. The probability of developing the disease of alcoholism and drug addiction is four times higher for those individuals who have one alcoholic or drug-addicted parent. The probability increases to eight times higher if both parents are alcoholics or addicts.

Children from alcoholic, dysfunctional, and shame-based family systems are at greater risk for developing problems with alcohol/drugs. The modeling of family members who use alcohol/drugs also greatly influences the development of alcohol/drug dependence. Exhibiting poor communication, the alcoholic/addict family has specific "no talk, no feel, and no trust" rules (see Chapter 7). Such a family system breeds childhood traumas of fear, rejection, abandonment, and sometimes violation (see Chapters 5 and 6).

Parents with substance-abuse problems have extreme difficulty in being effective parents. "Parenting is a difficult, time-consuming, complicated task. Staying on top of the situation requires quick, sensitive, and intuitive judgment of that which works best" (Kempher 1987). Parents with alcohol/drug problems are ill-equipped to provide the kind of patient, dedicated care necessary for children to develop and grow. Their parenting styles tend to be rigid and insensitive to the needs of children. These parents tend not to be nurturing and available. They often use coercive or abusive parenting techniques they learned from their own parents.

Adolescence

As children enter adolescence, they are at risk for alcohol/drug problems. (See Case Study 2.4 and 2.5.) In *Drugs and Drinking* (1985), Jay Strack classifies five major factors in adolescent abuse of drugs, using the mnemonic *PEACE:*

P—pressure (peer pressure)
E—escape
A—availability (of alcohol/drugs)
C—curiosity
E—emptiness

Poor Self-Concept

The most frequently generalized risk factor for problems with alcohol/drugs is a poor self-concept. Parents and schools talk about children's general under achievement,

Case Study 2.4

Adolescents and Alcohol/Drugs

After her birth, Joan was adopted into a wealthy family. Her birth mother had a history of emotional problems, and it is unknown whether she had problems with alcohol/drugs.

Joan, now 16 years old, was coming to counseling for an alcohol/drug evaluation. She was drunk at a party at her private high school. The parents described Joan's behavior as erratic, sometimes very loving and sensitive, and at other times explosively angry and out of control.

Joan was not adhering to simple boundaries that her parents had established (e.g., ignoring curfew, not calling if she is going to be late). They knew Joan was smoking marijuana but were unable to prevent her from using it.

The evaluation revealed that Joan is out of control. She blatantly told her parents that they were awful, and she was not going to listen to anything they said. Joan had a new older boyfriend (a 20-year old) and she was staying out overnight with him, doing cocaine and drinking alcohol. She had told her parents she was staying with friends.

Joan told the counselor her parents can't do anything. Joan did not see herself as having a drug problem, but did admit that she frequently lost her temper. Her grades in school were very good (3.8 GPA). She stated: "I just want to do what I want to do, and I am tired of my parents nagging all the time."

Discussion Questions

1. What role do you think being adopted plays in Joan's behavior and alcohol/drug use? Explain.
2. Do you think Joan has personality traits that are problematic? Explain.
3. Do you think Joan has an alcohol/drug problem? If so, explain with examples.
4. What kind of treatment counseling would you recommend for Joan and her family?

---

shyness, and aggressive or antisocial behavior as being a result of this lack of a good self-concept. Report cards and progress reports include comments such as "does not work up to his/her potential," "has difficulty finishing assignments and staying on task," "fails to participate in class, daydreams," and "more concerned with peers than teacher." It should be no surprise that the same evaluations occur for adults who have difficulty with work relationships and general achievement.

There are so many definitions of self-concept that isolating this variable as a causative factor for alcohol/drug problems is impossible. While exploring all of these definitions of self-concept, I developed a more workable behavioral definition that better explains what we are talking about. Instead of using the label *self-concept,* which implies something one gets from outside of oneself and is, therefore, beyond one's internal ability to develop, I relabeled it **sense of self**. A sense of self is less static than self-concept, involves more choices by the individual, and is active rather than passive. A sense of self comes from within to the outside world, rather than the outside world's defining who the individual is. This important point has implications for individuals who develop codependent

Case Study 2.5

Debra

Debra, 16 years old, is very bright, attractive, precocious, and looks like she is 18 or older. All her friends are older, and she prefers to spend time with college students. She has frequently attended fraternity parties.

Her parents are concerned because there is a family history of alcohol/drug addiction (i.e., her mother is a recovering alcoholic).

Recently, she confided to her parents that she drank too much and was date-raped by a boy she met at a college fraternity party.

Despite her parents' concerns about alcoholism, Debra believes she has no problem.

Discussion Questions

1. Do you think Debra has an alcohol problem? Explain why or why not.
2. What impact do you think the "date rape" had on Debra?
3. What developmental issues do you think need to be addressed?
4. If you were Debra's counselor, what would you want to work on?

relationships with addicts and alcoholics. (See Chapter 7.) Under this definition, a person with a sense of self is

1. A unique, worthwhile individual with emerging talents and skills.
2. An individual who can accomplish things (e.g., develop, prioritize, and achieve goals; solve problems; resolve conflicts; accept and carry out responsibilities; and have the maturity to develop and grow).
3. An individual who can trust and be trusted, one who sets appropriate boundaries for intimacy in relationships.

In his article "Beyond Drug Education," Paul Robinson (1975) argued that the goal is "not to convince people not to do drugs" but to empower them to enhance their development of self. Robinson suggests that we need to emphasize educational programs that help students acquire this sense of self, by helping students develop the skills to

- Control their destructive impulses.
- Understand their values, needs, and desires.
- Make wise decisions.
- Resist peer pressure when it endangers their welfare or inhibits their growth.
- Find nonchemical means of fulfillment and satisfaction.
- Think intelligently and rationally.

By focusing on programs that teach children and adults to develop and enhance a sense of self, we make them less at risk for alcohol and drug problems.

The more time I spend working in the fields of alcohol/drug recovery and mental health, the more clearly I see that a poor sense of self is a strong predictor of problems with alcohol/drugs. Families that do not promote the child's sense of self cause

TABLE 2.3	
Drugs and Their Effects	
Drugs	**Effects**
Narcotic analgesics	Kill pain, numb, shut out, and slow down
CNS depressants (e.g., alcohol)	Decrease activity, relaxation
CNS stimulants	Increase activity, excitation
Hallucinogens	Change the user's view of the world
Marijuana	Relaxation, stimulation of senses, and stimulation of thought

those children to be emotionally disabled (i.e., they develop a poor sense of self). In later chapters, I discuss these specific family issues in more detail.

Encouraging potential alcoholics and addicts to develop a sense of self is just one aspect of the problem; other factors must also be addressed. Even children and adults who possess a wonderful and creative sense of self can be at risk. Improving the sense of self is a preventive inoculation but is neither a cure nor a guarantee against having alcohol/drug problems. (See Chapter 11.)

Adolescence, in itself, is a time of risk for substance abuse. The developmental tasks of identify, self-worth, sexual and interpersonal identity, independence, school path toward career, achievement, motivation and direction, and other developmental issues are exacerbated by hormonal change, growth spurts, physical image and changes, peer identity and acceptance, and values clarification. Combine that with puberty, mood changes, conflicts with parents, school, driving, and other issues. It is no wonder that adolescents are at risk for substance abuse.

Hawkins, Catalono, and Miller (1992) have identified 17 risk factors for adolescent substance abuse of alcohol and other drugs and listed corresponding ways in which to prevent or address these factors. This comprehensive study, posted on the website at www.mhhe.com/fields8e, is an invaluable resource for helping you explore adolescent substance abuse.

People use drugs to get a variety of desired effects, such as pleasure, relaxation, excitation, relief from negative emotional states, and enhancement of positive emotional states (Table 2.3). For example, opiates (narcotic analgesics—e.g., heroin, morphine) are used to kill pain, numb, shut down, or shut out the world. In contrast, stimulants (e.g., cocaine, amphetamines) are used to increase stimulation, activity, and action. Unfortunately, continued drug use creates a negative cycle of abuse, dependence, and addiction.

✕ Other Factors that Contribute to Substance Abuse
Boredom and Altered States

Boredom is often cited as a major factor in alcohol/drug abuse by adolescents as well as adults. As previously described, the drive to alter one's consciousness is directly related to using alcohol/drugs to counter uncomfortable feelings of boredom.

Surprisingly there has been very little research to date into the nature of the relationship between boredom and alcohol/drug problems, alcoholism/addiction. Nor have there been concerted efforts to help addicts/alcoholics deal with boredom as a relapse dynamic.

McWelling Todman, Ph.D., an expert on the topic of boredom and psychiatric disorders, states:

> Despite its prominence in studies of human performance in industrial settings . . .
> the construct of boredom continues to be ignored by most clinicians. Even in the
> field of substance abuse, a field for which there has been no shortage of anecdotal
> and speculative commentary on boredom's motivational role in the addictive cycle,
> there has been surprisingly little in the way of empirical scrutiny. (Todman 2003)

The recent emphasis in the alcohol/drug recovery field of using meditation practices and mindfulness training is directly related to teaching people how to be more present and aware and to be able to deal more effectively with boredom by "showing up and being present" (see Chapters 12 and 13 on treatment and relapse prevention).

Boredom can involve many different issues. (See Chart 2.1.) Early research on boredom and alcohol use (Orcutt 1984) identified two different types of boredom. Existential boredom, which is defined as a lack of purpose in life, was found to have a strong, positive relationship to frequency of alcohol use among males. Another

---

C H A R T   2 . 1

Kinds of Boredom

Interpersonal Boredom

Being bored with "small talk" versus having feelings of "happiness with people"

Existential Boredom

Having difficulty with meaning or purpose in life

An inability to know what will make you happy leading to a pervasive sense of meaninglessness

Abandoning important life goals and dreams because of practical concerns or other pressures

Leisure Time Boredom

Not being able to find rewarding things to do during leisure time

Life Boredom

Neglect of life goals leading to a state of emotional ambivalence kind of boredom, interpersonal boredom, is defined as being bored with "small talk" versus having feelings of "happiness with people." Orcutt found that the more you are interpersonally bored, the more the quantity of alcohol consumed by males and females.

Impulsivity and Disinhibition

>It seemed like a good idea at the time.

Impulsivity/disinhibition includes personality traits such as sensation seeking and aggressiveness. I refer to some substance abusers as "edgewalkers"—people who are living on the edge of danger or risk. Impulsive/disinhibited individuals are at increased risk for alcohol-related problems (Caspi et al. 1997; Schukit 1998), and the traits of impulsivity/disinhibition are elevated in the children of alcoholics (Alterman et al. 1998; Scher 1991).

Alcohol/drug use involves taking the risks involved in using. There have always been individuals who, when told no, are curious and perhaps contrary and translate that no into yes. This is especially true of adolescents. Alcohol/drug use affects each individual's physical and emotional balance; for some, that balance is very delicate, even before they start to use alcohol/drugs. Individuals who have a need to be in control usually have a negative reaction when they use alcohol/drugs. People who enjoy losing control and are looking for an altered state of consciousness that approaches their outer limits of effective functioning become more involved in alcohol/drug use. Some thrill seekers may go further, to substance dependence and addiction.

The alcoholic/drug addict lifestyle, subculture, and environment are the most alluring features of addiction for some. Scoring drugs, hanging out in bars, associating with users, stealing, and engaging in other antisocial behaviors all reinforce the actual use of alcohol/drugs. The risk-taking behavior itself creates feelings of rebellion, aggression, rage, self-destructiveness, and "aliveness" (i.e., the adrenaline rush accompanying danger and fear).

The problems that result from these risk-taking behaviors lead to a vicious cycle of taking more alcohol/drugs to alleviate the feelings of pain, anxiety, and depression. This debilitating cycle continues until users recognize their own powerlessness and destructive behavior, or until they are in jail or dead.

Social Learning Theory

>It's fun to use and be with friends. . . . It's peer pressure. . . . It's cool to use and chill out. . . . I can use drugs and belong. . . . I can connect with others when we are together. . . . Sex is better. . . .

A variety of models can be considered psychosocial or social learning models. The key element of these models is the social learning aspect of alcohol/drug use. Social learning theory also incorporates other models, such as the tension-reduction model. For example, the young child who sees Dad drink his martini at the end of the day and witnesses the relief of tension may come to see drinking alcohol as an extremely positive experience. Children often experience their parents as more approachable and positive after they have used drugs or alcohol. Nathan (1983) describes alcohol use as a socially acquired, learned behavior pattern, maintained by antecedent cues (classical conditioning and expectancies), consequent reinforcements (operant conditioning and tension reduction), cognitive factors, modeling influences, and the interaction of behavioral and genetic mechanisms.

Marlatt and Gordon (1985) emphasize certain social learning and cognitive-behavioral points about addiction:

- Addictive behaviors are a category of "bad habits" (or learned maladaptive behaviors). Biological factors may contribute to predisposing an individual to alcohol problems, but specific patterns of use are learned.
- Addictive behaviors occur on a continuum of use—that is, behavior such as alcohol abuse is not categorical (e.g., present or absent) but instead varies in quantity and frequency of occurrence.
- All points along the continuum of addictive behavior are influenced by the same principles of learning. Therefore, the same mechanism that may be applied to explaining alcohol use can be invoked to explain alcohol-use disorder.
- Addictive behaviors are learned habits that can be analyzed in the same way as any other habit.
- The determinants of addictive behaviors are situational and environmental factors, beliefs and expectations, and family history and prior learning experiences with the substance or activity. Emphasis is also placed on the consequences of addictive behavior to understand its reinforcement and punishing features.
- Besides the effects of alcohol (or another substance or activity in question), it is also important to discern the social interpersonal reactions that the individual experiences before, during, and after engaging in the addictive behavior. Social factors are important in both the acquisition and later performance of the addictive behavior.
- Frequently, addictive behaviors are exhibited under conditions that are perceived as stressful. To that degree, they represent maladaptive coping behaviors.
- Addictive behaviors are strongly affected by the individual's expectations of achieving desired effects of engaging in the addictive behavior. Furthermore, self-efficacy expectancies (i.e., expectations of being able to use behavioral skills to cope with a situation without engaging in the addictive behavior) are important. If self-efficacy in a situation is low, and the individual believes (expects) that engaging in the addictive behavior would help him or her cope with it, then the likelihood of engaging in the behavior increases.
- The acquisition of new skills and cognitive strategies in a self-management program can result in changes in addictive behavior to new, more adaptive behaviors, which come under control of cognitive processes of awareness and decision making. Accordingly, the individual can assume and accept a greater degree of responsibility for changing the addictive behavior.

Sociocultural Models

In his review of cultural and cross-cultural studies, Bales (1946) identified factors in the influence of a culture or sociological organization on rates of alcoholism:

1. The degree to which a culture causes acute needs for adjustment of inner tension in its members.
2. The attitudes toward drinking that the culture produces in its members.
3. The degree to which the culture provides substitute means of satisfaction.

Societies, cultures, communities, socioeconomic groups, and even neighborhoods offering few or limited alternatives to drinking and drugging as tension relievers are more susceptible to addiction. The more these groups produce acute inner tensions (shame), suppressed or acted-out aggression, extreme conflict, dilemmas, mixed messages, sexual tensions, and the condoning of attitudes about alcohol/drugs as the normal, accepted way of relieving these tensions, the more prone individuals are to develop alcohol/drug dependence. When there is no limit on supply and distribution, attitudes are liberal, and cost is relative, the incidence of alcohol and drug abuse is high.

The attitude of the culture and ethnic customs may also facilitate patterns of alcohol/drug use. "The Irish and the American Indian groups positively sanction men's drinking to intoxication away from home; in these cultures the rates of alcoholism are high. Drug/alcohol dependence and addiction are influenced by sociological factors such as age, occupation, social class and subculture, and religious affiliation. In the United States, for example, young, single, unemployed urban men have a high incidence of abuse" (Donovan 1986).

Individuals who feel alienated from a larger society and who have no sense of belonging may feel that the society's rules and values about alcohol and drugs don't apply to them. This feeling of alienation from a larger social body may result in more favorable attitudes about alcohol/drugs. The application of this social model of alcohol/drug use is evidenced by the crack cocaine epidemic.

The lack of opportunity or hope that one can achieve the American Dream can contribute to feelings of despair that lead to alcoholism and/or drug addiction. This despair is most prevalent in the ghettos in America's inner cities. However, this sense of despair can occur in any locale, in any socioeconomic setting. From the blue-collar bars, to the shooting galleries in abandoned buildings, to middle-class suburban high schools, to the plush boardrooms of major corporations, drugs and alcohol infest our society.

Psychoanalytic Models—Psychoanalytic Meaning

The traditional psychoanalytic view of alcohol/drug dependence focused on a fixation at the oral stage of development, resulting in an oral and narcissistic premorbid personality. Otto Fenichel (1945) theorized that individuals use psychoactive drugs "to satisfy the archaic oral longing which is a sexual longing, a need for security, and need for the maintenance of self-esteem simultaneously." Menninger (1963) believed that alcohol may function as a coping device to alleviate stress and that the primary psychoanalytic root is a mother's denial of milk (security) in infancy.

Other psychoanalytic theories suggest drinking as a strategy for allaying anxiety over masculine inadequacy (Machover et al. 1959). Analytical theories also suggest that abusers use alcohol/drugs to suppress latent homosexuality and ego-dystonic feelings of homosexuality (i.e., the person's ego is not compatible with the possibility of being homosexual).

The dominant psychoanalytic explanation of alcohol/drug use today is that it is caused by "a structural deficit in object relations." This means that individuals have a hard time establishing effective interpersonal relationships due to their difficulty in managing their affect (feeling) and impulse controls. They often establish their defense mechanism of denial by defensive grandiosity. In 1986, James Donovan outlined psychoanalytic descriptions used by various researchers in identifying this difficulty in object relations:

> H. Krystal and H. A. Raskin (1970) indicated a defective stimulus barrier and an inability to desomatize emotions.
>
> Chein et al. (1964) described drug use to cope with painful feelings and overwhelming responsibilities in the outside world.
>
> L. Wurmser (1974) emphasized the maladaptive narcissism of the addict, a defensive stance against the potentially overwhelming feelings of rage and loneliness.
>
> E. J. Khantzian (1978) pointed to the impoverished self-esteem, the lack of capacity for self-care, and the poor emotional regulation of the alcoholic.
>
> Khantzian (1982) and Khantzian, Halliday, and McAuliffe (1990) described an inability to handle emotions and behavior characterized by swings from overcontrol to undercontrol. Feelings are often vague, ill defined, and confusing when expressed.
>
> Wurmser (1987) suggested drugs may be used to deny or "overthrow" a particularly burdensome and chafing inner authority figure.

Sometimes the choice of a particular drug is related to the meaning that drug has, both consciously and subconsciously, for that person.

Alcohol/Drugs as Power

Alcohol/drugs frequently denote power or feeling powerful to users. The expression *getting high* symbolizes feeling above others or above one's usual sense of self. Ironically, despite the original reason for using drugs to feel powerful, the ultimate state in the cycle of addiction makes the individual powerless. Cocaine is a drug that has a symbolic meaning of power. As a power drug, cocaine is attractive because of its status as well as its physical and psychological effects. An energizing stimulant, cocaine produces a sublime feeling of well-being; users describe being on top of the world, in control, able to accomplish a great deal, able to have tremendous capabilities and insights, and able to stimulate sexual arousal and performance. However, the reality today is that cocaine is one of the most addicting drugs, and one of the fastest addicting drugs, and it ultimately renders users powerless.

Alcohol and other drugs symbolize power in the forms of sensuality and sexuality; potency; the feelings of being supernatural, of pleasure, sensitivity, insensitivity, or not feeling pain; productivity; rebelliousness; high energy; and so forth.

Although cocaine may give users feelings of power, cocaine use can actually have many negative effects on personality and can quickly lead to addiction for some people. This photo is taken from a scene of the movie *Scarface*.
© Universal/The Kobal Collection/Art Resource

Our review of the research on why adolescents initially used marijuana indicated the following reasons: for pleasure, contentment, the joy of being high, relaxation, and recreation; to facilitate social interactions; to achieve status in one's peer group; to achieve friendship leading to better understanding; to defy authority, seek thrills, and flirt with danger; for curiosity and excitement, escapism, and enhancement of activity; to enhance aesthetic appreciation or sexual stimulation; to alleviate a sense of alienation; to make life better and more tolerable; to understand or find oneself; to expand one's mind for religious insights; to improve oneself.

Alcohol/Drugs as Self-Destruction

Alcohol/drugs can also have a powerful meaning as weapons of self-destruction and ultimately death. In *Family Therapy of Drug Abuse and Addiction,* M. Duncan Stanton and associates (1982) describe the addict as "part of a continuum of self-destruction." Stanton et al. report that, compared with the general public, addicts have a higher death rate, a shorter than average life expectancy, and a greater than normal incidence of sudden death. Compared to nonaddicts, addicts also have a more positive and potent view of death and are more likely to express a wish for death.

A number of clinicians have described alcoholism and drug addiction as an unconscious death wish. Self-destructiveness is the failure of ego functions involving self-care and self-protection. "We are all subject to our instincts, drives, and impulses, and if they are expressed indiscriminately, we are subject to hazard and danger" (Gottheil 1983).

Case Study 2.6

Lyn: Marijuana and Seduction

Lyn is a female client in outpatient therapy who successfully stopped smoking marijuana 10 months ago. At a party, a male acquaintance flirts with Lyn from across the room. She is very interested, so she returns the seductive eye contact. When they eventually make it to the same part of the room, they begin a conversation. He asks her out to the balcony where it is quieter. Even though Lyn has not smoked marijuana in 10 months and has a history of marijuana dependence, she accepts and smokes the marijuana he offers her, without much thought.

Discussion

Drugs are often linked to seduction and sexuality. For Lyn, the seductive nature and excitation of this new relationship was too powerful a draw for her to refuse the marijuana. She knew that marijuana had had significant negative consequences in her life, but the trigger of seduction overcame this awareness. Often people will say, "It seemed like a good idea at the time," rather than recognize the long-term consequences.

Discussion Questions

1. What role do alcohol/drugs play in seduction and sexuality?
2. Do you think alcohol/drugs can be cross-addicting with sexuality?
3. Explain the interaction dynamic of alcohol/drugs and sexuality (i.e., "Drugs, Sex, and Rock 'n' Roll").
4. What developmental problems can occur when alcohol/drugs are used to facilitate sexuality and intimacy?

Alcohol/Drugs in Seduction and Sexuality

Alcohol/drugs have important symbolic seduction and sexuality meanings. Practically all drugs and alcohol have been described at some time as aphrodisiacs. Unfortunately, no drug is truly an aphrodisiac. Alcohol/drugs may reduce inhibitions and stimulate sexual arousal at low doses; however, alcohol and other drugs impair sexual performance, especially with prolonged use.

The symbolic seduction and sexuality meanings of alcohol/drugs are exploited in advertisements for tobacco and alcohol products. If such advertising were legal, it would probably be used to advertise illicit drugs, too.

Whether celebrating an important event with a traditional toast of wine, champagne, or alcohol; passing around a pipe filled with marijuana; or sharing cocaine, heroin, or other drugs, the symbolic meaning is a shared altered state of consciousness (see Case Study 2.6).

Existential Issues

Existential issues have to do with the limitations of existence. These can include the limitations of life itself or how long we live, the unknowns related to death and dying, the pain of poor health, health-related problems and illness, the traumatic and untimely death of those close to us, ultimately being alone, the feelings of helplessness in not being in control, the dysphoria of life, boredom and ennui, the unknown, the betrayals, the loss or lack of spirituality, chronic long-lasting problems, even the eventual destruction of the planet Earth.

Drugs are a way to quiet, distract, or escape these existential issues and to gain a temporary relief and change in focus or perspective. However, it is a temporary and passive approach that doesn't resolve any issues but often leads to more drug use, and perhaps to a vicious pattern of substance abuse and/or addiction.

Poor Future Orientation and Hope

Michael Yapko, in his book *Breaking the Patterns of Depression* (1997), describes depression as having its roots in a "poor future orientation." Individuals who see their future as negative might abuse drugs, having a short-range view. Many addicts/ alcoholics report that they don't expect to live very long. Thinking that their life span is limited, they are not concerned about having good physical health. As one client put it, "I might as well party hearty, since I will die young, anyway."

Many adolescents have a poor future orientation because of a continued pattern of academic failure or a difficult family situation. Academic failure, especially in the late elementary grades, highly correlates with early antisocial behavior and alcohol/ drug abuse (Johnston et al. 1978; Kandel, Kessler, and Margulies 1978; Robins 1978). Many of these children fail to develop the skills necessary to learn, integrate concepts, and succeed in school. Many exhibit learning disabilities, emotional problems, and attention deficit disorder. These children's parents are frequently in denial of these emotional and learning disabilities, and the school system may not adequately address these problems, resulting in educational failure for the children. Some of these children do well during adolescence, some barely escape alcohol/drug problems, some develop addictions, and some die in alcohol/drug–related accidents and overdoses.

Some young adults might be frustrated that their careers are not developing. Middle-aged persons may be realizing that they face limitations and may not accomplish what they had intended. Older adults may have the existential despair about aging, future health problems, or death itself (see Case Study 2.7).

All of these issues may cause a person to have a poor future orientation. The adolescent, the young adult, the middle-aged person, and the elder may choose to abuse alcohol/drugs to cope with these discouraging issues. The obvious goal, whether the difficulty is poor future orientation, pessimism, or hopelessness, is to address these issues and to find new ways to enjoy life and relationships.

Hopelessness

It is hard to identify a single factor that leads to feeling hopeless, so hopeless that the person gives up (even if only temporarily) and stops trying to grow, achieve, and develop. Many clients feel as if they are getting nowhere, despite their continued efforts. It could be the hopelessness of poverty or financial disaster or of other socioeconomic loss. It could be the shattering of idealism in one's work or relationships.

Case Study 2.7

Poor Future Orientation

George: Recovering from Alcohol but Dying from Cigarettes

George had been in recovery from alcoholism for more than 2 years and recognized the benefits of sobriety. His financial situation was manageable and improving, he was losing weight gradually, he had a better relationship with his daughter, and even got along with his ex-wife.

When confronted in group therapy about his continued habit of smoking cigarettes, George maintained that he was going to smoke for one more year and then quit. His father had died of a heart attack at age 50, and George was now 49. He espoused a distorted belief that he had held for most of his life—that he was going to die by age 50. He rationalized that if he made it to 50, he would then stop smoking.

Discussion

Poor future orientation often involves limitations in one's view of future events and possibilities, whether financial, interpersonal, employment-related, or health-related. Poor future orientation is a major factor that exacerbates mood, often leading to depression.

This case illustrates George's pessimism about his own future health and his expectation and fear that he will (as his father did) die at age 50. George is living his life based on this belief, which is a distortion of reality. Although George is in recovery from alcohol and sees the benefits of his sobriety and working a recovery program, he is not committed to quit smoking. Exploring his belief that it may not be worth working on smoking cessation is an integral element to his taking action.

Discussion Questions

1. Do you think the addiction to "cigarettes" should be addressed when the person is in alcohol/drug treatment?
2. Do you think self-help meetings (e.g., Alcoholics Anonymous and Narcotics Anonymous) should be smoke-free?
3. How hard do you think nicotine addiction is to overcome, compared to other drugs?
4. Do you think people are still not in recovery if they are smoking cigarettes compulsively? Explain.

It could be the frustration of blocked goals and aspirations in employment, career, or interpersonal relationships. It could be the devastation of physical health, disease, physical injury, or the loss of a loved one. It could be the hopelessness of not knowing how to read or other blocks in learning or achievement. It could be the continual shame and loss of pride from emotional, physical, or sexual violation. It could be a single or continued exposure to a traumatic event or great loss that leads to feelings of hopelessness. One or all of these can lead to hopelessness, which can lead to increased drug use, alcohol/drug problems, and addiction.

Pessimism and Optimism

Many of my clients recovering from alcohol/drugs described their fathers as "pessimists." Their fathers (and sometimes their mothers) were extremely negative, sarcastic, shaming, critical of others, judgmental of their spouses and other family members, and pessimistic about the world in general. This pessimistic attitude was not limited to the fathers. Some family members were fearful and worried, expressing the philosophy that others would take advantage of people and "rip you off," either financially or emotionally. They viewed the world as hostile. As a result, they approached the world defensively, expecting to get hurt, looking for the negative. Some of these parents were alcoholics/addicts; some led lives that were limited, isolated in social and emotional connection, and not trusting or getting close to others.

Unfortunately, this pessimistic attitude contributes to alcoholism/addiction and is detrimental to recovery. Pessimistic individuals can maintain abstinence from alcohol/drugs, but they have difficulty trusting others or being vulnerable and real enough to get close to others, and they struggle with giving to others or attaining a spiritual sense of self. Developing and maintaining a support system for alcoholism/drug addiction is an integral element of recovery. However, developing the skills to overcome pessimism, and the mistrust of others and the world in general, is an ongoing developmental process.

Martin Seligman, in his book *Learned Optimism* (1991), describes pessimists as having a very negative view of the world and interpreting events as being **permanent, pervasive, and personalized.** These three *P*s of pessimism color the individuals' thoughts, beliefs, and attitudes about themselves and the world. Pessimists have these distorted thoughts about the world and over time continually approach situations with this distorted thinking process. They interpret a loss as permanent, verbalizing the all-or-none perception that "it will never get better, it will always be this way," making shaming self-statements, and seeing the world as hard, cruel, and uncaring. The pessimist takes one negative incident or a few negative situations or encounters and generalizes that they are pervasive (e.g., one or a few rejections lead to "No one loves me, there is nothing lovable about me, all of me is ugly"). Of course, the pessimist personalizes everything ("It was my fault," "If only I were . . ."). Most cognitive-behavioral therapists encourage their clients to take up these distorted thoughts by *disputing* the distorted reality and by *distracting* themselves from the incessant cycle or focus of these thoughts. This process of disputing and distracting from the distorted thoughts is a common strategy for cognitive-behavioral change.

> Distorted thought—"I can never be loved or find love."
> Dispute—"Love is precious but rare."
> Distorted thought—"No matter how hard I try, I can't ever be successful."
> Dispute—"Success is doing my best."

Seligman defines success as "talent/skill + drive + optimism." In his book, he has a test on optimism. I was very proud of how well I did on the test, soon to find out as I read the next page that even a little bit of pessimism can sabotage all the optimism you have.

Seligman says that an optimistic individual views setbacks, mistakes, and failure as *very temporary,* often confined to a *specific* situation, and *external,* or outside of

TABLE 2.4

Optimism and Pessimism

Dr. Seligman describes pessimists as thinking that a "negative event or interaction" is **permanent, pervasive** (in all parts of one's life), **and personalized** (caused by your own inadequacy). Whereas, an **optimist's** reaction to a negative event or interaction is very **temporary, specific** (related to this one event), and **external** (does not reflect the internal self).

Pessimism and Optimism	
Pessimism	**Optimism**
Permanent	Very temporary
Pervasive	Specific
Personalized	External

SOURCE: *Learned Optimism* by Martin Seligman, Pocket Press, 1991.

oneself (i.e., not an internal personalized flaw). Another term that many prevention specialists use to describe the optimistic personality is *resiliency*. Despite negative situations, resilient individuals challenge themselves to improve and don't think of themselves as victims. Optimists develop a plan to overcome the negative obstacles in their lives. They persevere through adversity (see Table 2.4).

You can certainly see how pessimism is a major characteristic of and contributing factor to alcoholism/addiction. The alcoholic/addict's sarcasm and sarcastic sense of humor underlie a **negative worldview.** Procrastination about organizing, cleaning up, or dealing with one's life is an ongoing aspect of this pessimistic view.

⚹ Appendix
Other Theories and Models

In this section, I highlight some of the many theories of drug abuse to help give you an orientation that will help you explore your own perspective of drug abuse.

- **Personality-Deficiency Theory—David P. Ausubel, M.D., Ph.D.** Describes narcotic addicts as having developmental personality traits of motivational immaturity, lacking in ego maturity of long-range goals, responsibility, self-reliance and initiative, volitional and executive independence, and the ability to defer the gratification of immediate hedonistic needs for the sake of achieving long-term goals.
- **The CAP Theory—Steven R. Gold, Ph.D.** The **cognitive-affective-pharmacogenic** (CAP) theory believes the cognitive style of the drug abuser is viewed as the pivotal factor in an individual's moving from drug experimentation to drug abuse. The abuse process begins with conflict,

having difficulty meeting society's demands or expectations, which leads to anxiety. The individual's interpretation of that anxiety is crucial. If he or she feels unable to alter or control the situation, the person feels powerless and is prone to using drugs to alter the anxiety and related feelings.

- **Existential Theory—George B. Greaves, Ph.D.** Individuals use drugs as a passive means of euphoria, or at least as a means of removing some of the pain and anxiety attending a humorless, dysphoric lifestyle.
- **An Ego-Self Theory of Substance Dependence—Edward J. Khantzian** Individuals are predisposed to drug use and dependence, as a result of severe ego impairments and disturbances in the sense of self, involving difficulties with drive and affecting defense, self-care, dependency, and the need for satisfaction.
- **An Availability-Proneness Theory of Illicit Drug Abuse—Reginald G. Smart, Ph.D.** Availability refers to the set of physical, social, and economic circumstances surrounding the ease or difficulty of obtaining drugs, especially the cost and the physical effort required to obtain them. The theory also looks at psychological problems as making individuals "prone" to certain drugs and drug abuse.
- **Drug Use as a Protective Defense—Leon Wurmser, M.D.** Drug use as a pharmacologically reinforced denial—an attempt to get rid of the feeling import of more or less extensive portions of undesirable inner and outer reality.
- **Problem-Behavior Theory—Richard Jessor, Ph.D., and Shirley Jessor, Ph.D.** In problem-behavior theory, the personality system is represented by a number of specific variables belonging to three component structures—a motivational-instigation structure, a personal belief structure, and a personal control structure.
- **Drug Subculture Theories—Bruce D. Johnson, Ph.D.** Explores the linkages between the parent subcultures, peer cultures, and drug subcultures.
- **Self-Esteem and Self-Derogation Theory of Drug Abuse—Howard B. Kaplan, Ph.D.** Adoption of the deviant response (drug abuse) has self-enhancing consequences if it facilitates intrapsychic or interpersonal avoidance of self-devaluing experiences associated with the traditional values of the culture.
- **The Iowa Theory of Substance Abuse Among Hyperactive Adolescents— Jan Loney, Ph.D.** Diagnostic evidence has centered upon the four As—activity (hyperkinetic reaction of childhood), attention (attention deficit disorder), aggression (conduct disorder), and/or achievement (learning disability).
- **A Family Theory of Drug Abuse—M. Duncan Stanton, Ph.D.** Symptoms occur and serve functions within a context (the family), both for the symptom-bearer and for the other family members. Accumulated data indicate that a high percentage of drug abusers' families have experienced premature loss or separation during the family's life cycle. Families of drug abusers show a high proportion of traumatic, untimely, or unexpected loss of a family member.
- **Self-Esteem Theory of Drug Abuse—R. A. Steffenhagen, Ph.D.** This theory is a developmental one emanating from an Adlerian approach in

which self-esteem is seen as the main psychodynamic mechanism underlying all drug use and abuse, including inferiority-superiority, social interest, goal orientation, and lifestyle.

- **Psychosocial Theory of Drug Abuse: A Psychodynamic Approach—Herbert Hendin, M.D.** In the case of the drug problem, social variables ranging from sexual activity to association with friends who use drugs have been shown to be related to drug use. There is a need for a psychodynamic approach to psychosocial problems.
- **Toward a Sociology of Drug Use—Irving F. Lukoff, Ph.D.** The view that it is less useful to speak of drug use alone, because those who are heavily invested in drug use are also part of more integrated lifestyles, different in the ghettos than on the campuses, but at variance with many aspects of conventional adult culture.
- **Achievement, Anxiety, and Addiction—Rajendra K. Misra, D.Phil.** Drug use is initiated as a time-saving device to cope with the stress of achieving. Drugs are used to relieve anxiety, to induce relaxation, and overcome boredom.
- **Addiction to Pleasure—Nils Bejerot, M.D.** Describes drug addiction as a chemical love. The pleasure mechanism may be stimulated in a number of ways and give rise to a strong fixation on repetitive behavior.
- **Brain and Neurotransmitters: Pharmacological Approach—William R. Martin, M.D.** The brain has a variety of receptors and several neurotransmitters that are involved in feelings of well-being. Further, many addicts and alcoholics have an affective disorder that appears to be the polar opposite of feelings of well-being produced by drugs of abuse.

SOURCE: Adapted from "Theories of Drug Abuse," National Institute on Drug Abuse *Research Monograph 30,* 1960.

❋ In Review

- Alcohol and drugs are used for a variety of desired effects, including altering consciousness, dealing with boredom, giving in to impulsivity, and engaging in a passive activity.
- In 1957, the American Medical Association (AMA) declared alcoholism a disease based on three criteria: (1) there is a known etiology (cause), (2) symptoms get worse over time, and (3) alcoholism has known outcomes.
- One researcher, Devor (1994), describes alcoholism in terms of a developmental-genetic model.
- Adoption studies and twin studies support the view that there is a genetic disposition to alcoholism.
- Various personality traits are more pronounced in addicts/alcoholics (e.g., risk taking, impulsivity).
- The two personality disorders most associated with alcoholism/addiction are narcissistic and borderline personality.
- The tension reduction theory (TRT) is one of the most widely researched theories of drug use.

- The family model sees alcoholism/addiction as a family disease in that all family members were affected by the alcoholic/addict's behavior.
- The probability of developing the disease of alcoholism and drug addiction is four times higher for those individuals who have an alcoholic or drug dependent parent. The probability increases to eight times higher if both parents are alcoholics or addicts.
- As children enter adolescence, they are at risk for alcohol/drug problems. The most frequently generalized risk factor is having a problem with poor self-concept.
- There are two major theories regarding trauma and substance abuse— individuals who use alcohol/drugs do so to assuage feelings related to traumatic experiences; chronic substance abuse can change the neurochemistry, making the user more susceptible to post traumatic stress disorder.
- Edward Khantzian (1985) makes the case that drug use is not a random phenomenon. Instead, he says it is a purposeful attempt by the user to assuage painful affective states and manage psychological problems and disorders.
- Cloninger (1987) in his neurological model of alcohol abuse that here dimensions of personality make an individual at risk for alcohol abuse and dependence.
- A very strong reinforcing factor in alcohol/drug use is the memorable feelings attached to using alcohol/drugs.

⚔ Discussion Questions

1. Using Worksheet 2.1, describe your rationale for rating the models and theories of addiction.
2. Alcoholics Anonymous is described by Borkman (2008) as a "voluntary mutual help association." What do you think of that statement?
3. Since altering consciousness is a natural drive, how do you satisfy that in healthy ways?
4. Discuss why adolescents are at risk for substance abuse problems.
5. Khantzian's self-medication model makes the case that drug use is not a random phenomenon. Discuss that contention.
6. Discuss drugs in relation to their use in seduction and sex, due to their ability to loosen inhibitions and spike arousal.
7. Rate family members and yourself on these traits that make an individual at risk for alcohol/drug problems. The sliding scale is as follows: 0 (none), 1 (low), to 10 (high).

   - Impulsivity
   - Novelty seeking
   - Pessimism
   - Tendency to be easily bored
   - Poor interpersonal skills
   - Disinhibition
   - Risk-tasking behaviors

Exploring Your Own Perspective

Please rate the following models and theories discussed in this chapter on the scale of 0 (no impact) to 7 (extremely strong impact).

Models and Theories of Alcohol/Drug Abuse

	0	1	2	3	4	5	6	7
Disease								
Genetic								
Personality Traits								
Tension Reduction								
Family								
Self-Medicating								
Social Learned Behavior								
Sociocultural								
Psychological								
Existential								
Moods/Feelings								
Personality								

✷ References

Alterman, A. I., et al. 1998. Personality pathology and drinking in young men at high and low familial risk for alcoholism. *Journal of Studies on Alcohol* 59: 495–502.

Bales, R. 1946. Cultural differences in rates of alcoholism. *Quarterly Journal of Studies of Alcohol* 6: 480–99.

Blane, Howard T., and Kenneth E. Leonard, eds. 1988. *Psychological theories of drinking and alcoholism.* New York: Guilford Press.

Caspi, A., et al. 1997. Personality differences predict health-risk behaviors in adulthood: Evidence from a longitudinal study. *Journal of Personality and Social Psychology* 73: 1052–63.

Chein, I., et al. 1964. *The road to H.* New York: Basic Books.

Cloninger, C. R. 1987. A systematic method for clinical description and classification of personality variants. *Archives of General Psychiatry* 44: 573–88.

Cloninger, C. R. 1987. Neurogenetic adaptive mechanisms in alcoholism. *Science* 236: 410–416.

Cloninger, C. R., M. Bohman, and S. Sigvardsson. 1981. Inheritance of alcohol abuse. *Archives of General Psychiatry* 38: 861–68.

Csikszentmihalyi, Mihalyi. 1992. *Flow: The psychology of optimal experience.* New York: Tarcher/Putnam.

Devor, Eric. 1994. A developmental-genetic model of alcoholism: Implications for genetic research. *Journal of Consulting and Clinical Psychology* 62(6): 1108–15.

Donovan, James M. 1986. Etiological model of alcoholism. *American Journal of Psychiatry* 143: 1–11.

Fenichel, Otto. 1945. *The psychoanalytic theory of neurosis.* New York: W. W. Norton.

Gitlow, S. E. 1972. The pharmacological approach to alcoholism. *Journal of Drug Issues* 2(3): 32–41.

Gitlow, S. E. 1985. Considerations on the evaluation and treatment of substance dependency. *Journal of Substance Abuse Treatment* 2: 175–79.

Goodwin, D. W. 1971. Is alcoholism hereditary? A review and critique. *Archives of General Psychiatry* 25: 545–49.

Gottheil, Edward, ed. 1983. *Etiological aspects of alcohol/drug abuse.* Springfield, Ill.: Charles C. Thomas.

Gurling, H. M., et al. 1984. Genetic epidemiology in medicine: Recent twin research. *British Medical Journal* 288: 3–5.

Hawkins, David, R. Catalono, and J. Miller. 1992. Risk and protective factors for alcohol and other drug problems in adolescence and early childhood: Implications for substance abuse prevention. *Psychological Bulletin* 112(1): 64–105.

Helzer, J. E., and T. R. Pryzbeck. 1988. The co-occurrence of alcoholism with other psychiatric disorders in the general population and its impact in treatment. *Journal of Studies on Alcohol* 49: 219–24.

Hennecke, Lynne. 1984. Stimulus augmenting and field dependence in children of alcoholic fathers. *Journal of Studies on Alcoholism* 45: 486–92.

Hesselbrock, M. N., R. E. Meyer, and J. J. Keener. 1985. Psychopathology in hospitalized alcoholics. *Archives of General Psychiatry* 42: 219–24.

Hosier, Steven G., and W. Miles Cox. 2011. Personality and motivational correlates of alcohol consumption and alcohol problems among excessive drinking university students. *Addictive Behaviors* 36: 87–94.

Hrubec, Z., and G. S. Omenn. 1981. Evidence of genetic predisposition to alcoholic cirrhosis and psychosis: Twin concordance for alcoholism and its end points by zygosity among male veterans. *Alcoholism* 5: 207–15.

Jellinek, E. M. 1960. *The disease concept of alcoholism.* New Haven, Conn.: Hillhouse Press.

Johnston, L. O., et al. 1978. Drugs and delinquency: A search for causal connections. In *Longitudinal research on drug use,* edited by D. B. Kandel. Washington, D.C.: Hemisphere.

Kaij, L. 1960. *Alcoholism in twins: Studies in the etiology and sequelae of abuse of alcohol.* Stockholm: Alonquist & Winkell.

Kandel, D. B., R. Kessler, and R. Margulies. 1978. Antecedents of adolescent initiation into stages of drug use: A developmental analysis. In *Longitudinal research on drug use,* edited by D. B. Kandel. Washington, D.C.: Hemisphere.

Kempher, Carol. 1987. Special populations: Etiology and prevention of vulnerability to chemical dependence in children of substance abusers. In *Youth at high risk for substance abuse.* Washington, D.C.: U.S. Department of Human Services.

Khantzian, E. J. 1978. The ego, the self, and opiate addiction: Theoretical and treatment considerations. *International Review of Psychoanalysis* 5: 189–98.

Khantzian, E. J. 1982. Psychopathology, psychodynamics, and alcoholism. In *Encyclopedia handbook of psychiatry,* edited by E. M. Pattison and E. Kaufman. New York: Gardner Press.

Khantzian, E. J. 1985. The self-medication hypothesis of addictive disorders: Focus on heroin and cocaine dependence. *Journal of Psychiatry* 142(11): 1–39.

Khantzian, E. J., K. S. Halliday, and W. E. McAuliffe. 1990. *Addiction and the vulnerable self.* New York: Guilford Press.

Krystal, H., and H. A. Raskin. 1970. *Drug dependence: Aspects of ego functions.* Detroit: Wayne State University Press.

Machover, S., et al. 1959. Clinical and objective studies of personality variables in alcoholism: An objective study of homosexuality in alcoholics. *Quarterly Journal of Studies in Alcohol* 20: 528–42.

Marin, Steven, and Roger D. Weiss. 1986. Psychiatric comorbidity in drug and alcohol addiction. *Journal of Drug Education.*

Marlatt, A., and J. Gordon. 1985. *Relapse prevention: Maintenance strategies in the treatment of addictive behaviors.* New York: Guilford Press.

Menninger, K. 1963. *The vital balance.* New York: Viking Press.

Nathan, P. E. 1983. A behavioral overview of alcohol abuse and alcoholism. In *Etiological aspects of alcohol and drug abuse,* edited by E. Gottheil, K. A. Druley, T. E. Skoloda, and H. M. Waxman, pp. 141–58. Springfield: C. C. Thomas.

National Institute on Drug Abuse. 1960. Theories of drug abuse. Research Monograph 30.

Orcutt, J. D. 1984. Contrasting effects of two kinds of boredom on alcohol use. *Journal of Drug Issues* 14(1): 161–73.

Petrie, A. 1960. Some psychological aspects of pain and the relief of suffering. *Annals of the New York Academy of Sciences* 86: 13–27.

Robins, L. W. 1978. Sturdy childhood predictors of adult antisocial behavior: Replication from longitudinal studies. *Psychology Medicine* 8: 617–22.

Robinson, Paul E. 1975. Beyond drug education. *Journal of Drug Education* 5(1): 183–91.

Rotgers, Frederick, et al. 2003. *Treating Substance Abuse: Theory & Technique.* New York: Guilford Press.

Scher, K. J. 1991. *Children of alcoholics: A critical appraisal of theory and research.* Chicago: University of Chicago Press.

Schukit, M. A. 1998. Biological, psychological, and environmental predictors of alcoholism risk: A longitudinal study. *Journal of Studies in Alcohol* 59: 485–94.

Seligman, Martin E. P. 1991. *Learned optimism: How to change your mind and your life.* New York: Pocket Books.

Stanton, M. Duncan, et al. 1982. *The family therapy of drug abuse and addiction.* New York: Guilford Press.

Strack, Jay. 1985. *Drugs and drinking: What every teen and parent should know.* Nashville: Nelson.

Tabakoff, Boris, and Paula L. Hoffman. 1988. Genetics and biological markers of risk for alcoholism. *Public Health Report* 103(6): 690–98.

Tarter, R., and K. Edwards. 1985. Neuropsychology of alcoholism. In *Alcohol and the brain,* edited by R. Tarter and Van Thiel, pp. 217–42. New York: Plenum.

Todman, McWelling. Summer 2003. Boredom and psychotic disorders: Cognitive and motivational issues. *Journal of Psychiatry* 66(2).

Whitlock, F. A., et al. 1967. Drug dependence in psychiatric patients. *Medical Journal of Australia* 1: 11–57.

Williams, Julie K., Douglas C. Smith, Hyonggin An, and James A. Hall. March 2008. Clinical outcomes of traumatized youth in adolescent substance abuse treatment: A longitudinal multisite study. *Journal of Psychoactive Drugs* 40(1).

Wurmser, L. 1974. Psychoanalytic considerations of the etiology of compulsive drug use. *Journal of the American Psychoanalytic Association* 22: 820–43.

Wurmser, L. 1987. Flight from conscience: Experience with the psychoanalytic treatment of the compulsive drug abuser. *Journal of Substance Abuse Treatment* 4: 169–79.

Yapko, Michael D. 1997. *Breaking the patterns of depression.* New York: Doubleday.

Drug-Specific Information

Drugs on the Street Where You Live

Outline of Chapter 3

Drugs in Our Society
- A New Era for Marijuana: Its Medical Usage
- Energy Drinks
- Crystal Methamphetamine
- MDMA (Ecstasy)
- OxyContin Abuse
- Heroin
- Inhalants

Definitions of Terms
- Physical Dependence
- Withdrawal
- Psychological Dependence (Formerly, Habituation)
- Tolerance
- Cross-Tolerance
- Synergism
- Antagonism
- Routes of Administration
- Set and Setting

Definition of Addiction
- Drug Absorption, Distribution, and Elimination

Classification of Drugs
- Narcotic Analgesics
- Central Nervous System Depressants
- Central Nervous System Stimulants
- Hallucinogens

Athletes and Drugs
- Steroids
- Amphetamines
- Chewing Tobacco
- Other Drugs/Alcohol in Sports

Objectives

1. Explain the current changes in marijuana use, including medical uses of marijuana.
2. Explain the dangers of energy drinks when they are consumed with alcohol.
3. Outline the problems with the following drugs—methamphetamine, MDMA, heroin, OxyContin, and inhalants.

4. Define the following terms—physical dependence, withdrawal, psychological dependence, tolerance, cross-tolerance, synergism, and antagonism.
5. Define and describe addiction, routes of administration, set and setting, drug absorption, distribution, and elimination.
6. Define addiction using the three Cs of addiction.
7. Identify and list the drugs for each of the five classifications of drugs.
8. List and describe the hazards in using alcohol and other sedative-hypnotics.
9. Identify and describe the major effects of central nervous system stimulants.
10. Identify and describe the major effects of hallucinogens.
11. Identify and describe the major effects of all cannabis sativa products.
12. Identify and describe the major effects of inhalants and phencyclidine.
13. Explain the relationship of drugs and athletic performance in sports.

✺ Drugs in Our Society

The 1960s and 1970s were truly the birth of the modern drug revolution. Marijuana, hallucinogens (especially LSD), and other drugs became a major part of the hippie movement of that time. It was a time when young people rebelled against their parents' traditional values by using drugs, dressing differently, growing their hair long, espousing open love, and listening to rock 'n' roll. They also staged protests against civil rights violations, the war in Vietnam, and the traditional values of our political system.

In the 1980s, cocaine became the rage—a drug that was first thought to produce only psychological dependence. However, over the next 10 years, this drug would cause us to dramatically change our definition of addiction and our whole outlook on drug abuse. Cocaine was soon being used intravenously and smoked in the form of *freebase cocaine.* Comedian Richard Pryor set himself on fire while smoking freebase cocaine, and John Belushi died when he overdosed by injecting cocaine and heroin ("speedballing"). Both of these unfortunate tragedies brought cocaine to the forefront. A dramatic and tragic victim of cocaine was Len Bias, a talented college basketball player who had been drafted by the Boston Celtics. Boston fans were elated at the prospect of Bias and Larry Bird being on the same team. Unfortunately, on the evening he was drafted by the Celtics, Bias celebrated with freebase cocaine and died.

Soon cocaine was being converted to *crack cocaine.* Crack addicts in the inner cities became a major addict population that quickly challenged our treatment and criminal-justice system. Babies born to mothers who were addicted to crack cocaine were another casualty of this new drug.

It is fair to say that cocaine changed our entire outlook about addiction. Even individuals who thought that drugs were rather benign and produced only psychological dependence could not ignore the high addiction potential of cocaine. This short-acting drug created addicts very quickly, with dramatic and disastrous effects on their lives. It also affected people from all socioeconomic levels.

Another group of drugs that came to our attention in the mid-1980s was synthetically produced drugs. In an attempt to subvert existing controlled substance laws, underground chemists created new drugs that were chemically different (by a molecule or two) from those banned by existing drug laws.

Donald Wesson, an expert in the alcohol/drug field, defined designer drugs as "substances wherein the psychoactive properties of a scheduled drug have been retained, but the molecular structure has been altered in order to avoid prosecution under the Controlled Substance Act." The potency and volume of production of these drugs challenged our perception of illicit drug manufacturing. There was no need for the large production and distribution networks like those used for cocaine and marijuana. There was no harvest of the drug. Instead, one chemist with the basic raw materials could produce enough of the drug to supply the entire United States.

In the early 1990s, another new drug brought to public attention was *ice*. Ice is a transparent, sheetlike crystalline structure that is a purified form of the drug methamphetamine hydrochloride. In the early 1990s, ice was imported to the mainland United States by eastern drug cartels operating out of Oahu, Hawaii. In January 1990, authorities busted the operation of an ice factory in northern California. At that time, the National Institute on Drug Abuse reported the use of ice in cities such as Atlanta, Dallas, Los Angeles, Phoenix, San Diego, and Seattle. Attempts to develop ice on the East Coast did not pan out. Much as crack is to cocaine, ice is to methamphetamine. Ice is a smokable and more powerful form of methamphetamine hydrochloride. Smoking ice allows more rapid absorption into the blood via the lungs. Unlike the extremely short-acting high of freebase and crack cocaine, the ice high can last from 7 to 30 hours.

A New Era for Marijuana: Its Medical Usage

As outlined in Chapter 1, the legalization of medical marijuana is the single most significant change in recent drug history. The federal government is leaving it up to the States to legalize medical marijuana and approve medical marijuana dispensaries.

The problem is the limited research on medical marijuana. "A review by researchers in Canada (where medical marijuana is legal) identified only 31 studies [that] focused on medical benefits of the drug. A separate review by the American Medical Association (AMA) also concluded that the research base remains sparse."

Marijuana research has some inherent problems because of marijuana's illicit status. There are also research difficulties because of variables that are hard to control (e.g., potency, method of ingestion, frequency of use, etc.).

There is no denying some of the many benefits and applications of marijuana for medical conditions. We are even seeing marijuana as being helpful for treating osteoporosis in the elderly and for hospice patients. We do not know whether medical marijuana users will experience significant adverse effects such as dependence, addiction, increased anxiety, and/or increased depression.

Three key points made in the Harvard Mental Health Letter in April 2010 stated that

- Medical marijuana may be an option for treating certain conditions, such as nerve pain or chemotherapy-related nausea.
- There is not enough evidence to recommend medical marijuana as a treatment for any psychiatric disorders.
- The psychiatric risks are well documented and include addiction, anxiety, and psychosis.

Financial and Future Implications for Medical Marijuana

There is a potential for financial benefit for States to legalize medical marijuana and medical marijuana dispensaries. At a time of economic recession, medical marijuana has the potential to bring States much needed sources of revenue. If the system is effective and expands, it would reduce the money spent on enforcement of cannabis prohibition, estimated at $7.7 billion per year (Temple et al. 2011). It could eventually lead to a reduction in illegal drugs from Mexico and other countries and savings in the federal budget for programs of interdiction and supply. Marijuana could become a "cash crop" product, much like alcohol and tobacco, and has the potential to surpass profits from both alcohol and tobacco. An interesting point is that pharmaceutical companies who produce sleep aids and medications for anxiety, depression, nausea, and pain will probably see decreased revenue if medical marijuana becomes a staple for medical treatments.

Lollipops to Vaporizing Marijuana

The health-related concerns of smoking marijuana (especially lung and throat cancer) have led to a marketplace of marijuana products that are ingested without smoking. Medical marijuana dispensaries are producing lollipops, chocolate bars, and baked goods. Vaporizers are also available at various levels of sophistication and price. Inhaling the marijuana vapors is less harmful than smoking marijuana.

Resurgence of Marijuana Use by the Young and Old

Another part of the marijuana story is the resurgence of marijuana use by high school students. They are increasing their use of marijuana, and they see marijuana as less harmful. Adults 50 and over are increasing their use of marijuana as well. A portion of these adult users are "resumers," that is those who recently emerged from a long hiatus of smoking marijuana. In his article, Daniel Enger jokingly describes these older resumers as "Puff Daddies" and "Pot Mommies." Some of these Baby Boomer adults get their marijuana from their adult children.

Energy Drinks

Energy drinks (ED) appear to be innocuous, but combined with alcohol they can be deadly. Energy drinks are very popular with college students and young adults, especially athletes and students who are physically active. A jolt from an energy drink is attractive to this age group, who discount the impact. That jolt contains mega doses of taurine, B-vitamin, and other substances, which with prolonged use can be toxic. "With increases in ED strength and the introduction of energy shots . . . containing 350 mg. of caffeine in 2.5 ounces the dangers of EDs are greater than just a few years ago" (Woolsey 2010).

Combine these drinks with alcohol and you have a potentially fatal cocktail. The ED can mask the effect of the alcohol, so more alcohol is consumed and can be potentiated by an increase in ED consumption. Unfortunately, there has not been significant research on the safety of ED ingredients. As Woolsey points out ED manufacturers in the United States, avoid FDA regulations by classifying EDs as dietary supplements.

Crystal Methamphetamine

The United States is currently experiencing an upward cycle of stimulant abuse, with a dramatic increase in the availability and use of crystal methamphetamine, in a potency, purity, and accessibility unlike that found at any previous time in our history. This is a substance that does not occur in nature and thus must be synthesized in a laboratory.

Street names for this drug include speed, crank, crystal, ice, meth, chalk, chicken powder, peanut butter-crank, go-fast, crystal meth, shabu-shabu, glass, go qip, chris, and christy, depending on the geographical area, the dealer, and the physical form, crystal versus powder.

The name *ice* has been used by dealers to represent methamphetamine as well as other substances, including methamphetamine mixed with heroin, cocaine, or other adulterants, quartz, and rock salt.

Part of this alarming trend is ascribed to the takeover of the manufacture and distribution of speed, formerly the province of outlaw fringe individuals, by Mexican nationals, who already had a strong, well-organized distribution network. This has resulted in a much purer, significantly more potent, and lower priced drug, precipitating a sharp increase in the number of users, including much younger users.

Methamphetamine enters the brain more rapidly than any other CNS stimulant, rapidly producing a "rush" of euphoria when injected or smoked. Many people who try methamphetamine go on to compulsive abuse of the drug. Typically, small doses can have a profound effect, including stimulated movement and increased speech, feelings of excitement and euphoria, and decreased appetite. A significant rise in pulse rate and blood pressure occurs, as well as a sensation often described by users as "my heart pounding out of my chest." This may progress to irregularities in heart rhythm, a dramatic rise in body temperature, convulsions, cardiovascular collapse, and death.

Populations Using Methamphetamine

- Traditionally associated with white, male, blue-collar workers, methamphetamine is now reportedly being used by diverse groups in all regions of the country.
- Use is increasing among men who have sex with men and use other drugs, making this population more vulnerable to contracting and spreading sexually transmitted diseases, especially HIV/AIDS.
- Young adults who attend "raves" or private clubs are increasingly using methamphetamine.
- Notable increases are occurring among homeless and runaway youth.
- Increasing use of methamphetamine is reported among male and female commercial sex workers who also trade sex for drugs and among members of motorcycle gangs. Also, people in occupations that demand long hours, mental alertness, and physical endurance (such as long-haul truckers) have been using this drug at increased rates (National Institute on Drug Abuse 1998).

Methamphetamine Use by Adolescents

There are mixed reports on methamphetamine use by young people. The U.S. federal government statistics in a nationwide survey of 12th graders indicates a significant downward trend of lifetime methamphetamine use by adolescents from 1999 to 2005 (4.75 to 2.5 percent). Yet, state and local drug treatment programs report that more than 20 percent of adolescent admissions report methamphetamine abuse and dependence (Rawson 2007).

Methamphetamine use by adolescents can also cause significant problems including:

- Different types of neurological and psychiatric consequences (since the adolescent brain is still developing)
- High levels of depression and suicidal ideation compared to other substance abuse (e.g., marijuana, alcohol)
- Implications in risky sexual behavior
- Problematic among girls (i.e., much higher admissions to treatment programs than boys) (Rawson 2007)

You Can Identify Methamphetamine Users by . . .

- Signs of agitation, excited speech, decreased appetites, and increased physical activity levels. Other common symptoms include dilated pupils, high blood pressure, irregular heartbeat, chest pain, shortness of breath, nausea and vomiting, diarrhea, and elevated body temperature.
- Occasional episodes of sudden and violent behavior, intense paranoia, visual and auditory hallucinations, and bouts of insomnia.
- A tendency to compulsively clean and groom and repetitively sort and disassemble objects, such as cars and other mechanical devices (National Institute on Drug Abuse 1998).

Chronic use leads to a state of paranoia, with individuals displaying behaviors strikingly resembling those of someone experiencing an acute episode of paranoid schizophrenia. Tolerance develops quickly, and chronic users must increase their dose, which, in turn, leads to magnification of the side effects and may lead to permanent brain damage.

In addition to the physical symptoms, the chronic user will experience a profound depression, with low energy levels, anhedonia (the total inability to experience any pleasurable feelings), and such a profound craving for the drug, remembering when the drug "worked" for them, that the cycle is often repeated many times, often with tragic results.

Ice, the smokable form of methamphetamine, is of extremely high purity—greater than 90 percent—and can lead to "runs" of 4 to 5 days without any sleep and often without food or even fluids. Then, a "crash" of 4 days or so occurs, before the user begins another "run."

The drug, regardless of form, is often used concurrently with alcohol, either to blunt some of the stimulant effect or to help the user "come down" after a protracted period of use. The use of other depressant psychoactive substances leads to a polydrug use pattern that can be extremely dangerous.

MDMA (Ecstasy)

MDMA is better known as Ecstasy, XTC, X, Rave, or Adam. Although MDMA was first synthesized and patented in 1914 as an appetite suppressant, it became popular in the 1980s with college students. Prior to July 1985, when it became illegal to sell MDMA, or Ecstasy, the drug was legally sold in bars in Texas catering to college students. A major factor that contributed to MDMA's emergence in the rest of the country was publicity—associated with the drug being blatantly sold in bars and then with its being scheduled as a controlled substance. In 1985, *Newsweek, Time, Life,* and other magazines sensationalized the euphoric, therapeutic, and aphrodisiac qualities of the drug. MDMA is related to both mescaline and amphetamines and could be best described as a "mood-enhancing stimulant." It is often perceived as "mild speed," and users often claim that it increases empathy and communication, which is why it is also called the "hug drug." A subculture has evolved around the drug, with resultant Ecstasy and rave parties, which are often clandestine (although most young adults seem to have no problem knowing where they are), changing location as often as every weekend.

Even though it is often referred to as hallucinogenic, it rarely produces delusions. MDMA is most frequently taken orally, with reports of a variety of psychological effects, including the following:

- Positive mood change
- Dramatic drop in defense mechanisms
- Increased empathy for others
- Increased self-esteem and elevated mood

Combined with the stimulant effect, these also may produce an increase in communication, intimacy, and enhanced pleasure of touching, yet MDMA inhibits orgasm and interferes with erection.

Negative effects include overdose potential, extreme fatigue with too much use, dilated pupils, dry mouth and throat, tension in the lower jaw, grinding of the teeth, and too much stimulation.

Although users tend to perceive MDMA as harmless, there are reports of cases of acute and chronic paranoia associated with usage, and even panic reactions requiring emergency care. As with other central nervous stimulants, a rise in blood pressure accompanies its use; this is of no consequence to most otherwise healthy young adults but can have a potentially deadly effect on someone with an underlying cardiac problem or a congenital abnormality.

There often appears to be a hangover effect, consisting of muscle aches, especially of the jaw and facial muscles (clenching of the teeth is common); generalized fatigue; decreased concentration; and insomnia. Tolerance to the mood- and mind-altering effect does develop, with subsequent increase in the "unwanted" side effects. See Table 3.1 for a summary of the effects of MDMA.

OxyContin Abuse

OxyContin is a semisynthetic opioid analgesic prescribed for chronic pain. It is often prescribed for cancer patients with chronic, long-lasting pain, or for other related

T A B L E 3 . 1
Effects of MDMA

Minor Adverse Effects (relatively common and generally short-lived reactions, which occur shortly after taking a dose)

Mydriasis (dilated pupils)

Photophobia (discomfort when looking at bright lights)

Headache

Anorexia (diminished appetite), nausea, dry mouth, abdominal cramps, and diarrhea

Sweating, tachypnea (rapid breathing), tachycardia (rapid heart rate), palpitations, and tremor

Bruxism (grinding of teeth)

Trismus (uncomfortable rigidity of the jaw muscles)

Gait disturbance, ataxia (difficulty walking)

Serious Acute Adverse Effects (uncommon reactions)

Hallucinations, severe anxiety, agitation, panic attacks, and paranoia

Hypertension (increased blood pressure)

Cardiac arrhythmias (irregular heart rhythms)

Severe central chest pain (probably due to intercostal muscle spasm)

Severe abdominal cramps

Urinary retention (due to alpha-adrenergic stimulation of bladder neck)

Adverse Effects Only in Certain Circumstances

Overexertion, dehydration, and collapse

Hyperpyrexia (increased body temperature)

Convulsions (seizures)

Rhabdomyolysis (muscle breakdown)

Disseminated intravascular coagulation (blood clots throughout the body)

Cerebrovascular accident (stroke), intracerebral hemorrhage

Acute renal failure

Polydipsia (excessive drinking), low sodium levels, and stupor

Road traffic accidents

Facial dermatosis (pimples)

Delayed Reactions to Exposure

Jaundice, hepatotoxicity

Tooth wear

Possible congenital anomalies

Poor concentration and attention, memory impairment, and depression

Sleep disturbance

Weight loss, exhaustion

SOURCE: Holland, Julie, ed. 2001. *Ecstasy: The complete guide: A comprehensive look at the risks and benefits of MDIUIA*. Rochester, Vt: Park Street Press. www.InnerTraditions.com.

chronic pain. It is effective and beneficial for chronic pain sufferers because it is a long-acting medication that is time-released over 12 hours, so patients need to take it only twice a day.

The active ingredient in OxyContin is oxycodone. OxyContin contains a much larger amount of oxycodone than other prescription opiate pain medications— between 10 and 150 milligrams of oxycodone in each time-release tablet.

OxyContin abusers are seeking a quick, powerful rush. They crush the OxyContin tablets and inject or snort the powder, or mix it in water and drink it. This disarms the timed-release mechanism, resulting in a quick, powerful high.

By prescription, OxyContin costs about $4 for a 40-milligram pill. On the street, the cost escalates to $20 to $40 for a 40-milligram pill. As a result, many pharmacies are being robbed for OxyContin, and many prescriptions are being forged to obtain OxyContin (CSAT Advisory 2001).

Heroin

The 1990s saw a significant increase in the use of heroin. The number of hard-core users, estimated by the National Institute of Drug Abuse (NIDA), has remained fairly constant over the past 25 years, at 750,000 to 1 million. However, the past several years have seen a disturbing number of heroin users who are dramatically unlike the stereotypical heroin addict. The profile now contains well-educated, often, female individuals, frequently employed in white-collar and even professional capacities. The age of users is also alarming, considering reports of use in high schools and even middle schools.

The reasons for this trend are many. For one, heroin use has assumed the trappings of glamour, often associated with the "arts," fashion, and entertainment world. It is now much purer, and thus more potent, which enables the user to inhale it, either through smoking it, "chasing the dragon," or snorting it in its powder form. The very fact that it does not have to be injected makes it more attractive by alleviating the aversion most people have to needles (i.e., needle phobia, stigma, and risk of AIDS virus). There is also the widespread misbelief, and rationalization, that if one smokes or snorts heroin, it will be nonaddicting.

To add to its "attractiveness," it is also relatively inexpensive, especially compared with crack cocaine. A bag of heroin containing enough to get the user high for 6 to 8 hours may be purchased for as little as three dollars in New York City and will be of significant purity and potency, whereas a ten-dollar bag of heroin purchased on the streets in 1980 was about 4 percent pure. Today, it is not uncommon for a sample to be 65 percent pure, or even higher.

Another factor is that the drug is more easily obtained. The neophyte user is no longer forced to venture into dangerous neighborhoods to purchase the drug. It may be as easy as paging the dealer, who then delivers it, or it may be available on certain street corners in middle-class or industrial neighborhoods or even at the workplace.

One of the more insidious aspects of the drug is that, unlike cocaine and even alcohol, heroin use may exist for a significant period of time before its use is suspected. Individuals may be fairly high and functioning for quite a while, and, if they are careful, it may take months before they have to increase their dose and risk getting toxic. By the time it becomes obvious, the problem has progressed to the point where medical treatment and appropriate intervention is most often necessary to treat the addiction.

Heroin-related emergency department visits doubled from 33,900 in 1990 to 70,500 in 1996. In 1993, more than 3,805 deaths nationwide were related to heroin. "Both urban and suburban emergency departments treat patients with heroin overdoses daily and hospitalize 3 to 7 percent of these patients for related complications" (Sporer 2000).

Heroin use can no longer be confined along geographic, economic, or social lines. It is in "Heartland USA," as well as in suburbia and in the urban centers of the nation. It is found among the unemployed and disadvantaged, blue-collar workers, professional workers, the economically advantaged, and even homemakers.

Inhalants

In addition to glue, paint, room deodorizers (e.g., Glade), butane, and even propane, there are commercial products that are often inhaled to get high. This includes ethyl chloride and nitrous oxide, which are known as "whippets," found in whipped cream canisters. It is estimated that at least 10,000 common household products contain ingredients that can be abused.

The most commonly used inhalants by young people are glue, shoe polish, and gasoline. Other inhalants include nitrous oxide, lighter fluid, and aerosol sprays. There are also gender differences in inhalant use, with boys more likely to use gasoline or nitrous oxide, while girls favor glue, shoe polish, spray paints, correction fluid, and aerosol sprays (*Washington FOCUS* 2004).

The earlier children use inhalants, the more likely they will become dependent.

> Adolescents who reported first use of inhalants at age 13 to 14 were six times more likely to be dependent on inhalants than those who started using inhalants at age 15 to 17. (*Washington FOCUS* 2004)

✷ Definitions of Terms
Physical Dependence

Physical dependence is the altered state that develops when a person cannot stop taking a certain drug without suffering from withdrawal.

Withdrawal

Withdrawal symptoms are physical symptoms resulting from stopping the use of a drug (see Table 3.2). These vary according to the specific drug, the amount used, and the length of time over which it has been used. Because the body has actually adapted metabolically to the presence of the drug, when it is withdrawn (or even tapered off too rapidly), the reactions may vary from mild, flulike symptoms for a person coming off of opiates to a severe, potentially life-threatening situation when withdrawing from alcohol or other sedative hypnotics.

Psychological Dependence (Formerly, Habituation)

A user with a profound emotional or mental need for the repetitive use of a drug or a class of drugs is **psychologically dependent.** The user becomes so preoccupied with taking the drug to achieve the optimal level of functioning or to maintain a sense of

TABLE 3.2

Drug Withdrawals
Here are some common signs of withdrawal from opiates, alcohol, cocaine, and nicotine.

Drug	Common Signs
Opiates	Dysphoric mood (depression), nausea and vomiting, muscle aches, runny nose, dilated pupils, goose bumps, diarrhea, fever, and insomnia
Alcohol	Hand tremors, hyperactivity, insomnia, nausea and vomiting, psychomotor agitation, anxiety, seizures, and hallucinations (auditory and visual)
Cocaine	Dysphoric mood, fatigue, paranoia (e.g., seeing people who are not there—police), psychomotor agitation, and increased appetite
Nicotine	Dysphoric mood (depression), insomnia, irritability, anxiety, difficulty concentrating, decreased heart rate, increased appetite, and weight gain

well-being that it becomes extremely difficult to abstain. Psychological dependence is a subjective state that is almost impossible to quantify; therefore, it is of limited usefulness in establishing a diagnosis of chemical dependency.

Tolerance

Tolerance to a drug develops when the individual requires increasingly larger doses to achieve the desired optimal effect. In other words, users require larger doses to achieve the same high produced previously by a smaller dose of the same drug.

Cross-Tolerance

Cross-tolerance is a diminished or reduced response to the effect of a psychoactive drug. This response is due to prior use of other psychoactive drugs, usually in the same drug category.

Synergism

In a synergistic process, one chemical enhances, or adds power to, the effect of another. The combined effect of two or more drugs is therefore greater than the effect of each agent added together (e.g., $1 + 1 = 3$ or more).

Antagonism

The opposite of synergism, antagonism, occurs when the combined effect of two drugs is less than the sum of the drugs' effects acting separately (e.g., $1 + 1 = $ less than 2). For example, the depressant effects of alcohol are counteracted by the stimulant effects of cocaine.

Routes of Administration

The route of administration is the method by which the alcohol/drug is ingested. Ingestion may be oral, through the skin, by injection, by smoking, or through other orifices (e.g., suppositories). The most rapid reaction occurs after inhalation while smoking a drug; injection is the next most rapid route. Oral administration and absorption through the skin are the slowest routes. (See Figure 3.1.)

Set and Setting

Set refers to the user's state of mind at the time of use. *Setting* refers to the physical environment or environmental factors surrounding alcohol/drug use. The differences in set and setting can account for different reactions to the drug. The same individual using the same dose and same drug can vary in reaction to the drug based on the set and setting. The hallucinogens are the most dramatic example of the importance of set and setting. A "bad trip" can occur under the influence of hallucinogens if the set and setting are negative. For example, a man takes a hallucinogen and goes to a party with his girlfriend. She breaks up with him at the party, telling him she has been cheating on him for months, and leaves the party with the other guy. He's now at the

1. Mouth—Alcohol is drunk.

2. Stomach—Alcohol goes right into the stomach. A little of the alcohol passes through the wall of the stomach and into the bloodstream. Most of the alcohol continues down into the small intestine.

3. Small intestine—Alcohol goes from the stomach into the small intestine. Most of the alcohol is absorbed through the walls of the intestine and into the bloodstream.

4. Bloodstream—The bloodstream then carries the alcohol to all parts of the body, such as the brain, heart, and liver.

5. Liver—As the bloodstream carries the alcohol around the body, it passes through the liver. The liver changes the alcohol to water, carbon dioxide, and energy. The process is called *oxidation*. The liver can oxidize only about one half ounce of alcohol an hour. Thus, until the liver has time to oxidize all of the alcohol, the alcohol continues passing through all parts of the body, including the brain.

6. Brain—Alcohol goes to the brain almost as soon as it is consumed. Alcohol continues passing through the brain until the liver oxidizes all the alcohol into carbon dioxide, water, and energy.

FIGURE 3.1   *How Alcohol Is Absorbed in the Body*
SOURCE: National Institute on Alcohol Abuse and Alcoholism. *Alcohol Health and Research World.* Washington, DC: U.S. Department of Health and Human Services, 1988.

party, alone, and doesn't know anyone. He is pretty angry and upset and accidentally bumps into a bunch of rowdy, drunk guys. You can imagine the rest.

A woman gets a promotion at work and is affirmed for her diligence, intellect, and good management of a major project. Several co-workers invite her out for a drink on Friday at the close of business. Compare her reaction to that of another woman in the same office who is warned that her performance is poor and placed on probation pending a review by her supervisors. She is not invited to go out with the first group, but instead goes off by herself to a bar with the express intention of getting drunk. You can clearly predict based on set and setting the different reactions that each woman will have to drinking alcohol that Friday evening.

⚕ Definition of Addiction

Historically, there has been a wide range of definitions of addiction—for example:

> A chronic, progressive, and potentially fatal disease. It is characterized by tolerance, psychological and physical dependence, pathogenic organ changes, all of which are the direct or indirect consequence of the alcohol ingested. (National Council on Alcoholism)

> An illness characterized by preoccupation with alcohol and loss of control over its consequences, which usually leads to intoxication if drinking is begun; by chronicity; by progression; and by the tendency to relapse. Typically associated with physical disability and impaired emotional, occupational, and/or social adjustments as a direct consequence. (American Medical Association 1957)

As described throughout this textbook, the current definition of addiction used in the alcohol/drug field is the one developed by Dr. David Smith. An expanded version of that definition of addiction follows:

1. Compulsion and obsession

   a. The compulsive use of the chemical despite its no longer having the desired effect.
   b. The fear of being without the substance.
   c. The compulsion to substitute other drugs if that particular substance is unavailable.
   d. Thoughts about the drug as a dominant theme or integral part of one's life.

2. Loss of control or inability to stop

   a. The inability to limit the amount of use.
   b. The inability to refuse the substance if available.
   c. The inability to stop using the substance for 3 months or longer.
   d. Binge patterns of use.

3. Continued use despite known adverse consequences

   a. Medical complications.
   b. Psychiatric complications ranging from mood swings and anxiety to depression, panic disorders, and paranoid-schizophrenic reactions or other psychoses.

   c.   Social consequences, the deterioration of family and other significant relationships, work status, and legal complications.

A simple way to remember this behavioral definition is the 3Cs mnemonic:

- **C**ompulsion
- **C**ontrol
- Continued use despite negative **C**onsequences

A more diagnostic definition of substance abuse and dependence can be found in Chapter 4.

As of 2011, the American Society of Addiction Medicine (ASAM) issued a public policy statement with a new definition of addiction. The new definition was a result of a 4-year process involving noted addictionologists, addiction medicine clinicians, and leading neuroscience researchers. It focuses more on the brain reward system and the neurological changes that occur with addiction. For example, it states:

> Addiction is a primary, chronic disease of brain reward, motivation, memory and related circuitry. Dysfunction in these circuits leads to characteristic biological, psychological, social, and spiritual manifestations. This is reflected in an individual pathologically pursuing reward and/or relief by substance use and other behaviors.

The new definition expands addiction to other behaviors—sexual addictions, addiction to gambling, and other behaviors that are compulsive/addictive and involve changes in brain chemistry. ASAM emphasizes the point that addiction is more than a behavioral disorder; it is also a brain disorder.

Based on this new definition, treatment needs to focus more on neuroscience and new ways to address and enhance recovery and relapse prevention. It makes sense that meditation and mindfulness practices are a natural bridge to help those in recovery to slow down, change reactivity, and rewire their brains.

Drug Absorption, Distribution, and Elimination

Drug absorption is the process and actions that occur when drugs are taken into the body and absorbed into the bloodstream. Several factors determine the absorption, including the route of administration, the dose of the drug, and the dosage form (e.g., pill/tablet, capsule, liquid, injection, spray, patch, or gum). For the desired effect or effective administration, the drug must be absorbed in adequate concentrations over time and must reach the desired site of action.

There are nine methods of absorption, or routes of administration (see Tables 3.3 and 3.4):

- Oral
- Rectal
- Inhalation
- Mucous membranes
- Skin
- Injection
- Intravenous
- Intramuscular
- Subcutaneous

TABLE 3.3

Methods of Absorption

Oral
Must be soluble and stable in stomach fluids
Contents of stomach drain into intestine
Pass through lining of intestines into bloodstream
Liquid form faster than tablets
75 percent of drug is absorbed within 2 to 3 hours
Can lead to vomiting and stomach pain
Amount of absorption varies between individuals

Rectal
Most commonly used when vomiting, unconscious, or can't swallow
Not good absorption; irritates lining

Inhalation
Popular method
Lungs large surface area, fast absorption into bloodstream
Into pulmonary capillaries to heart and out to body
Very fast effects
May even have faster effects than intravenous injection

Mucous Membranes
Mouth or nose

Skin
Patches provide continuous metered release of drug over long time
Absorbed into systemic circulation
Slowly absorbed so level of intake is easily kept constant

Injection
Intravenous
Intramuscular
Subcutaneous
Faster absorption than oral administration
Easy to give accurate dose because it's not absorbed through membranes
Rapid rate of absorption can make it dangerous for overdose or reaction
Can be exposed to bloodborne pathogens

Intravenous
Directly to bloodstream
Precise dosage
Allows for slow administration of drug to watch for symptoms
Most dangerous because enters straight into bloodstream

Intramuscular
Absorbed faster than through stomach
Not as fast as intravenous
Need larger amount than intravenous

Subcutaneous
Fast when injected under the skin

T A B L E   3 . 4

Three Types of Injection of Drugs

Route	Site	Reactions	Problems
1. Intravenous	Directly into a vein	Immediate impact	Risk of overdose and adverse reactions
2. Intramuscular	Into a muscle	Slow and sustained impact	Intramuscular problems
3. Subcutaneour	Under the skin	Liquids—prompt action otherwise slow	Problem with large volumes
			Pain from irritation

The drug enters the bloodstream at the site of absorption and is pumped throughout the body. It takes approximately 1 minute for the drug to circulate throughout the body, depending on the size of the individual. Side effects occur because the drug is everywhere in the body, not just at the desired site of action. Drugs leave the body through the kidneys, the lungs (breath), the bile, and the skin.

⚹ Classification of Drugs

Drug may be most simply defined as a nonfood substance intended to affect the structure and function of the body, most often to diagnose, cure, mitigate, treat, or prevent disease.

There are many ways to classify drugs, such as by chemical structure or by specific effects on particular organ systems. Most frequently, drugs are classified as nonpsychoactive and psychoactive. **Nonpsychoactive drugs** are substances that in normal doses do not directly affect the brain, such as vitamins, antibiotics, and topical skin preparations. **Psychoactive drugs** affect brain functions, mood, and behavior and are subdivided primarily on the basis of physiological and psychological effects. The psychoactive drug classification includes the following:

1. Narcotic analgesics: painkillers and designer drugs (fentanyl)
2. Central nervous system depressants: sedative hypnotics, alcohol, tranquilizers, and barbiturates
3. Central nervous system stimulants: amphetamines, cocaine, nicotine, and caffeine
4. Hallucinogens
5. *Cannabis sativa:* marijuana and hashish
6. Inhalants: volatile solvents
7. Phencyclidine (PCP)

Narcotic Analgesics

The term *narcotic* comes from the Greek word *narkosis,* which means "to numb or to be in a stupor." *Analgesia* means "to relieve pain, without producing unconsciousness."

The narcotic analgesics (morphine, codeine, and heroin) come from the poppy plant (*Papaver somniferum*). (See Table 3.5.) The narcotic analgesics category also includes synthetic and semisynthetic drugs that have morphinelike action, such as meperidine (Demerol), methadone, Dilaudid, and Percodan.

The term *narcotic* was often incorrectly applied to a wide variety of drugs, including marijuana, alcohol, and cocaine. This was the result of a legal classification system rather than a medical classification. The emotional overtone of *narcotic* was frequently misapplied to those drugs considered dangerous by legislators and policymakers.

The term *narcotic* has a variety of meanings. Its scientific meaning is drugs related botanically to the opium poppy and pharmacologically to opium, morphine, and heroin. Its medical meaning is synthetic drugs having morphinelike effects on a user. Its legal meaning is anything the legislature of a state wants to classify. Its public meaning is anything the general public wants to label as belonging to a particular drug category. In some states, this includes all drugs having morphinelike action. Elsewhere the term may also be applied to drugs chemically unrelated to narcotics (e.g., cocaine and marijuana).

Additional analgesics are nonnarcotic and satisfy other functions, such as reducing fever (antipyretic) and reducing inflammation (anti inflammatory). Other nonnarcotic analgesics include aspirin, phenacetin, and Darvon. Nonsteroidal anti-inflammatory drugs (NSAIDs) include Naprosyn and Motrin.

Heroin

There are an estimated 166,000 heroin users in the United States (SAMHSA 2004). Common street names for heroin include big bag, big H, blanco, bomb, boy, brother, brown, brown rocks, brown sugar, caballo, cat, chich, Chinese red, Chinese white, chiva, crap, dogie, doojee, dope, duji, dust, eighth, flea powder, garbage, good stuff, H, hard stuff, harry, H-caps, henry, him, horse, hombre, jones, joy powder, junk, Mexican mud, mojo, muzzle, pack, poison, powder, pure, red chicken, red rock, rock, scag, schmeck, smack, stuff, tecata, thing, white boy, white junk, and white stuff.

Brief History of the Narcotic Analgesics   The opiates have been used for medicinal purposes and pleasure since prehistoric times. Opium eating has been known in Asia for thousands of years. A brief history follows:

   1806: Friedrich Wilhelm Adam Serturner, a German chemist, isolated
        morphine from opium.
   1832: Codeine was isolated.

TABLE 3.5

Narcotic Analgesics Classification

Natural Opioids	Synthetic	Semisynthetic	Antagonists
Morphine	Demerol	Dilaudid	Narcan
Codeine	Meperidine	Percodan	Naloxone
Opium		Talwin	

1845: Alexander Wood invented the hypodermic syringe.

1861–65: Approximately 45,000 U.S. Civil War soldiers were addicted to morphine.

1874: Alder Wright, a London chemist, first synthesized heroin from morphine.

1875: A San Francisco ordinance prohibited the smoking of opium in public houses and opium dens.

1906: U.S. Pure Food and Drug Act required all medicines containing opiates and certain other drugs to list them on the labels.

1914: Harrison Narcotics Act required licensure of drug manufacturers, importers, pharmacists, and physicians marketing or prescribing narcotics. Patent medicine manufacturers were exempt from the act, provided that their products did not contain more than two grains of opium, or one-eighth grain of heroin per ounce.

1942–43: During World War II, a German chemist, Aschenbrenner synthesized methadone and named it Dolophine, after Adolph Hitler.

1970s: Most addicted U.S. soldiers returning from Vietnam withdrew from heroin on the trip back to the United States or shortly thereafter. The anticipated need for heroin treatment was not realized.

1978: Scientists discovered endorphins; these proteins play an important role in the body's pain suppression system.

Chemists first isolated morphine in the early nineteenth century. During the Civil War, doctors widely used morphine in injectable form. Addiction to morphine was very common at that time, resulting in a significant addict population. Fortunately, society attached no stigma to the soldiers' addiction to morphine; it was commonly referred to as "soldiers' disease." Most soldiers withdrew from morphine on their own or under medical supervision, and there was minimal social impact.

Around the 1870s, manufacturers added tincture of opium to many patent medicines sold over the counter for treatment of diarrhea in infants and children. When first introduced at the end of the nineteenth century, heroin was thought to cure opium dependence and morphinism.

Routes of Administration Users may inject narcotics either intravenously, subcutaneously (under the surface of the skin—known as skin popping), or deep within the muscle. They can also snort narcotics intranasally, smoke it, or absorb it into their bodies via the mucous membranes of the mouth or rectum (using suppositories). The route of administration determines how quickly the drug affects the brain: A drug that is smoked reaches the brain in 5 seconds; one injected intravenously reaches the brain in 14 seconds. A drug taken by mouth takes 30 to 45 minutes to hit the brain.

The intensity of the drug effect and the complications are also influenced by the route of administration. Intravenous use can lead to infection, local abscesses, disseminated infections (HIV, hepatitis B, and pulmonary emboli), and local damage to the lungs and lining of the nose.

Major Effects

1. Pain relief (analgesia)
2. Euphoria (sense of well-being)

3. Cough suppressant (antitussive)
4. Respiratory depression
5. Sedation or drowsiness
6. Constriction of the pupils (pinpoint pupils)
7. Nausea and vomiting
8. Itching
9. Decrease in gastrointestinal activity (constipation)

Hazards Even while using low to moderate doses, users face many hazards related to the circumstances of illicit use, such as drug impurities, infection, and the consequences of the addict lifestyle. By using dirty and shared needles, they contract infections such as HIV/AIDS, hepatitis, tetanus, and all other bloodborne infections (septicemia) leading to endocarditis and to liver, brain, and skin abscesses.

Other hazards include allergic (anaphylactic) reactions to the narcotic or substances used to cut or dilute the narcotic. Overdosing causes cardiac arrest, lung reaction, and the narcotic's direct actions on the brain, leading to coma, shock, respiratory arrest, and death.

Tolerance Tolerance develops to a rapid degree with the effects of analgesia, respiratory depression, sedation, and feelings of euphoria. In effect, users must take more and more of the narcotic to get the original effect.

The rate of tolerance depends on the pattern of use, route of administration, and physical aspects of each individual. Even though some addicts build to phenomenally high doses, inevitably there is always a final dose that can produce death from respiratory depression.

Tolerance often returns to normal after withdrawal. Many narcotic addicts have fatally overdosed by returning to their normal and customary doses after detoxification.

Cross-tolerance exists even between chemically dissimilar opioids.

Withdrawal Withdrawal symptoms and their severity depend on the specifics of the drug being used. With low doses of intermittent narcotic use, withdrawal symptoms may be negligible or perhaps resemble mild, flulike symptoms. Anyone who has ever been seasick can identify with these feelings. Withdrawal symptoms include the following:

- Appetite suppression
- Nausea and vomiting
- Dilated pupils
- Gooseflesh, or increased pylomotor activity—the skin resembles a plucked turkey, hence the expression "going cold turkey"
- Restlessness
- Intestinal spasms
- Abdominal pain
- Muscle spasms
- Kicking movements—hence the expression "kicking the habit"
- Occasional diarrhea

- Increased heart rate and blood pressure
- Chills alternating with flushing and sweating
- Irritability
- Insomnia
- Violent yawning
- Severe sneezing and runny nose (rhinorhea)
- Crying and tearing, nasal inflammation
- Depressive mood and tremor

The peak intensity of withdrawal occurs at 48 to 72 hours (2 to 3 days) for heroin, but for methadone the peak withdrawal is from 5 to 7 days.

Despite these symptoms, the management of withdrawal from opiates is far less dangerous than the management of alcohol withdrawal. The effects of the withdrawal are not life threatening but may need medical attention. The medical conditions worthy of attention may be excessive weight loss, dehydration, body chemistry disturbances, and stress on the cardiovascular system. Without treatment, symptoms usually disappear in 7 to 10 days for heroin but may last 2 to 3 weeks for methadone (see Table 3.2).

Opiates and Pregnancy Chronic use of opiates, especially heroin, results in a variety of obstetrical compromises. Because withdrawal in an addicted mother may lead to spontaneous miscarriage, the consensus of the medical community to date is to stabilize the heroin-addicted mother on methadone during the pregnancy. However, these babies tend to be born prematurely, with a lower birth weight. Born addicted, these babies may display withdrawal symptoms and have significant neonatal difficulties, with lifelong negative effects on psychomotor development.

Central Nervous System Depressants

Most central nervous system (CNS) depressants are sedative hypnotics. These include alcohol, barbiturates, and tranquilizers.

Alcohol

Alcohol acts as a depressant on the central nervous system. Once absorbed, it is distributed throughout the body, enters the brain easily, and is uniformly found in all body fluids. In pregnant women, alcohol crosses the placental barrier into the fetus.

A blood alcohol level of 0.05 percent or higher produces some driving impairment. In all U.S. states, anyone driving with a 0.10 percent blood alcohol level is driving under the influence. Alcohol is metabolized at a relatively constant rate, which depends primarily on the body weight of the drinker. A 150-pound man metabolizes approximately three-quarters to one ounce of alcohol in an hour.

Brief History of Alcohol

1500 B.C.: Book of the Dead mentioned "hek," a form of beer made from grain.
2225 B.C.: The Code of Hammurabi, Assyria, involved rules for the keeping of beer and wine shops and taverns.

400 B.C.: Plato wrote rules for the leader of the "symposia" to try to control the excessive drinking that went on. This was probably an ancient version of the "designated driver" (of course, back then it was the chariot driver).

Eighth century: Numerous taverns and beer houses were established in Britain.

Sixteenth century: Through the distillation process, Irish settlers manufactured and distributed "usquebach," or whiskey.

1660: Distilleries were licensed and the popularity of gin became widespread.

1770s: The British brought beer and alcohol to Colonial Americans.

1777: After the American Revolution, there was an increase in rum consumption as a new American freedom, when prior to the revolution there was some success in regulating taverns. Corn whiskey became popular after the Louisiana Purchase added new American corn-growing territories.

Late 1700s: Dr. Benjamin Rush, champion of the temperance movement and author of *An Inquiry into the Effects of Ardent Spirits,* inspired the nineteenth-century American temperance movement.

1917: Alcohol Prohibition came about with the Eighteenth Amendment to the Constitution.

1920s: The Roaring Twenties brought bootlegging, bathtub gin, homemade beer, and speakeasies.

1932: The Twenty-first Amendment to the Constitution repealed the highly unpopular Eighteenth Amendment.

1970–present: Numerous alcohol products have been developed and marketed, especially to young people (e.g., malt liquors, wine coolers, and a variety of beers).

These alcoholic beverages contain equal amounts of alcohol.
© McGraw-Hill Education/Jill Braaten, photographer

Estimates of Alcoholism Other than tobacco products containing nicotine, beverage alcohol (ethanol) is the most widely used psychoactive drug known to humanity. In 2004, about half (50.3 percent) of Americans aged 12 or older reported being current drinkers of alcohol. This translates to an estimated 121 million people. About 16.9 million Americans (6.9 percent of the population) reported heavy drinking (SAMHSA 2004).

Major Effects The range of physical reactions to varying doses of alcohol is vast. The effects depend on the amount consumed, the circumstances of consumption (set and setting), the drinker's body size, and the experience of the drinker. Someone unaccustomed to alcohol use is more likely to show signs of impairment than a conditioned drinker who has learned to compensate for impaired behavior. One or two alcoholic drinks may induce talkativeness in one individual, along with slight flushing, and reduce the drinker's inhibitions, so he or she appears more expansive and more animated, perhaps grandiose at times. The same amount of alcohol in another individual may induce drowsiness and lethargy.

Alcohol in even moderate doses generally reduces one's performance in tasks that require physical coordination or mental agility, such as driving a car. Larger doses can alter perception and cause staggering, blurred vision, and the manifestations of drunkenness. However, one person may become emotional or amorous, while another becomes aggressive and hostile. Extremely high doses—typical during binges—can knock out a drinker, even kill the person, if the central nervous system is depressed to the point that body functions, such as breathing, cease altogether.

Alcohol is a toxic drug with irritating as well as sedative properties. It can have a negative effect on every tissue in the human body, as shown in the following:

1. Brain

    a. Amnesia—most commonly called blackouts—causes partial, or sometimes temporary, loss of memory, often following binge patterns of alcohol use. Blackouts can occur even after low-dose alcohol consumption, or first-time alcohol consumption by someone who has a family history of alcoholism. Blackouts may be a significant early indicator of a diagnosis of alcoholism.
    b. Permanent loss of memory and mental confusion, as in Wernicke-Korsakoff's syndrome.
    c. Damage to the cerebellum, affecting balance and coordination.

2. Peripheral nerves

    a. Usually in the legs and sometimes other extremities, alcoholics experience pain, loss of sensation, and general weakness.
    b. Optic nerves are damaged, causing blurred or dimmed vision.

3. Gastrointestinal tract

    a. Gastritis and esophagitis, irritation of the lining of the esophagus and stomach, causing mild to severe pain; may aggravate an ulcer.
    b. Peptic ulcer at the outlet of the stomach (duodenal).

    c.   Fatty liver, hepatitis, or cirrhosis (a scarring of the liver that destroys the tissue and is a leading cause of death from alcohol).

    d.   Pancreatitis, in which muscle spasms block the duct from the pancreas, causes the acidic juices to back up and start digesting the pancreas. This is often very painful and can also cause death.

4.   Heart and blood vessels

    a.   Heart muscle becomes weaker, and heart expands because it is working harder. Alcohol complicates problems with heart disease.

    b.   Peripheral blood vessels are dilated by alcohol. Initially, this causes a sensation of warmth, followed by serious heat loss in the cold. The old habit of drinking alcohol to fend off the cold actually makes the person more susceptible to the cold.

    c.   High blood pressure is often associated with alcoholism, but the relationship is not clearly established.

5.   Lungs: emphysema occurs most frequently in the alcoholic who also smokes. Alcohol seems to have a direct toxic effect on the cells lining the alveoli, or small air sacs in the lungs, as the alcohol is excreted into the air.

Sobering Up Contrary to much public opinion, steam baths, vigorous exercise, black coffee, and other sobering-up agents have no effect on the rate at which alcohol is metabolized. Time is the only thing that works.

Tolerance Tolerance to most of the immediate effects of alcohol develops with frequent use. Regular heavy drinkers may be able to consume two or three times as much alcohol as novice drinkers. Heavy drinkers have to drink more and more to achieve the desired effect.

Stage 1 Withdrawal Symptoms Withdrawal from alcohol usually begins 6 to 12 hours after the last drink and may even begin in the presence of significant blood alcohol levels. Table 3.6 lists the Stage 1 withdrawal symptoms. These symptoms, in varying degrees, may last anywhere from 3 to 5 days and are relieved by drinking more alcohol.

TABLE 3.6

Stage 1 Alcohol Withdrawal Symptoms

1. Psychomotor agitation
2. Anxiety
3. Insomnia
4. Appetite suppression
5. Gastrointestinal disturbances
6. Elevated heart rate, blood pressure, sweating, and tremors

Stage 2 Withdrawal Symptoms The onset of Stage 2 withdrawal symptoms is usually within 24 hours after the last drink but may occur as long as 3 days later. Stage 2 consists of the symptoms in Stage 1, plus hallucinations. These may be visual, auditory, tactile, olfactory (smell), or mixed. Although the visual hallucinations usually predominate, olfactory hallucinations are a particularly more ominous sign and may be accompanied by seizures. The delirium tremens—disorientation to person, place, or time—also can be life threatening; this is a true medical emergency, with a 15 percent mortality rate if untreated.

Related Illnesses Alcoholics have twice the chance of experiencing premature deaths as nonalcoholic persons. Liver disease of varying types is one of the most prominent manifestations of alcoholism. Among young males 20 to 40 years of age, liver cirrhosis is the third fastest growing cause of death, after heart disease and lung cancer. Alcoholics also show higher than normal rates of peptic ulcers, pneumonia, cancer of the upper digestive and respiratory tracts, heart and artery disease, tuberculosis, and suicide.

Many heavy drinkers also suffer vitamin deficiencies, gastritis, sexual impotence, and infections. The more serious alcohol-related neurological disorders include peripheral neuritis (loss of sensation), Korsakoff's psychosis (loss of memory), and Wernicke's encephalopathy (mental confusion).

Fetal Alcohol Syndrome Alcohol use and abuse by pregnant women is the third leading cause of birth defects, exceeded only by Down syndrome and spina bifida. The four basic abnormalities characteristic of fetal alcohol syndrome (FAS) are as follows:

1. Distorted facial features. A baby born with FAS has short fissures in the eyelids, a small or underdeveloped upper lip with thinned vermilion, and a diminished philtrum, the line running between the upper lip and nose.
2. Prenatal onset growth deficiency. Babies with FAS are usually two standard deviations below normal in weight and height; they exhibit little or no indication of growth spurts to catch up after birth.
3. Reduced central nervous system performance. As a result, babies with FAS have mild to moderate mental retardation; microcephaly, or disproportionately small heads; poor coordination; irritability in infancy; and hyperactivity in childhood.
4. Increased frequency of major abnormalities. Such disorders range from gross cardiovascular abnormalities and congenital heart disease to abnormal and malformed limbs.

Alcohol use during the first trimester is often responsible for stillbirths. Research further supports the position that even small doses of alcohol affect the development of the fetus, especially in the first trimester. The only safe dose of alcohol during pregnancy is no alcohol at all.

Antabuse Some alcoholics have extreme difficulty in abstaining from alcohol. Usually, they choose Antabuse (disulfiram) when other methods to stop drinking have failed. At early stages of recovery, alcoholics may use Antabuse as a deterrent to drinking alcohol, but it must not be viewed as the only modality. (See Chapter 11.)

Alcohol is metabolized by a liver enzyme (aldehyde dehydrogenose) to form acetaldehyde. Normally, acetaldehyde is rapidly metabolized by another enzyme, which breaks it into inert substances, eventually becoming carbon dioxide and water. Antabuse interferes with the enzyme that breaks down acetaldehyde. A person taking Antabuse and drinking alcohol would have a sharp increase in acetaldehyde, resulting in extreme feelings of discomfort, which include nausea and vomiting, flushing, sweating, palpitations, increased heart rate, breathing difficulty, and anxiety. Blood pressure may first rise and then fall, making the person appear to be in shock. Feelings of drowsiness may occur later. People rarely die from an alcohol-Antabuse reaction, but they feel so sick they think they will die. Nevertheless, some people continue to drink alcohol while on Antabuse.

Barbiturates

Barbiturates also belong to the sedative-hypnotic class of drugs and are widely prescribed to decrease central nervous system activity (e.g., induce sleep, relax the nervous system). Barbiturates and barbiturate like drugs seem to affect the cortex of the brain or those areas related to sleep more than other sedative hypnotics.

Medical Uses In low doses of 25 to 50 milligrams, the short- or intermediate-acting compounds such as amobarbital (Amytal), pentobarbital (Nembutal), secobarbital (Seconal), and butabarbital (Butisol) treat or prevent acute convulsions associated with tetanus; epilepsy; and an overdose of stimulants such as strychnine, nicotine, or cocaine and the withdrawal symptoms associated with alcoholism and other sedative drug dependence. (See Table 3.7.)

For years, doctors prescribed barbiturates in the treatment of asthma, premenstrual tension, motion sickness, nausea and vomiting, peptic ulcer and other gastrointestinal disturbances, hyperthyroidism, high blood pressure, and other cardiovascular diseases. Now doctors can prescribe many newer drugs, which have fewer side effects and less potential for abuse.

TABLE 3.7

Classification of Barbiturates and Their Street Names

Short-Acting

Amobarbital (Amytal)—known as blues, blue angels, bluebirds, blue devils, and blue bullets

Pentobarbital (Nembutal)—known as yellows, yellow jackets, yellow bullets, and nembies Butabarbital (Butisol)

Intermediate-Acting

Phenobarbital (Luminal, Eskabarb)—know as phennies

Secobarbital (Seconal)—known as reds, pinks, red birds, red bullets, red dolls, seccies, and F-40s

Long-Acting

Pento-secobarbital (Tuinal)—known as trees, tootsies, double trouble, gorilla pills, and rainbows

Estimates of Use and Addiction After minor tranquilizers, barbiturates are prescribed more than any other psychoactive drug in the United States. Most individuals are introduced to barbiturates by physicians, who prescribe them as mild tranquilizers or sleeping pills.

Many individuals find barbiturates make coping with life easier. As tolerance to the tranquilizing and sedating effects set in, individuals increase their doses, often without their physicians' knowledge. Teenagers and young adults take enough barbiturates orally to produce highs the same way as alcohol might be taken. The sources of the supply for these young people are often the black market, the family medicine cabinet, and sometimes manipulation of otherwise legitimate prescriptions.

Illicit use of barbiturates has been on the decline for the past several years in North America. Because they are still prescribed so often for a variety of medical conditions, however, their pharmaceutical use remains widespread, as is their abuse by those who have obtained legitimate prescriptions.

Routes of Administration Usually taken orally, barbiturates are readily absorbed by the stomach and small intestine. Absorption into the bloodstream can be rapid, especially on an empty stomach. Most barbiturates are white powders, odorless but with a slightly bitter taste. Most often packed in capsules and tablets of varying colors, they are also available as liquids, injectable solutions, and suppositories.

Major Effects The short-term effects of barbiturates are very similar to those of alcohol. At low doses, barbiturates tend to induce relaxation, a sense of well-being, and drowsiness. At higher doses, the drug reduces the individual's ability to react quickly and to perform skilled, precise tasks. Often there is a feeling of sedation, and the individual may alternate between feelings of euphoria and hostility and aggressiveness. This is very similar to the high-dose reactions under the influence of alcohol.

At still higher doses, the symptoms may be similar to those of drunkenness, with confusion and difficulty communicating. The person may fall into a stupor or sleep. If the dose is high enough, it may impair the respiratory function so severely that the individual stops breathing and dies.

Barbiturates and Sleep Barbiturates are generally considered by the public as sleep medication. However, long-term barbiturate use can interfere with the rapid eye movement (REM) phase of sleep. REM sleep is associated with an essential feature of healthy sleep—dreaming. Normal functioning is further disturbed with the disruption of REM sleep. When the individual stops taking barbiturates, there is often a rebound effect and more REM sleep occurs. But the dreaming is more intense and frequently turns into a nightmare. The user interprets this as poor sleeping and again takes sleeping pills, often escalating the dose, and a vicious cycle is put into play.

Barbiturates and Pregnancy Barbiturates should never be taken during pregnancy, unless advised by a physician, because they could cause birth defects. Also, the baby may be born addicted to barbiturates and have potentially dangerous withdrawal symptoms.

Tolerance Barbiturates used repeatedly over a long period can induce tolerance and physical and psychological dependence. Tolerance to the euphoric effects of the drug develops quickly in many users, so larger and larger amounts of the drug must be taken to achieve the same high.

The lethal dose is usually only 10 to 15 times the therapeutic dose, so the margin of safety is low. As tolerance develops, the difference between the amount needed to get high may be only one or two pills away from an overdose; such an amount is also potentially lethal in combination with alcohol use.

Withdrawal Table 3.8 lists typical symptoms of barbiturate withdrawal; these and other symptoms may last for days or even months. Anyone greatly addicted to barbiturates also runs a risk of having a grand mal seizure. Grand mal seizures can occur up to 2 weeks after the barbiturates are withdrawn and can be fatal. This is why it is essential that barbiturate addicts withdraw under a doctor's supervision, preferably in a medical facility.

Overdose Signs and Symptoms The signs and symptoms of an overdose include the following:

1. Mood alteration ranging from depression to euphoria.
2. Sedation or drowsiness proceeding to stupor and coma with increasing doses. Paradoxical excitement rather than drowsiness may occur, especially in the young or the old.
3. Confusion and disorientation.
4. Slurred speech (dysarthria).
5. Staggering gait (ataxia), indicating that motor coordination is impaired.
6. Nystagmus, or involuntary rapid eye movement from side to side.
7. Pupils constricting a little at first; later as the level of unconsciousness deepens, they dilate.
8. Respiratory depression, with a decrease in the oxygen supply to the brain; this can cause death.

TABLE 3.8

Barbiturate Withdrawal

The withdrawal symptoms may include
1. Physical weakness
2. Dizziness
3. Anxiety
4. Tremors
5. Sleeplessness
6. Nausea
7. Abdominal cramps and vomiting

From day 3 to day 7 of withdrawal, the user may experience
1. Delirium
2. Delusions
3. Hallucinations

Barbiturates Used with Other Drugs Barbiturates are often used in conjunction with stimulants. Amphetamine users often use barbiturates to come down after a prolonged period of amphetamine use. Barbiturates are also used by heroin addicts when their drug of choice is not available.

Barbiturates plus other central nervous system depressants can have a synergistic effect when taken together. People who drink alcohol and use barbiturates run the risk of accidental overdose. Overdoses on barbiturates plus alcohol are more common than on barbiturates alone.

Methaqualone Methaqualone is one of several nonbarbiturates that have barbiturate like effects (see Table 3.9). Methaqualone was introduced to the American medical market in the mid-1960s for the treatment of insomnia and anxiety. It was originally believed to have none of the abuse potential of short-acting barbiturates. It was alleged to be a safe, nonaddictive sedative; however, this drug has an extremely high abuse potential.

The popularity of methaqualone grew swiftly, given its enthusiastic medical use and street use. Among its most enthusiastic users were college students in the 1970s. Since then, methaqualone has spread not only to high school and college campuses throughout the United States but also into the adult population. Methaqualone use has also become popular among methadone maintenance patients because of the additive high the drug produces in combination with methadone.

Some street names for methaqualone are sopors, ludes, and love drug.

Principally, younger age groups use this illicit drug, with the heaviest concentration of use between high school age and people in their mid-30s. The cost of illicit methaqualone ranges from four- to eight-dollars per tablet.

Methaqualone is usually taken orally in pill form. Since 1984, pharmaceutical companies can no longer legally produce methaqualone in the United States. The drug is most often found on the street in bootlegged forms, which look real but may or may not contain actual methaqualone.

Following its ingestion, methaqualone is readily absorbed from the gastrointestinal tract. Once transported into the blood plasma, it is distributed in body fat, the liver, and brain tissue.

Relatively low doses (75 milligrams four times a day) produce sedation; larger doses of 150 to 300 milligrams lead to sleep. Those who use the drug to get high

---

TABLE 3.9

Nonbarbiturates with Barbiturate like Action

- Chloral hydrate (Noctec)—known as Mickey Finn, or knockout drops when used with alcohol
- Methaqualone (Quaalude, Sopor)
- Flurazepam (Dalmane)
- Glutethimide (Doriden)—known as goofers
- Ethchlorvynol (Placidyl)
- Methyprylon (Noludar)
- Paraldehyde

often take far larger doses, sometimes 600 to 900 milligrams and much more if they have been using the drug steadily enough to develop a tolerance.

Users describe the sensation produced by methaqualone as "a peaceful calm, a rush, a drunk." Some describe it as a love drug due to methaqualone's alcohol like symptoms (e.g., loss of motor and muscle control, and loss of inhibitions), although, just as with alcohol, actual sexual performance is reduced.

Basically, intoxication with methaqualone is similar to intoxication with barbiturates or alcohol and subjects the individual to similar risks: death by overdose and accidents due to confusion and impaired motor coordination.

Methaqualone has induced headaches, hangovers, fatigue, dizziness, drowsiness, torpor (extreme sluggishness, apathy, dullness), menstrual disturbances, dry mouth, nosebleeds, diarrhea, skin eruptions, lack of appetite, numbness, and pain in the extremities. Researchers have found that a coma occurs following 2.4 grams of Quaalude. Eight to 20 grams have produced severe toxicity and death.

Methaqualone overdoses are less often associated with cardiac and respiratory depression than are overdoses of the oral barbiturates. However, shock and respiratory arrests may occasionally occur. Methaqualone overdose can also result in delirium, restlessness, hypertonia (excessive tension), and muscle spasms leading to convulsions.

As with barbiturates, tolerance to the intoxicating effects of methaqualone develops more rapidly than does tolerance to the lethal dose. Withdrawal from methaqualone dependence carries approximately the same risks as withdrawal from the short-acting barbiturates and can be quite severe for a large addiction.

Japanese researchers have provided a good deal of the information about methaqualone's addiction potential. In Japan, where this drug was once available over the counter, it was widely abused by young people (Tamura 1989). From 1963 to 1966, a survey of drug addicts in Japan found that 176 out of 411 (41.8 percent) were addicted to methaqualone. Withdrawal convulsions occurred in 7 percent of the methaqualone addicts, and 9 percent developed delirium tremens symptoms. Subsequent studies in England and in the United States have documented cases of physical dependence as manifested by a withdrawal syndrome. The symptoms include insomnia, abdominal cramps, headaches, anorexia, and nightmares.

Research conducted in Philadelphia and at the Haight-Ashbury Free Clinic in San Francisco has also documented the high abuse potential and dependence-producing properties of methaqualone, as well as its cross-tolerance with the short-acting barbiturates.

Tranquilizers

Minor tranquilizers are drugs that act primarily as antianxiety agents (Table 3.10). They reduce anxiety and tension. Major tranquilizers—drugs that are used over the long term in the treatment of mental illnesses, such as schizophrenia—are antipsychotic agents (Table 3.11).

All of the antipsychotic drugs can produce Parkinson-like signs and symptoms with tremor, rigidity, and shuffling gait. To counteract these side effects, one of the following anti-Parkinsonism drugs is often prescribed along with the antipsychotic drug: Artane, Cogentin, Kemadrin, or Benadryl.

TABLE 3.10

Classification of Minor Tranquilizers (Antianxiety Agents)

Benzodiazepines	Meprobamate	Sedating Antihistamines
Valium (diazepam)	Equanil	Atarax, Vistaril (hydroyzine)
Librium (chlordiazepoxide)	Miltown	Benadryl (diphenhydramine)
Serax (oxazepam)		Sleep-Eze, Sominex, Nytol
Tranxene (chlorazepate)		
Ativan (lorazepam)		
Xanax (alprazolam)		
Halcion (triazolam)		

TABLE 3.11

Classification of Major Tranquilizers (Antipsychotic Agents)

Phenothiazines	Butyrophenones	Thioxanthenes	Other
Thorazine (chlorpromazine)	Haldol (haloperidol)	Navane (thiothixene)	Serpasil (reserpine)
Mellaril (thioridazine		Taractan	Moban (molindone
Stelazine (trifluoperazine)		(chlorprothixene)	hydrochloride)
Compazine (prochlorperazine)			Loxitane
Trilafon (perphenazine)			
Prolixin (fluphenazine)			

Because the major tranquilizers do not produce pleasant psychological effects, they are rarely used nonmedically and have no illicit attraction. The focus of this section is on the minor tranquilizers, which do have an abuse and dependence potential.

Medical Uses Doctors prescribe the minor tranquilizers mainly for treatment of tension, insomnia, behavioral excitement, and anxiety. Some treat convulsive disorders, symptoms of barbiturate-alcohol dependence, and the anxiety and panic that sometimes result from the use of hallucinogenic drugs. Although fairly high doses are necessary, some minor tranquilizers are also effective muscle relaxants (e.g., Valium may be used in injectable form for this purpose).

Estimates of Use Most Americans are introduced to minor tranquilizers by physicians, and most use them according to prescription, but there are large numbers who do not stay within the physician's guidelines. Recent statistics show that the prescribing of tranquilizers is on a downward trend, and some authorities believe this trend may continue.

Routes of Administration Most minor tranquilizers are usually taken orally as tablets, capsules, or liquids. Occasionally, they are injected for both medical and nonmedical purposes.

Major Effects With normal therapeutic doses, individuals usually feel well, feel relaxed, and may lose some of their inhibitions. They feel a lessening of anxiety, tension, and agitation.

As the dosage is increased, patients usually feel more sedated and may have a sensation of floating. Many individuals at this dosage level experience some depression of nervous and muscular activity, mental confusion, and physical unsteadiness. High doses may produce the following:

- Drowsiness
- Loss of muscle coordination
- Lethargy
- Disorientation and confusion
- Low blood pressure
- Memory impairment
- Rage reactions
- Moodiness and personality alterations
- Symptoms resembling drunkenness

Obviously, the ability to drive a car under high-dose levels is also impaired. Other side effects may include skin rashes, nausea, loss of sex drive, and menstrual and ovulatory irregularities.

The margin of safety of minor tranquilizers is so wide that death rarely results from use of these drugs alone, with the lethal dose being 100 or more times the effective dose. Where death has occurred, it has often been due to an interaction between the tranquilizer and other drugs, such as alcohol.

Tolerance With regular use, tolerance can develop to most of the effects of these sedatives. This means that the user has to take increased doses to get the desired effect.

Dependence and Withdrawal Even though physical dependence and withdrawal can occur with most tranquilizers, these effects are infrequent in relation to the large number of people who take these drugs. On a therapeutic dosage level, addiction may still occur. Escalation of the amount and frequency of the dose without a doctor's orders increases the chance of physical dependence.

Withdrawal from a large habit may involve anxiety states, apprehension, tremors, insomnia, rapid pulse, fever, loss of appetite, nausea, vomiting, stomach cramps, sweating, fainting, and other symptoms. Withdrawal from high-dose tranquilizer dependence is often done gradually as the individual is tapered off of the medication. A quick withdrawal can produce life-threatening withdrawal symptoms.

Addiction Potential with Alcoholics/Addicts Physicians should not prescribe minor tranquilizers for patients who are addiction-prone. Pharmaceutical manufacturers warn physicians through medical journal ads and the *Physicians' Desk Reference* that tranquilizers are capable of abuse and dependence, especially when prescribed to addiction-prone individuals. Many patients deny or are unaware of their problems with alcohol and/or drugs, however, and fail to report this to their physicians. A thorough assessment for alcohol/drug problems is necessary before prescribing minor tranquilizers. "Non medical use of benzodiazepines in the general population is rare and of little or no consequence; on the other hand, benzodiazepines are used with some frequency among populations with histories of drug abuse" (Woods et al. 1988).

Central Nervous System Stimulants

Amphetamines

Overview Amphetamines are central nervous system stimulants (Table 3.12). Until recently, they were widely prescribed by physicians for conditions such as obesity, depression, and narcolepsy (uncontrolled fits of sleep). For certain kinds of hyperactive behavior in children, Ritalin is most commonly prescribed.

Doctors also prescribe amphetamines for Parkinson's disease, epilepsy, nausea during pregnancy, bed-wetting, asthma, sedative overdoses, and hypotensive states associated with anesthesia. Because amphetamines relieve sleepiness and fatigue, they are widely used nonmedically by students cramming for exams, long-distance truck drivers, night-shift workers, and individuals seeking general stimulation.

In the mid-1960s, a phenomenon new to North America emerged: intravenous use of massive doses of amphetamines (usually methamphetamines) by chronic abusers, or speed freaks. This abuse pattern had been common in Japan and some parts of Europe following World War II, when stockpiles of amphetamines used by the military were diverted to more general use.

As a result of amphetamines' abuse potential, physicians have sharply restricted their use. Now they prescribe amphetamines primarily for narcolepsy, hyperkinetic syndrome in children, certain mental conditions, and short-term weight control. David Smith and Donald Wesson (1988) note that in 1972, when the U.S. government put federal control over stimulants in the same category as narcotic control, legitimate production of stimulants was reduced by 80 percent.

Street Names for Amphetamines Common street names are A, AMT, bam, beans, bennies, black beauties, black mollies, brain ticklers, brownies, bumblebees, cartwheels, chalk, chicken powder, crank, Christmas trees, crossroads, cross tops, crystal, dexies, diet pills, dolls, double cross, eye openers, fives, footballs, forwards,

T A B L E 3 . 1 2		
Classification of Stimulants		
Amphetamines	**Cocaine (Benzoylmethylecognine)**	**Other Stimulants**
Benzedrine (amphetamine)		Ritalin (methylphenidate)
Dexedrine (dextroamphetamine)		Preludin (phenmetrazine)
Methedrine, Desoxyn (methamphetamine)		Tenuate (diethylpropion)
		INH (isoniazid)
		Coffee, colas, tea (caffeine)
		Tobacco (nicotine)

hearts, jam, jellybeans, leapers, lid poppers, lightning, meth, pep pills, purple hearts, rippers, sparkle plenties, sparklers, speed, splash, sweets, tens, thrusters, truck drivers, turnabouts, uppers, uppie, ups, wake-ups, water, and white crosses.

Estimates of Use The Substance Abuse and Mental Health Services Administration (SAMHSA 2004) reports that the number of recent methamphetamine users was 318,000 in 2004.

Routes of Administration Amphetamines are available in a variety of forms; tablets and capsules are the most common. Amphetamines are usually taken orally or injected intravenously.

Methamphetamine (speed) is usually in powder or crystal form and is made illicitly. The solid form of methamphetamine with the street name ice was first cooked up in Hawaii. Ice is smoked much like freebase or crack cocaine.

Major Effects Typical therapeutic doses of amphetamines stimulate the central nervous system, increase blood pressure, widen the pupils, increase respiration rate, depress the appetite, relieve sleepiness, and decrease fatigue and boredom. Other effects include increased awareness and alertness, slight euphoria, elevation of mood and self-confidence (although the ability to perform complex tasks is usually diminished), increased talkativeness and excitement, reduced nausea and gastrointestinal upset, and dry mouth.

Adverse Effects In some individuals, even a moderate dose of amphetamines can have adverse effects, such as agitation, an inability to concentrate, anxiety, confusion, blurred vision, tremors, and heart palpitations. Higher doses of amphetamines can produce quite severe adverse reactions, which include the following:

- Tremors, palpitations
- Dilated pupils (mydriasis)
- Sweating and flushing, abdominal cramps, nausea
- Tachycardia (rapid heartbeat), heart abnormalities
- Hypertension (later hypotension), circulatory collapse
- Anxiety, agitation, and panic
- Aggression and violent behavior often associated with paranoia
- Rapid breathing, respiratory collapse
- Hallucination (visual and auditory), delirium
- Extremely high fevers
- Convulsions and seizures

Although death reports from amphetamine use are rare, some individuals who are unusually sensitive to these drugs have died as a result of burst blood vessels in the brain, heart failure, or high fever. Amphetamine psychosis, a mental disturbance similar to paranoid schizophrenia, is sometimes associated with high-dose amphetamine use, but many of its symptoms have been observed with moderate dose levels.

Injecting amphetamines causes other complications: unsterile and shared needles cause problems with tetanus, AIDS, abscesses, and hepatitis. The injection of insoluble particles in street speed also causes many problems.

Dependence and Withdrawal Abruptly stopping amphetamines after chronic heavy use is often followed by symptoms such as fatigue, brain wave abnormalities, prolonged sleep, voracious appetite, stomach cramps, muscle pains, lethargy, and severe emotional depression. Some of these symptoms seem just as dramatic as withdrawal symptoms from depressant drugs.

Withdrawing amphetamines from chronic users does not seem as physically distressing as withdrawal from depressant drugs. There is little evidence of any physical dependence on moderate doses of amphetamines, but researchers frequently report psychological dependence on even low doses.

Prolonged use of amphetamines leads to a broad range of illnesses. Chronic users suffer dehydration, weight loss, and vitamin deficiency. Their reduced resistance to disease allows sores, nonhealing ulcers, and chronic chest infections. Users have a higher than normal rate of liver and cardiovascular disease, hypertensive disorders, and psychiatric problems.

Bootlegged Amphetamines The newer, tighter regulations imposed on the legitimate prescribing of amphetamines have caused the widespread bootlegging of amphetamines and substitution of other substances to mimic the amphetamine high. The most common substitutes include ephedrine—a mild stimulant found in some over-the-counter asthma remedies—and phenylpropanolamine, or PPA, the ingredients in most legal diet capsules. The moderate to large amounts of caffeine in most illicit amphetamines sometimes account for the bulk of the ingredients.

Cocaine

Cocaine is a central nervous system stimulant that has gained great popularity in a variety of drug forms. At first, cocaine was expensive; only the wealthy could afford it. Today, crack cocaine is used by every socioeconomic class, making it the scourge of humanity.

Brief History of Cocaine

2500 B.C.: Coca leaves were found in burial sites in Peru.

500 B.C.: In Colombia, South America, large stone monolithic idols possessed puffed-out cheeks, representative of a coca chewer.

Tenth century: Incas started to use the plant referred to as "Mama Coca," and the coca tree was pictured as a beautiful woman.

Eighteenth century: The Spanish took coca leaves back to Europe. However, there was general disinterest in coca by Europeans. One can speculate that the sample of coca leaves taken from South America lost its potency during the trip.

1786: Lamarck named the species of the coca plant *Erythroxylum coca.*

1844: Conflicting reports stated that either Albert Nieman or Gaedecke isolated cocaine.

1878: W. H. Bentley espoused cocaine as a cure for morphine addiction.

1883: Aschenbrandt prescribed the use of cocaine to counteract the battle fatigue of the Bavarian troops.

Sigmund Freud.
© Corbis

1883: Sigmund Freud wrote *Über Coca* praising the medicinal effects of cocaine.
1887: Sigmund Freud recognized cocaine addiction and wrote a book titled *Fear of and Craving for Cocaine.*

Cocaine is obtained from the leaves of *Erythroxylum coca,* a bush grown in parts of South America. Mountain Indians of Peru and Bolivia have chewed coca leaves as a social ritual for more than a thousand years.

The coca leaf was taken to Europe in the nineteenth century and became quite popular in certain circles. Sigmund Freud, the father of psychoanalysis, used cocaine extensively. In 1883, he recommended cocaine for treatment of morphine addiction, alcohol dependence, asthma, digestive disorders, and depression and fatigue. Freud frequently recommended the drug for what was then called neurasthenia (i.e., nervous anxiety). Freud soon realized cocaine was addictive; in 1887, he wrote *Fear of and Craving for Cocaine,* describing dependence on cocaine.

One of the most popular soft drinks of all time, Coca-Cola, originally contained extracts of the coca leaf. Coca was also present in wines such as Vin Mariani, a wine that was extremely popular with the pope and the royal families in Italy and other countries. Today, a little more than 100 years after the cocaine problems of the 1880s, we have another cocaine problem caused by coca products that are far more addicting than those of the past. Cocaine was also used as a topical anesthetic (e.g., in eye surgery) and as a local vasoconstrictor.

Street Names for Cocaine There are several street names for cocaine: Bernice, bernieds, big C, blow, bombita, bouncing powder, burese, C, charles, charlie, coke, cola, corrine, dream, dust, flake, fly, girl, gold dust, heaven, heaven dust, her, ice (not to be confused with the form of methamphetamine), incentive, jay, joy powder, lady, lady snow, nose candy, nose powder, paradise, poison, powder, rock, schoolboy, snow, star dust, sugar, white, white lady, white powder, and white stuff.

Estimates of Use An estimated 2 million Americans are current cocaine users, 467,000 of whom use crack (SAMHSA 2004).

Routes of Administration Cocaine can be inhaled, injected, or smoked. Cocaine hydrochloride is snorted or injected, while crack cocaine is smoked.

Freebase cocaine is another smokable form of cocaine. Heating up cocaine hydrochloride with a volatile solvent (usually ether) and a base (baby laxative) results in cocaine free of its hydrochloride base, with by-products of water and salt.

$$\text{Cocaine HCl} + \text{ether} + \text{base} + \text{heat} =$$
$$\text{pure cocaine} + \text{NaCl (salt)} + \text{H}_2\text{O (water)}$$

Because this cocaine is extremely pure, the volatile point, or the temperature at which cocaine burns, is raised. This allows freebase cocaine to be smoked without burning it. Simply burning cocaine does not produce a high. Freebase cocaine smoke goes from the lungs to the brain in 6 seconds, resulting in an immediate and intense high. This high lasts only 40 to 50 seconds and requires repeated doses, making it extremely expensive to maintain a habit. Crack cocaine is formed by combining cocaine with baking soda; this overrides the hydrochloride acid and allows the crack to be smoked. Crack is sold in small rocks at lower prices to lower economic populations.

Major Effects The cocaine user experiences 15 to 30 minutes of excitation and euphoria, tends to talk a lot, and feels energetic and self-confident. The effect of cocaine often gives the individual a supreme feeling of well-being, control, and enjoyment of activities that may previously have been mundane. At early stages of use, men report feeling a stimulation of sexuality. Cocaine is very short-acting because it has an extremely short half-life; after the euphoria, psychological depression, nervousness, fatigue, and irritability set in. (See Table 3.13.)

Adverse Effects With heavy regular use, depression and anxiety can be so severe that the user continues to snort, smoke, or inject cocaine every 20 minutes or so for several hours to avoid the onset of depression. This pattern may develop into binges—or 24 to 48 hours of cocaine use.

Another method to take the edge off cocaine is to inject heroin with cocaine (speedballing). This form of cocaine use was implicated in the death of comedian and actor John Belushi. Addicts frequently turn to the sedative hypnotics (alcohol, tranquilizers, and barbiturates) to counteract the downside after using cocaine. This

---

TABLE 3.13

Cocaine Clinical Syndromes

Cocaine Euphoria	Cocaine Dysphoria	Cocaine Schizophreniform Psychosis
Euphoria	Sadness	Anhedonia (inability to feel pleasure from what would have normally given pleasure)
Affective lability	Melancholia	
Increased intellectual function	Apathy	Disorientation
Hyperalertness	Inability to concentrate	Hallucinations
Hyperactivity	Painful delusions	Concern with minutia
Anorexia	Anorexia	Stereotyped behavior
Insomnia	Insomnia	Paranoid delusions (parasitosis)
Hypersexuality		Insomnia
Proneness to violence		Proneness to violence

pattern of sedative hypnotic use may also cause a dependence on drugs in this classification. Acute toxicity can occur from any method of cocaine use. In the past, cocaine was thought of as a rather benign drug. Today, we know that cocaine-related deaths are more common than once thought. Cases of sudden death from cocaine use are increasing. Large doses of cocaine may cause shallow breathing, fever, restlessness, anxiety, and confusion. Even small doses of cocaine can cause a slowing of the heart rate. Cocaine use can also result in arrythmia and heart attack. High doses also have an impact on the motor systems in the brain and spinal cord, resulting in tremors and convulsive movements. Long-term chronic snorting of large amounts of cocaine can destroy tissue in the nose. Nausea, vomiting, and abdominal pains can occur. Death from cocaine overdose is usually due to convulsions, respiratory arrest, and/or the Casey Jones reaction, a condition during which the body acts like a runaway train exceeding its own metabolic limits. People have done and seen some bizarre things under the influence of cocaine. Case studies in Chapter 5 describe these in more detail.

Tolerance and Withdrawal According to our behavioral definition of addiction, cocaine is the most addicting drug known today, especially freebase cocaine. However, a physical tolerance to cocaine does not develop. When cocaine is used, the dopamine neurotransmitters are blocked from reuptake, stranding them in the synaptic clefts. This causes a cessation of stimulant response. However, this is not a classical tolerance reaction. This was one of the factors that led to the tragic miscalculation that cocaine was not an addicting drug. Its intense high and the user's need to avoid the crash or depression makes cocaine highly addicting and contributes to the binge patterns of cocaine use. Cocaine is one of the few chemicals (other than amphetamines and other stimulants) that exist outside of the body and stimulate catecholamine. Catecholamines are responsible for extraordinarily intense reactions to stressful situations (e.g., a father lifts a car to release his child pinned beneath it). The Casey Jones reaction mentioned above is directly related to this catecholamine-enhancing property

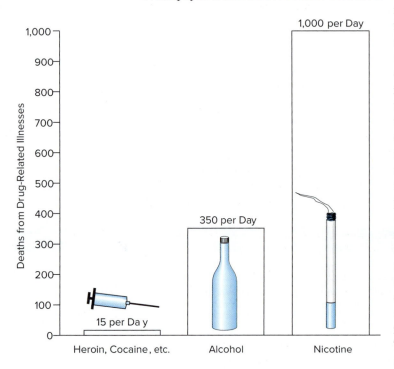

This graph shows the number of deaths from drug-related illnesses for illicit drugs (heroin, cocaine, etc.) and licit drugs (alcohol and nicotine).

of cocaine. Once this reaction is set in motion, it usually results in death. Some people die from nontoxic doses of cocaine due to a phenomenon known as the kindling effect. The brain is primed for, sensitized to, the effect of cocaine, so that one additional dose may trigger firing or discharge, leading to sudden death.

Cocaine Additives Cocaine purchased on the illicit market is very seldom, if ever, pure by the time it reaches the consumer. As it makes its way from the original source down to the illicit market, the drug's purity is cut with various substances. These additives include mannitol (a mild baby laxative), lactose (milk sugar), or the psychoactive drugs procaine (Novocain), Lidocaine (Xylocaine), benzocaine, tetracaine, and amphetamine. Some individuals have allergic reactions to these substances.

Tobacco

Tobacco is the most widely abused drug. Despite warnings regarding the health hazards, approximately 70.3 million Americans (29.2 percent of the population aged 12 or older) were current users of tobacco products in 2004: 59.9 million smoked cigarettes, 13.7 million smoked cigars, 7.2 million used smokeless tobacco, and 1.8 million smoked tobacco in pipes (SAMHSA 2004). Tobacco use remains the single leading cause of preventable death in this country. The numbers of tobacco-related deaths are far higher than those related to alcohol or other drugs.

Diseases Related to Smoking Tobacco

1. Heart disease (coronary heart disease, increased artherosclerotic disease). Smoking elevates low-density lipoproteins (LDL, or bad cholesterol) while reducing high-density lipoproteins (HDL, or good cholesterol).
2. Peripheral vascular disease.
3. Cerebrovascular disease.
4. Cancer (lung cancer; cancer of the larynx, mouth, esophagus; contributing factor in urinary cancer, kidney cancer, and pancreatic cancer).
5. Chronic obstructive lung disease and colds (chronic bronchitis and emphysema).

Health Consequences

- More women die from lung cancer than breast cancer each year.
- Twenty to 25 percent of female smokers don't stop during pregnancy.
- Over three-fourths of smokers start during the developmental teenage years.
- One out of every five high school seniors smokes cigarettes on a daily basis.
- Chewing tobacco (smokeless tobacco) is the leading cause of oral cancer.
- Approximately 75 to 80 percent of recovering alcoholics smoke cigarettes.

In recent years, there has been a decrease in use of tobacco products by the general public, yet the use of tobacco, especially by young people, makes them a significant population at risk for the development of smoking-related diseases.

Hallucinogens

Definition

The term *hallucinogen* is derived from the Latin word *hallucinari,* which means "to dream or to wander in the mind." Other terms describing hallucinogens are *psychedelic* ("alters consciousness"), *psychotomimetic* ("mimics psychosis"), and *psychotogenic* ("produces psychosis").

Hallucinogens are capable of altering time and space perception; of changing feelings of self-awareness and emotion; of changing one's sense of body image; and of increasing sensitivity to textures and shapes, sounds, and taste. In addition, these drugs bring visions of luminescence, flashes of light, kaleidoscopic patterns, and landscapes. They can also induce hallucinations and feelings of enlightenment and spiritual or religious awakening.

In the past, any substance whose function is to change the habitual way of perceiving and orienting oneself toward one's physical, psychological, and social environment was considered a hallucinogen. As a result, many drugs such as marijuana, PCP, and even cocaine are inappropriately classified as hallucinogens because that is the category they seem to fit best.

In the 1960s, Timothy Leary advocated LSD as a means of "turning on, tuning in, and dropping out" of mainstream lifestyles and thinking. Of the many natural and synthetic hallucinogens, LSD is the most potent by weight and the most thoroughly researched.

Other hallucinogens include mescaline, which is derived from the dried buttons or heads of the peyote cactus; peyote buttons, which can be eaten or made into a tea; and psilocybin, which is found in a wide range of American and Mexican mushrooms. Some street names for peyote are bad seed, big chief, buttons, cactus, P, peyotl, and topi. Common street names for mescaline include beans, big chief, buttons, cactus, cactus buttons, mesc, mescal, and moon topi. (See Table 3.14.)

LSD

Common street names for LSD are acid, barrels, beast, Big D, blotter, blue acid, blue cheer, blue heaven, blue mist, brown dots, California sunshine, cap, chocolate chips, contact lens, cubes, cupcakes, D, deeda, domes, dots, electric Kool-Aid, flash, ghost, hawk, haze, L, lysergic, mellow yellows, microdots, orange cubes, paper acid, peace,

Panther mushroom
© Sally A. Morgan/Ecoscene/Corbis

Psilocybe mushroom
© John Wright/Science Source

T A B L E   3 . 1 4

Classification of Hallucinogens

LSD-25 (lysergic acid diethylamide)
Dimethyltryptamine (DMT)
Psilocybin (mushrooms)
Psilocin
Bufotenine
Harmine
Mescaline (active part of peyote cactus)
Diethytryptamine (DET)
Dipropryltryptamine (DPT)
Dimethoxymethamphetamine (DOM/STP)
Methylenedioxyamphetamine (MDA)
Belladonna alkaloids (atropine, scopoliamine, and stramonium are found in many
      medicines for asthma and stomach cramps)
Nutmeg (myristicin)

---

pearly gates, pellets, pink owsley, purple haze, sacrament, strawberries, strawberry fields, sugar, sugar cubes, sunshine, tabs, ticket twenty-five, wedges, white lightning, window pane, and yellow.

Brief History of LSD and Other Hallucinogens

1000 B.C. or earlier: Hallucinogenic mushrooms were used in religious and tribal use.

700 B.C.: Hallucinogenic mandrake root was referred to by the Assyrians and mentioned in the Bible as a fertility substance.

38: Datura was used by the early Incas and other Indians of South America. Peyote cactus (mescaline) was used by Incas and later by Native Americans.

1899: Oklahoma was the first state to outlaw the use of peyote.

April 16, 1943: Albert Hoffman, a chemist who discovered aspirin, working at Sandoz Laboratories in Basel, Switzerland, discovered LSD-25 and experienced the first LSD-25 trip.

Until mid-1960s: LSD was used in experiments in mental hospitals and laboratories to explore the treatment of mental disorders and as a means of studying psychotic behavior.

1960: Timothy Leary, Ph.D., a research professor in the Department of Social and Human Relations at Harvard University, reported a "full-blown conversion experience" after eating psilocybin mushrooms. He and Richard Alpert, Ph.D. (today known as lecturer Ram Dass), distributed psilocybin.

1961: Leary and Alpert distributed LSD.

1963: Leary and Alpert were dismissed from Harvard, giving them tremendous publicity. They coined the famous phrase "Turn on, tune in, and drop out."

1965: At an LSD conference, Sidney Cohen summarized the research on LSD use with psychiatric patients and other experiments.

1969: The Woodstock Festival took place in Woodstock, New York.

Timothy Leary was influential in the popularization of LSD in the early 1960s.

© Bettmann/Corbis

1960s and 1970s: LSD was extremely popular on the streets, especially among young people and college students.

1992 to 1993: An increase in the trend of LSD use by young people became evident.

Estimates of Use In comparison with the use of hallucinogens in the late 1960s, today's use rate is smaller. But, contrary to media reports, that use has not all but died out. These drugs continue to be taken by almost a million people in the United States each year (929,000 per SAMHSA 2004). LSD is the most commonly used hallucinogen. LSD is manufactured, and hallucinogenic mushrooms grow wild in some states, as do many plants with hallucinogenic or toxic-hallucinogenic properties.

Routes of Administration Hallucinogens are usually ingested orally, but they may be smoked, snorted, or injected. Because such small amounts are required at any one time (25 to 150 millionths of a gram), LSD is often impregnated in sugar pills, blotter paper, or small gelatin squares. The nasty taste of some hallucinogens requires mixing them with other substances to counteract their taste. Teas and broths are a common method of ingesting hallucinogens.

Major Effects The effects of hallucinogens are influenced by the personality of the user, the expectations of use, the user's general experience with drugs, the mindset of the individual, and, most important, the setting. The right group of trusting friends, a comfortable, soothing environment (e.g., dim lights and soft music), and someone experienced with hallucinogens are described as integral in developing a good hallucinogenic trip.

As a result of all these variables, users of hallucinogens report a wide range of reactions. Some individuals feel an insight and expanded consciousness, while others report a discomfort and fear of losing control that is quite disturbing. Generally, low to moderate doses of hallucinogens produce mood and perceptual alterations. LSD and other hallucinogens can produce profound effects on the user's thinking, self-awareness, and emotions. Hallucinogens distort time and space perception and induce hallucinations.

Adverse Effects Hallucinogenic experiences can sometimes add to existing neuroses, or character disorders, and can produce transient waves of mild anxiety, paranoia, or severe panic. Flashbacks (recurrences of negative hallucinogenic experiences) usually occur within a year or less from the previous use of hallucinogens. However, the incidence of flashbacks is relatively small. Flashbacks can occur in individuals who have used hallucinogens excessively and in the occasional or first-time user.

Accidents are very common under the influence of hallucinogens. The high degree of suggestibility and perceptual distortions and hallucinations often lead to accidents. Such accidents include walking through a plate glass window; jumping from a roof due to the coaxing of a friend (high degree of suggestibility); and suffering accidental falls, drownings, and car accidents.

Tolerance and Dependence Researchers have observed psychological dependence in long-term LSD users but have rarely reported dependence as a consequence of other hallucinogenic use. Hallucinogenic trips can be of long duration, compared with other drug use. Users tend to trip for from 4 to 6 hours to 12 to 24 hours. Following these trips, users are usually quite tired. This often necessitates periods of getting back to normal functioning before again using hallucinogens. Because of this pattern of occasional or intermittent use of hallucinogens, physical dependence is unlikely under most conditions. Tolerance has been shown to develop to some of the psychological and physiological effects of LSD. Quite frequently, there is cross-tolerance to other hallucinogens. For example, an individual who has recently been taking LSD generally shows a reduced response to mescaline and psilocybin.

Cannabis Sativa

Cannabis refers to any product of the plant *Cannabis sativa,* which grows in most parts of the world. In North America, the most commonly used products derived from this plant are marijuana and hashish. Marijuana is the unprocessed, dried leaves, flowers, seeds, and stems of the plant. Hashish is a more potent product processed from the resin of this herb. Researchers have obtained more than 300 cannabis products (cannabinoids) from cannabis. They have isolated and synthesized the most active ingredient in marijuana. This product, tetrahydrocannabinol (THC), is the psychoactive compound found in the greatest amount in the plant; it is thought to produce most of the high.

Street Names Common street names for marijuana include Acapulco gold, ace, African black, aunt mary, baby, bale, bomb, boo, brick, broccoli, bush, Canadian black, charge, Colombian, doobie, dry high, fatty, fingers, flowers, gage, ganga, gauge, giggleweed, grass, green, grefa, greta, grifa, grillo, grunt, hay, hemp, herb, home-grown, Indian hay, Indian hemp, J, jane, jay smoke, joint, joy stick, juanita, kick sticks, kif, killer, killer weed, kilter, loco, mary, maryann, maryjane, mary warner, mary weaver, meserole (messerole), Mexican brown, Mexican green, Mexican locoweed, MJ, mooca, moota, mooters, mootie, mota, mother, mu, muggles, muta, number, Panama gold, Panama red, panatella, pin, pode, pot, ragweed, rainy day woman, red dirt, reefer, roach, root, sassafras, sinsemilla, smoke, snop, stick, sweet lucy, tea, Texas tea, twist, weed, wheat, yerba, and Zacatecas purple. Street names for hashish include black hash, black Russian, blond hash, canned sativa, hash, Lebanese, and mahjuema.

Brief History of Marijuana

2737 B.C.: The earliest reference to marijuana by a Chinese treatise on pharmacology was attributed to Emperor Shen Nung.

Marijuana leaves.
© Travelib India/Alamy

Second century B.C.: The Scythians, a warlike and mobile Middle Eastern tribe, spread cannabis into Egypt and then northward to Russia and Europe.

They had a ritual of throwing hemp seeds on heated stones and inhaling the vapors (funeral rite).

650 B.C.: The use of cannabis was mentioned in Persia and Assyria.

400 B.C.: The use of cannabis was mentioned in Rome.

1545: The first record of a marijuana plant in the New World occurred when Spanish traders introduced marijuana to Chile.

1611: Sir Walter Raleigh was ordered by the British to grow hemp in his Virginia colony. Hemp was much needed for the strong shipbuilding industry of the time.

1765: George Washington grew marijuana hemp and is said to have experimented with the medicinal or intoxicating potency of the plants.

1804–44: Jacques-Joseph Moreau of France used marijuana in the treatment of melancolia, hypomania, and other forms of mental disorder.

1839: W. B. O'Shaughnessy, a young chemistry professor, used marijuana for medicinal use as an anticonvulsant and an appetite stimulant.

1846: A group of French writers formed the "Club des Hachichias," meeting in Paris once a month, where they often smoked marijuana. The meetings were attended by Victor Hugo, Baudelaire, Dumas, Gautier, and De Nerval.

Early 1900s: It is believed that the drug and use of the word *marijuana* were introduced to the United States by migrant Mexican laborers.

1937: Henry Anslinger, commissioner of the Bureau of Narcotics, campaigned on the dangers of marijuana.

1937: The federal government developed the Marijuana Tax Act and used taxes to outlaw the drug.

October 1969: A Gallup Poll estimated that 10 million Americans, half of them under 21 years of age, have smoked marijuana.

1970: The Controlled Substance Act, supported by the American Medical Association, reported that marijuana had no potential medicinal use, ignoring years of medical evidence to the contrary.

2011: Medical marijuna is licensed in 14 states and Washington, DC and pending in another 10 states.

Estimates of Use Marijuana is the most widely used of all illicit drugs. Past-month users number 14.6 million (61.1 percent of U.S. population) (SAMHSA 2004).

Medical Uses Cannabis, primarily in the form of synthetic THC, has been under scientific investigation in recent years to ascertain its potential therapeutic uses. One approved therapeutic use is as an antiemetic (antivomiting) agent for the nausea and vomiting associated with chemotherapy treatment for cancer patients. It is also medically used to relieve the intraocular pressure accompanying glaucoma. Both of these medical uses are the most well researched. Other potential medical uses of marijuana researched thus far include spasm relief, asthma relief, anxiety reduction, and relief of alcohol withdrawal symptoms. Studies in these areas have not been as prolific, or as conclusive, as those regarding chemotherapy and glaucoma (Solomons and Neppve 1989).

As of 2001, 34 states had statutes on the books allowing marijuana, typically in the form of THC, to be used in medical research and/or medical treatment as a part of a clinical investigation. The number of states that have actually implemented these procedures is much smaller. The political and moral/ethical emotionality of our times may further hinder these investigations into the effectiveness of marijuana in medical research. For this reason, other synthetically produced cannabis derivatives are also under investigation.

Routes of Administration Marijuana can be smoked in hand-rolled cigarettes, or joints. Today's higher potency marijuana is usually smoked in a pipe—most frequently, a water pipe. This allows the most intense high with the least waste of the marijuana.

Generally, hashish has a much higher THC content, though it varies widely in potency. Hashish can be crumbled and rolled into a cigarette for smoking; often, it is mixed with a lower grade marijuana or tobacco. In this country, hashish is normally smoked in a water pipe.

Marijuana and hashish can also be eaten in cookies, brownies, and other food or made into a tea. In this form, the high lasts longer, since it is slowed down by the digestive processes.

Cannabis resin is not water soluble, so the drug cannot be injected. The few who have tried using it this way usually experienced violent convulsions.

Major Effects The effects of cannabis depend on the potency of the drug, the method of use, and the experience and expectations of the user regarding what will happen. For low-dose periodic use, the common effects of marijuana use are:

- Intensification of thoughts and feelings
- Feelings of exhilaration, relaxation, and giddiness
- Minor increase in heart rate
- Drowsiness, dry mouth and throat, bloodshot eyes
- Impaired short-term memory
- Altered states of time and space
- Dilated pupils

TABLE 3.15

Aspects of Life Experience Adult Daily Users Most Frequently Described as Positively Affected by Marijuana

- Ability to relax and enjoy life
- Enjoyment of food
- Ability to overcome worry and anxiety
- Ability to sleep well
- Ability to avoid feeling bored
- Enjoyment of sex
- Understanding of others
- Creativity
- Ability to avoid feeling angry
- Ability to enjoy varied activities
- Self-understanding
- Overall happiness
- Ability to avoid feeling depressed
- Ability to be tolerant and considerate of others

SOURCE: Herbert Hendin et al., *Living High: Daily Marijuana Use by Adults.* Human Sciences Press, 1987.

For a list of experiences that adult users tend to describe as positively affected by marijuana use (see Table 3.15).

Increased Potency of Marijuana You might remember hearing about types of marijuana such as Acapulco gold, Maui Wowi, or Panama red. Most of the potent marijuana in the 1960s was imported from these places. Today, homegrown marijuana is the staple of American pot smokers. The more than 14 million pot smokers in the United States prefer the high-potency sinsemilla grown in hidden caches throughout the United States. Humboldt County in California is a well-known locale of this homegrown cultivation. The California gold rush continues there in the form of marijuana crops, despite increased eradication efforts.

In the 1960s, the THC content of marijuana was 1 to 2 percent in potency. Most users would smoke half a joint to get high. Two or three joints passed among friends could get everyone high. Today, the THC content of marijuana averages 6 percent. One hit is enough to keep an individual loaded. Today, hashish is 10 percent THC and hash oil is 20 percent THC. This increase in the potency of marijuana means we are looking at a new drug with new problems. The research of the past with marijuana in the 1 to 2 percent THC level does not apply to marijuana now in use.

Subjective effects of cannabis intoxication have been reported in hundreds of different ways. Common reports include happiness, warmth, conviviality, camaraderie, and the ability to enjoy music and art better than when sober. Reactions to marijuana depend a great deal on the attitude of the user and the compatibility of the surroundings (set and setting). Cannabis is sometimes classified as a mild hallucinogen. With the increase in potency of marijuana, this classification may be warranted.

Adverse Effects The long-term effects of chronic cannabis use are at the heart of the current medical debate on this drug. Strong psychological dependence does develop in many regular users of marijuana, as evidenced by a need for cannabis use every day to perform certain tasks, to relax and unwind, or to sleep. The individual's life begins to revolve around the use of marijuana as a primary activity. The user tends to use marijuana more frequently throughout the day and evening.

Withdrawal symptoms after steady use may include irritability, decreased appetite, restlessness, sleep disturbances, sweating, nausea, or diarrhea. Hangovers are not uncommon. However, unlike the alcohol hangover, which causes headaches and sensitive optic nerves, the cannabis hangover is more likely to be light-headedness characterized by the inability to gather thoughts. When the drug is ingested, the effect can linger on for an entire day, along with nausea, body aches, and other symptoms.

Despite the lack of classic withdrawal symptoms, some patterns of marijuana use fit the behavioral definition of addiction. Researchers have well established the fact that chronic marijuana use can cause physical dependence by identifying full-blown withdrawal symptoms in the newborn babies of marijuana-dependent mothers. Treatment for the addiction to marijuana requires the support of an outpatient treatment counselor knowledgeable about alcohol/drug recovery and marijuana dependence. Marijuana Anonymous groups have also developed to meet the rising incidence of dependence on marijuana.

Anxiety and panic reactions are common with chronic marijuana use. Many individuals who have used marijuana to self-medicate affective disorders, such as depression and bipolar disorder, can experience severe anxiety and panic reactions. Individuals experiencing psychologically negative reactions may require temporary hospitalization so they don't lose control and hurt themselves or others.

Damage to the Respiratory System The tars in cannabis smoke are 50 percent greater by weight than tobacco tars and 70 percent higher in cancer-producing substances. Considering that marijuana is deeply inhaled and the smoke is held in the lungs, instead of passively inhaled, as in cigarette smoking, the cancer-causing risk is increased by marijuana smoking.

Long-term, heavy smoking of cannabis is associated with bronchial problems, sore throat, and chronic coughing. These conditions may be more severe in chronic hashish users. In addition, those who smoke tobacco as well as cannabis products have an added risk of bronchial problems and cancer.

Immune System Effects Research suggests that cannabis, particularly when used regularly, tends to suppress the body's immune response and ability to combat infections (Cohen 1986). Marijuana temporarily arrests the maturation of developing T cells, which protect the body from colds and other bacterial infections. This increases the chances of illness due to either bacteria or viruses. The most prominent indication of this effect is the higher incidence of bronchial infections, coughing, bronchitis, and pneumonia noted among chronic, heavy marijuana users.

Reproductive System Effects Chronic use of cannabis decreases sperm motility and serum testosterone in men and interferes with the menstrual cycle in women, thus affecting fertility. Most of these effects are reversed after marijuana use is discontinued. Marijuana is suspected to be harmful to the fetuses in pregnant women; research with rhesus monkeys has shown pregnancy problems such as stillbirth and spontaneous abortion. Reduced birth weight is also a characteristic of surviving fetuses.

Brain System Effects Considerable debate continues over the effects of cannabis on the brain. A certain percentage of users develop lethargy, apathy, and disorientation, which persist long after chronic use has been discontinued. Fortunately, these effects appear to wear off gradually. Some researchers claim that long-term changes occur in some brain wave patterns; these claims are being investigated further.

Impairment of Maturation Process Most researchers agree that cannabis use, during the primary developmental years of 11 to 15, in particular, interferes with physical and mental maturation processes and impedes emotional development. Research describes an amotivational syndrome with symptoms of apathy, lethargy, and a general lack of involvement and motivation in growth and developmental activities.

Marijuana and Driving Cannabis intoxication and chronic marijuana use impair short-term memory, alter the user's sense of time and space, and impair overall coordination and motor functioning. The ability to track other vehicles is also impaired and is a major problem in driving a car. Tracking involves judging time, distance, and the speed of other cars. Skills such as merging into traffic, making U-turns, and performing other driving tasks require tracking skills. Adding another drug, such as alcohol, only makes the situation worse. Many persons insist that their driving performance is improved under the influence of marijuana. This is due to their increased sensitivity to enjoying driving, not to a realistic evaluation of driving ability.

Smoking marijuana also makes it very dangerous to operate machinery and other equipment, since perception and timing are off, and the drug may also produce fatigue and drowsiness.

A study of airplane pilots reported that, after smoking marijuana, performance was impaired up to 2 to 3 days later, despite the pilots' thinking that they did extremely well on simulated tests (Rohr 1989). Other problems include (1) true allergic reactions to cannabis for a small minority of users, (2) gastrointestinal disturbances and weight loss among a small percentage of heavy users, and (3) difficulty in medical control of some diabetic users.

Inhalants

From time to time, the phenomenon of inhalant use is brought to public attention. In the 1960s, there was an epidemic of glue sniffing. Nowadays, there is still a consistent use of various solvents, aerosols, and other gases that people inhale to get

TABLE 3.16
Classification of Inhalants

A wide variety of names apply to inhaled substances. Many liquids also contain alcohol and petroleum distillates.

Naphtha	Fluorocarbon propellants
Benzene	Nitrous oxide
Acetone	Amyl nitrite, butyl nitrite
Toluene	Anesthetic gases (e.g., ether and chloroform)
Carbon tetrachloride	Gasoline

high. Inhalant use is more prevalent in young people, people of color, and minorities who do not have the money to buy drugs. And, in certain locations, the problem is much more serious because of the number of young people who use inhalants to get high, yet this is hardly a modern-day phenomenon. Table 3.16 lists some common inhalants.

Brief History Some inhalants and anesthetics, such as nitrous oxide, ether, and chloroform, were used recreationally in the nineteenth century, especially during times of liquor scarcity. This occurred in Europe, Great Britain, and North America, where ether inhalation parties were common among students and physicians.

In the 1960s, the inhalation of volatile substances such as plastic model glue, nail polish removers, and aerosol sprays occurred frequently among adolescents. A wave of anti glue-sniffing publicity at the time resulted in many local and state laws prohibiting minors from buying such substances. In spite of these laws, inhalant vapors and sprays continue to be used today, partially because of the widespread application of such products in household use and partially because of ineffective legislation and enforcement.

In the 1970s and 1980s, paint became the primary inhalant of abuse. Users sprayed cans of paint, preferably gold and silver, into rags that they stuffed under their noses to inhale the fumes. These huffers (paint inhalers) were often inner-city Latinos and other young people of color. Native American youth have an extremely high incidence of gasoline inhalant use. In 2004, an estimated 856,000 persons had used inhalants for the first time in the past 12 months (SAMHSA 2004). Inhalants—particularly volatile solvents, gases, and aerosois—are often among the first drugs that young children use. One national survey indicates that about 6 percent of U.S. children have tried inhalants by fourth grade (NIDA 2004).

Route of Administration Inhalation is accomplished in any number of ways, depending on the ingenuity of the user. Inhaling fumes can be accomplished by placing the substance on a rag; placing or spraying the substance in a plastic bag; or, in the case of some pressurized gases, filling up a balloon, then waiting for the frozen vapor to warm up (if necessary) before inhaling. Users also sometimes go into a food market, smash the bottom of whipped cream cans, and squirt the gas from the broken containers into the backs of their throats. This aerosol freon gives them a cheap high.

Absorption of gases and volatile liquids is efficient and rapid. Absorption into tissues begins with the nasal mucous membranes. The major absorption site is the lungs, where substances enter the bloodstream. From the lungs, substances are distributed directly to the brain and other organ systems. They also enter fatty tissue.

Available Forms of Inhalants Glue, model cement, fingernail polish removers, various cosmetics, various cleaning solvents, gasoline, paint, paint thinners, lighter fluids, antifreeze, aerosol cans, and white correction fluids can all be inhaled.

Major Effects Users report a feeling of well-being, a reduction of inhibitions, and an elevated mood. In many respects, the effects are similar to those produced by alcohol and other sedatives. Higher doses often produce laughing and giddiness, feelings of floating, dizziness, time and space distortions, and illusions. (See Table 3.17.) Some substances induce psychedelic effects. An inhalant's effects may last anywhere from 5 minutes to an hour, depending on the substance and the dose.

Many people do not understand why anyone would actively seek a high from inhalants. They forget how young children often twirl to feel the effect of dizziness and how children, adolescents, and even adults are exhilarated by the rides at amusement parks, especially the rides that give them feelings of vertigo. These effects are altered states of consciousness that are reinforcing to many individuals. Such is the case with inhalant abusers. Other reasons for using inhalants include (1) recreation (fun, mood elevation, the high); (2) peer group influence ("it was what everyone was doing"); (3) cost effectiveness (a quick and cheap high); and (4) easy availability.

Tolerance and Dependence When use of volatile substances continues for a long time and becomes heavy, tolerance may develop. Physical dependence with withdrawal symptoms has also occurred among some chronic users. These withdrawal symptoms include hallucinations, headaches, chills, delirium tremens, and stomach cramps. Hangovers lasting several days have also occurred.

There is cross-tolerance between some solvents and central nervous system depressants. For example, skid row alcoholics inhale hydrocarbon vapors from

---

TABLE 3.17

Signs and Symptoms of Inhalant Use

1. Slurred speech
2. Odor of the substance being used
3. Mental disorientation or confusion
4. Headaches, dizziness, and weakness
5. Muscle spasms in the neck, chest, or lower extremities
6. Euphoria, exaggerated feeling of well-being
7. Loss of balance and ataxia (uncoordinated walk)
8. Nystagmus (eye movement from side to side)

kerosene or spray paint when they run out of liquor. These solvents forestall withdrawal symptoms from the alcohol, especially delirium tremens.

Alcohol and barbiturates potentiate some of the adverse effects of certain solvents. Consequently, users risk unconsciousness or even heart failure if they add the effects of alcohol to the effects of volatile solvents.

Acute Adverse Effects Acute use of solvents often brings on confusion, drunkenness, slurred speech, numbness, runny nose, tears, headache, and muscular incoordination. Frequently, there is nausea and vomiting. Due to impaired judgment from solvent use, users often feel confusion, panic, irritation, tension, and hyperactivity and become physically aggressive.

In cases of high dosage, the general sedative-anesthetic effects take over, resulting in drowsiness, stupor, respiratory depression, and unconsciousness. Extremely heavy use can inhibit breathing and bring on death.

Many of these substances are capable of sensitizing the heart to adrenaline. Since the early 1960s, heart failure due to this effect has been suspected in hundreds of users. This has been referred to as sudden sniffing death syndrome (SSD).

Some deaths have been directly attributed to solvent use. Most of them are due to suffocation when the users faint from inhalation and their noses and mouths remain covered by the plastic bags or when they suffocate in their own vomit. Additional acute adverse effects depend on the specific products and their chemical makeup.

Long-Term Effects Some temporary abnormalities take place in liver and kidney function and bone marrow activity; gastritis, hepatitis, jaundice, blood abnormalities, and peptic ulcers also occur.

Chronic users have exhibited slow-healing ulcers around their mouths and noses. Other effects are loss of appetite, weight loss, and nutritional disorders. Brain damage also results from regular solvent use; most of the time, this has been reversible (without permanent effect) once the use was stopped.

With so many different kinds of solvents and hydrocarbons with chemically different structures, it is impossible to predict the long-term effects of the inhalation of all possible substances. Recent information suggests that some substances, such as toluene, may actually be less harmful than previously believed. On the other hand, long-term use of other substances, such as n-hexane, which is commonly found in some plastic cements, gasoline, various adhesives, and rubber cements, may cause permanent damage to the muscles. Because spray paint, aerosols, glues, and other such substances often contain a half-dozen or more ingredients in combination, researchers have had a great deal of difficulty ascertaining the exact damage potential for humans (Ashton 1990).

Phencyclidine

Phencyclidine (PCP) is a drug that cannot be classified properly as a hallucinogen, a stimulant, or a depressant, causing it to be listed in a separate drug category. Originally, PCP was developed in the 1950s as a sedative, general anesthetic and analgesic. In clinical testing, it worked fine as a painkiller, although subjects often developed visual disturbances, severe agitation, and other unpleasant side effects.

These side effects caused its discontinued use with humans. Until 1978, phencyclidine was sold as a veterinary medication for immobilizing primates and other large animals. Its use as an illicit drug began in the mid-1960s.

Street Names for PCP Common street names for PCP are angel dust, animal trank, aurora borealis, DOA, dust, elephant, hog, peace, peace pill, rocket fuel, supergrass, and tic tac.

Estimates of Use The geographic patterns of PCP use are haphazard. It has long been popular on the West Coast and in certain large cities; recently, the geographical pattern of use has become more widespread.

The majority of users are young, approximately 12 to 18 years of age, though there is use by young children and adults. (PCP users inadvertently exposed infants to PCP when they stored their drugs in empty milk bottles.) Few users have been involved for as long as 10 years, probably due to negative effects, resulting in discontinuance or a switch to another intoxicant (Thombs 1989).

Routes of Administration PCP is a white, crystalline powder, soluble in water. Most commonly smoked or ingested, it may occasionally be injected. As tablets or capsules, PCP commonly comes in various sizes and colors. When PCP is smoked, users sprinkle the drug over mint leaves, marijuana, tobacco, or other substances, or they spray PCP liquid onto the substance to be smoked. One popular method is to dip cigarettes into liquid PCP. Given all these possibilities, this drug may appear as a drug or be disguised to look like any number of other substances.

Major Effects With a moderate or low dose, PCP produces a state of euphoria lasting 3 to 5 hours when smoked or 5 to 8 hours when eaten. Reactions to the drug vary greatly; much depends on the personality of the user and the circumstances surrounding the use (set and setting). Users who have bought this drug thinking it was THC have sworn that the high was like a heavy marijuana intoxication. When PCP is misrepresented as a hallucinogen, users report LSD experiences. Users who believe they are getting PCP, however, seldom have these convictions.

The most common reactions from moderate to low doses are auditory, visual, time, and other sensory disturbances. The most consistent effect is deadening of the extremities. Due to the drug's anesthetic properties, users lose control of their muscles. Depending on the individual, the overall reaction may vary anywhere from hyperactivity to complete immobility. The drug, though not a true hallucinogen, may mimic hallucinogenic drugs in some ways. It has been described by one authority as a *delusionogen,* a term that may more accurately describe its effect on the user.

Intoxication by PCP produces an experience of tranquilization, euphoria, inebriation, dissociation, and usually tactile and auditory hallucinations. The most common effects are changes in body imagery, perceptual distortions, and feelings of apathy and estrangement. The experience often includes drowsiness, inability to verbalize, and feelings of nothingness or emptiness. Reports of difficulty in thinking, poor concentration, and preoccupation with death are frequent.

Adverse Effects As with most other drugs, for some users occasional recreational or social use of small amounts of PCP does not cause undesirable side effects. However, this situation is likely to change when users take or smoke larger doses or smaller amounts consistently day after day. Users often smoke or ingest other drugs in addition to PCP, causing many unusual reactions.

Accidents With high doses of PCP, accidents are common. Because PCP produces a loss of feeling, users frequently report cuts, bruises, and torn muscles and ligaments. The dissociative effects of PCP may make users believe these injuries are happening to someone else at the time.

In the heyday of PCP use in southern California in the 1960s, high doses resulted in many drownings. In those drownings, the individuals under the influence of PCP became disoriented; once underwater, they did not know which way was up. Drownings also result when users are so anesthetized that they forget to breathe; friends who are also stoned may not realize what is taking place (Thombs 1989).

Violence Higher or consistent doses of PCP have also led to incidents of violence. These vary widely, but many are characterized by the user's inability to feel pain. The result is a situation where the user feels extraordinary strength and immunity to pain. Police have reported high-dose PCP users breaking out of steel handcuffs, failing to stop an attack even though shot several times, coming forward and attacking police, or bleeding to death because of an inability to feel the injury inflicted during an attack. Despite several hundred reports of incidents like these, in relation to the millions who use this drug, they are considered rare.

More common adverse reactions include the following:

- Paranoia
- Severe agitation
- A severe withdrawn or isolated feeling
- Bizarre delusions
- Increases in heart rate, blood pressure
- Sweating, salivation, and flushing of the skin (these increase according to the dose)
- Nystagmus (jerky eye movements) and other reactions

PCP is unsafe to use during pregnancy, though the exact potential for damage to the fetus is unknown. PCP may also interfere with the hormones governing normal growth and development in the adolescent user. The principal proven negative effects on youthful users, however, relate to a decreased learning capacity, difficulty in concentration, poor grades, and poor social adjustment.

Unpredictable episodes of panic may occur. Latent psychopathology may be unmasked or triggered either by acute doses or by patterns of chronic use, as evidenced by episodes of violence, paranoia, and so forth. With prolonged regular PCP use, the effects can linger after the intoxication has worn off, necessitating therapy or rehabilitation. Flashbacks are also reported from prolonged PCP use. With very large doses, convulsions or coma may occur.

Several PCP deaths have been due to the direct effects of the drug. Other deaths have been attributed to PCP combined with other drugs, particularly central nervous system depressants. As mentioned earlier, deaths are more frequently due to accidental causes while under the influence.

Tolerance and Dependence PCP does not appear to be physically addictive, even though some tolerance does develop in regular users. When used orally, PCP is most often used only occasionally. When smoked, it is very often used more frequently and can create a very strong psychological dependence. Few data substantiate a withdrawal syndrome with PCP, though the drug often produces aftereffects lasting many months after use is discontinued. One of these aftereffects is depression, which can last up to a year; if untreated, it can lead to relapse and suicide.

✺ Athletes and Drugs

Athletes have been using drugs to enhance their performance since ancient times. The use of drugs by athletes is almost as old as the Olympic Games themselves.

In the marathon event of the 1904 Olympic Games in St. Louis, Missouri, the winning runner was American Thomas Hicks, who was aided by a heady cocktail of brandy and strychnine (a stimulant at low doses, a poison at high doses). Today, more than 50 psychomotor stimulant drugs are banned from use during an Olympic competition.

The use of performance-enhancing drugs continues to be a current problem. Professional baseball players Roger Clemens, Barry Bonds, and many others were implicated in the use of these drugs. Olympic gold-medal winner Marion Jones has admitted to doping. The Tour de France has had drug-related scandals as well. Practically every professional and amateur sport has had concerns about athletes using these drugs to improve their performance.

Steroids

All of the previously described drugs used in sports and athletics can be labeled *ergogenic* because they are performance-enhancing substances. By far, the most controversial ergogenic drug used by many athletes—especially young, developing boys and girls—is steroids.

Brief History

Steroids were developed in the 1930s for the treatment of anemia and a variety of diseases that wasted away muscles. Physicians have also used steroids to treat cancer, burns, intestinal problems, asthma, and emaciation. After World War II, steroid use restored body tissue to victims of starvation. The increased aggressiveness caused by steroid use was one of the benefits sought by German soldiers in World War II.

In 1988, Canadian sprinter Ben Johnson lost his Olympic gold medals because he tested positive for steroids. Today, steroid use is a problem not only with world-class Olympic athletes but also with teenagers. Steroid use became the adolescent rage of the 1990s. Studies indicate that 6 to 10 percent of high school boys will use steroids by graduation, as will 1 percent of girls. Unfortunately, two-thirds of these young people will start to use steroids before the age of 16. Most young people who use steroids do so to enhance their performance in sports, yet a surprisingly large percentage (25 percent) use steroids for appearance. The skinny boy on the beach who gets sand kicked in his face no longer chooses the old Charles Atlas weight-training program to bulk up. Instead, steroid use with weight training and diet create the hulking bodies that young men desire. Beefing up and strengthening their bodies give these young people added self-confidence because they feel attractive (Hough 1988).

Steroids are illegal without a prescription. Federal officials estimate the illicit steroid market at $400 million.

Terminology

Androgenic steroids, which include testosterone, primarily develop and maintain male sex characteristics. So-called **anabolic** steroids are synthetic derivatives of testosterone developed in an attempt to minimize testosterone's androgenic or masculinizing effects on the individual while promoting protein synthesis and muscular growth.

Because none of these compounds is purely anabolic or purely androgenic in its effects, and since athletes usually stack, or use the steroids in combination, technically the more correct designation is "anabolic-androgenic steroids (A-AS)" rather than just anabolic steroids (AS).

Major Effects

Many of the early studies regarding the effectiveness of steroids produced conflicting results. More recent studies have clearly indicated significant increases in strength as a result of steroid use. The American College of Sports Medicine in its position statement on steroids in 1989 concluded that "gains in strength can occur through a variety of mechanisms in the highly trained athlete who takes steroids."

Increases in lean body mass do occur in A-AS steroid use. In the past, this was thought to be the result of water retention. It is now clear that there is an actual increase in muscle tissue and enhancement of muscle contractility. In addition, some reports cite an increase in actual bone density. However, most of these changes do not increase strength unless their use is combined with high-intensity weight training and a properly balanced diet.

Anabolic-androgenic steroids also increase the ability to perform high-intensity training sessions. In part, this is due to increased protein metabolism as well as the inhibition of the metabolic (breaking down) effects of corticosteroids, which are released in increased amounts whenever the body is stressed. The result is that the body requires less recuperation time between intensive workouts to repair itself. However, most studies have also shown that aerobic capacity is not affected or improved at all with steroid use.

Adverse Effects

The problem with steroids is that they do not act exclusively on one muscle or tissue group. Therefore, they stimulate all muscles and tissues, making the individual at risk for other adverse effects. The body's homeostasis is disrupted with the use of steroids, causing a variety of physical problems. "Heart disease will probably be the most widely noted side effect with anabolic steroid abuse. Blood pressure elevates significantly when an individual takes anabolic steroids due to the retained fluid and increased blood volume. . . . High Density Lipoproteins (HDL-C) that aid the body in removing cholesterol, and are important to cardiac longevity, are drastically reduced with the use of androgens" (American Osteopathic Academy of Sports Medicine 1989).

For adolescents, the drug can cause stunted growth and the premature closing of growth plates. Other problems resulting from steroid abuse by men include the following:

- Liver and kidney damage
- Breast development
- Acne, baldness
- Cysts
- Shrinking of the testicles and sterility
- Reduced sex drive
- Headaches, nausea, and dizziness

For women the drug can cause the following:

- Infertility
- Clitoral enlargement
- Breast atrophy
- Menstrual irregularities
- Male pattern baldness and voice change

More and more evidence is accruing that the most significant effect of A-AS use may be psychiatric. Psychological reactions such as extreme aggressiveness, mood swings, depression, and delusions are reported in some individuals. Signs and symptoms similar to drug and alcohol dependence (e.g., loss of control; continued use despite known adverse consequences, tolerance, and withdrawal) suggest that both physical and psychological dependence can occur with A-AS use.

Amphetamines

The first widespread abuse of drugs in professional sports occurred in the late 1960s and early 1970s, when professional football players used amphetamines. Mandell

(1979) reported this as a so-called Sunday syndrome of amphetamine use to enhance performance. However, athletes in many other sports—notably, those involved in endurance events—also have used amphetamines.

Amphetamines have an appetite-suppression effect attractive to a variety of athletes for whom making and keeping a required weight is essential (e.g., jockeys, gymnasts, wrestlers, and boxers). Numerous studies have attempted to document the effects of amphetamines on performance. Some have looked at psychomotor tasks, others have examined certain variables related to overall performance, and still others have studied athletic performance (Derlet and Heischober 1990).

Smith and Beecher (1959) reported that approximately 75 percent of trained swimmers, weight lifters, and runners showed improvements in performance after administration of amphetamines. However, Karpovich (1969) found improvement in only 3 of 20 athletes, and one athlete actually performed more poorly. A review in 1981, using criteria based on knee-extension strength and running to exhaustion, showed that performance usually improved by only a small percentage. However, in highly competitive sports, even a 1 percent improvement can mean the difference between victory and defeat.

Most people also would probably agree that the alertness of the fatigued person, whether an athlete, a truck driver, a student, or a subject of an experiment, increases with the use of amphetamines. However, Chandler and Blair concluded in 1980 that "amphetamines do not prevent fatigue but rather mask the effects of fatigue and interfere with the body's fatigue-alarm system which could lead to disastrous results, especially under extreme environmental conditions."

Deaths caused by amphetamine use have involved cerebral vascular accidents (strokes) secondary to hemorrhages in the brain, acute heart failure with arrhythmias, and hyperthermia. The elevation of body temperature, if not fatal, can combine with heat exhaustion and circulatory collapse to cause heat stroke, because amphetamines obscure the athlete's normally protective physiologic fatigue level.

By diminishing pain thresholds, amphetamines allow athletes to continue to compete despite injury, thus potentially causing more tissue damage to the injured areas. Finally, there is an added potential for injury to others in contact sports because of the increase in aggressiveness caused by amphetamine use.

Chewing Tobacco

Epidemiologically, the percentage of smokers among athletes in the United States has declined, along with the decreasing trend in the general population. The use of chewing tobacco, however, remains inordinately high among athletes. Part of this can certainly be ascribed to new marketing and promotion campaigns by the tobacco companies, as well as the almost mythic, traditional relationship of "chawing" tobacco to the great American pastime of baseball. Ironically, the original baseball cards advertised tobacco. Long ago, politicians recognized the health hazards and declared chewing and spitting tobacco illegal in most places—except the baseball park.

From 1978 to 1985, celebrity athletes promoted chewing tobacco. Free supply programs and heavy advertising at sporting events stimulated the sale of chewing tobacco. As a result, chewing tobacco saw a 55 percent rise in sales at a time when cigarette sales dropped off. In 1970, men 55 and older were the heaviest users of chewing tobacco. By 1985, males under the age of 20 displaced them. Smokeless tobacco, a marketing label for chewing tobacco, is used by kindergarten children in Arkansas and Alaska; in Texas, reportedly, up to one-third of varsity football and baseball players use smokeless tobacco.

Many people have been misled into thinking that smokeless tobacco is a safe alternative to smoking. The surgeon general's *Report on the Health Consequences of Smokeless Tobacco Use* concluded that smokeless tobacco is causally related to oral cancer and gum recession, that it can lead to dependence on nicotine, and that it is not a safe alternative to cigarettes (U.S. Surgeon General 1988). In 2004, 7.2 million Americans used smokeless tobacco (SAMHSA 2004).

Nonetheless, some athletes use nicotine products for their perceived stimulating effect before their events, while others paradoxically use the tobacco for its calming effect. Still others state they use nicotine for its effect on the satiety center ("I'll gain weight if I stop smoking"). Some just use tobacco products for personal rather than performance reasons.

Regarding the widely held misconception that smokeless tobacco enhances performance, it is critical to make known that nicotine does not heighten energy or strength. In reality, the user who smokes, chews, or snorts nicotine is simply experiencing elevation in heart rate and blood pressure. The perceived relaxation is actually relief from the craving associated with nicotine withdrawal.

Clearly, young people will continue chewing smokeless tobacco unless professional athletes, coaches, and managers act as role models and point out the negative effects of all tobacco products.

Other Drugs/Alcohol in Sports

The pressures of professional athletic competition and the accompanying lifestyle can create a situation in which athletes seek both relief and the enhancement of performance by using alcohol or other drugs. Many high school, college, and even professional athletes are ill prepared for these pressures.

The widespread use of cocaine, marijuana, alcohol, amphetamines, and other drugs in professional sports came to the attention of the general public in the drug scandals of the past three decades. This was an indicator of the high level of denial and enabling behavior by players, coaches, and management. Today, teams are making more concerted efforts at education, assessment, and treatment. They have programs that help athletes develop the skills to deal with the pressures. However, alcohol/drug problems are still enabled and/or denied at many levels of athletic competition. Additional efforts are needed to resolve the issue of alcohol/drug abuse and addiction at all levels of athletic endeavor.

⚹ In Review

- Alcohol and other drugs are found in each neighborhood and community in our society, and every family is vulnerable to the problems associated with alcohol/drugs.
  - The legalization of medical marijuana is the single most significant change in recent drug history. More research is needed to understand the effective medical benefits, problems, and financial implications.
  - Adults over age 50 are coming back to marijuana use. Many of these "renewers" are getting their marijuana from their adult age children.
  - Energy drinks (EDs) are dangerous when combined with alcohol. College students and college athletes are vulnerable to using EDs.
- You can identify methamphetamine users by
  - Signs of agitation, excited speech, decreased appetites, and increased physical activity levels. Other common symptoms include dilated pupils, high blood pressure, irregular heartbeat, chest pain, shortness of breath, nausea and vomiting, diarrhea, and elevated body temperature.
  - Occasional episodes of sudden and violent behavior, intense paranoia, visual and auditory hallucinations, and bouts of insomnia.
  - A tendency to compulsively clean and groom and repetitively sort and disassemble objects, such as cars and other mechanical devices.
- The most commonly used inhalants by young people are glue, shoe polish, and gasoline. Other inhalants include nitrous oxide, lighter fluid, and aerosol sprays.
- A simple way to remember the behavioral definition of addiction is the 3Cs mnemonic:
  - **C**ompulsion
  - **C**ontrol
  - Continued use despite negative **C**onsequences
- Nine methods of absorption:
  - Oral
  - Rectal
  - Inhalation
  - Mucous membranes
  - Skin
  - Injection
  - Intravenous
  - Intramuscular
  - Subcutaneous
- *Set* refers to user's frame of mind at time of use. *Setting* refers to the physical environment or environmental factors surrounding alcohol/drug use.
- Drugs are classified as nonpsychoactive and psychoactive. *Nonpsychoactive drugs* are substances that in normal doses do not directly affect the brain, such as

vitamins, antibiotics, and topical skin preparations. *Psychoactive drugs* affect brain functions, mood, and behavior and are subdivided primarily on the basis of physiological and psychological effects.

- The psychoactive drug classification includes the following:
  - Narcotic analgesics: painkillers and designer drugs (fentanyl)
  - Central nervous system depressants: sedative hypnotics, alcohol, tranquilizers, and barbiturates
  - Central nervous system stimulants: amphetamines, cocaine, nicotine, and caffeine
  - Hallucinogens
  - *Cannabis sativa:* marijuana and hashish
  - Inhalants: volatile solvents
  - Phencyclidine (PCP)
- Definition and sources of narcotic analgesics: The term *narcotic* comes from the Greek word *narkosis,* which means "to numb or to be in a stupor." *Analgesia* means "to relieve pain, without producing unconsciousness."

    The narcotic analgesics (morphine, codeine, and heroin) come from the poppy plant (*Papaver somniferum*). The narcotic analgesics category also includes synthetic and semisynthetic drugs that have morphinelike action, such as meperidine (Demerol), methadone, Dilaudid, and Percodan.
- Narcotic analgesics have the following major effects:
  - Pain relief (analgesia)
  - Euphoria (sense of well-being)
  - Cough suppressant (antitussive)
  - Respiratory depression
  - Sedation or drowsiness
  - Constriction of the pupils (pinpoint pupils)
  - Nausea and vomiting
  - Itching
  - Decrease in gastrointestinal activity (constipation)
- Most central nervous system (CNS) depressants are sedative hypnotics. These include alcohol, barbiturates, and tranquilizers.
- Amphetamines are central nervous system stimulants. Until recently, they were widely prescribed by physicians for conditions such as obesity, depression, and narcolepsy (uncontrolled fits of sleep). For certain kinds of hyperactive behavior in children, Ritalin is most commonly prescribed.

    In some individuals, even a moderate dose of amphetamines can have adverse effects, such as agitation, an inability to concentrate, anxiety, confusion, blurred vision, tremors, and heart palpitations. Higher doses of amphetamines can produce quite severe adverse reactions, which include the following:
  - Tremors, palpitations
  - Dilated pupils (mydriasis)
  - Sweating and flushing, abdominal cramps, nausea
  - Tachycardia (rapid heartbeat), heart abnormalities
  - Hypertension (later hypotension), circulatory collapse
  - Anxiety, agitation, and panic
  - Aggression and violent behavior often associated with paranoia
  - Rapid breathing, respiratory collapse

- Hallucination (visual and auditory), delirium
- Extremely high fevers
- Convulsions and seizures
- Cocaine is obtained from the leaves of *Erythroxylum coca,* a bush grown in parts of South America. Mountain Indians of Peru and Bolivia have chewed coca leaves as a social ritual for more than a thousand years.
- Diseases related to smoking tobacco include the following:
  - Heart disease (coronary heart disease, increased artherosclerotic disease). Smoking elevates low-density lipoproteins (LDL, or bad cholesterol), while reducing high-density lipoproteins (HDL, or good cholesterol).
  - Peripheral vascular disease.
  - Cerebrovascular disease.
  - Cancer (lung cancer; cancer of the larynx, mouth, esophagus; contributing factor in urinary cancer, kidney cancer, and pancreatic cancer).
  - Chronic obstructive lung disease and colds (chronic bronchitis and emphysema).
- The health consequences of tobacco use include the following:
  - More women die from lung cancer than breast cancer each year.
  - Twenty to 25 percent of female smokers don't stop during pregnancy.
  - Over three-fourths of smokers start during the developmental teenage years.
  - One out of every five high school seniors smokes cigarettes on a daily basis.
  - Chewing tobacco (smokeless tobacco) is the leading cause of oral cancer.
  - Approximately 75 to 80 percent of recovering alcoholics smoke cigarettes.
- *Cannabis* refers to any product of the plant *Cannabis sativa,* which grows in most parts of the world. In North America, the most commonly used products derived from this plant are marijuana and hashish. Marijuana is the unprocessed, dried leaves, flowers, seeds, and stems of the plant. Hashish is a more potent product processed from the resin of this herb. Researchers have obtained more than 300 cannabis products (cannabinoids) from cannabis. They have isolated and synthesized the most active ingredient in marijuana. This product, tetrahydrocannabinol (THC), is the psychoactive compound found in the greatest amount in the plant; it is thought to produce most of the high.
- Glue, model cement, fingernail polish removers, various cosmetics, various cleaning solvents, gasoline, paint, paint thinners, lighter fluids, antifreeze, aerosol cans, and white correction fluids can all be inhaled.
- Signs and symptoms of inhalant use are the following:
  - Slurred speech
  - Odor of the substance being used
  - Mental disorientation or confusion
  - Headaches, dizziness, and weakness
  - Muscle spasms in the neck, chest, or lower extremities
  - Euphoria, exaggerated feeling of well-being
  - Loss of balance and ataxia (uncoordinated walk)
  - Nystagmus (eye movement from side to side)
- The substances that athletes use to enhance athletic performance include caffeine, chewing tobacco, amphetamines, and steroids. Steroid use by athletes, especially young people, can be a major tragedy.

✴ Discussion Questions

1. Rank the following drugs in terms of hazards and problem, with 1 (least harmful) to 10 (most harmful). Defend your rationale.

Example	DRUG	RATIONALE
10	Alcohol	Most widely used drug
		Binge drinking by young people/college students
		Family problems—impact on children
		Lost cost of business—sick days, injury, illness
9	Methamphetamine	Physical and health problems
		High addiction potential with young people

   - Alcohol
   - Methamphetamine
   - Glue sniffing
   - Smoking marijuana
   - Smoking freebase cocaine
   - Snorting heroin
   - OxyContin
   - Xanax
   - LSD
   - Snorting cocaine

2. Rank the following drugs in terms of hazards and problem, with 1 (least harmful) to 10 (most harmful). Defend your rationale.

   - Coffee and tea
   - Cigarettes
   - Marijuana
   - Performance enhancing steroids
   - Alcohol
   - Energy drinks
   - Chocolates
   - Fatty foods
   - Fast foods
   - Xanax

3. List at least five drugs in each of these drug classifications:

   - Narcotic analgesics (painkillers)
   - Sedative-hypnotics
   - Stimulants
   - *Cannabis sativa*
   - Hallucinogens

   If you feel comfortable, talk about your experiences, if any, with these drugs and discuss their effects.

4. Define and explain addiction using the three Cs model.

5. Explain the role of "set and setting" with alcohol, marijuana, and hallucinogenics.
6. Debate the issue of medical marijuana—pros, cons, and potential future benefits and drawbacks.
7. Debate the issue of legalizing marijuana entirely—pros, cons, and potential future benefits and drawbacks.

✷ References

American Osteopathic Academy of Sports Medicine. 1989.

Ashton, C. H. 1990. Solvent abuse: Little progress after 20 years. *British Medical Journal* 300: 135–38.

Chandler, J. V., and S. N. Blair. 1980. The effect of amphetamines on selected physiological components related to athletic success. *Medicine and Science in Sports and Exercise* 12: 65–9.

Cohen, S. 1986. Marijuana research: Selected recent findings. *Drug and Alcohol Newsletter, Vista Hill Foundation* 15(1).

CSAT advisory: Breaking news for the treatment field: Oxycontin. 2001. *Prescription Drug Abuse* 1(1).

Derlet, R., and B. Heischober. 1990. Methamphetamine: Stimulant of the 1990s. *Western Journal of Medicine* 153(6) (December): 625–28.

Holland, Julie, ed. 2001. *Ecstasy: The complete guide: A comprehensive look at the risks and benefits of MDMA.* Rochester, Vt.: Park Street Press.

Hough, D. 1988. Anabolic steroids and ergogenic aids. *Academy of Family Practice* 41: 1157–64.

Goldstein, Avram. 2001. *Addiction: From biology to drug policy,* 2nd edition. New York: Oxford University Press.

Mandell, A. J. 1979. The Sunday syndrome: A unique pattern of amphetamine abuse indigenous to American professional football. *Clinical Toxicology* 15(2): 225–32.

National Institute on Drug Abuse [NIDA]. 1998. *Community drug alert bulletin.* Rockville, Md.: Author.

National Institute on Drug Abuse [NIDA]. March 2004. Inhalant abuse. NIDA Research Report Series. Publication Number 04-3818.

Rawson, R., et al. 2007. Use of methamphetamine by young people: Is there reason for concern? *Addiction* 102(7)(July).

Rohr, V. 1989. Withdrawal sequelae to cannabis use. *International Journal of the Addictions* 24: 627–31.

Smith, David, and Donald Wesson. 1988. *Treating cocaine dependence.* Center City, Minn.: Hazeldon Foundation.

Smith, G. M., and H. G. Beecher. 1959. Amphetamine sulfate and athletic performance. *Journal of American Medical Association* 170(5): 542–57.

Solomons, K., and V. M. Neppe. 1989. Review article: Cannabis: Its clinical effects. *South American Medical Journal* 78: 476–81.

Sporer, Karl A. 2000. Acute heroin overdose. In *Heroin overdose: Research and interventions.* San Francisco: Linden Center.

Substance Abuse and Mental Health Services Administration [SAMHSA]. 2004. Overview of findings from the 2004 National Survey on Drug Use and Health. NSDUH Series H-27.

Tamura, M. 1989. Japan: Stimulant epidemics, past and present. *Bulletin on Narcotics* 1: 83–93.

Temple, Elizabeth C., Rhona F. Brown, and Donald W. Hine. 2011. The 'grass ceiling': Limitations in the literature hinder our understanding of cannabis use and its consequences. *Addiction* 106(2) (February).

Thombs, D. 1989. A review of PCP abuse, trends, and perceptions. *Public Health Reports* 104(4): 325–28.

U.S. Surgeon General. 1988. *The health consequences of smoking: Nicotine addiction.* Rockville, Md.: U.S. Dept. Health and Human Services.

Washington FOCUS. 2004. Risk factors identified in inhalant abuse. *Washington FOCUS,* 14(3).

Woods, James H., et al. 1988. Use and abuse of benzodiazepines. *Journal of the American Medical Association* 260(23): 3476–80.

Woolsey, Conrad. 2010. Energy drinks: A dangerous combination for athletes and beyond. *Journal of Alcohol and Drug Education* 54(3) (December): 41–59.

Assessment of Substance Abuse, Dependence, and Addiction

Outline of Chapter 4

Introduction

Diagnostic Categories
    A Behavioral Definition of Addiction

Assessment Stages of Alcohol and Drug Use

Set and Setting
    Alcohol/Drug Use—A Progressive Disease
    Addiction

Vulnerability to Relapse

Assessment for Relapse
    Denial—A Problem in Accurate Assessment

Identification of Adolescent Alcohol/Drug Problems

Alcohol/Drug Assessment

Consequences of Alcohol/Drug Use

Alcohol/Drugs and Suicide

Objectives

1. Identify diagnostic criteria for substance abuse and substance dependence.
2. Explain and give examples of the three Cs in our behavioral definition of addiction—compulsion, control, and consequences.
3. Describe the differences between early and late stages of alcohol/drug use.
4. Define and describe denial by the addict/alcoholic and his or her family members.
5. Identify important alcohol/drug assessment questions.
6. Identify the varied consequences of alcohol/drug abuse and dependence.
7. Identify the various issues that make adolescents more at risk for substance abuse.
8. Explain the relationship between alcohol/drugs and suicide.
9. Identify the differences between a screening tool and an assessment tool.

�ખ Introduction

The most difficult challenge in the assessment process is in differentiating those individuals who fall in the gray area between occasional, or nonproblematic, use of alcohol/drugs from those who use excessively and/or have an alcohol/drug problem. Assessment is also complicated by the fact that people strongly deny problems with alcohol and drugs. Individual, family, and societal perceptions of alcohol/drugs are distorted by this denial system.

The major goal of this chapter is to help the reader define substance abuse, substance dependence, and addiction and to identify the various stages of use. The chapter also focuses both on screening and assessment tools and on clinical questions and assessment strategies.

✰ Diagnostic Categories

The *Diagnostic and Statistical Manual of Mental Disorders,* 5th edition, *(DSM-V)* (American Psychiatric Association [APA] 2013) is a primary reference used by mental health practitioners to diagnose both mental disorders and substance-related disorders.

Substance-related disorders are divided into two major categories:

1. *Substance-use disorders.* These include substance dependence and substance abuse.
2. *Substance-induced disorders.* These include substance intoxication and substance withdrawal.

For information on the features and diagnostic criteria of substance-use disorders and substance-induced disorders, please refer to the *Diagnostic and Statistical Manual of Mental Disorders, Fifth Edition. pp. 483–486; 577–583.* Copyright © 2013. American Psychiatric Association.

A Behavioral Definition of Addiction

In the early 1980s, the rise in cocaine use challenged the basic framework of our definition of alcohol/drug addiction. Cocaine was previously thought to be a drug that incurred psychological dependence with no physical dependence. At that time, we defined addiction as a physical dependence measured by a significant and noticeable medical withdrawal symptom. Although cocaine had no significant, medically noticeable withdrawal symptoms, users reported a severe addiction to it. David Smith (Smith and Wesson 1988) was aware of this discrepancy and proposed a more behavioral definition of addiction. Because Smith's definition is more functional, counselors in the fields of chemical dependency treatment and addictionology use it. In fact, counselors can apply this behavioral definition of addiction to a wide variety of types of disorders, including eating, gambling, sex, workaholism, television, smoking, video games, spending/consumerism, and other activities.

Alcoholism and drug addiction are best described metaphorically as "the dragon in the corner, eating its own tail."

The three basic components of the behavioral definition of addiction are the three *Cs—compulsion, control,* and *consequences.*

1. **Compulsion with obsession.** Users think about alcohol and drugs in a vicious negative cycle; their obsessive concern and preoccupation follow an incessant use of alcohol/drugs in a continuous pattern and compulsive lifestyle.
2. *Control*—**Inability to stop** using the substances. Users cannot stop using alcohol/drugs for at least 3 months and/or make feeble attempts to cut back in a stop-then-start pattern. They are unable to refuse readily available drugs.
3. **Continued use despite adverse *consequences.*** Users are caught up in their addictions, illustrating the pervasive defense mechanisms of denial (rationalization and minimization). Eventually, the alcoholic/addict suffers family, social and interpersonal, economic, and spiritual bankruptcy.

⚸ Assessment Stages of Alcohol and Drug Use

The most successful preventive approach is not to use drugs and alcohol, especially at early ages. Not smoking cigarettes at early ages highly correlates with not developing addictions later in life. Children are less likely to develop chemical dependencies later in life, if parents

1. Do not model alcohol/drug use and encourage a healthy approach to life.
2. Encourage children to participate in activities that enhance the development of a strong sense of self.
3. Promote positive alternative activities to alcohol/drug use (see Chapter 10).
4. Are sensitive to what children feel while parents are setting appropriate boundaries.
5. Provide structure, discipline, and consistency.
6. Develop a climate of discussion, which facilitates an effective exploration of values and the development of coping skills in goal setting, decision making, and conflict resolution.

Parents can establish nonuse of drugs and alcohol by teaching children to make positive lifestyle choices that they can maintain throughout adult life. Although the drive or desire to alter one's consciousness is innate, learning to alter one's consciousness with alternatives other than chemicals is a developmental task of childhood. Children can be encouraged to be more active in choosing things to do that change their mood and develop their sense of self, instead of choosing a passive solution, the use of alcohol/drugs.

⚸ Set and Setting

The three major components of alcohol and drug use are the individual, the drug, and the set and setting in which the drug is taken. Set and setting often determine the individual's reaction to alcohol/drugs.

As mentioned in an earlier chapter, **set** refers to the psychological and emotional frame of mind of a person when using alcohol/drugs. Those who are relaxed, comfortable, and secure in the knowledge that they can handle possibly losing control usually have less trouble with the initial use of alcohol/drugs. Individuals who have a set that can be described as anxious, extremely nervous, or overly concerned with maintaining control are more prone to a negative drug reaction. If a person is not emotionally stable and/or has psychiatric problems, alcohol/drug use can exacerbate those problems. (See Chapter 11.) This is especially true for hallucinogens and marijuana. Set can also be influenced by the person's mood or emotional state at the time of alcohol/drug use. The individual who has just received some bad news or has had a negative experience might be feeling down or depressed; this may result in a negative set and a negative experience with alcohol/drugs. Significant trauma, shame, and embarrassment can also contribute to a negative experience with alcohol/drugs.

Setting involves not only the physical environment but also the social and interpersonal environment. Negative drug reactions may be the result of being in an uncomfortable setting, with unknown people who are not trusted.

Alcohol/Drug Use—A Progressive Disease

Certainly, the beginning of alcohol/drug use starts with initial contact. Because alcohol/drug use is a progressive disease, individuals get more involved as they progress through the stages, as shown in Figure 4.1. A positive initial contact usually leads to the next stage of drug use—experimentation. Experimentation may lead to the subsequent stages, which end in addiction. Richard Rawson (1989) has written about his outpatient treatment of cocaine addicts. He describes the progressive themes at various stages of cocaine addiction, as shown in Table 4.1. These descriptions can easily be adapted to alcohol and other drugs and illustrate the progressive nature of addiction.

As stated earlier, a positive initial contact may be the beginning of a progressive cycle to addiction. This is especially true for those who grew up in alcoholic/addict and/or dysfunctional family systems.

The alcoholic's life is limited, with significant negative consequences, as if he or she "is trapped in a shot glass."
© Dream Pictures/Getty Images

Addiction

Addiction is the last stage. Based on our definition of addiction and the disease model, an addict cannot return to any of the previous stages of alcohol/drug use. The best recovery strategy is to abstain from alcohol/drug use and to participate in a 12-step recovery program. This usually involves an inpatient program; strong development in self-help support groups, such as Alcoholics Anonymous, Narcotics Anonymous, and Cocaine Anonymous; a relationship with a sponsor; and an aftercare treatment program on completion of the inpatient program. (See Chapter 12.)

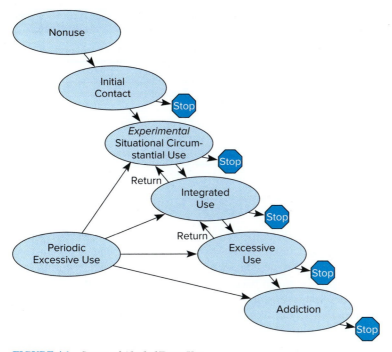

FIGURE 4.1 *Stages of Alcohol/Drug Use*
SOURCE: Richard Fields Ph.D. 1986, revised, 1988.

TABLE 4.1	
Phases of Cocaine Addiction	
Initial contact	"Isn't this a great drug?"
Experimentation	"It's sure expensive, but it's worth it."
Excessive use	"I really should cut down."
Addiction	"I know I have to stop, but I can't."
SOURCE: Rawson 1989.	

Chronic alcoholics and drug addicts spend major portions of their lives addicted to alcohol/drugs. In this late stage of chronic addiction, they are extremely difficult to treat. (See Table 4.2.) Some new approaches are required for this population. Such programs provide basic needs for shelter, food, other health-related services, and educational and counseling services. These programs for chronic alcoholics emphasize maintaining the individual's dignity while providing access to recovery services.

TABLE 4.2	
Early and Late Stages of Alcohol/Drug Use	
Early Stage	**Late Stage**
More freedom	Lack of freedom
Fewer risks and less damage	More damage
Possible abuse	Present abuse
No illness	State of illness
Linear operating factors	Vicious cycles

⚹ Vulnerability to Relapse

At each of the stages of recovery, individuals are vulnerable to relapse, or a return to alcohol/drug abuse or addiction. Therefore, all chemical dependency treatment programs must address relapse issues. Many experts agree that a longer-term inpatient or residential program is much needed (although financially difficult, due to limitations in insurance reimbursement and managed care). Experts agree that a 6- to 9-month inpatient program would be most effective, considering the high relapse rates. In addition, a 1-year outpatient aftercare program would further enhance the probability of recovery without relapse. It is not surprising that the relapse statistics are high following the traditional 28-day inpatient stay, making it even more important to counsel patients in relapse prevention. (See Chapter 13.)

Many people find it extremely difficult to stop using alcohol/drugs. Danaher and Lichtenstein (1978) describe the natural cycle of smoking, which is similar to the cycle of alcohol/drug use.

For more information on relapse, relapse prevention, recovery-prone behaviors, and relapse-prone behaviors (see Chapter 13).

⚹ Assessment for Relapse

We have diagnostic criteria for the different alcohol/drugs disorders, but no criteria for relapse, nor descriptions of the different types of relapses.

This is symbolic in the need to shift more focus on relapse dynamics and relapse prevention. As Samuel Clemens (Mark Twain) put it:

"It is easy to quit smoking, I have done it hundreds of times."

You can read more about some of the ways one can be vulnerability to relapse in Chapter 13.

Denial—A Problem in Accurate Assessment

D-E-N-I-A-L can stand for I **D**on't **E**ven k**N**ow **I A**m **L**ying.

The denial of alcohol/drug problems is a major factor in the difficulty of assessment. There is widespread denial, not only by individuals who have drug problems but also by family and friends, as well as society at large. It is often difficult to break through denial and have the courage to admit a problem with alcohol/drugs. Family members often experience a sense of shame or embarrassment or feelings of responsibility for the alcohol/drug problem of a family member.

The two major defense mechanisms used to deny problems with alcohol and drugs are minimization and rationalization. The following are common examples of minimizations and rationalizations of alcohol/drug problems:

"Now, if I drank and drugged like Shawn, then I would really have a problem."
"I use alcohol and drugs only on weekends; a person with a problem uses everyday."
"I never miss work, no matter how much [alcohol/drugs] I've used."
"The media are just trying to get you scared."
"I don't have a problem. Now, Tiffany has a problem. Why don't you get her into treatment?"

Additional consequences of minimization and rationalization include the following:

- Neglect; emotional, physical, or sexual abuse
- Loss—death, trauma, divorce, separation
- Numerous relocations and unstable home environment
- Parental dysfunction, creating feelings of parental unavailability and/or feelings of abandonment, rejection, or shame

Another reality is that substance abusers often are deceptive, tell half-truths, and outright lie about their use and the behaviors around their use. Of course, the larger the lie, the more unbelievable it is, yet abusers might defend themselves by saying, "Would I make up such an outrageous story?" The answer is often Yes!

✄ Identification of Adolescent Alcohol/Drug Problems

Adolescent alcohol/drug problems are often harder to assess than adult substance abuse. Trying to clarify and sort out what is "normal" adolescent behavior versus what is an alcohol/drug problem is very difficult.

The following eleven questions can help in identifying an adolescent alcohol/drug problem:

1. *Mood.* Has the child been extremely moody or more upset than usual? Adolescence is a time of fluctuations in mood. A child might be as happy as a lark one minute and quite despondent the next. Therefore, it is difficult to isolate change in mood as being related to alcohol/drug use. However, if a child's mood seems more intense than usual, it could be related to the irritability associated with withdrawal from marijuana, alcohol, or other drugs.
2. *Changes.* Are there some significant changes in the child's choice in friends, grades, dress, general hygiene, and responsibilities? Adolescence is a time of change, a time to explore different aspects of one's identity and personality.

However, when these changes are self-damaging and seem more than just the trying on of a different role, it could be a sign for concern.

3. *Responsibility.* Is the child more irresponsible about his or her commitments (e.g., chores, schoolwork, friends)? Is he or she not coming home on time or disregarding rules? It is common for young people to push limits and boundaries. However, doing this on a consistent basis or pushing boundaries beyond reasonable expectations may be a sign of alcohol/drug abuse.

4. *Motivation.* Is there a noticeable decrease in motivation, interest, or activity? Has the child shown disinterest in things he or she is normally interested in (e.g., friends, school, sports, extracurricular activities)? Loss of motivation is indicative of regular marijuana use. Alcohol and other drugs can also impair interest and/or performance in activities normally seen as pleasurable.

5. *School.* Are there signs of problems at school and difficulty in studying, completing assignments, and so on? Has the teacher complained that the youngster is sleeping or inattentive in class? Some common signs of problems are ditching school, having problems with teachers, acting out behavior, getting failing or lowered grades, and having fights and arguments with friends. School problems are usually the first sign of negative consequences that may be related to an alcohol/drug problem.

6. *Negative activities.* Is the child engaging in activities that are not healthy or productive and potentially damaging? Such activities include those that might provoke physical violence; emotional abuse of others; disregard for others' property; dangerous use of motor vehicles; weekend-long parties or excessive isolation and secrecy about activities; and no accountability or supervision of time. A youngster having problems with alcohol or other drugs will abandon old friends and seek out those with similar attitudes and behaviors.

7. *Lying, stealing, and cheating.* Is money, household objects, or personal property missing? Is alcohol, prescription medication, or perhaps a parent's own stash of drugs missing? Does the child make up stories and lie compulsively? The expense of alcohol/drugs can be overcome by taking things that can be used for cash or bartered for alchohol/drugs. It is probably not forgetfulness or memory loss that has caused things to be either "misplaced" or "missing."

8. *Community.* Has the child been in trouble with neighbors, storekeepers, or other community members? Have concerned friends, neighbors, relatives, or others talked about this child's behavior? Have former friends, teachers, or parents of the child's friends expressed concern or given information that indicates this child may have a problem with alcohol/drugs? You can't go on ignoring the problem when others in the community have seen the child's misbehavior or actual alcohol/drug abuse.

9. *Criminal justice problems.* Has the child been involved in an activity that has caused investigation or charges being made by the police? Examples of these behaviors include disorderly conduct, drunkenness, driving under the influence, stealing, bouncing checks, shoplifting, vandalism, fighting, and

breaking and entering. As outlined earlier, alcohol/drug use and antisocial behavior are highly correlated.

10.   *Physical signs.* Are there physical signs of alcohol or drug use? Have some of the following been noticed?

- The smell of alcohol or marijuana on the breath or body
- Dilated pupils
- Increase in activity
- Grandiosity
- Talkativeness
- Extreme quietness
- Slurred or incoherent speech
- Bizarre behavior
- Moodiness
- Aggressiveness and show of temper
- Fatigue, lethargy

Has drug paraphernalia been found in the child's room (e.g., rolling paper, syringes, pipes [water pipes], mirrors, razors, baggies)?

11.   *Parents.* Do you find yourself justifying your child's behavior? Are you saying things like the following?

- "He or she will grow out of it."
- "This is just a stage."
- "Kids will be kids."
- "I went through the same kind of behavior when I was a kid."

If so, you may be denying signs of alcohol/drug abuse. Remember: *Believe the behavior,* not necessarily what the person says.

Case Study 4.1 illustrates that it is not necessary to catch children red-handed using alcohol/drugs. If there is enough evidence of possible alcohol/drug abuse, seek professional help early—don't wait until the problem gets out of hand.

✳ Alcohol/Drug Assessment

Recovery from alcohol/drugs also involves the family of the alcoholic/addict. The family system is an integral part of the development of the disease. The most difficult work in recovery is dealing with family issues and relationships to help family members recover from dysfunctional patterns in the family system. (See Chapter 5.)

This section is not intended as a clinical skill training, but it lists things you need to be aware of when taking an alcohol/drug history.

The most important task in assessing the potential for problems with alcohol/drugs is determining if there is a family history of alcohol or drug abuse and addiction. Family members may deny the extent of alcohol/drug use in their family. It might take additional questioning to clarify the true dimensions of family use of alcohol/drugs.

Case Study 4.1
The Marijuana Search

Despite Mr. and Mrs. Green being aware of signs of drug use by their 13-year-old son, John, he kept denying he was using. John seemed to have an answer for everything. He would make them feel guilty for doubting his word and not trusting him. As time went on, the deceptions and lies got more and more complicated. John, despite being caught in these lies, insisted that he was not smoking marijuana. The parents were frustrated and felt the only way they could have their son acknowledge his problem was for them either to catch him using marijuana or to find his marijuana.

One day, while their son was out of the house, they searched his room. Despite looking everywhere in the room, they couldn't find any tangible evidence of marijuana use. Curiously, the room seemed cleaner and neater than usual—almost as if their son suspected a search was imminent. Perhaps he heard them talking on the phone to the neighbors when they suggested a search. By chance, the father decided to expand the search to other rooms in the house—bathrooms, family room, bedrooms. They found what they were looking for in the hall closet. They unscrewed the rubberized handle of the vacuum cleaner and found a small stash of marijuana.

When John came home, his parents calmly held a family meeting. They asked him if he had any marijuana in the house. Again, he said he didn't. When they produced the marijuana and told him where they found it, John didn't blink an eye while saying, "Oh, that stuff. I forgot all about it. I've been holding that for the kid down the block for months now—you know, the one who went into drug treatment. I forgot all about it."

Discussion Questions

1. Explain and describe "parental denial" in acknowledging their child's drug use.
2. Do you think parents have the right to search their kids' room, etc.?
3. What do you think about drug testing of children,
    By parents?
    By schools? As a requirement for extracurricular activities? . . .
4. Are drug tests reliable? Explain "false positives."
5. Class Project: Visit a drug-testing lab and report on the procedure, tests available, and reliability of tests.

Some education for family members and the individual who may have a drug problem might also be necessary to establish a clear perception of the dimensions of substance abuse and addiction. To assess an individual's alcohol/drug problem, counselors need the following information:

- Age of initial drug and alcohol use
- Frequency of use, amounts used, set and setting of use
- Patterns of use, binges, periods of nonuse
- Stage of current use—experimentation, integrated use, excessive use, addiction
- History of negative consequences—physical, psychological, financial, familial, and spiritual

- Medical history—conditions that might be affected by use of drugs/alcohol
- Use of coffee, cigarettes, and medication

⚹ Consequences of Alcohol/Drug Use

An extremely important area of assessment is the consequences of alcohol/drug use. Remember, the third criteria of addiction is "continued use despite adverse consequences."

A client, who was referred for outpatient counseling after 120 days in a residential and extended care program, was now dealing with significant criminal, civil, and other legal problems, as well as financial, marital, business, and relationship problems. He said, "You can do all the drinking and drugging you want as long as you are willing to pay the consequences."

Perhaps this is a straightforward way of looking at addiction, but it does point out the significant consequences that come with substance abuse and addiction. Pointing out the consequences may be a valuable tool in breaking through denial. A very common exercise used in most drunk driving programs is to have clients figure out how much their conviction has cost them. For some, the amount is staggering when they stop to consider the cost of legal fees, the diversion program, loss of work, and so on.

Arnold Washton (1995) asks several questions in the assessment stage about consequence, covering the physical, psychological, sexual, relationship, job, financial, and legal consequences of alcohol/drug use (Table 4.3).

⚹ Alcohol/Drugs and Suicide

Another key assessment issue with alcohol/drugs is the potential for suicide. Stanton and Landau-Stanton (1985) state that the "recognition of substance abuse as a suicidal endeavor stems from as far back as 1938 when Menninger likened addiction to chronic suicide." Table 4.4 highlights key facts about suicide.

Some common assessment questions for suicide are as follows:

1. Is there a family history of alcohol/drug problems, suicide, or depression?
2. Do you use alcohol/drugs to

   a. overcome bad/shameful feelings?
   b. deal with sleeping problems, depression, or stress?
   c. quiet suicidal or self-destructive thoughts?

3. Do you have suicidal thoughts?
4. How will you do it? Do you have a plan? (Assess the availability or means to commit suicide and the lethality of the means.)
5. Have you previously had suicidal thoughts and have you attempted suicide before? How frequently do these thoughts occur?
6. What role does alcohol/drug use have in relation to suicide? Does it make you more likely or less likely to follow through?
7. On a scale of 1 to 10, how likely are you to kill yourself?
8. How much do you want to die? to live?

TABLE 4.3

Consequences Related to Alcohol or Drug Use

Check below any PHYSICAL problems caused by or worsened by your use of alcohol or drugs:

- Convulsions with loss of consciousness
- Nasal sores, bleeding
- Chest congestion, wheezing
- Hepatitis or other liver problems
- Severe or frequent headaches
- Drug overdose requiring treatment in an emergency room or hospital
- Coughing up black phlegm
- Severe weight loss (without dieting)
- Sinus problems
- Ulcers or other stomach problems
- Heart palpitations
- Other (specify)

Check below any PSYCHOLOGICAL problems caused by or worsened by your use of alcohol or drugs:

- Irritability, short temper
- Panic attacks
- Violent thoughts
- Severe depression
- Memory problems
- Paranoia, suspiciousness
- Suicidal thoughts
- Other (specify)

Check below any SEXUAL problems caused by or worsened by your use of alcohol or drugs:

- Loss of sex drive
- Sex with strangers
- Sexuality out of control
- Sexual obsession or preoccupation
- Risking of AIDS through sexual behavior
- Other (specify)

Check below any RELATIONSHIP or SOCIAL problems caused by or worsened by your use of alcohol or drugs:

- Arguments with spouse or mate
- Thrown out of household
- Loss of friends
- Arguments with parents, brothers, or sisters
- Spouse or mate has threatened to leave or has already left
- Social isolation
- Other (specify)

Check below any JOB or FINANCIAL problems caused by or worsened by your use of alcohol or drugs:

- In jeopardy of losing my job
- Late to work
- Less productive at work
- In debt
- Already lost at least one job
- Missed days of work
- Missed opportunity for promotion or raise
- Behind in paying bills
- Other (specify)

Check below any LEGAL problems caused by or worsened by your use of alcohol or drugs:

- Arrested for possession of illicit substances
- Arrested for forging prescriptions
- Auto accident while driving under the influence
- Arrested for assaulting someone
- Arrested for embezzlement or check forgery
- Arrested for sale of illicit substances
- Arrested for DWI or DUI
- Arrested for violent or disorderly conduct
- Arrested for theft or robbery
- Other (specify)

SOURCE: Washton, Arnold M. 1995. *Psychotherapy and substance abuse: A practitioner's handboo.* New York: Guilford Press.

T A B L E   4 . 4

The Facts about Suicide

1. Suicide is preventable. Most suicide victims do not want to die.
2. Suicide is the eighth leading cause of death and ranks ahead of homicide.
3. Talking about suicide does not cause someone to be suicidal.
4. Suicidal behavior is not inherited, but the risk is higher for family members who have lost a close relative to suicide.
5. The suicide rate is higher for the elderly than any other age group.
6. Suicide is the second leading cause of death among young people. Accidents are number one, but even some of these accidents could be suicides.
7. Suicide claims the lives of at least 30,000 people annually in the United States.
8. Five states have passed legislation providing for school suicide prevention programs.
9. The incidence of suicide among young people has nearly tripled during the past three decades.
10. Three times as many men as women kill themselves, yet three times as many women as men attempt suicide.
11. More than 80 percent of people communicate their intent to kill themselves before they attempt to do so. They leave clues as to their distress and/or plans.

SOURCE: American Association of Suicidology, 4201 Connecticut Ave. NW, Suite 310, Washington DC 20008, (202) 237–2280.

9. What would prevent you from committing suicide?
10. What might occur to make life worth living?

These questions can help you to assess potential suicide:

- Have you been thinking about suicide?
- Do you have a plan to take your life?
- Do you feel hopeless about the future?
- Do you think you are a burden to your loved ones?
- Are you feeling so bad you are considering ending your life?
- Do you ever wish you could go to sleep and never wake up?
- Have you ever wanted to stop living?

If a client is suicidal, an extremely important question to ask is, "What would prevent you from committing suicide?" This will often lead to a dialogue and plan of action that will prevent suicide. Fortunately, the vast majority of suicidal people do not want to die so much as they want to find a way to live. A common practice involves a written contract with a client who may be suicidal. The client agrees to not take action or to call the therapist or a suicide hot line before making an attempt. (See Case Study 4.2.)

(Alcoholics Anonymous)—Silence is the enemy of recovery.

Case Study 4.2

Alcohol, Depression, and Suicide

The names and details of this case study have been changed to maintain anonymity.

Cheryl, a 43-year-old manager of a telecommunications company, struggled with bouts of alcoholism and depression. She originally called, seeking help for marital problems. During the assessment session, Cheryl reported her struggles with alcohol and drugs. She admitted that she was probably addicted to cocaine. She was convinced that she could no longer use cocaine. She still struggled to control her drinking. Cheryl had been through one inpatient treatment program and sporadically attended AA but was able to sustain only short periods of abstinence. Her job was extremely stressful, demanding more of her time and energy. She frequently lost her temper with people she worked with. The counselor listened to her "gripes" about her husband and their marital problems but astutely brought the conversation back to Cheryl's alcohol abuse.

In the third session, Cheryl acknowledged the need to strengthen her efforts to seek recovery from alcohol. She began attending AA and was encouraged to obtain an AA sponsor and attend counseling sessions once a week, yet, as time went on, she got distracted from committing to AA and chose a sponsor whom she rarely interacted with. Despite the counselor's efforts to get her to develop a stronger recovery program, she resisted. In future sessions, Cheryl began to talk about overwhelming feelings of depression and suicidal thoughts. She was referred to a psychiatrist for evaluation and was put on antidepressant medication. At the same time, the counselor and Cheryl wrote a contract that she would not attempt suicide and, if she felt suicidal, she would call the counselor or the suicide helpline.

Several months into treatment, Cheryl's depression was stabilizing and she was attending AA meetings more regularly, but she still had not established an active relationship with a sponsor or others in the program. The counselor suggested a woman's recovery therapy group. Cheryl agreed and attended the therapy group each week. At this time, her marriage was headed for a divorce, and her job was getting worse. She eventually moved out of her house and rented an apartment. During this time, she lapsed back to using alcohol and was more depressed. The counselor and group encouraged her to get more active in AA and to continue with her medication. Unfortunately, Cheryl did the opposite. She stopped taking her medication, rarely went to AA, and immersed herself in her work. She spent excessive hours working overtime and eventually dropped out of group counseling, stating that her schedule and finances made it impossible to attend. Despite efforts by her counselor to have her continue in group at a reduced fee, Cheryl decided against it. She continued, only briefly, with her individual counseling. Despite the counselor's best efforts to point out the need for counseling and renewed recovery efforts, Cheryl did not follow through. She began to miss counseling appointments. The counselor pointed out her pattern of "isolating" and continued to try to reengage her into counseling and recovery. Despite the counselor's best efforts, Cheryl went to counseling less frequently and eventually stopped going.

Nine months later, the counselor received news that Cheryl had killed herself. The combination of alcoholism, depression, marital problems, stress at work, and Cheryl's inability to seek connection with others had led to her suicide.

Discussion Questions

1. Describe the role "pride" and "shame" can play in not seeking help.
2. As a counselor, what boundaries would you set to deal with a client with suicidal ideation? Would you set up a contingency contract?
3. List some questions you might ask a client whom you suspect may be suicidal.
4. What does "silence is the enemy of recovery" mean?
5. What signs might make you aware of the potential for suicide?
6. Have you ever considered suicide? What is your view on suicide?
7. What conditions increase a person's vulnerability to suicide?

✖ In Review

- The *Diagnostic and Statistical Manual of Mental Disorders* (APA 2000) establishes standards for assessing mental disorders and substance-related disorders.
- The behavioral definition of addiction is expressed by the three Cs mnemonic:
    - **C**ompulsion
    - **C**ontrol (inability)
    - Continued use despite negative **C**onsequences
- Denial is the major defense, due to users' minimization and rationalization of their level of involvement with alcohol/drugs, which makes accurate assessment more difficult.
- Assessment of adolescent alcohol/drug problems is very difficult. Trying to clarify the truth and sort out what is "normal" adolescent behavior versus what is an alcohol/drug problem is often difficult. Assessing these eleven topics can help identify an adolescent alcohol/drug problem:
    - Mood
    - Changes
    - Responsibility
    - Motivation
    - School
    - Negative activities
    - Lying, stealing, and cheating
    - Community
    - Criminal justice problems
    - Physical signs
    - Parents
- Assessment involves not only taking a good alcohol/drug history but also assessing the individual's vulnerability to alcohol/drugs, the consequences of the alcohol/drug use, and the person's suicide potential.
- The most important task in assessing the potential for problems with alcohol/drugs is to determine whether there is a family history of alcohol or drug abuse and addiction. It might take additional questioning to clarify the true dimensions of family use of alcohol/drugs.
- Alcohol and suicide are strongly interrelated. Use these questions to assess potential suicide:

    Have you been thinking about suicide?
    Do you have a plan to take your life?
    Do you feel hopeless about the future?
    Do you think you are a burden to your loved ones?
    Are you feeling so bad you are considering ending your life?
    Do you ever wish you could go to sleep and never wake up?
    Have you ever wanted to stop living?

- Some important questions to ask clients at risk for suicide:

  On a scale of 1 to 10, how likely are you to kill yourself?
  How much do you want to die? to live?
  What would prevent you from committing suicide?
  What might occur to make life worth living?

❊ Discussion Questions

1. Explain and discuss the three Cs of addiction—compulsion, inability to control use, and continued use despite significant negative consequences. Continued use, despite significant negative consequences, is a good indication of addiction.
2. A family history of alcoholism and/or drug addiction is the strongest indicator that someone might be genetically vulnerable to the disease. Discuss this and other factors that contribute to vulnerability to alcohol/drug abuse, dependence, or addiction.
3. Role play an assessment session:
   - One person plays the counselor doing an informal assessment of another person playing the client.
   - The class can create a client profile for someone to play.
   - The counselor would not know this profile, so he or she would need to determine the profile the client is portraying.

Note: In each session, you might ask questions to get the following information:
- Age of initial drug and alcohol use
- Frequency of use, amounts used, set and setting of use
- Patterns of use, binge, periods of nonuse
- Stage of current use—experimentation, integrated use, excessive use, addiction
- History of negative consequences—physical, psychological, financial, familial, spiritual
- Medical history—conditions that might be affected by use of drugs/alcohol
- Use of coffee, cigarettes, and medication

❊ References

American Psychiatric Association. 2000. *Diagnostic and statistical manual of mental disorders*, 4th edition, text rev. Washington, D.C.: Author.

Danaher, B. G., and E. Lichtenstein. 1978. *Becoming an ex-smoker*. Englewood Cliffs, N.J.: Prentice-Hall.

Rawson, Richard. 1989. *Cocaine recovery issues: The neurobehavioral model*. Beverly Hills, Calif.: Matrix Institute on Addictions.

Smith, David, and Donald Wesson. 1988. *Treating cocaine dependence*. Center City, Minn.: Hazeldon Foundation.

Stanton, M. D., and Judith Landau-Stanton. 1985. Treating suicidal adolescents and their families. In *Handbook of adolescent and family therapy,* edited by M. P. Mirkin and S. L. Koman. New York: Gardner Press.

Washton, Arnold M. 1995. *Psychotherapy and substance abuse: A practitioner's handbook*. New York: Guilford Press.

Family

❖ **Chapter 5:**

Substance Abuse and Family
Systems

❖ **Chapter 6:**

Parents and Family: At-Risk
Factors for Substance Abuse

❖ **Chapter 7:**

Growing Up in an Alcoholic Family
System

C H A P T E R   **5**

Substance Abuse and Family Systems

Outline of Chapter 5

Introduction

Families as Systems

Family Rules

Imbalanced versus *Dysfunctional*
    Rigid Family Systems
    Ambiguous Family Systems
    Overextended Family Systems
    Distorted Family Systems
    Entitled Family Systems

Satir's Family Patterns of Communication

Family System Roles
    Wegscheider-Cruse's Alcoholic/Addict Family System Survival Roles
    Family Roles Played Out at the Dinner Table
    Five Styles of Managing Anxiety
    Enabling Behavior

Stages in Family Recovery from Substance-Abuse Problems
    Denial
    Anger
    Bargaining
    Feeling
    Acceptance

Objectives

1. Identify families as systems with key elements of rules, values, verbal and nonverbal methods of communicating, boundaries, roles, and patterns of interaction.
2. Identify the characteristics of family metaphorically as a mobile (Satir) trying to maintain balance.
3. Explain the three rules that children of alcoholics learn, as identified by Claudia Black: "Don't talk. Don't trust. Don't feel."
4. Identify the reasons for using the term *imbalanced* instead of *dysfunctional* family system.
5. Identify the rules, values, and communication styles of the rigid, ambiguous, overextended, and distorted family systems.
6. Identify the ways in which placaters, blamers, intellectualizers, and distracters discount themselves and/or others, as described by Virginia Satir.

7. Identify the characteristics of the roles described by Sharon Wegscheider-Cruse:
   - Family hero
   - Family scapegoat
   - Lost child
   - Family mascot
8. Define and classify enabling behavior as
   - avoiding and shielding
   - attempting to control
   - taking over responsibility
   - rationalizing and accepting
   - cooperating and collaborating (Nelson 1988)
9. Identify and describe the five stages of grieving—denial, anger, bargaining, depression (feeling stage), and acceptance—as they relate to family recovery from an alcohol/drug problem.

⚛ Introduction

This book is perceiving alcoholism/drug addiction and substance-abuse problems as having a major impact on the family and its members—the family system. Drug/alcohol abuse does not happen in isolation. This chapter explores the imbalances created in the alcoholic/addict family systems, with specific imbalances in communication, roles, and actions. The chapter lays the foundation for understanding the personal impact on children who grow up in the alcoholic system, which is further explored in Chapter 7 as these children become adults, or adult-children of alcoholics.

⚛ Families as Systems

Initially, one must look at the family as a system. Some key elements of family systems are that they all have rules, values, verbal and nonverbal methods of communicating, boundaries, roles, and patterns of interaction. Systems always seek some level of homeostasis, or balance. Alcoholism and drug dependency are dysfunctional elements in family life. The result is a disequilibrium, or imbalance, forcing family members to compensate and give up aspects of their own sense of self in an attempt to keep the family in balance. The alcoholic/addict family system could be compared with an unbalanced toy top, one so top-heavy that when it tries to spin in a functional pattern, it instead swerves to one side and skids in a diagonal direction until it stops. The individuals in this system are all compensating in different yet similar ways. It's as if they are walking around with a heavy weight on one shoulder; they have to either lean to one side to walk properly or use all their energy to try to compensate and look as if they are walking upright. Both positions require a great deal of energy. Family therapist Carl Whitaker (Whitaker and Napier 1978) has described the family as the source of all kinds of electrical energy, with positive and negative voltages.

Virginia Satir (1967), a famous family therapist, was the first to describe the family using the metaphor of a mobile: if the wires on one of the pieces of the mobile are twisted, the mobile spins improperly. Instead of a delicately balanced mobile, each piece gets entangled and out of balance at the slightest breeze. A well-balanced mobile, or family system, sways and flexes with the strong gusts and heavy winds of life. The family with alcohol/drug problems is described as an imbalanced, or dysfunctional, family system. In a healthy family, the system is flexible and fluid, open (not rigid), predictable (not inconsistent), and balanced in meeting both the individual's and the family's needs.

Looking at the family as a system is imperative in addressing the problem of alcohol/drug dependence and addiction. If the family system does not change and the family members do not do their recovery work, the same dysfunctional styles of communication and interaction make the alcoholic/addict at risk for alcohol/drug relapse or the development of another dysfunctional behavior.

To effectively treat the alcoholic/addict, the rest of the family system also needs treatment. The high alcohol/drug relapse rate is often attributable to the lack of recovery by the family members. Too frequently, the alcoholic/addict is the focus of help, and the family members deny their own enabling and codependent behavior. The messages from the family are "Just fix the alcoholic/addict" and "Just get him or her to stop using alcohol/drugs and then everything will be O.K."

Family members avoid being active in treatment because they resist looking at their own behavior; they fear getting in touch with painful feelings, which may be overwhelming.

Another fear is whether the family system can survive reexperiencing these feelings. They wonder, "Has the family been hurt beyond repair?" and "Will the family be able to work through the violations of the past?" These questions and others need to be addressed for the effective recovery of the alcoholic/addict and the family members.

The expression *dry drunk* refers to the alcoholic/addict who is abstaining from alcohol/drug use but either is unaware of other behavioral, personality, and relationship problems or is choosing not to address these maladaptive behaviors. The overall behavior and personality styles of dry drunks are very similar to when they were using alcohol/drugs. Essentially, they have chosen not to deal with the underlying issues that contributed to the negative aspects of their personalities. For some, it is certainly enough that they are sober. Others who are still experiencing feelings of depression, fear, rage, and anxiety may decide to get help and address the problem "What you resist, persists"—Carl Rogers.

After 1 to 5 years of being sober, many recovering alcoholics/addicts realize that they are still having problems, especially in interpersonal relationships. This is often described as the addicts' "second bottom." The first bottom is the realization that they can no longer continue to use alcohol/drugs. The second bottom is the realization that they are still not having fun, due to unresolved personality issues. They ask themselves the question, "Now that I am years sober, am I having fun yet?" The answer frequently is, "No, my life is more manageable but I'm still not feeling better."

The family of the alcoholic/addict also goes through a kind of dry drunk. The family may glow in the joy of the alcoholic/addict's initial sobriety and may now feel validated that he or she is, indeed, okay. From the viewpoint of friends, neighbors, and community, he or she "did the right thing." There is no discounting that the family members were courageous in struggling to get the alcoholic/addict into treatment. However, they must continue the struggle to develop a healthier family system. In many cases, the family returns to old dysfunctional patterns. It is fair to say that recovery from the diseases of alcoholism and drug addiction is an ongoing process for the individual and the family.

⚹ Family Rules

Each family makes decisions and choices based on the rules, boundaries, and alliances of family members.

Claudia Black (1982) referred to the three rules that children of alcoholics often learn to live by: "Don't talk. Don't trust. Don't feel."

> Talking, especially about the substance abuse, might cause even more problems. Trusting usually leads to disappointment when parents do not come through with their promises. Feeling is too painful, and expression of feelings is not allowed because it might cause more trouble. (Lawson and Lawson 1998)

⚹ *Imbalanced* versus *Dysfunctional*

Nathan Ackerman first coined the term *dysfunctional family* in 1958, when referring to alcoholic family systems. Throughout the literature of the alcohol/drug and mental health fields—and even in this textbook—we frequently use the term dysfunctional in describing families, systems, relationships, parenting, behavior, and individuals. The term dysfunctional is often a shame-based, negative label, with a negative emotional tone. Labeling them as dysfunctional discourages families and individuals who are struggling with the problems of alcohol/drug dependence. Many people have been annoyed and discouraged at being told they are dysfunctional. It sounds hopeless. For example, what good does it do to tell a patient, relative, or friend, "You come from a shame-based, dysfunctional family system" or "You have a codependent, enabling, dysfunctional relationship with your spouse and children"? This doesn't really help people and it shames them, making them feel helpless and hopeless. Most people feel a sense of betrayal in even thinking about their families in such a derogatory manner.

Instead of using *dysfunctional,* replace it with the term *imbalanced,* for this is truly what we are looking at—an imbalance in the individual and in the family members' lives. Remember Satir's image of an out-of-balance mobile. It is so much more hopeful to seek treatment if one has the expectation of becoming balanced. It is also a far more positive approach.

There is truly an emotional imbalance in the alcoholic/addict family system. The term *imbalance* gives hope that there is a way to get help and better manage the system. The goal is to establish balance and order by addressing the problems in the family.

There are different kinds of imbalance in family systems. Alcohol/drugs serve a different function in each of these imbalanced systems. Next, we examine rigid, ambiguous, overextended, and distorted family systems to better understand imbalanced family systems. In each family system, the drug of choice and its function are for illustration, not an empirically proven fact.

Rigid Family Systems

Rules—Strict interpretation of the rules with no exceptions; inflexibility with no extenuating circumstances. The rules keeper (usually a critical/judgmental father or mother) is exempt from the rules.

Values—"There is only one way to do things and that is the right way—my way." Things are always black or white, right or wrong.

Motto—"Do it right, or else."

Communication—Linear, hierarchical. The father is usually dominant, powerful, and unapproachable. The mother softens the impact of the father's harshness. Or the mother is critical-judgmental, often moralistic and controlling, and the father goes along with the mother, deceptively avoiding conflict and the rage of the mother.

Drugs of choice—Alcohol and/or heroin, other sedative hypnotics, and narcotic analgesics.

Functions of drug—Suppress feelings, especially anger, and stay numb to the trauma in this family system.

Ambiguous Family Systems

Rules—We have rules but we don't enforce them, and we change them to avoid conflict.

Values—Forever changing, based on the situation.

Motto—"Keep peace at all costs; avoid conflict."

Communication—Mixed messages that are confusing. "Do what you know we want, without us letting you know what it is we want."

Drugs of choice—Alcohol and/or heroin, marijuana, and hallucinogens.

Functions of drug—Suppress feelings of discomfort, kill pain, shut out reality, and/or distort reality.

Overextended Family Systems

Rules—Be productive, get busy, stay on the move.

Values—Look good, achieve, do it with willpower, feelings are for wimps.

Motto—"We can achieve anything we set our minds to." "The right stuff."

Communication—Feelings are not expressed or integrated; decisions are based on results and what will please the parents.

Drugs of choice—Cocaine, methamphetamine, and other stimulants, alcohol.

Functions of drug—Keep on working/doing, even though feelings are not congruent with work or intimate relationships.

Distorted Family Systems

Rules—Don't let outsiders know we are crazy. Act as if we were a normal family, just a bit eccentric.

Values—Maintain an illusion of normalcy, despite significant physical, emotional, and interpersonal problems of the family. Keep outsiders guessing about us.

Motto—"Aren't most families like ours?"

Communication—Mixed messages; parents and children are unavailable and have limited common perceptions of situations.

Drugs of choice—Alcohol, hallucinogens, marijuana, and inhalants.

Functions of drug—Distort reality, which is already distorted, to try and make sense, or no sense, of it.

Entitled Family Systems

Rules—Rules don't necessarily apply to us because we are special.

Values—Money, status, and who you know.

Motto—We are entitled.

Communication—We are better than others, so we see others as less entitled.

Drugs of choice—Fine wines, champagne, cocaine, Ecstasy, marijuana, and anything we want.

Functions of drug—Pleasure, party, embue life.

⚹ Satir's Family Patterns of Communication

Virginia Satir, author of *Conjoint Family Therapy* (1967) and *Peoplemaking* (1972) and co-author of *Helping Families to Change* (1983), emphasizes the feeling component of family patterns of communication. She describes a dysfunctional family as one that maintains rules that do not fit the reality of what is felt and believed.

Satir's work is monumental and popular. According to Satir, individuals with poor self-concepts see pots that are half-empty. Individuals with the ability to differentiate (i.e., those with good self-concepts) see their pots as half-full. The former group feels hopeless and negative; the latter group is positive and hopeful.

Satir identified the following dysfunctional styles as well as a functional style of communicating:

1. Placaters discount themselves. Their goal is frequently to avoid conflict and to avoid others' anger. Their communication patterns feature the following:

   a. Words that agree and avoid conflict: "Whatever you want is O.K." The placaters' worth is based on others accepting, not rejecting, what they say.

   b. Bodies that placate: "I am helpless." The placaters' worth is based on being physically available, even when that may not be consistent with what they feel.

   c. Feelings: "I am worthless." Placaters believe they have no choices but to be dependent in dysfunctional relationships because there is no way out, and they are not strong enough or worth the struggle.

2. Blamers elevate themselves by discounting others. Their goal is to avoid looking at themselves, their own issues, and their own responsibility. Others' feelings are often discounted. If others would only do it the right way—which is their way—then things would work out. Their communication patterns feature the following:

   a. Words that are critical, judgmental, shaming put-downs: "You never do anything right." "It's all your fault."

    b.   Bodies that blame: "I am more powerful, more dominant."

    c.   Feelings: "It is your fault that I am unhappy."

3.   Intellectualizers discount their own feelings. Their goal is to place rigid emphasis on the cognitive to figure out problems, to deny the role feelings play in relationships and decisions, and to avoid the emotional impact of feelings. Intellectualizers are the brains, the computers, the cognitive persons who think, "If I can only understand this, I'll be O.K." They often feel that, if they can only find that missing piece of the puzzle, they will find the cause of their problems. They fail to integrate the key elements of the puzzle—their feelings—and fail to realize that the puzzle may not be solvable, especially with their linear approach. Their communication patterns feature the following:

    a.   Words that are extremely logical: "That makes sense and is reasonable."

    b.   Bodies in control or shut down.

    c.   Feelings: "I am vulnerable and feel threatened when I get in touch with my feelings, especially feelings of vulnerability."

4.   Distracters discount context. Their goal is to keep others and themselves away from painful feelings, to distract and avoid conflict. Distracters are the elusive, sometimes charming, magicians. They are difficult to hold accountable or responsible because they keep the focus elsewhere, not on themselves. Many alcoholics and addicts are masters of this style of communication and avoid or deny their problems with alcohol and drugs. Their communication patterns feature the following:

    a.   Words that are confusing and irrelevant. They are unable to establish clarity or to set specific goals.

    b.   Bodies that act as if they are somewhere else when the content gets too specific and focused. They want to frustrate, discount, and escape from others.

    c.   Feelings: "Nobody cares. I am not happy."

According to Satir, **leveling** is the healthy state of communication. Words, body, and feelings are consistent with the message. The individual is congruent and acts in a congruent fashion.

❈ Family System Roles

Wegscheider-Cruse's Alcoholic/Addict Family System Survival Roles

Sharon Wegscheider-Cruse was trained by and has worked closely with Virginia Satir. Wegscheider-Cruse is best known for her books *The Family Trap* (1976) and *Family Reconstruction Therapy: The Living Model* (1994). She is a leader in the field of adult children of alcoholics and family reconstruction and has popularized the concept of survival roles in the alcoholic/addict family system. These roles are labeled in terms of the coping mechanisms members use to survive in a dysfunctional alcoholic/addict family. They include the chief enabler, family hero, family scapegoat, lost child, and family mascot.

The *chief enabler* assumes primary responsibility for the chemically dependent family member. The chief enabler shelters and protects, even denies, the dysfunctional aspects of a family member's alcohol/drug use.

The *family hero* is the achiever, the responsible child, the good child, and the model child. The family hero is often the firstborn, who escapes the dysfunctional aspects of the alcohol/drug family through personal achievement. The family's sense of self-worth is often the conscious or unconscious responsibility of this family member. Unfortunately, the family hero achieves for the family and ignores personal feelings, values, and goals. The family hero in adulthood often experiences a depression or sense of loss due to the incongruency of internal feelings with external behaviors. The hero may be outwardly successful but feel like a charlatan, or empty inside. When this conflict is not dealt with, the family hero is vulnerable to alcohol/drug problems and/or problems in interpersonal relationships.

The primary function of the *family scapegoat* is to divert the family members away from the real issues in the family (e.g., marital discord, marital infidelity, or parental alcohol/drug problems) and the painful emotionality of these family issues. The family members can then blame the scapegoat for all of the family problems. The family scapegoat often exhibits acting-out behavior in school and at home, antisocial behavior, and substance abuse due to underlying feelings of anger and resentment.

The *lost child*'s role (see Case Study 5.1) is often the most tragic. This is the child whose primary function is to allow the dysfunctional family—especially the parents—to expend less energy. This child often identifies with the pain of his or her parents and other siblings and wants to decrease the family members' level of pain by not contributing to the problem, perhaps even taking on the family's pain. The family inadvertently reinforces this child for not having needs. The child denies feelings and needs, frequently disconnecting emotionally and even physically from the family. At some point, the child can no longer deny personal feelings and pain. Thus, lost children frequently get overwhelmed with emotions and are at risk for suicide.

The primary function of the *family mascot* is to divert attention away from the family issues and family pain. The mascot uses humor, silliness, and even self-disparaging ineptness (making fun of oneself) as a way of diverting the family from its pain. Frequently, the mascot discounts a sense of self as the price to pay for calm in the family. As a result, the mascot may feel unworthy of love, unless able to alleviate someone's pain.

These are just a few family roles. The roles are stereotypic classifications for purposes of identifying some common role features in dysfunctional, or imbalanced, family systems. Please note that the roles are illustrations of dysfunctional patterns of family interaction and should not be used to pigeonhole someone into a static classification. Usually, people maintain a variety of traits from each of the roles. Family roles may also change based on different family situations and adjustments in the family process.

Case Study 5.1

The Lost Child

Michelle

Michelle was beginning her senior year in high school when her family began therapy. At that time, her stepbrother, Jack, was heavily into drugs (marijuana, hallucinogens, speed, and cocaine) and alcohol. Her other sisters were extremely angry with Jack's attitude and behavior. Michelle was an A student and the student body president. She was on the cross-country team and very popular. She had a quiet, affable presence and acted older than her 17 years. She was the only one in the family to whom Jack related. During the course of treatment, it was very difficult for Michelle to express any feelings. Even in individual sessions, she would deny feeling any pain or negative emotions.

Later that year, Michelle was accepted to a college a few hours' drive from home. During her first semester away at school, despite good study habits, she ended up dropping a course and receiving C grades. Also, she didn't make any friends at school. Michelle was running on the college track team but was unmotivated and not running to her true potential. This was quite traumatic for Michelle because she had been so popular and such a good student and athlete in high school. Michelle set up an individual counseling appointment during her college break. For the first time, she was in touch with her pain and grief. If she had not reached out for help, Michelle would have been another college student unable to cope with the pressures or to deal effectively with backlogged feelings, which eventually might have caused her to take her own life.

Discussion Questions

1. Describe some behaviors of the "lost child" in coping with stress and imbalance in the family.
2. Describe some of your own "lost child" behaviors.
3. Describe what you would do if you were counseling a family about the "lost child."
4. What role could self-compassion play in helping a "lost child"?
5. Identify some of the negative feelings that a lost child might have.

Other important family therapists—Salvador Minuchin, Theodore Lidz, Lieman Wynne, James Framo, Ron Jackson, and Jay Haley—emphasize a systems approach in their work with families and changing dysfunctional patterns of family communication and interaction. These family therapists have different styles, theories, and methods of working with families. Some see the entire family together in a counseling session. Others may see family members separately or sometimes see the father and son, mother and daughter, or just the children. Family therapists even use a multigenerational approach that includes grandparents, or an expanded family approach of including other relatives. The key element of all of these approaches is looking at the family as a system, a system that is affected and changed by the actions and events in the lives of each of the family members.

Family Roles Played Out at the Dinner Table

The Green family, like many families, had the ritual of having dinner together. When the children were younger, the minor irritations of "spilled milk" (literally and metaphorically) gave rise to Dad's rage. Mr. Green was usually exhausted at dinnertime, stressed out by his job. Mr. Green's father was a mean-tempered, negative, emotionally disconnected, and nasty alcoholic, who didn't model any form of connection or caring toward his children. Mr. Green, like his father, had little patience with his children and would lose his temper easily. As the children got older, the dinner table became a battle zone. The youngest child was the "lost child," the middle child the "scapegoat," and the oldest child the "hero."

The middle child (the scapegoat) would spark the battle by antagonizing his father, challenging him. This son would argue politics, religion, current events, and so on, taking a position that would irritate his father. This son was the brightest child, aware and well read, and would use these skills to mock his father's ignorance on issues.

Mr. Green would soon escalate and explode. The youngest child (lost child) would plead for a truce, which was ignored. She would burst into tears and retreat to her room. The oldest child (the hero) would make jokes and tell the family they were too serious about all this. Sometimes this approach worked, but many times it didn't. Mr. Green would usually explode, grab his dinner plate, and retreat to the den. The oldest child was aligned and enmeshed with his mother. Mom would then sit down by this son and blame the middle child (scapegoat) for causing the conflict.

This is just one scenario of family roles and alliances. The family imbalance is played out night after night at the dinner table.

Five Styles of Managing Anxiety

Harriet Lerner (1997) describes five styles or roles of managing anxiety—underachievers, overfunctioners, blamers, pursuers, and distancers (see Table 5.1). Anxiety about substance abuse in the family often leads to these coping roles.

Enabling Behavior

The major enabling approaches are the following:

1. Avoiding and shielding
2. Attempting to control
3. Taking over responsibilities
4. Rationalizing and accepting
5. Cooperating and collaborating (Nelson 1988).

In an attempt to avoid recognizing problems, the family enables the continued use of alcohol/drugs and other dysfunctional behaviors. Enabling is described as an unhealthy doing-for, or killing with kindness (Table 5.2). Parents may have good intentions in enabling their children. Their lack of insight into the dynamics of the enabling process, however, causes problems to continue and to get progressively worse. (See Case Study 5.2.)

T A B L E 5 . 1	
Five Styles of Managing Anxiety	

Underfunctioners

- Tend to have several areas where they just can't get organized.
- Become less competent under stress, thus inviting others to take over.
- Tend to develop physical or emotional symptoms when stress is high in either the family or the work situation.
- Earn such labels as the "patient," the "frail one," the "sick one," the "problem," the "irresponsible one."
- Have difficulty showing their strong, competent side to intimate others.

Overfunctioners

- Know what's best not only for themselves but for others as well.
- Move in quickly to advise, rescue, and take over when stress hits.
- Have difficulty staying out and allowing others to struggle with their own problems.
- Avoid worrying about their own personal goals and problems by focusing on others.
- Have difficulty sharing their own vulnerable, under-functioning side, especially with those people who are viewed as having problems.
- May be labeled the person who is "always reliable" or "always together."

Blamers

- Respond to anxiety with emotional intensity and fighting.
- Have a short fuse.
- Expend high levels of energy trying to change someone who does not want to change.
- Engage in repetitive cycles of fighting that relieve tension but perpetuate the old pattern.

- Hold another person responsible for one's own feelings and actions.
- See others as the sole obstacle to making changes.

Pursuers

- React to anxiety by seeking greater togetherness in a relationship.
- Place a high value on talking things out and expressing feelings, and believe others should do the same.
- Feel rejected and take it personally when someone close to them wants more time and space alone or away from the relationship.
- Tend to pursue harder and then coldly withdraw when an important person seeks distance.
- May negatively label themselves as "too dependent" or "too demanding" in a relationship.
- Tend to criticize their partner as someone who can't handle feelings or tolerate closeness.

Distancers

- Seek emotional distance or physical space when stress is high.
- Consider themselves to be self-reliant and private persons—more "do-it-yourselfers" than help-seekers.
- Have difficulty showing their needy, vulnerable, and dependent sides.
- Receive such labels as "emotionally unavailable," "withholding," "unable to deal with feelings," from significant others.
- Manage anxiety in personal relationships by intensifying work-related projects.
- May cut off a relationship entirely when things get intense, rather than hanging in and working it out.
- Open up most freely when they are not pushed or pursued.

SOURCE: Lerner, Harriet. 2005. *The Dance of Anger.* New York: Harper Collins. Used with permission of Harriet Lerner.

Case Study 5.2
Enabling Behavior
Jerome

Jerome's marijuana use and related behaviors were driving his family crazy. Mom tried persuasion and pleading to Jerome's sense of "doing the right thing." She picked up after Jerome, believed his stories, denied his abuse of marijuana, and buffered him from his dad's anger.

Dad vacillated from trying to control the situation, to buying and doing things for Jerome. He would "throw money" at the problem and then get angry when Jerome was irresponsible. This cycle continued for quite some time. The family entered family counseling, but most sessions were just "rag on Jerome sessions." Mom and Dad decided to do their own individual counseling, which eventually led to marital counseling. Eventually they stopped blaming each other for Jerome's problems, diminished their enabling behavior, and held Jerome responsible for his behavior. Progress was slow but eventually led to all three of them feeling like they were a more functional and balanced family.

Discussion Questions

1. Describe and list the enabling behavior of "Mom" and "Dad."
2. What is the difference between being supportive and helpful and "enabling behavior"?
3. Enabling behavior is sometimes gray and difficult to clearly identify. Do you think people overuse the term (enabling) and mislabel behavior as enabling, when it isn't? Explain.

Protecting one's child is normal and appropriate, but overprotection can cause problems. Enablers overprotect and find it difficult to separate what their child needs from what their child wants. The price of overprotection is prolonging the dependency of immaturity and thereby aiding the progression of chemical dependency. (MacDonald 1984)

Enabling behavior has been defined as taking responsibility for someone else's lack of responsibility, or softening the consequences for someone's irresponsibility. Enablers are under the delusion that no one knows about the problems and they can continue to cover them up. The reality is that others are aware of the problems and are directly and indirectly letting the family know they need help. Only the family maintains this denial to the real dimensions of the problem.

⚜ Stages in Family Recovery from Substance-Abuse Problems

Families have a wide range and variety of reactions to alcohol/drug problems, yet there are some common, generalizable patterns to a family's response.

TABLE 5.2

Enabling Behavior

Charles Nelson (1988) identified the following four styles of enabling behavior.

Avoiding and Shielding

Avoiding and shielding constitute any behavior by a family member that covers up or prevents the user or the family member from experiencing the full impact of the harmful consequences of the drug use. Enabling behavior includes

- Making up excuses to avoid social contact during drinking and drugging periods
- Side-stepping or avoiding participation in discussions about drugs
- Taking alcohol, sedatives, and/or other drugs to try to lower one's own anxiety or stress about a family member's problems with drugs
- Not standing up for one's rights in fear of the family member going into a binge cycle of drug use
- Cleaning up the family member's vomit after an alcohol/drug episode
- Staying away from home as much as possible to get away from the situation
- Shielding the addict from a crisis that could send her/him into therapy
- Telling the alcoholic to leave until he/she quits drinking but then immediately going out and looking for that family member
- Helping the addict keep up appearances or cover up around relatives, friends, neighbors, or her/his employer

Attempting to Control

Attempting to control is any behavior by a family member that is performed with the intent of taking personal control over the alcoholic/addict's use of the drug. Enabling behavior includes

- Trying to buy things that might divert the addict from drug use (sports equipment, tools, car, house, etc.)
- Spending the night at a hotel or motel to get the user to quit

- Spending the night at a friend's house to get the user to quit
- Screaming, yelling, swearing, or crying in an attempt to get a family member to stop drinking or drugging
- Threatening to hurt oneself in an attempt to get a family member to quit
- Threatening physical violence to get the user to quit
- Checking or measuring the addict's drug stash to determine how much he has been using
- Encouraging the addict to do the drug at home to avoid more problems away from home
- Using or withholding sex as a way to control a partner's alcohol/drug use
- Throwing away, hiding, or destroying the family member's stash or paraphernalia

Taking Over Responsibilities

Taking over responsibilities is any behavior by the family member designed to take over the user's personal responsibilities (e.g., finances, household chores, or employment). Enabling behavior includes

- Cleaning the family member's drug paraphernalia when left out
- Waking the alcoholic in time for work
- Reminding the user to eat at times
- Staying home from work to take care of the family member's problems resulting from drug use
- Preaching to the addict about her failures as a warning about the personal effects of the drug use
- Doing the family member's chores
- Waiting hand and foot on the family member
- Paying all the bills
- Taking a second job to cover the bills piling up after money has been diverted to drugs
- Covering the alcoholic/addict's bad checks

Rationalizing and Accepting

Rationalizing and accepting are any behavior by the family member that conveys a rationalization

(continued on next page)

T A B L E 5 . 2 (*c o n t i n u e d*)	
Enabling Behavior	
or acceptance of the alcoholic/addict's use of the drug. Enabling behavior includes	• Believing and/or communicating that the use of the drugs was safe
• Believing and/or communicating that the family member's episodes of drug use were only isolated instances and not patterns of use	• Believing and/or communicating that the family member's use of drugs increased that person's self-confidence

One model describes the following stages in the family's adjustment to the substance-abuse problem:

1. Denial and minimizing
2. Tension and isolation
3. Frustration and disorganization
4. Attempts to reorganize, shifts in family member alliances
5. Separation in roles, escape
6. Reorganization without the addict/alcoholic
7. Recovery and reorganization with the addict/alcoholic

The application of the stages of grieving can also be used as a model to describe the stages in recovery for the alcoholic/addict and his or her family members.

1. Denial
2. Anger
3. Bargaining
4. Feeling (or depression)
5. Acceptance

Often the stages are positioned differently or combined. Remember, such models are meant to highlight different aspects of the recovery process, not to describe a rigid linear process.

Denial

At the denial stage (see Table 5.3), family members rarely acknowledge that something is wrong, although they sense something might be different about their family.

T A B L E 5 . 3
Denial Stage in Imbalanced Family Systems
Feelings—embarrassed, humiliated, shamed *Defenses*—minimization, rationalization *Linkage to society*—friends and relatives "maintain the denial" *Motto*—"normal family illusion"

The spouse or family members may seek help in an indirect, nonspecific manner, such as talking to friends and/or relatives. Unfortunately, those friends and relatives often reinforce the denial. One such example is the following:

Denial Transaction Between Mary and Her Sister-in-Law, Maureen

Mary: The other night at the party, do you think Harry drank too much?
Maureen: Oh, that happens to everyone once in a while.
Mary: You don't think he has a problem with alcohol, do you?
Maureen: No, of course not. He drinks like most of us in the family, and we certainly don't have a problem. You're overreacting.

In reality, Harry and Maureen grew up in alcoholic family systems and they both have drinking problems.

Anger

Anger is an effective defense to keep family members from talking about issues and feelings that might indicate an alcohol/drug problem in the family. Anger can be expressed as verbal, physical, emotional, and/or sexual threats, abuse, and/or violation. Anger can be actual or threatened rejection and abandonment. Alcoholics/addicts use anger to blame and shame other family members as inadequate and responsible for their predicament. In reality, the anger is a way for the alcoholic/addict to avoid feelings of shame, to control others in the family, and to deny responsibility for problems in the family system.

Once in recovery, many adolescent and adult patients/clients admit that causing a conflict or big fight was a way to get out of the house and use alcohol/drugs. Many clients rationalized that they were already in trouble with the family, so what was the difference if they got into more trouble?

An adolescent patient/client once described her alcoholic/addictive family system as "raging and ragging" (nagging): "Dad is the one who rages around the home, and Mom attempts to control him by ragging at Dad and everyone else. It is no wonder that I don't spend much time at home."

The combined effect is an unsafe, unpredictable family system with underlying feelings of confusion, fear, anxiety, and shame and sometimes immobilizing trauma.

This conflict among family members creates a climate of confusion and a lack of clarity as to what is an appropriate approach to the problem of alcohol/drugs. The result is often a trial-and-error approach. At first, family members try extreme control or rigid threats: "The next time you use alcohol/drugs, I will . . . " (not let you in the house, confine you to your room for 1 month, get a divorce or separation). When this doesn't work, the next approach might be to let go, or to try to ignore the addictive behavior completely, as if the addict didn't exist. The resulting pattern of control-release is chaotic. This trial-and-error approach creates further anger, confusion, and feelings of hopelessness.

At this stage, the family might go beyond relatives and friends and talk to a minister, priest, rabbi, family physician, or school counselor. The family members may be vague in disclosing the degree to which alcohol/drugs are used. At this stage, family members

T A B L E   5 . 4
Anger Stage in Imbalanced Family Systems
Feelings—confusion, fear, anxiety
Defenses—"raging and ragging"
control to chaos
trial and error
Linkage to society—search for magical solutions
Goal—cover up real issues and feelings

are still not quite sure they need help and are embarrassed in seeking help. They may start to get help, get frightened, or be resistant to experiencing the pain associated with acknowledging the problem and then back off from getting help (see Table 5.4).

Bargaining

The bargaining stage (see Case Study 5.3) is usually preceded by a major crisis. The family can no longer deny or ignore the problem and cannot cover up the feelings of frustration and anger. The family is essentially saying, "We have had enough of

Case Study 5.3
A Bargain That Doesn't Work
Marilyn

Marilyn is a very bright, attractive, outgoing 17-year-old. She puts forth minimal effort at school and barely passes her classes, despite her superior intelligence.

She smokes marijuana regularly, drinks alcohol, uses cocaine, and has begun free-basing cocaine. She has been staying out late, and sleeping in every day during the summer. This is the second marriage for her mother, and Marilyn's mother and father are always trying to bribe Marilyn to get her to straighten out. Bribes have included a new car, clothes shopping excursions, and vacations. There have been so many conflicts at home between Marilyn, her mother, and her stepfather, that her real father has agreed to let Marilyn live in the condo on the waterfront for the rest of the summer. It only took a few weeks for the place to be trashed, and the police became regular visitors to Marilyn's parties. Her parents also became aware of Marilyn's freebase cocaine use and took her in for an alcohol/drug evaluation.

Discussion Questions

1. What is the difference between bargaining and compromising?
2. What "bargains" have you made that have backfired?
3. How can you tell when you are "bargaining" that the other person has no intention or motivation to change?

this; it's too chaotic." The family is still not ready to effect change in the system; instead, the goal is to strike some arrangement or bargain. Being held hostage by the addict, the family is willing to pay a ransom to have the addict stop bothering them with outrageous behavior. Unfortunately, the ransom often goes beyond what is reasonable or tolerable, and the family initially agrees to do almost anything to survive in this chaos. Many of the bargains are financial or object-related: "If you stop abusing alcohol/drugs, I'll buy you. . . ."

The underlying and false assumption of most bargains is that the addict can stop using. The assumption is that the addict can override the drive and allure of the alcohol/drugs for a reward. Unfortunately, the drive to use alcohol/drugs is stronger than the reward of the bargain, and willpower alone is not strong enough to overcome the drive to use alcohol/drugs.

Some of the bargains are far more subtle. Couples, families, and friends develop lives based on the bargain of maintaining addiction (see Table 5.5). Following are some common bargains related to alcoholism and drug addiction, and their weaknesses:

- *Let's ignore the addict's behavior and it might just stop.* The more you ignore the destructive behavior, the more intense and dramatic the situation becomes.
- *Let's separate or withdraw from the addict temporarily.* Unless there is strong therapeutic and personal support, the addict feeds on the partner's or family members' weaknesses. The individual usually does not have the support to break the codependent dance of addiction. (See Chapter 7.)
- *Avoid making a decision; maybe it will get better with time.* It's very rare that a spontaneous recovery occurs from alcohol/drugs. Chapter 9 discusses alcohol/drug intervention and "raising the addict's bottom" in an attempt to salvage and avoid further damage. Rarely do addicts decide on their own to get help. Sometimes it is so late that scary consequences are involved, such as the threat of physical harm, criminal justice and legal problems, job and financial problems, or death.

T A B L E   5 . 5

Bargaining, Feeling, and Acceptance Stage in Imbalanced Family Systems

Goal—"maintain the chaos of addiction"
Bargains—compromise values
        love/hate—let go/hold on
        avoid making a decision
        confused—doesn't know what is appropriate
Depression/feelings—feelings are experienced
Acceptance—there is a problem on road to recovery

At the bargaining stage, family members might seek help from experts in the field because their bargains are not working and they need advice and direction. Even when family members are fortunate in finding a counselor who knows about alcohol/drug intervention and treatment, the family members may still not follow through. The attitude at this stage is still a form of bargaining. The therapeutic bargain is to fix the identified patient (the addict) so the bargainer can avoid feeling pain. In some situations, family members may even sabotage counseling to avoid the pain of looking at their roles in the dysfunction. In a distorted sense, the failure of the trained professional validates the failure of the family member: "If the counselor can't help, then I guess we didn't do such a bad job." Many families seeking counseling soon find out that addiction is a family disease and effective treatment involves the entire family.

Feeling

At the feeling stage, family members can no longer deny, cover up with anger, or bargain their feelings away. Many feelings come to the surface and are easily accessed. Family members cry at the slightest provocation, anxious to the point of being hypervigilant (checking things out obsessively) and, in some cases, feeling immobilized. These feelings are undeniable and force the family to seek help.

Acceptance

At the acceptance stage, the family has recognized that they have a problem. They are ready to do the work necessary to heal and develop healthier ways of relating. Recognizing that all the family members are suffering, they have the courage to get help. At this stage, the alcoholic/addict and the family members have begun to work on the problem. This is when treatment and recovery begin.

⚓ In Review

- The alcoholic/drug addict family system is a system in disequilibrium, often trying to counterbalance the extent of the problem with denial. Therefore, instead of *dysfunctional family system*, we can use the term *imbalanced family system*. This term is recommended because it is a more accurate description and avoids the shame connotations of the term *dysfunctional*.
- Families have specific rules, alliances, and patterns of communication.
- There is truly an emotional imbalance in the alcoholic/addict family system. The term *imbalance* gives hope that there is a way to get help and better manage the system. The goal is to establish balance and order by addressing the problems in the family. The term *dysfunctional* implies hopelessness and shame. It is best to avoid using the term.
- Virginia Satir describes unhealthy styles of communication:
    - *Placaters* discount themselves.
    - *Blamers* elevate themselves by discounting others.

- *Intellectualizers* discount their own feelings.
- *Distractors* keep others and themselves away from painful feelings; distract and avoid conflict.
- The alcoholic/addict family system has survival roles—chief enabler, family hero, family scapegoat, lost child, and family mascot.
- Enabling behaviors include avoiding and shielding, attempting to control, taking over responsibilities, and rationalizing and accepting.
- During family recovery, the family goes through the stages of grieving—denial, anger, bargaining, depression/feeling, acceptance. However, the family might skip or go back and forth through the stages of grieving.

✴ Discussion Questions

1. Describe some imbalances in your own family system, and describe the crisis or conflict that may have caused that imbalance.
2. What is your emotional (gut) reaction to using the term *dysfunctional family system* versus *imbalanced family system*. Explain.
3. Identify some family rules in your family of origin, and list the ones you like and those you don't like. If you have children, what are the rules in your family? If you don't have children, what rules do you think would be important if you had children?
4. Please rank your use of these styles of communication, from 1 (least frequently) to 5 (most frequently), and explain.

   - Placater
   - Blamer
   - Intellectualizer
   - Distracter
   - Leveler

5. From the following list, please identify the role you might have played in your family, and the roles that any siblings played. Explain and describe the characteristics and circumstances played out by each role.

   - Hero
   - Lost child
   - Mascot
   - Scapegoat
   - Chief enabler

✴ References

Black, Claudia. 1982. *It will never happen to me!* Denver, Colo.: M.A.C.

Lawson, Ann, and Gary Lawson. 1998. *Alcoholism and the family: A guide to treatment and prevention,* 2nd edition Gaithersburg, Md.: Aspen.

Lerner, Harriet. 1997. *The dance of anger.* New York: HarperCollins.

MacDonald, Donald Ian. 1984. *Drugs, drinking and adolescents.* Chicago: Year Book Medical.

Nelson, Charles. 1988. The style of enabling behavior. In *Treating cocaine dependency,* edited by D. E. Smith and D. Wesson. Center City, Minn.: Hazeldon Foundation.

Satir, Virginia. 1967. *Conjoint family therapy.* Palo Alto, Calif.: Science and Behavior Books.

Satir, Virginia. 1972. *Peoplemaking.* Palo Alto, Calif.: Science and Behavior Books.

Satir, Virginia, et al. 1983. *Helping families to change.* New York: Aronson.

Wegscheider-Cruse, Sharon. 1976. *The family trap.* Palo Alto, Calif.: Nurturing Network.

Wegscheider-Cruse, Sharon, et al. 1994. *Family reconstruction therapy: The living model.* Palo Alto, Calif.: Science and Behavior Books.

Whitaker, Carl, and Augustus Y. Napier. 1978. *The family crucible.* New York: Harper & Row.

Parents and Family: At-Risk Factors for Substance Abuse

Outline of Chapter 6

Introduction

Early Attachment with Parents
> Abandonment Depression
> Impact of Early Abandonment on Adult Interpersonal Relationships

Traits and Temperament: At-Risk Factors for Substance Abuse
> Adoptees: At-Risk for Substance Abuse

Parental Support and Control

Shame and Imbalanced Parenting
> Shame and Feelings

Parental Imbalance and Boundary Setting
> Boundary Inadequacy
> Boundary Ambiguity
> Triangulation—Another Boundary Issue

Parents' Use/Abuse of Alcohol and Drugs
> Criticism, Anger, and Blame

Family Cohesion, Flexibility, and Communication Clarity
> Other Obstacles to Reaching Parents and Family
> Parents' Shame

Compassion, Self-Compassion, and Mindfulness

Objectives

1. Outline the problems that can occur as a result of poor "early parent-child attachment" with infants and children.
2. Identify the six elements of "abandonment depression."
3. Identify the different traits and temperaments that put children more at-risk for substance abuse disorders.
4. List at-risk problems that adoptees are prone to.
5. Describe a healthy balance of parental support and control.
6. Define "shame" and describe its impact on childhood, adolescence, and adulthood, especially with regards to problems with self-worth and ability to balance feelings.

7.   Identify the differences between shame and guilt.
8.   Classify the escalation of feelings caused by the affect-shame bind.
9.   Describe parental imbalance and problems in parental boundaries.
10. Describe the following conditions: boundary ambiguity, triangulation, and parental use and abuse of alcohol/drugs.
11. Describe family cohesion, flexibility, and communication clarity.
12. Describe how criticism, anger, and blame play a negative role in parenting.
13. Describe the dimensions of "self-compassion."
14. Define the role of "compassion" in parenting and family systems.

✳ Introduction

This chapter focuses on some of the parent and family factors that contribute to increased risk of substance use disorders (SUDs) in their children. The factors discussed in this chapter are:

- Early attachment with parents (guardians)
- Abandonment depression
- Abandonment—impact on adult interpersonal relationships
- Traits and temperament
- Parental and control factors
- Shame and imbalanced parenting
- Shame and feelings
- Parental imbalance and boundary setting
- Boundary inadequacy
- Boundary ambiguity
- Triangulation
- Parents' use and abuse of alcohol and drugs
- Criticism, anger, and blame
- Compassion

✳ Early Attachment with Parents

A child's development is often impaired as a result of inadequate nurturing, lack of bonding, and poor attachment during infancy and early childhood. "The insecure-avoidant style emerges when a significant caring figure is unavailable, or when relationships with the family are incongruent and unpredictable." The result is that these children often have trouble forging healthy and intimate interpersonal relationships throughout their lives. They are at-risk for developmental, interpersonal, and substance abuse problems later in life.

Often, because of certain circumstances, parents are not available. A variety of conditions may take the parents from the child—death of a parent, a parent away at war, divorce, illness, mental breakdown, criminal-justice problems, financial problems, job relocation (e.g., military), and so on. All of these circumstances prevent bonding between child and parent and are extremely disruptive to the child's life. The child may even suffer depression as a result of times when he or she felt abandoned or rejected.

Perhaps the parent is ill, suffering from depression, or withdrawn due to a personality and/or psychiatric disorder and finds it hard to nurture his or her child. Maybe the parent didn't grow up in a family system that modeled nurturing, caring, and empathetic connection with the children. Masterson (1976) describes three elements that may produce separation stress in children:

1. *Nature:* Possible genetic or constitutional deficiencies such as inability to tolerate separation anxiety or to synthesize positive and negative effects as well as such conditions as attention deficit disorders and developmental disharmonies.
2. *Nurture:* "Maternal libidinal unavailability for the child's move toward separation-individuation or self-activation (i.e., the mother is unable or has difficulty in identifying, acknowledging, and supporting the child's emerging self-activation, experimentation, and exploration). The reasons for maternal libidinal unavailability may be many—death, divorce, physical or emotional illness, etc."
3. *Fate:* "Any accident of fate that impairs the child's ability to separate and/or individuate. On the separation side, events such as death or divorce can prevent the mother from being emotionally available. On the individuation side, events can impair or prevent the child from practicing his emerging individuation. For example, the child may be sickly or in a restricted environment."

Children of fathers with SUD have been found to have higher levels of insecure-avoidant style of attachment to their children (Peleg-Oron Rahav, and Tecichma 2008). "The insecure-avoidant style emerges when a significant caring figure is unavailable, or when relationships with the family are incongruent and unpredictable" (Peleg-Oron Rahav, and Tecichma 2008). The result is that these children often have trouble with "emotional regulation," which manifests in having trouble maintaining healthy and intimate interpersonal relationships.

Certainly, the parent's alcoholism/drug addiction also makes the parent either unavailable or inconsistent in the quality of the parent-child relationship.

Patrick Carnes, author of numerous books on sexual trauma and addiction, describes the importance of developing healthy bonds with caring adults outside of the family system for children who have been sexually violated/traumatized by a family member. In a 1995 interview in *Professional Counselor Magazine,* Carnes states, "One of the things that emerges in trauma literature is why some kids, who have the same identical history of trauma, rebound from that and have resiliency. As near as I can tell from the literature and what I have seen clinically, the primary factor is the ability of children to have healthy bonds around them that are not traumatic. As an antidote to trauma bonding, you need healthy bonds."

Two prevailing hypotheses regarding parental bonding in adolescent substance abusers are the *overinvolvement hypothesis* and the *functional hypothesis* (Volk et al. 1988). The overinvolvement hypothesis is that one parent (frequently the mother) is overly involved in the adolescent's life to compensate for the lack of availability by the other parent. The functional hypothesis is that the adolescent's substance abuse distracts the family from focusing on other familial problems, such as marital discord, infidelity, and parental abuse of alcohol/drugs.

Abandonment Depression

A young child needs nurturing and connection with a caring parent. Masterson (1976), in his work with borderline-personality-disordered individuals, identifies an affective (feeling) disorder that he labeled "abandonment depression." Masterson believes that a significant separation stress precipitates abandonment depression (see Table 6.1). It is also likely that this separation occurs early in life, at 18 to 24 months of age. The individual suffering from abandonment depression is metaphorically described as "an egg with the insides removed." All the good stuff—the nutrients, the seed, the juices of life—has been removed, has rotted, or has been destroyed by a lack of nurturing.

The six key elements of abandonment depression are

1. Homicidal rage
2. Suicidal depression
3. Panic
4. Feelings of hopelessness and helplessness
5. Emptiness and void
6. Guilt

Impact of Early Abandonment on Adult Interpersonal Relationships

Individuals suffering from abandonment depression express complaints having to do with intimacy. They have difficulty emotionally entering into healthy relationships and are unable to differentiate their needs from others' needs. They experience difficulty in identifying and communicating feelings or in accepting feelings and

---

TABLE 6.1

Negative Parenting

- Lack of physical and emotional availability of parents
- Negative blaming; verbal and nonverbal behavior or attacks
- Mixed messages (double binds), saying one thing and meaning something else
- Unreasonably high expectations or standards; ambiguous expectations of behavior, performance, and affect
- Lack of warmth, sensitivity, security, safety, or high regard for feelings, situations, and conflicts
- Discounting of the child's sense of self or physical and psychological boundaries
- Disparaging, blaming, and generally rejecting attitude about the child's difficulty-with developmental tasks
- Disregard, ridicule, blaming, teasing, or other verbal and nonverbal behavior that is either rejecting or shaming
- Threats to abandon or leave a child in a joking or real manner
- Negative and rejecting statements, actions, and comments about something that is of minor or major importance to the child

communication from others. There is either a fusing of others into self or a fission, causing them to break away emotionally from others.

Masterson (1976) described persons suffering from abandonment depression as experiencing difficulty in establishing intimacy in relationships due to a limited capacity for spontaneity, empathy, and sensitivity. These persons have difficulty in making an emotional commitment to a relationship. Such individuals experience twin fears—the fear of losing (abandonment), which leads to clinging behavior, and the fear of being engulfed (smothered), which leads to feelings of depersonalization, shutting down, distortion of reality, and desensitization (numbing, disconnecting from the body).

At first, using alcohol and drugs to facilitate feeling in interpersonal relationships may seem effective; however, as time goes on, this becomes dysfunctional and destructive. Persons feeling pain also use alcohol/drugs to alleviate the core feeling of abandonment.

Those suffering feelings of abandonment may also choose to enter into dysfunctional and/or alcoholic/addict relationships, or relationships with individuals emotionally and physically unavailable.

The *Diagnostic and Statistical Manual of Mental Disorders* (American Psychiatric Association 2000) lists diagnostic criteria for borderline personality disorder that include the following. These often result from early childhood experiences of abandonment. (See Chapter 11 for more information.)

1. Impulsivity or unpredictability in at least two areas that are potentially self-damaging
2. A pattern of unstable and intense interpersonal relationships
3. Inappropriate, intense anger or lack of control of anger
4. Identity disturbances manifested by uncertainty about several issues relating to identity, such as self-image, gender identity, long-term goals or career choice, friendship patterns, values, and loyalties
5. Affective instability

❧ Traits and Temperament: At-Risk Factors for Substance Abuse

Each child has his or her own temperament. Temperament is described as a behavioral characteristic that researchers believe is present at birth, within the first few months of life, and during infancy (Garrison and Earls 1987; Kohnstamm, Bates, and Rothbart 1999).

There is emerging evidence that extremes in certain temperament traits, such as high activity level, emotionality, attention span, and sociability, are associated with children of alcoholics. These temperaments also put the child at risk for alcoholism/drug addiction and other problem behaviors. The parents of these children are faced with challenges beyond the average parenting techniques. Early evaluation and early intervention are essential to address the issues of children with these temperaments. Children who exhibit these genetically determined temperaments may benefit from prevention efforts, which include special educational and counseling programs. Parents also benefit from parenting skills and education in helping these children to cope better.

Aspects of temperament may predict the behavior problems and substance-abuse problems that frequently arise during adolescence. There also appear to be gender differences in temperament that put children at risk for behavior problems and substance abuse. A study by Block, Block, and Keyes (1988) found that nursery school girls who were low in ego resiliency and ego control were using marijuana at age 14, and boys' marijuana use was predicted by low ego control but not by early ego resilience. Masse and Tremblay (1997), in a study of kindergarten boys, found that high novelty seeking and low harm avoidance measured at age 6 predicted early onset of cigarette smoking, drunkenness, and other drug use in adolescence. Dobkin et al. (1995), in a study of 755 6-year-old boys, found that disruptive behaviors (fighting, hyperactivity, oppositional behaviors) measured at 6 years of age predicted having been drunk or using other drugs—or both—before age 14.

Adoptees: At-Risk for Substance Abuse

One would think that adopted children would thrive considering all the benefits of being adopted into a family. However, adopted children are at risk for many problems, including substance abuse in adolescence and adulthood. "Despite having numerous psychological advantages in their adopted families, adopted children have had higher rates of academic and behavioral problems in childhood than have non-adoptees. . . . Problems with higher than expected prevalence among adoptees have included: learning disabilities, eating disorders, somatoform disorders, criminality, suicide attempts, substance abuse, and psychiatric disorders."

� Parental Support and Control

A *supportive* parent with a healthy relationship with her or his child is less likely to have a child who gets involved with alcohol/drugs.

Rollins and Thomas (1979) explained the differences between a supportive and a controlling parent. They defined a supportive parent as possessing "parental behaviors toward the child such as praising, encouraging, and giving physical affection, which indicate to the child that she or he is accepted, approved of, and loved." In contrast, the controlling parent is defined as having "parental behavior toward the child which is intended to direct the child's behavior in a manner acceptable to the parent."

The goal of parenting is to develop a high level of parental support and a moderate level of parental control. Parents who are highly rigid, authoritarian, and controlling tend to have children who are resentful, frustrated, and angry. These children are then prone to problem behaviors, causing them to rebel or passive-aggressively get back at the rigid parent. "Children whose relationships with their parents lacked love, warmth, and closeness and exhibited signs of hostility, have children who exhibit increased levels of substance abuse, delinquency, and dysfunctional coping strategies" (Johnson and Pandina 1991).

The children of parents who are unable to establish moderate control and effective disciplining techniques often experience problem behaviors and associate with other children who have problem behaviors.

The availability of the parent(s) is extremely important in the child's development, as is the quality of the parent-child relationship. Frequently, parents will spend a quantity of time with their children and mislead themselves into thinking they are effectively developing the relationship. The quality of the parent-child relationship is the essential ingredient. The parent needs to be fully present, listening reflectively, and exchanging ideas, while giving full attention to the child. Quality time also involves understanding, touching (hugging), playing, and sharing. Making a genuine, heart-to-heart connection is at the core of a good parent-child relationship.

⚹ Shame and Imbalanced Parenting

Shame is a deep-rooted feeling, often a result of traumatic childhood experiences that are excessively shaming (e.g., sexual, physical, and emotional abuse). (See Table 6.2.) Parental imbalance and parenting dysfunction are at the core of these feelings of shame. Fossum and Mason (1986) defined shame as "the self looking in on itself and finding the self lacking or flawed." Individuals may feel exposed, vulnerable, and fearful that others know they are feeling inherently bad and inadequate. Shame is more powerful than simple embarrassment, which is a temporary situation with little long-term impact. In shame, people feel that they will never recover from the negative way others see them.

Shame is a feeling that has an integral role in the individual's development. "Shame is a basic, natural human emotion, which in moderation is adaptive, healthy,

---

TABLE 6.2

Characteristics of Shameful Experiences

1. Unexpected exposure; being judged on a vulnerable aspect of oneself
2. Feeling as if there is a loss of choice
3. Feeling out of place, flawed, defective, or inadequate
4. A threat to the core of one's identity
5. Mistrust in ability to perceive things properly; unsure of self in making decisions or relating to people
6. Trust of self and others is jeopardized; boundaries are distorted; and physical, emotional, and/or sexual violations may occur
7. Difficulty in assessing what is reality
8. Feeling helpless, powerless, and trapped, with no way out

SOURCE: Fossum, M, and M, Mason, 1986, *Facing shame: Families in recovery.* New York: W. W. Norton.

and absolutely essential for development. We could not eliminate shame even if we wanted to. It's inbred in the species" (Kaufman 1989).

Sigmund Freud used the word *guilt* to describe feelings of shame. Famed family therapist Erik Erikson, in his description of the human life cycle, outlined two developmental stages that focused on guilt and shame: (1) autonomy versus doubt and shame and (2) initiative versus guilt.

Growing up in an alcohol/addict family system or an imbalanced family system creates a foundation of shame. Additional feelings of shame are perpetrated by peers, the school system, other institutions, and other authority figures in the child's life. These shame-based messages are internalized by children. The result is a vicious pattern of feelings and behavior, which perpetuates the feelings of shame.

Individuals from shame-based family systems often feel that (1) there is no hope for change; (2) shame is inescapable and inevitable; (3) shame is exterior-based, not an internal process; and (4) they are bad, no good, flawed, or worthless as individuals (Fossum and Mason 1986). For these individuals, feelings of shame can include thoughts like these:

No matter what I do, it's never going to be good enough, so why try?
Each time I try, I fail, anyway. The result is always negative.
I must try so much harder than others. It's so much easier for others, so I must be inferior and inadequate.
You have to be perfect to be O.K.
Look at _____. Now, if I could only be like them.
It's never going to get any better, no matter how hard I try.
If only others would feel good. Then I would be happy.

Shame is a fascinating topic because it affects us all in some way (see Table 6.3). Most individuals can overcome feelings of shame and grow as a result of it, getting on with their lives. However, some individuals have been shamed dramatically and frequently, especially during early developmental years, and are unable to overcome it. These individuals are at risk for alcoholism and drug dependence or developing

TABLE 6.3

Shame

Definition: self looking in on self, finding the self lacking or feeling exposed—"seen"—in a public way and wanting to cover—feeling hunted

Shame-Based System	Balanced System
1. No hope—hopelessness	1. Hope—choice
2. Inescapable	2. Can make amends
3. Exterior-based	3. Internally based

SOURCE: Adapted from Fossum, M, and M, Mason, 1986, *Facing shame: Families in recovery.* New York: W. W. Norton.

relationships with alcoholics/addicts. Too much trauma creates shame, which leads to feelings of hopelessness and helplessness.

There is almost a resignation that life is painfully unfulfilling—not worth trying to change. Expectations and aspirations are only indirectly acknowledged, for fear of reexperiencing rejection and shame. Shame-based individuals perceive themselves as trapped, inescapably destined to again experience the shame message of self-inadequacy and powerlessness. The shame-based orientation is external. The individual's sense of self is formed by others' evaluations and judgments of his or her performance and behavior. The orientation is outside (external world) in versus inside (internal self) out. Three characteristics—no hope, inescapable shame, and an exterior base—are found in shame-based systems and shame-based individuals.

In contrast, in a balanced family system, the individual has a much healthier way of approaching life and others. The individual receives feedback from the world and evaluates the feedback. The individual then chooses to make changes or adjustments in decision making, goal setting, and interpersonal communication, based on his or her evaluation of the validity of the feedback. The major focus is on *hope* and *choice*.

In a balanced-system, individuals can recognize their mistakes and not feel that they themselves are the mistake. They can make amends to those who might have been hurt by their mistakes and can learn from their errors. The experience is valued, and there is an opportunity for self-growth. Individuals from a balanced family system have an orientation that is inside out (internal). These individuals relate well to and have empathy for others, balancing their own sense of self with the judgments and reactions of others.

Shame is different than embarrassment. Embarrassment is temporary, one can recover from embarrassment; shame is more long-lasting and deep-rooted. Often, shameful experiences are unresolved and take a very long time and much effort to overcome. For example, finding that your home was burglarized while you were away can elicit feelings of violation and victimization. However, letting someone in to your home, who then robs you at gunpoint, ties you up, and terrorizes you, brings a far greater level of helplessness and horror, which is shattering to your perception of being safe.

Fossum and Mason (1986) make the distinction between shame and guilt. Many people believe the feelings of guilt and shame are the same, but they are very different emotions. Table 6.4 illustrates the differences of shame and guilt as they relate to self. The key point is that shame affects the core of your being, whereas guilt is about things you have done.

The following are ways in which parents can avoid instilling shame in their young children:

1. Provide unconditional love. Let their child know that they really like him or her. Talking, touching with affection, hugging, and, most important, paying attention to the child are some of the ways in which parents express unconditional love.
2. Provide safety, nurturance, security, and care.
3. Communicate clearly with and support their spouse or partner.

TABLE 6.4

Primary Characteristics of Shame and Guilt

Central Trait	Shame	Guilt
Failure	Of being	Of doing
Involvement of Self	Damage to global sense of self	Damage to active or moral sense of self
Action Tendency	To withdraw; to escape	To confess; to repair damage
Focus	On inadequate self	On impaired relationships
Sense of Self	Inadequate, deficient, defective, worthless, exposed, disgraced	Bad, selfish, evil, remorseful, irresponsible
Key Phrases	I am no good I am not good enough I am unlovable I do not belong I should not be	I have done wrong I have hurt someone It is my fault I must make amends
Primary Response	Strong affective/physical response: eyes down, blush, shrinking, feel small, exposed	Strong cognitive and behavioral response: need to take action
Central Fear	Abandonment: not belonging (not getting in)	Punishment: ostracism (being cast out)
Primary Defenses	Withdrawal, denial, arrogance, exhibitionism, rage, perfectionism	Rationalization, selflessness, paranoia (projection)

SOURCE: Potter-Efron 2002.

4. Resolve conflicts with their spouse or partner (invoking the Alcoholics Anonymous motto "Would you rather be right or happy?").
5. Play with their infants and children.
6. Be available and enjoy the growth and development of their children.
7. Recognize that at times parenting is overwhelming—take a break and get support.
8. Protect their children from others who may hurt, violate, or shame them.
9. When parents "don't like their child's behavior" or are frustrated and annoyed, they need to minimize the impact of those negative feelings.
10. Use appropriate discipline and good judgment in parenting, and learn about parenting by taking classes on parenting and child development.
11. Seek help from teachers, family members, counselors, doctors, clergy, and so on when "shame-based" family issues arise. Do not isolate or deny (minimize or rationalize) these issues, but take early, proactive action, which can prevent a more significant problem later on.
12. Encourage children to express themselves (what they feel and think) in play, verbal and nonverbal communication, and other activities.

Shame and Feelings

Shame-based messages that are internalized have a major impact on feelings. When shame is attached to normal, everyday feelings, it tends to escalate those feelings. For example, when an internalized shame-based message is attached to normal, everyday feelings of frustration or anger, it tends to escalate those feelings to rage (anger + shame = rage). The person feeling shame then directs this rage toward others, blaming and holding them responsible for feelings of anger and frustration. The rage violates others, pushes them away, and creates more of a feeling of isolation, loneliness, and hopelessness with no way out. This out-of-control emotional freight train picks up speed from all the memories of shame experienced in the family of origin. Some may think that the way to slow down this runaway emotional pain is to self-medicate with alcohol/drugs. Unfortunately, this temporary solution may even speed up the emotional turmoil or cause it to be repeated. When people do not deal with feelings of shame, this pattern continues. The next time, even less anger and shame are needed for the escalation to rage (see Table 6.5).

One of the largest domains of shame is human sexuality, as evidenced by our society's problems in establishing intimate and caring relationships. Let's look at three areas in particular: adolescent sexual identity, sexual violation, and drugs and sex.

Adolescent Sexual Identity and Shame

The developmental task of exploring and defining one's sexual identity is probably the most difficult task of adolescence. Shame-based messages by parents, schools,

TABLE 6.5
Affect-Shame Binds
anger + shame = rage
anxiety + shame = panic
fear + shame = terror
sadness + shame = depression
depression + shame = despair
despair + shame = suicidal thoughts
suicidal thoughts + shame = suicide attempt
hurt + shame = pain
pain + shame = trauma (deep or chronic pain)
trauma + shame = phobia
phobia + shame = loss of reality
unavailability + shame = lack of trust of others
lack of trust of others + shame = paranoia
paranoia + shame = loss of reality

institutions, and peers may be devastating to adolescents and delay the development of a secure sense of sexual identity. Shame-based messages include the following:

You are bad if you _____. (masturbate, are feeling sexual, are aroused, etc.)
Having sexual feelings before marriage is unnatural.
Sex is dirty.
That's all that men want. Men are bad and evil.
Women use sex to manipulate you to get what they want.
Don't watch television; it promotes sexual arousal.
In our family, we don't talk with others about sex.

Sexual Violation and Shame

Sexual violations are common in alcoholic/addict and imbalanced family systems. Children often feel responsible for sexual violation, as if they caused the violation (e.g., I must be responsible for this sexual feeling in others because I am so cute, attractive, shy, or outgoing). Usually, the violation is not talked about or is enabled by the mother or, in some cases, the father. When told of the violation, the parent often denies that it happened or that it is possible and rationalizes the action: "Your uncle is that way with everyone. Try to stay away from him." Such parents fail to adequately protect children from future violations. When the behavior is acknowledged by children, usually no one in the family seeks therapeutic help for the victim and/or the perpetrator. Families deny sexual violations for fear of exposing the inappropriate and violating behavior and to avoid familial shame. Instead of families getting help, they maintain denial and scapegoat the victims by not acknowledging the violations or their pain. They take no or limited action to prevent future violations to the victim or to someone else.

Drugs, Sex, and Shame

Cocaine, marijuana, alcohol, methaqualone, and other drugs are often described as sex drugs, or aphrodisiacs. At early stages, alcohol/drugs do reduce inhibitions. This confuses people who define them as aphrodisiacs. In reality, all drugs impair performance, especially at middle and later stages of use.

Under the influence of alcohol/drugs, individuals also experience impaired judgment and may take part in sexual activities in which they would not normally engage if they were sober. The shame of these sexual experiences can be devastating, so they use alcohol/drugs to blot out these feelings of shame. This can become a vicious, negative, addictive cycle. This cycle involves alcohol/drug use, followed by sexual activity, followed by feelings of shame. More alcohol/drug use follows (to numb the feelings of shame), succeeded by sexual activity and more shame and feelings of loss of control.

⚹ Parental Imbalance and Boundary Setting

In her review of the literature, Kempher (1987) identified various factors that contribute to parental imbalance. Often parents are imbalanced as caregivers; sometimes they are overwhelmed by problems of their own. (See Table 6.6.) This prevents them from providing the kind of care, support, structure, and healthy encouragement that children require to develop effectively and grow. Kempher summarized these characteristics of parental imbalance:

1. Increased alcoholism, drug use, and nicotine dependence
2. Increased antisocial or sexually deviant behavior in parents
3. Increased mental and emotional problems, such as depression, personality disorders, or narcissism
4. Increased marital conflict
5. Increased parental absenteeism due to separation, divorce, or death

Parents who are not aware of their own emotional and psychological issues may deny the impact their anger, rage, and physical and emotional unavailability have on their children. Parents play an integral role in the development of their children.

It is natural and essential for parents to set appropriate boundaries with their children. Boundaries act as guideposts for children to bump into as they test their own independence and developmental skills. Good boundaries are a sign of good communication, respectful negotiation, and connection between parents and children. Poor boundaries escalate conflict and frustration, leading to disrespect and poor communication.

It is natural for children to test the limits of parental authority as they explore their own capacity for taking on more responsibility as they grow up. Poor boundary setting causes children to be exposed to situations before they have the developmental skills to handle the situations.

Boundaries are not rules for behavior of children; nor are they processes of limit setting. Boundaries exist between all members of the family, between subsystems, and between the family and society. These are the rules of interaction and the methods of functioning (Lawson and Lawson 1998).

TABLE 6.6

Parental Imbalance

Chemically dependent and/or imbalanced parents often

- Lack knowledge and skill in parenting
- Have unrealistic expectations and lack information on what is developmentally appropriate behavior at various ages
- Are insensitive to the special needs of their children
- Have decreased family-management skills
- Have inappropriate disciplining techniques and maintain inconsistent, rigid, or ambiguous boundaries
- Have decreased positive responses to and reinforcement of their children
- Have decreased parental involvement and poor bonding or parent-child attachment

Minuchin (1974) defined three types of boundaries: Clear boundaries are essential to balanced families. Enmeshed and disengaged boundaries are characteristic of imbalanced families.

Clear boundaries allow mutual respect and concern by allowing separateness for each member yet maintaining closeness. Freedom and flexibility in these healthy relationships are developed by clear, direct, and understanding communication. Clear boundaries allow children to develop, grow, and differentiate from the family. Individuation can be accomplished only when clear boundaries are functioning within the family system.

Enmeshed boundaries are inflexible, are unyielding, and leave no room for differences. Differentness or separateness is not tolerated; individuation is not a goal of enmeshed relationships. Families with enmeshed boundaries view differentness as disloyalty and as a threat to the rules of the system. The needs of the individual are subjugated to the needs of the parents or system. Satisfying the parents' definition of unity and sameness is stressed. Individual boundaries are blurred, and the individual is often swallowed up by the system. Individuals discount their own feelings, needs, and desires; they feel smothered and numb. They often use alcohol/drugs to counteract these feelings and the underlying resentment and anger.

Disengaged boundaries are overly rigid, with little or no opportunity for communication. Individuals in families that maintain disengaged boundaries have little sense of belonging, often feeling isolated from one another. The family also isolates from community and society. The parents are emotionally unavailable to each other, to the children, and, for that matter, to anyone else.

Boundary Inadequacy

Boundary inadequacy has been defined as the inability to set consistent and appropriate boundaries in relationships. The three major forms of boundary inadequacy identified by Coleman and Colgan (1986) are ambiguous, overly rigid, and invasive.

Ambiguous boundary inadequacy involves a pattern of double messages exchanged within the relationship. The double messages create an atmosphere of tension wherein the recipient of the communication can never be sure what can be believed. The inability of the communicator to send clear messages lays the groundwork for the cycle of ambiguity to begin.

Overly rigid boundary inadequacy is characterized by patterns of behavior wherein smooth and efficient functioning is a priority over being responsive and adaptable. Adherence to a preset code of behavior is maintained, regardless of intervening situational variables, wherein roles are played and rules are strictly enforced.

Invasive boundary inadequacy involves patterns of behavior wherein an imbalance of power is used to objectify people. Other people become objects for the person to use in satisfying all needs (e.g., sexual and physical abuse).

Boundary Ambiguity

Boss and Greenberg (1984) use the term *boundary ambiguity* for confusion in family members' perceptions of who is in and out of the family and who is performing various family roles and tasks. The alcoholic family system organizes around the alcoholic or the family member(s) who exhibit dysfunctional behavior. In recovery, the family is challenged to reorganize as a viable system or become dysfunctional with continued boundary ambiguity (i.e., the dry-drunk family).

Ziter (1988) describes the alcoholic/imbalanced family as going through four recovery stages to overcome boundary ambiguity. These stages are very similar to the grieving stages of denial, anger, bargaining, depression, and acceptance described earlier in this chapter.

- *Stage 1—Clustering.* This is described as an early denial stage, when the family members sacrifice in order to maintain family harmony. The family task at this stage is to assure themselves that a family exists and to try to keep the alcoholic in the family system.
- *Stage 2—Conflict.* The reality of the situation is beginning to be understood at this stage. Individual differences are penetrating the denial system, and the family members are experiencing the stress and uncertainty of these ambiguous differences. It is at this stage that anger replaces denial to control family differences.
- *Stage 3—Individuation.* At this stage of family recovery, the family members are able to recognize the individuality of each person. The family's task is to support each other in exploring "self" while negotiating living together. Boundaries are becoming clearer.
- *Stage 4—Connection.* Family members are making connections with each other. There is a new way of relating that perhaps was not experienced before—an intimate linking. Mutuality emerges, and family members maintain boundaries through their own assertiveness and the respect of other members.

One can see how family members move from a system with imbalance and boundary ambiguity to a balanced system with connection and clarity in boundaries.

Coleman (1987) underscored the importance of setting appropriate boundaries for members of imbalanced families:

> Developing skills at boundary setting is an essential ingredient in the recovery from chemical dependency or codependency. For many it is learning to say "no" to someone's request for physical, sexual, or emotional intimacy. Through saying "no," the individual learns that he or she can have a personal boundary and have it respected. This leads to a clear sense of self-wants and self-desires and it develops a sense of power and control in interpersonal relationships. After learning to say "no," the individual can learn to say "yes," and not lose a sense of individuality.

Triangulation—Another Boundary Issue

Jay Haley, a noted family therapist, defined triangulation (Figure 6.1) as at least two adults involved in an offspring's problem, where the parent-child dyad is

FIGURE 6.1   *Triangulation*

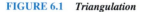

pitted against a more peripheral parent, stepparent, or grandparent. The triangle may involve a parent's lover, an estranged parent, or another relative (Haley 1971).

The destructive nature of the triangle is that the parent-child dyad, or alliance, is established at the expense of the peripheral parent. Often the parent-child dyad creates a marital conflict. The parent is overly enmeshed in this alliance, seeking the child's favor despite the reality of the situation.

❧ Parents' Use/Abuse of Alcohol and Drugs

Kandel and Andrews (1987) postulated that parents can influence their offspring's behavior by modeling actions and defining norms, by controlling the child's susceptibility to the influence of others, and by providing positive attachments.

The modeling of drug use and alcohol use by parents, inadequate supervision of children, and lack of physical and emotional availability are factors that may put children at risk for substance abuse.

Criticism, Anger, and Blame

Do No Harm
Do not take lightly small misdeeds,
Believing they can do no harm:
Even a tiny spark of fire
Can set alight a mountain of hay.

Acting for the Good
Do not take lightly small good deeds,
Believing they can hardly help:
For drops of water one by one
In time can fill a giant pot.
(Patrul Rinpoche, *The Words of My Perfect Teacher*)

Words, actions, emotions, and even thoughts can impact a child. Criticism, anger, and blame are just a few of the negative actions that can do great harm, especially during children's formative years, putting young people at risk for future problems with alcohol/drugs.

Blame is another form of criticism that is so quick to invoke instead of looking at one's own responsibilities for the problem. Blaming and holding on to resentment keeps us stuck, isolated, and alone, like the proverbial "dragon in the corner eating its own tail."

> "We habitually erect a barrier called blame that keeps us from communicating genuinely with others, and we fortify it with our concepts of who's right and who's wrong."
>
> (Pema Chodron, *When Things Fall Apart*)

⚹ Family Cohesion, Flexibility, and Communication Clarity

Barnes (1990) describes the three major family system variables necessary to prevent problem behaviors by children: **family cohesion, flexibility,** and **communication clarity.**

Cohesion is defined as the emotional bonding of family members toward each other. Family members respect one another, support each other, and have appropriate boundaries. Cohesion is not possible if family members are enmeshed or disengaged from each other. Instead, there is a balance in roles, tasks, and ability to resolve conflicts.

Flexibility is the family members' ability to alter family roles and rituals in response to situational stress.

Communication clarity is the ability of family members to develop coalitions and to understand each other.

Parental competence is described by Burton White, director of the Harvard Preschool Projects, as the ability and willingness of parents to

- Sensibly design the world of the child
- Serve as a child's personal consultant
- Set limits effectively, for the sake of the child (not the parent)
  (White, Kaban, and Attanucci 1979)

Other Obstacles to Reaching Parents and Family

One of the major stumbling blocks in getting adolescents into counseling for alcohol/drug problems is parental resistance. Logically, parents want the best for their children, and the parents' intentions are to do the best they can. Parents may deny adolescent substance abuse, because it brings up their own "shame" at being judged "bad parents." This denial can persist as the problems get worse, the adolescent escalates the substance abuse, and the negative consequences increase as well.

Table 6.7 lists the many obstacles that caregivers must overcome to reach parents and family. Parents make the assumption that "things will be O.K." and may have other reasons for not asking for help and resisting taking action. Asking for help, and thereby admitting that a problem exists and that we (parents and family) are not being successful at addressing the adolescent's substance abuse, is a difficult and painful first step for many parents and family members.

T A B L E   6 . 7

Obstacles to Reaching Parents and Family

- Denial
- Skepticism, incongruence
- Assumption that things will be O.K.
- Distorted, depressed view of life
- Fear of being labeled
- Fear of loss of confidentiality
- Narcissism of parents
- Lack of energy/time of parents
- Distrust of the system
- Lack of credible messages—cultural/racial
- Lack of concern/respect for experts
- Lack of awareness of community resources
- Need for services for basic survival
- Cultural mores

Parents' Shame

Parents who have not done a good job of parenting may experience feelings of shame. Gomberg (1988) describes this parental shame as falling short of expectations in being a good parent. Jessup (1983) also describes a sense of failure for mothers that is shameful. Eliason and Skinstad (1995) describe the deep sense of identity and self-esteem that many women gain from their children:

> When they perceive failure at meeting the needs of their children, the sense of
> hopelessness that follows can be devastating. The sense of shame . . . about
> mothering in substance using women has been heightened by the media's attention
> to Fetal Alcohol Effects and 'cocaine babies' in recent years. This press is often
> sensationalized and contains blatant mother-blaming implications.

❊ Compassion, Self-Compassion, and Mindfulness

Compassion is the practice of recognizing and understanding others' suffering as well as one's own. Being self-compassionate means not personalizing or being over reactive to difficulties and suffering. This involves having "equanimity towards difficult and uncomfortable thoughts and experiences—rather than over identification" (Van Dam et al. 2011). Compassion has been described as the core of mindfulness, as in self-compassion.

> ". . . within a traditional mindfulness context . . . compassion is viewed as a
> necessary underpinning for the whole (mindfulness) path, a kind of pilot light for
> the other virtues." (Rosch 2007)

Many generations have been trained to be self-critical, competitive, judgmental, argumentative, and critical of others. Self-criticism can lead to a vicious cycle of self-condemnation, blaming, rumination, and depression.

Compassion is a cornerstone of Buddha's teaching (dharma). The Dalai Lama, along with noted authorities in the psychology/counseling field, has been conducting large public conferences (2008) focusing on helping parents teach children to be more compassionate.

Shame, aggression, emotional and physical violations can be quite traumatic. Children are sometimes shaming, bullying, and violating their peers. By teaching respect and compassion, we can counter the peer culture from hurting and harming one another.

The ultimate goal of teaching compassion is to help establish safety and trust in relationships—a trust that promotes peace, cooperation, and well-being between peoples in our communities and our world.

⊁ In Review

- A poor bond between parent and child can often impair the child's development. Self-concept, social and interpersonal relationships, achievement, and identity are negatively affected by inadequate parent-child bonding. A positive, caring relationship is essential for healthy development.
- A child's development is often impaired by inadequate nurturing, lack of bonding, and poor attachment. This creates at-risk factors for developmental, interpersonal, and substance abuse problems.
- There are two prevailing hypotheses regarding parenting styles in adolescent substance abusers. The over-involvement hypothesis is that one parent (frequently the mother) is overly involved in the adolescent's life to compensate for the lack of availability by the other parent.
- The functional hypothesis is that the adolescent's substance use distracts the family from focusing on other familial problems.
- There are clusters of temperaments that are related to substance use/abuse disorders, such as high activity level, low flexibility, mood instability, social withdrawal, and low positive mood.
- The individual suffering from abandonment depression is metaphorically described as "an egg with the insides removed."
- An individual's suffering from abandonment depression often has difficulty in affect (feeling) regulation, which impairs interpersonal relationships.
- The goal of parenting is to develop a high-level of parental support and moderate level of parental control.
- Problems in boundary setting include enmeshed boundaries, disengaged boundaries, boundary ambiguity, and triangulation.
- Parents' abuse of alcohol/drugs is an at-risk factor for substance abuse disorders.
- Critical, angry, and blaming thoughts, feelings, and actions by parents negatively impact children.

- Shame is defined by Fossum and Mason as the self looking in on itself; finding the self lacking, flawed, or inadequate; and feeling exposed in a public domain.
- Shame is a deep-rooted feeling that often results from traumatic childhood experiences.
- One way to counter shame and anger is to teach and model compassion for self and others.

✳ Discussion Questions

1. Rank the seven factors listed below in order from the most influential (7) to the least influential (1) parenting factors that make children at risk for substance abuse problems. Explain your rationale.

   - Attachment
   - Temperament of the child
   - Parenting style
   - Parental imbalance and substance abuse
   - Boundary problems (e.g., triangulation)
   - Parent criticism, anger, and blaming of children
   - Shame

2. Give examples and describe incidents of shame at various ages. Explain how the incidents fit the definition of shame.
3. Give examples and describe a situation where shame attached to a feeling escalated. Explain the sequence and why this occurred.
4. Explain the role of compassion in promoting healthy parent-child relationships. List some people who have shown you compassion growing up. Write a letter to those people who showed you compassion and helped you, and consider mailing it to them.

✳ References

American Psychiatric Association. 2000. *Diagnostic and statistical manual of mental disorders.* 4th ed. Washington, D.C.: Author.

Barnes, Grace M. 1990. Impact of the family on adolescent drinking patterns. In *Alcohol and the family,* edited by R. Collins et al. New York: Guilford Press.

Block, J., J. H. Block, and S. Keyes. 1988. Longitudinally foretelling drug usage in adolescence: Early childhood personality and environmental precursors. *Child Development* 59(2): 336–55.

Boss, P., and J. Greenberg. 1984. Family boundary ambiguity: A new variable in family stress theory. *Family Process* 23: 535–46.

Carnes, Patrick. 1995. Patrick J. Carnes: Riding the tides, navigating counseling's turbulent waters [Interview]. *Professional Counselor Magazine,* December, pp. 47–52.

Chodron, Pema. 2002. *When things fall apart.* Boston: Shambhala.

Coleman, Eli. 1987. *Chemical dependency and intimacy dysfunction.* New York: Haworth Press.

Coleman, Eli, and Philip Colgan. 1986. Boundary inadequacy in drug dependent families. *Journal of Psychoactive Drugs* 18: 21–30.

Dobkin, P. L., R. E. Tremblay, L. C. Masse, and F. Vitaro. 1995. *Child Development* 66: 1198–1214.

Eliason, M. J., and A. H. Skinstad. 1995. Drug/alcohol addictions and mothering. *Alcoholism Treatment Quarterly* 12(1): 83–95.

Fossum, M., and M. Mason. 1986. *Facing shame: Families in recovery.* New York: W. W. Norton.

Garrison, W. T., and F. J. Earls. 1987. Temperament and child psychopathology. *Developmental Clinical Psychology and Psychiatry* 12.

Gomberg, E. S. L. 1988. Shame and guilt issues among women alcoholics. *Alcoholism Treatment Quarterly* 5: 139–55.

Haley, Jay. 1971. *Changing families: A family therapy reader.* New York: Grune & Stratton.

Jessup, M. 1983. *Chemically dependent women in San Francisco: A status report.* San Francisco: California Department of Public Health, San Francisco Community Substance Abuse Services.

Johnson, Valerie, and Robert J. Pandina. 1991. Effects of the family environment on adolescent substance use, delinquency, and coping skills. *American Journal of Drug and Alcohol Abuse* 1(17): 71–88.

Kandel, D. B., and K. A. Andrews. 1987. Processes of adolescent socialization by parents and peers. *International Journal of Addiction* 22: 319–42.

Kaufman, E. 1989. The psychotherapy of dually diagnosed patients. *Journal of Substance Abuse Treatment* 6(1): 9–18.

Kempher, Carol. 1987. Special populations: Etiology and prevention of vulnerability to chemical dependency in children of substance abusers. In *Youth at high risk for substance abuse,* edited by B. S. Brown and A. R. Mills. NIDA monograph. Washington, D.C.: U.S. Department of Health and Human Services.

Kohnstamm, G., J. Bates, and M. K. Rothbart. 1999. In *Alcohol use among adolescents,* edited by M. Windle. Thousand Oaks, Calif.: Sage.

Lawson, Ann W., and Gary W. Lawson. 1998. *Alcoholism and the family: A guide to treatment and prevention,* 2nd edition. Gaithersburg, Md.: Aspen.

Masse, Louise C., and Richard E. Tremblay. 1997. Behavior of boys in kindergarten and the onset of substance use during adolescence. *Archives of General Psychiatry* 54(1): 62–68. Available at http://archpsyc.jamanetwork.com/journal.aspx

Masterson, James F. 1976. *Psychotherapy of the borderline adult: A developmental approach.* New York: Brunner/Mazel.

Minuchin, Salvador. 1974. *Families and family therapy.* Cambridge, Mass.: Harvard University Press.

Peleg-Oron, Neta, Giora Rahav, and Meir Tecichma. 2008. School-age children of fathers with substance use disorders (SUDs): Are they a high-risk population? *Journal of Alcohol and Drug Education* 52(2): 9–30.

Potter-Efron, Ronald. 2002. *Shame, guilt, and alcoholism: Treatment issues in clinical practice,* 2nd edition. New York: Haworth Press.

Rinpoche, Patrul. 1994. *The words of my perfect teacher.* New York: Harper-Collins.

Rollins, B. C., and D. L. Thomas. 1979. Parental support, power, and control techniques in the socialization of the child. In *Contemporary theories of the family,* vol. 1, edited by W. R. Burr et al. New York: Free Press.

Rosch, E. 2007. More than mindfulness: When you have a tiger by the tail, let it eat you. *Psychology of Inquiry* 18: 248–64.

Van Dam, Nicholas T., Sean C. Sheppard, John P. Forsyth, and Mitch Farleywine. 2011. Self-compassion is a better predictor than mindfulness of symptom severity and quality of life in mixed anxiety and depression. *Journal of Anxiety Disorders* 25: 123–30.

Volk, R. J., et al. 1988. Family systems of adolescent substance abusers. *Family Relations* 38: 266–72.

Werner, R. J., and C. A. Smith. 1999. In *Alcohol use among adolescents,* edited by M. Windle. Thousand Oaks, Calif.: Sage.

White, B., B. Kaban, and J. Attanucci. 1979. *The origins of human competence: The final report on the Harvard Preschool Project.* Lexington, Mass.: Lexington Books/D. C. Heath.

Ziter, MaryLou Politi. 1988. Treating alcoholic families: The resolution of boundary ambiguity. *Alcoholism Treatment Quarterly* 5: 221–33.

Growing Up in an Alcoholic Family System

Outline of Chapter 7

Introduction

The Adult Children of Alcoholics Movement

Characteristics of Adult Children of Alcoholics

Growing Up in an Alcoholic Home as Post traumatic Stress Disorder

Childhood in an Alcoholic Home

Identification of Children of Alcoholic Families

Denial of Feelings in an Alcoholic Family

Perspective of the Child in an Alcoholic Family

Family Disease Model

Alcoholism/Drug Addiction—Impact on Marriage

ACA in Relationships
    ACA Define Self Through Others
    The Disengaged ACA
    Atypical Depression
    Codependency
    Boundary Inadequacy
    Overattachment and Overseparation
    Codependent Dances

Recovery for Adult Children of Alcoholics
    Inherited Family Belief Systems
    Overview of ACA Recovery
    Powerlessness in the Alcoholic Family System
    Feeling Awareness
    Identifying Feelings for ACA
    Grief Work
    Group Psychotherapy

Objectives

1. Describe and define what we mean by adult children of alcoholics.
2. Identify the basic facts about children of alcoholics that the National Association of Children of Alcoholics developed in its charter statement in 1983.

3. Identify at least seven characteristics of adult children of alcoholics.
4. Compare the symptoms of post traumatic stress disorder (PTSD) to growing up in an alcoholic family system.
5. Identify the behaviors of children in alcoholic family systems.
6. Identify and describe how role-reversal, unpredictability, unavailability, and social isolation impact the child in the alcoholic system.
7. Describe the dimensions of the family disease model and the impact of alcoholism/drug addiction on the marriage.
8. Describe adult children of alcoholics (ACA) in adult relationships.
9. Define and describe codependency and some "codependent dances."
10. List characteristics and thoughts of both the overattached and the overseparated individual.
11. Describe the various modalities and methods for recovery for adult children of alcoholics.
12. List the eleven curative factors of group psychotherapy, and describe them for recovery of adult children of alcoholics.

⋊ Introduction

This chapter focuses on children of alcoholics. In the 1980s, this was an emerging issue that shifted the focus away from the alcoholic/addict to the children in the alcoholic/addict family system.

Alcoholism is a family disease that includes codependency, enabling behavior, and marital discord. The children in an alcoholic system, much like the nonalcoholic spouse, compensate to keep the system in homeostasis. The family is organized around the alcoholic's behavior and drinking. The alcoholism is the central organizing principle around which the family focuses.

Children growing up in an alcoholic/addict family system experience traumas, which result in specific adult behavioral characteristics and developmental disabilities. Adult children of alcoholics (ACA) have trouble establishing effective boundaries in relationships and are often either overseparated or overattached in partner relationships. Recovery for adult children involves dealing with unresolved feelings of childhood grief and working through feelings of shame, abandonment, and rejection.

By understanding the healing and recovery process for adult children, perhaps this pattern of imbalance can be broken for the next generation.

⋊ The Adult Children of Alcoholics Movement

In the 1980s, one of the most significant alcohol/drug issues brought to the attention of the general public was the awareness of the characteristics of adult children of alcoholics. Children who grew up in alcoholic families are now adults, hence the term *adult children of alcoholics*. These adults report difficulties in establishing effective, intimate, interpersonal relationships.

The talent and dedication of people such as Timmen Cermak, Claudia Black, Stephanie Brown, Janet Woititz, Sharon Wegscheider-Cruse, Robert Ackerman, and Lori Dwinell created an awareness of the trauma of growing up in an alcoholic family system. Because of this awareness, our society not only has recognized but today is dealing with how the imbalanced aspects of alcoholism affect all family members.

In 1979, a *Newsweek* article about adult children of alcoholics reported the early work of Claudia Black (1982) and Stephanie Brown, who both described and labeled the characteristics of ACA. Brown (1988) described the reaction after the *Newsweek* article as "a prairie fire of interest." The proliferation of articles, materials, books, general information, workshops, and speakers on ACA issues was dramatic from 1979 to the late 1980s. Adult children of alcoholics were finally recognized as a treatment population that had generally been ignored for years. This explosion of interest was in direct proportion to the neglect and oversight that occurred as professionals focused myopically on the alcoholics, while ignoring the children who grew up in alcoholic families. In 1983, the National Association for Children of Alcoholics (NACOA) was formed. Timmen Cermak, one of the founders, was its first president. Numerous planning meetings established the NACOA as a central organizing force in disseminating information, providing direction, and developing resources for adult children of alcoholics. The NACOA organized national conferences to provide a forum for the dissemination of ACA treatment information for both professionals and the lay public.

In 1983, the NACOA developed some basic facts about children of alcoholics in its charter statement:

- An estimated 28 million Americans have at least one alcoholic parent.
- More than half of all alcoholics have an alcoholic parent.
- Children of alcoholics are at the highest risk of developing alcoholism themselves or marrying someone who is alcoholic.
- In up to 90 percent of child abuse cases, alcohol is a significant factor.
- Children of alcoholics are frequently victims of incest, child neglect, and other forms of violence and exploitation.

The popularity of the ACA movement also brought with it some concerns for overgeneralization and a lack of clinical foundation. Appropriately, this point is made by Stephanie Brown (1988), one of the pioneers of the movement.

> Like many social movements, the sudden recognition, widespread interest, and emotional intensity have been powerful and helpful for many children and adults. However, there continues to be a lack of a solid clinical research and theoretical foundation on which to base important decisions for intervention, education, prevention, and treatment.

✷ Characteristics of Adult Children of Alcoholics

Following are some of the behavioral characteristics of ACA:

1. Fear of losing control
2. All-or-none, black-or-white thinking
3. Fear of experiencing feelings
4. Overdeveloped sense of responsibility or irresponsibility

5. Difficulty with intimacy and with asking for what is wanted or needed
6. Flashbacks of childhood but many memory gaps
7. Feelings of being little, or like a child, when under stress
8. Unreasonable loyalty
9. Addiction to excitement
10. Difficulty relaxing
11. Feelings of guilt, abandonment, and/or depression
12. Tendency to confuse love with self-pity
13. Backlog of shock and grief
14. Compulsive behaviors
15. Living in a world of denial
16. Guessing at what is normal
17. Tendency toward physical symptoms (e.g., headaches, gastrointestinal problems)

⚹ Growing Up in an Alcoholic Home as Post traumatic Stress Disorder

Timmen Cermak (1984) stated that the effect of growing up in an alcoholic family system is analogous to the post traumatic stress disorder (PTSD) (see Case Study 7.1) of war veterans or survivors of the Holocaust because the same coping mechanisms are used. The soldier who helplessly watches as a buddy is shot and killed shuts down his own emotions to survive the trauma, which can later be reexperienced in a safe environment. This same reaction of shutting down emotionally occurs in the children of alcoholics. After these children become adults, they reexperience feelings of childhood traumas and suffer chronic symptoms of acute anxiety, depression, sleep disturbances, and nightmares, as well as an inability to work or function effectively at daily activities.

The following major symptoms of PTSD are similar to symptoms experienced by ACA:

1. Reexperiencing the trauma, as evidenced by

    a. Nightmares
    b. Recurrent obsessive thoughts
    c. Sudden reemergence of survival behavior in the face of events that resemble the original trauma
    d. Emotional overload

2. Psychic numbing, as evidenced by

    a. A sense of depersonalization
    b. A sense of not fitting into one's surroundings
    c. A feeling of emotional anesthesia
    d. Constriction of emotions, especially in situations demanding intimacy, tenderness, or sexuality
    e. Lack of feelings during times of stress
    f. Sudden experience of a wall between the self and the feelings

Case Study 7.1

The ACA and Post traumatic Stress Disorder

Joe

Joe was a client who had experienced both the trauma of growing up in an alcoholic family system and post traumatic stress as a result of military service in Vietnam. Joe was referred to me by a colleague, who was counseling Joe's 12-year-old daughter.

Joe came home drunk one evening, went to his daughter's bedroom to kiss her good night, and began crying and talking about how unhappy he was. Although there was no sexual violation, the daughter was extremely upset by her father's behavior. She was frightened and concerned about his drinking and his deep emotional sadness.

Joe was one of those patients for whom I initially had very little hope; he turned out to be a case that reinforced my belief in the inherent goodness in people. He was 25 minutes late for his first counseling session. He insisted that his lateness was due to a business appointment and wondered why I was so concerned with time. He believed that his only problem was his business. Joe said, "If I could only get out from under the financial pressure, everything would be back to normal." He agreed to come back for counseling to help with stress management although he felt that his daughter needed assistance, not him.

Gradually, I was able to establish a therapeutic bond with Joe. Once I got to know him, I soon realized that he had the heart of a puppy dog and he had suffered significant disappointments and trauma in his life.

Joe's alcoholic father, who was well read and extremely bright, owned his own business. His dad spent most of his time drinking at the office and the local bar while discussing many topics with his customers and friends; he was well versed in politics, philosophy, religion, physics, even psychology. Although he was a friendly and entertaining drunk with his friends, he was emotionally unpredictable at home. At times, Joe's dad was maudlin about his childhood and his father's death when he was 8. At other times, he raged around the house, screaming resentments for his need to work so hard to support his wife and children. Once Joe was so angry with his father that he took a baseball bat and was going to smash him in the face.

Sometimes Joe felt sorry for his father and put him to bed after a drinking binge; when things got to be overwhelming, Joe just ran out of the house. On those evenings, Joe frequently went down to the school and threw rocks at the classroom windows. This and similar aggressive behavior kept him in trouble throughout his childhood. Joe was extremely bright and, despite his aggressive behavior, pulled good grades in high school. Because he spent more time drinking than studying in college, in 1968 his military deferment was revoked.

In the service, Joe was put through training for military intelligence and could have avoided Vietnam if his alcoholism and aggressive anger hadn't gotten him into trouble with his top sergeant. In Vietnam, Joe's major job was to fly to battle zones after conflicts and get a body count for Vietnamese and American soldiers.

Joe felt sadness for the Vietnamese children; he described them stealing, cheating, and manipulating the GIs to survive. It reminded him of his own childhood anger and aggressive behavior. In counseling sessions, Joe initially denied the emotional trauma of his experiences in Vietnam. He insisted that he had had it good, compared with others.

(continued on next page)

Case Study 7.1 (continued)

The ACA and Post traumatic Stress Disorder

Joe

Joe suffered from this traumatic exposure as well as from survivor's guilt. He experienced all the traditional signs of post traumatic stress: sleep disorders and nightmares, night sweats, inability to concentrate, hypertension, disorientation, and explosive temper. All of these symptoms were complicated by his alcoholism.

After a year and a half of individual counseling, followed by group counseling with other ACA, Joe was able to maintain sobriety, grieve the loss of his father, and grieve his experiences in Vietnam. After some time in counseling, Joe and some other group members visited the Vietnam War Memorial in Washington, D.C. This was an important event in his painful journey to recovery.

Discussion Questions

1. Do you think people are inherently motivated to change negative and unhealthy behaviors?
2. Do you believe people can work only on themselves?
3. What role does getting angry play in relationships?
4. What are some healthy ways of expressing anger?

---

g. Confusion instead of having feelings
h. A lump in the throat instead of allowing feelings to emerge, or pressure and tightness in the jaw, shoulders, or other parts of the body
i. Feelings that emotions will be overwhelming if one gets in touch with them

3. Hypervigilance, as evidenced by

a. Inability to relax
b. Frequent startle responses
c. Chronic anxiety
d. Panic attacks

4. Survivor guilt, as evidenced by

a. Chronic depression
b. A sourceless sense of guilt

5. Intensification of symptoms by exposure to events that resemble the original trauma

In order to constitute post traumatic stress disorder, the trauma must be significant. Severe emotional or physical abuse and/or sexual violation can be so traumatizing to the child that symptoms of PTSD might occur. Unfortunately, the diagnosis of PTSD has frequently been used too loosely, without evidence of significant trauma. Just growing up in an alcoholic family does not mean one suffers from PTSD. Cermak is using PTSD as a model to understand the symptoms of ACA, not as a generalized label.

✎ Childhood in an Alcoholic Home

Children growing up in an alcoholic family often suffer from both trauma and stress during childhood and beyond.

© Stockbyte/Getty Images

Children in alcoholic families learn to distrust their own observations (what they see and hear) and feelings (what they sense), and they feel powerless to change the family system. They cannot speak out and cannot trust their feelings because the rules in an alcoholic family system are don't talk, don't feel, and don't trust. Because these children distrust their own observations and feelings, they must wonder or guess at what is normal. At a time when most functional families are providing structure, discipline, and natural consequences for their children's behavior, alcoholic families provide control, rigidity, fear, irresponsibility, immaturity, and, most important, *unpredictability*. Children in alcoholic families try to control the behavior of the alcoholic parent and the codependent spouse by becoming super-responsible and trying to do everything correctly to obtain the parent's approval. They soon find out that, despite their best efforts to be perfect, the parent always finds fault with something. While desperately trying to predict or control the behavior of their parents, children do not realize that alcoholism and drug addiction is a disease that results in unpredictable behavior.

✎ Identification of Children of Alcoholic Families

Robert Ackerman (1978) described various behavioral characteristics of children of alcoholics, including the following:

- Being superachievers or perfectionists or exhibiting efforts that go far beyond the reasonable criteria of every task
- Exhibiting an inordinate need to control their environment and therefore becoming anxious with the slightest threat to their security (e.g., a teacher's comment on homework or an unusually low grade may provoke emotional upset)
- Displaying social disengagement from or excessive attention to the peer group (as an isolated loner or a class clown)
- Exhibiting signs of physical neglect (untidiness, soiled clothing, poor hygiene) and/or physical abuse (bruises, cuts, etc.)
- Being unable to concentrate and sometimes showing marked variations in academic performance, especially when parents are in a binge pattern of alcohol use or in codependent conflict

⚹ Denial of Feelings in an Alcoholic Family

The alcoholic family swears an allegiance to the family secret of alcoholism. Family members dedicate themselves to denying that Dad and/or Mom is out of control. The children hope that perhaps their family secret will change and continually explore ways to make it change.

Sometimes this becomes an almost magical quest by the children to find that special way of being or ritualistic behavior that can make Dad and/or Mom change. Children give up their own sense of self in their search for the key that will change their parents' dysfunctional behavior.

A friend tells this story illustrating how children's feelings are discounted: When the alcoholic dad falls down, drunk, and spends the night on the front lawn, still in his work clothes, does the child really believe Mom's explanation? "You know your dad loves astronomy; he came home late last night, lay down to gaze at the stars, and, since he was tired from working late, just fell asleep, gazing at the constellations."

Children must maintain the *illusion of normalcy,* the illusion that their families are normal. The child defensively maintains the belief that this is what other families go through.

Howard Clinebell (1985) reported that the following factors produce damage in the lives of children of alcoholics:

1. *Role reversal:* Children may undertake parental duties because the parent is unable to be responsible or because the parent forces responsibilities on the children. The alcoholic may be treated as a child and, in return, act helpless. In incestuous families, the daughter and mother often switch roles.
2. *Unpredictability:* An inconsistent and unpredictable relationship with the alcoholic emotionally deprives the children.
3. *Unavailability:* The nonalcoholic, inadequate parent is struggling with major problems; because this parent's own needs are unmet, he or she is unable to attend to the needs of the children.
4. *Social isolation:* The damaging factor is the social isolation of the family, as protection from further pain and suffering, due to embarrassment.

Even periods of parental sobriety have negative effects on the children in alcoholic families. This is due primarily to the inconsistency and shattered hope that this time it will be different. The alcoholic father "inspires the natural love of his offspring, who build there from an ideal father image of omnipotence and loving kindness. This disillusionment of the drunken episode is shattering to the frail superego structure of the child who is subjected to alternating experiences of exalted hopes and blighting disappointments" (Newell 1950).

⚹ Perspective of the Child in an Alcoholic Family

M. Cork (1969) interviewed 115 children living in alcoholic families in an attempt to understand the child's perspective. Cork found that the children react to the alcoholic family system in a number of common ways. The interviewed children in alcoholic families

1. would not go to a friend's house because they would not dare reciprocate and invite friends to their homes due to the unpredictability and embarrassing behaviors of their parents.
2. were angry at everybody.
3. were preoccupied at school with worry about what would happen when they returned home.
4. envied their friends who seemed to have fun with their families.
5. felt alone when they were only children.
6. felt neglected when both parents were drinking.
7. felt they had to be parentlike, especially if the mother was drinking.
8. worried about each parent's loneliness if the parents were separated; wished for their parents to reunite, even if their home was calmer during the separation; seemed to feel an even deeper loss if the alcoholic parent moved out of the house.
9. were unable to separate and individuate from their parents as adolescents; it was difficult to break away from somebody with whom they had no ties; one child poignantly said, "I want to be somebody, but I feel like nobody."
10. excused the alcoholic's behavior and often condemned the nonalcoholics for being hostile and angry; children could deduce from this that love and caring would come from alcoholics; research, unfortunately, indicates that many ACA do marry alcoholics to try out their hypothesis.
11. experienced multiple separations and reunions of their parents and learned not to expect any state to continue consistently.
12. continued to have problems, even when the alcoholic stopped drinking.

✺ Family Disease Model

Just as alcoholism is classified as a disease (i.e., it has a known etiology, progressive nature, and known outcome), the alcoholic family is often described in the context of a "family disease." The family members are described as suffering from alcoholism, codependency, and enabling behavior, perpetuating both the alcoholism- and alcohol-related problems. The family is organized around the alcoholic's drinking and the consequences of that drinking. The central organizing principle of the family is focused around the alcoholic's behavior (e.g., Is she drinking? Will she drink? How much will she drink? When and with whom will she drink? Will she get drunk?). The family responds to the alcoholic in a codependent (giving up of self) fashion or enables both alcoholic behavior and drinking. The family disease model describes the family as trying to maintain homeostasis, compensating for the disequilibrium of the alcoholic's behavior and drinking. This results in family members' disconnecting from their own feelings, distorting their perceptions, and invoking the "no-talk, no-feel, no-trust" rule.

❈ Alcoholism/Drug Addiction—Impact on Marriage

Marriages are at risk when there is a substance-abuse problem. Feelings of betrayal, continuous conflict, chaos, loss, resentments, and pain are constant parts of the marital cycle when one partner is alcoholic/drug-addicted. Ironically, some studies indicate that if spouses drink together and with approximately equal patterns and amounts of use, it may not initially create a problem. However, problems will arise when one partner goes out to drink with friends, or a partner cuts back his or her drinking, enters into treatment, or voluntarily seeks sobriety.

Sexual problems related to substance abuse are very common, confounded by problems of intimacy. John Gottman, author of *Why Marriages Fail* (1995), describes the four horsemen of the apocalypse of marriages—criticism, contempt (nonverbal), defensiveness, and withdrawal. The codependent dance of couples where there is an alcohol or drug problem frequently involves an "in the marriage," "out of the marriage," and "on the fence" attitude toward the marriage and each other. Frequently, all four horsemen are present. There is also a strong ambivalence that the wife of an alcoholic has toward her husband. There is a vacillation between being supportive and understanding and feeling hopeless and withdrawn.

Certainly, recovery not only involves treatment for alcoholics/addicts or problem users but also involves treatment for the spouse.

> Behavioral marital therapy focuses on teaching partners how to communicate with each other, solve problems together and resolve their conflicts. Husbands and wives look directly for ways to break the cycle of criticism, denial and blame that characterizes a chemically dependent family and develop new roles and new ways of interacting that will support recovery. ("After Drug Treatment" 1999)

❈ ACA in Relationships
ACA Define Self Through Others

ACA define their sense of identity by the impressions others have of them. ACA have a strong, often imbalanced need for affirmation from others that they are indeed worthwhile. They approach their world from the outside in versus the inside-out stance of self-confident people.

Even though many of my ACA patients have been extremely successful in their professional lives, they still feel inadequate and don't trust their talents, skills, and accomplishments. Many feel that they are charlatans and will be exposed as inadequate persons. They fear that at any time their professional abilities may all be taken away from them. Then they will relive their ultimate fear of being all alone, helpless, abandoned, and rejected; the fears they felt growing up will be played out again. Successful careers and stylish and attractive lifestyles camouflage their poor sense of self, and they are surprised when others don't see through their disguises.

The Disengaged ACA

Growing up in alcoholic families with parents who are unavailable, children often develop patterns of interpersonal disengagement. ACA may maintain this pattern of disengagement in most interpersonal relationships. Cermak (1984) describes disengaged ACA as having the following behaviors:

1. Hard-driving, workaholic; always preoccupied by projects and things that have to be done; rarely satisfied with accomplishments; in denial of feelings, relationships take a back seat
2. Defensive, fearful of closeness to others; plays cards close to the vest; unable to deal honestly on an emotional level; longing for relationships; chronic anger
3. Overwhelmed by feelings, buffeted by emotional storms; desperately trying to get other people to behave properly; often unable to work effectively.

Disengaged ACAs exhibit behaviors that on the surface make them seem self-sufficient and self-actualized; in actuality, they are depressed and suffering from deep emotional pain.

Atypical Depression

Another diagnostic category recently associated with ACA and others who grew up in imbalanced family systems is atypical depression. Atypical depression is an impairment in interpersonal and social skills due to an extreme sensitivity to rejection. Because these individuals are highly sensitive, they overreact, thinking others' remarks, opinions, and/or actions are personal attacks. Many individuals suffering from atypical depression report that this sensitivity began in early childhood and have histories of physical, emotional, and/or sexual violation.

Codependency

Timmen Cermak quotes a metaphor from Charles Alexander: that codependency is "like being a lifeguard on a crowded beach, knowing that you cannot swim, and not telling anyone for fear of a panic." This is the sense of desperation that ACA feel as they guess at what is normal.

Cermak, himself an adult child of an alcoholic, defined codependency in diagnostic terms in the hope that codependency would be recognized as a psychiatric disorder. The following are diagnostic criteria for codependent personality disorder:

1. Continual investment of self-esteem in the ability to influence or control feelings and behaviors in the self and others in the face of obvious adverse consequences
2. Assumption of responsibility for meeting others' needs to the exclusion of acknowledging one's own needs
3. Anxiety and boundary distortions in situations of intimacy and separation
4. Enmeshment in relationships with personality-disordered, drug-dependent, and impulse-disordered individuals

5. Maintenance of a primary relationship with an active substance abuser for at least 2 years without seeking outside support and/or exhibiting three or more of the following characteristics:

    a. Constriction of emotions with or without dramatic outbursts
    b. Depression
    c. Hypervigilance
    d. Compulsions
    e. Anxiety
    f. Excessive reliance on denial
    g. Substance abuse
    h. Recurrent physical or sexual abuse
    i. Stress-related medical illnesses

An individual who has all five criteria of codependency would be diagnosed as having codependent personality disorder. A personality disorder affects all aspects of one's life because pervasive personality traits become inflexible and maladaptive. The results are significant subjective distress and social and occupational impairment. Treatment for codependent personality disorder often involves extensive education, counseling, therapeutic interventions, and sometimes medication to deal with major anxiety and depression.

If you find yourself identifying with some of the diagnostic criteria for codependent personality disorder but not all of them, you might have some codependent traits but not a full-blown disorder. If these codependent traits result in significant difficulties in establishing effective, caring, and intimate relationships, they probably need to be investigated.

Boundary Inadequacy

Boundary inadequacy is the inability to set consistent and appropriate boundaries. The result is vascillating or ambiguous boundaries, overly rigid boundaries, and invasive boundaries. As a result, ACA have difficulty in relationships; often they choose an alcoholic, addict, or a generally dysfunctional partner, or develop codependent relationships. If one were to ask persons with strong codependent traits and difficulties in setting appropriate boundaries to choose persons they were interested in from 100 people—90 of whom are fairly functional and stable—their choices would probably come from the 10 dysfunctional people.

For ACA, boundaries are often distorted in interpersonal relationships; sometimes they are excessively involved (overattachment) or excessively detached (overseparation).

Overattachment and Overseparation

In their work on chemical dependency and intimacy dysfunction, Eli Coleman and Philip Colgan (1987) focused on overattachment and overseparation in men who grew up in alcoholic families. They identified thoughts, feelings, and behaviors common to both the overseparated and the overattached individuals. Table 7.1 lists these thoughts, feelings, and behaviors.

The thoughts of the overattached and overseparated sound like common lyrics to country-western songs. These codependent lyrics include "You should be grateful," "I want so little," "You don't care," "What am I doing wrong?" and "I'm nobody without you." Many people identify strongly with either the overseparated or the overattached column in Table 7.1; others cross over, having both overattached and overseparated characteristics. Overseparated individuals tend to develop relationships with overattached individuals and vice versa. Frequently, ACA duplicate the kind of relationship their codependent parents had. Just as the disease of alcoholism and drug addiction progresses from generation to generation, so do the patterns of inadequate boundary setting and codependent relationships.

TABLE 7.1

Overseparation and Overattachment

Overseparation	*Overattachment*
Thoughts	
You're not good enough.	I'm not good enough.
They want so much.	I want so little.
They give so little.	I give so much.
I'm ambivalent.	You don't care.
If only they would . . .	What am I doing wrong?
I am a rock.	I'm nobody without you.
You should be grateful.	I'm so unappreciated.
Feelings	
Fear, smothering	Fear, abandonment
Self-controlled	Out of control
Indifferent	Needy, burdened
Unsafe with others	Unsafe alone
Trapped	Shut out
Numb	Desperate
Behaviors	
Is self-protective	Is self-sacrificing
Controls others	Pleases others
Acts to guard feelings	Acts contrary to feelings
Denies	Explains
Is compulsively independent	Is compulsively dependent

SOURCE: Eli Coleman and Philip Colgan, "Chemical dependency and intimacy dysfunction" in *Journal of Chemical Dependency*, Vol. 1 (1), 1987. New York: Haworth Press.

Codependent Dances

The most traditional codependent dance is between alcoholics/addicts and their codependent partners. Alcoholics/addicts and their partners are both codependent; alcoholics/addicts need partners who enable them to continue to use drugs/alcohol and not suffer the full impact of their addiction. Their partners need alcoholics/addicts to avoid their own fears of abandonment and depression. Both of them fear feelings of loneliness, isolation, anxiety, and depression.

The fear of abandonment and rejection is so strong for ACA that they choose not to develop an individual sense of self. This neglect of oneself while preoccupied or obsessed with changing the partner is codependency. The codependent dances these couples perform have some common features: (1) shame-based styles of communicating and interacting; (2) a denial by at least one partner of dysfunctional and/or codependent behavior; (3) a relationship of bargaining, not an intimate partnership; and (4) shame-based litany of the past. Each partner holds on to unresolved conflicts and continues to use them to shame the other.

⊗ Recovery for Adult Children of Alcoholics

An ACA's prognosis for treatment is directly related to the severity of the parental alcoholism and the levels of abuse, violation, and trauma experienced while growing up in the alcoholic/addict family system. The onset of the alcoholism is also a factor in the ACA's recovery. The earlier the alcoholism in the family, and the younger the child when exposed to direct or indirect consequences of the parents' alcoholism, the more extensive the damage, and therefore the deeper the wounds. Impact at early ages can have dramatic developmental consequences (Brown 1988).

Inherited Family Belief Systems

A major recovery issue at the heart of all ACAs' problems is their core belief system. The "process of recovery involves challenging the deepest core beliefs about others and the self that were constructed to preserve core attachments" (Brown 1988). As discussed earlier in this chapter, these core beliefs serve to deny the ACAs' feelings and maintain the illusion of their parents' normalcy. ACA avoid exploring these holes in their belief systems for fear that their swiss cheese system might fall apart. When ACA can acknowledge how the belief systems acquired from their parents have prevented them from attaining what they want, recovery can begin.

In *Struggle for Intimacy,* Janet Geringer Woititz (1985) devotes an entire chapter to some of the misconceptions, or inappropriate beliefs, that ACA have when it comes to establishing intimate relationships.

Overview of ACA Recovery

Once ACA are aware that their belief systems are not serving them and are preventing, blocking, or sabotaging the development of effective relationships, the next step is to develop a more reality-based belief system.

The first step in developing this reality-based belief system is to recognize the dysfunction and trauma of the past and unlock the feelings denied by this dysfunctional belief system.

A trusting therapeutic alliance with a counselor/therapist allows ACA to feel the loss, grief, and trauma of the past. This difficult process involves (1) giving up the old defense mechanisms and dysfunctional beliefs, (2) feeling, and (3) choosing to honor and integrate those feelings in a new more functional belief system.

Eventually ACA loosen their defensive controls and develop the ability to respond to different situations and circumstances with flexibility. ACA can now establish effective boundaries in relationships, stop engaging in dysfunctional behavior and relationships, and establish a core belief system that allows for effective choicemaking and change.

Powerlessness in the Alcoholic Family System

Just as alcoholics/addicts must first admit they are powerless over drugs/alcohol, so must ACA admit that as children they were powerless to change the alcoholic family system. They were innocent children whose feelings were ignored while living in unhealthy imbalanced situations. Recognizing that as children they were not responsible for their parents' disease of alcoholism frees ACA to honor their own feelings.

Feeling Awareness

For ACA who have spent a major portion of their lives denying feelings, the most difficult task of recovery is recognizing and integrating feelings in making decisions, resolving conflicts, and developing interpersonal relationships.

Jerry, a patient of mine who is a recovering alcoholic and an ACA, quizzically and candidly commented, "Feelings, I am not quite sure what you mean when you ask 'What do you feel?' I don't know what you mean or want from me. When you ask me if I feel sad, or I sound angry, I don't recognize that I am experiencing those feelings until you mention it."

Many ACA have similar reactions. Unaware of what they feel, they are equally inexperienced in recognizing what others feel. This makes it difficult to effectively communicate with others—especially family members—and to establish sensitive, caring, and intimate relationships.

Identifying Feelings for ACA

Jael Greenleaf, an ACA counselor in Los Angeles, describes ACA as having an emotional learning disability. (See Case Studies 7.2 and 7.3.) ACA have learned not to trust their feelings; thus they make decisions based on what they think is appropriate, without integrating what they feel. Feelings are what make us, or define us as, human. The famous television series *Star Trek* gave us Mr. Spock, the cognitive logical unemotional alien, and in the later version of the series, Data, a robot with extensive computer capabilities. Data was often fascinated by and marveled at human feelings and emotions and tried to understand them. Mr. Spock does not understand human emotions that may override the logic of a decision. The captains

Case Study 7.2
Rejection Sensitivity
Frank

A colleague, old friend, and workshop training partner of mine tells a story of his fear of rejection. Growing up in an imbalanced, alcoholic family system, Frank learned how to defend against shame by being likable and by avoiding conflict. He figured that if everyone liked him and he avoided conflict, he would not be subject to rejection, attack, or shame. Unfortunately, his likable quality put him in a real dilemma back in the third grade.

As Frank tells the story, his classmates really liked him and nominated him for third-grade class president. Normally, he would be just likable enough, but not too popular, because that would bring the unwanted attention he feared. That year, there were no outstanding choices for class president, and his likable, nonaggressive style became the qualities that the class wanted in its president. His classmates reacted to the nomination with genuine acceptance and encouragement. Frank felt this put him in a lose-lose position. Frank thought that if he ran and lost, he would experience tremendous feelings of rejection and shame. If he ran and won, he would disappoint his classmates by being an inadequate class president, unable to meet the responsibilities of the office. Ultimately, this would lead to the same feelings of rejection and shame. Either way, Frank felt he would be rejected and shamed. His only choice was to reject the nomination for office. He did this rather adroitly by taking the nomination as an opportunity to lend his support to another, more popular classmate. "Thanks for the nomination," he said, "but my support goes to Larry. He would make a far more capable class president than me, and he was the one I had intended to nominate." Unfortunately, Frank missed out on the opportunity to grow from experiencing what it is like to run for office and perhaps the opportunity to be class president.

Discussion Questions

1. How do you deal with conflict?
2. Are you a conflict-avoider or do you like conflict? Where are you on the continuum of avoidance or attraction to dealing with conflict?
3. What behaviors do you employ to avoid rejection?

of the *Enterprise* remind Spock and Data that human emotions are essential and part of the human equation in approaching life.

By being sensitive to what we feel, we can begin to understand our feelings (affective self) and integrate them with what we know (cognitive self). When our affective self is congruent with our cognitive self, the application (whatever action we take) is often more successful. Decisions become easier to make when feelings are balanced with the cognitive side, and there is an interplay of these two sides of our self. Our decisions become more fulfilling, our goals more attainable, and our relationships more effective, when we integrate our feelings. The struggle for the ACA begins with identifying, understanding, and integrating feelings.

Case Study 7.3
Difficulty in Making Decisions
Norman

Norman, 29, is an adult child of an alcoholic. He grew up in an extremely abusive and physically violating dysfunctional family system. During one alcoholic rage, Norman's dad shoved his mom's head through the front window of their living room. Another time, his mom hid his dad's car keys in the garbage because his dad was drunk. They both struggled with the garbage, and she severely cut her hand on the jagged edge of a coffee can. Later, two tall police officers came to quiet them down during another domestic dispute. These were just a few of Norman's memories.

His parents' fighting had a far-reaching impact on Norman and the other children in the family. The fear of abandonment, shame, and rejection caused Norman to act out during his childhood in many destructive ways. He did not achieve at school, despite being very bright and capable.

One day in individual counseling, Norman talked about a trip he took to Reno, Nevada. This trip was a metaphor for his fear of making a career change. After watching for some time at the roulette table with his wife and a friend, he decided to place his bet. Norman placed a two-dollar bet on the red and a two-dollar bet on the black. He surmised that this was a secure bet. He smiled to himself smugly as the roulette wheel spun and the ball bounded around from number to number. When it landed on a red number, the croupier just pushed his two dollars from the black spot to the red spot, and Norman collected his bet. Despite the odd looks from the croupier, and his friend's efforts to explain why this was a stupid bet, Norman continued to play two dollars on black and two dollars on red simultaneously. After several spins, he stopped betting. He felt entertained and justified that he had played roulette. I didn't hesitate to point out to Norman that the numbers zero and double zero on the roulette wheel are green. If either of those numbers had come up, he would have lost both bets.

This was analogous to what Norman was doing in his conflict about his career. He was betting on his current job for security, but not actively putting himself on the line to find a more fulfilling job. The longer he waited to take action, the more time he was wasting, and the more likely it was that zero or double zero would come up, in the form of either losing his current job due to his dissatisfaction projected to the work setting or not being able to motivate himself to find a better job because he was suffering from feelings of rejection, shame, and abandonment.

Even with this therapeutic insight, Norman waited several months to take any direct action. After a great deal of work, he eventually landed a new job in the field that he really wanted. That job didn't work out but it led to another job. After 2 years of struggle, Norman found himself in a career position that was consistent with his feelings of entitlement and accomplishment; his job affirmed his skills and capabilities.

Discussion Questions

1. What role does ambivalence play in your life?
2. What "passions" are you acting on?
3. What "passions" are you not acting on? Why?
4. What decisions are you avoiding making, and how are you procrastinating in taking action?

A good technique to help ACA access their feelings is journaling, or writing a feeling diary. Often a counselor asks the ACA to buy a special notebook and keep it nearby—in the car, at work, and at home. Whenever the ACA is aware of an emotional reaction, thought, or feeling, he or she writes about it in the journal. By writing rather than thinking, ACA soon find that they are accessing feelings that they may not have been aware of previously.

Another method of feeling awareness involves ACA verbalizing and communicating what they feel directly to others. One method would be using the statement:

"I feel _____, when I_____." For example:

"I feel upset when I notice you haven't taken the garbage out, after you said you would."

"I feel confused, and both sad and angry, when I don't get a present for Valentine's Day."

"Right now, I am not feeling close and caring toward you. I do not want to have sex. I am still feeling hurt by the fight we had earlier today. I would prefer talking about it tomorrow when our emotions are not running so deep."

Therapists help ACA identify and explore a wide variety of feelings (shame, rejection, abandonment, loss, loneliness, isolation, and grief) that were experienced growing up in an alcoholic family system. ACA therapists use various treatment methods to access feelings, including guided imagery, gestalt exercises, art therapy, role plays, workbooks, and books and articles on ACA issues (bibliotherapy).

Grief Work

Children who grow up in alcoholic families experience loss, violation, and trauma growing up in imbalanced alcoholic family systems. Many never have an opportunity to mourn what they have lost or missed out on. Mourning is a process of allowing feelings of loss to come to the surface, to be felt, and to be grieved. (See Case Study 7.4.)

An analogy is the improper healing of a cut. In the child's case, an emotionally damaging cut or violation of self has occurred. The cut has healed over but was not cleaned out first; the dirt (leftover unresolved issues and feelings) was not removed. The result is a numbing pain, which is tolerated and denied for years and is thought to be quite normal. Grief work involves going back and cleaning out this wound by gently and sensitively removing the dirt. By avoiding the feelings and pain accompanying proper healing of this infected wound, individuals are unable to function to a fuller potential. Once their wounds are cleaned, true healing allows ACA to make more effective choices.

Grief work requires the help of a professional therapist trained and experienced in ACA recovery. The counselor/therapist must be sensitive to the patient's ego strength, general level of functioning, underlying psychiatric issues, and support system. Attempting to do ACA grief work without an experienced professional may cause unnecessary emotional harm by going too deep, too quickly into traumatic issues of the past. A professional trained and experienced in ACA recovery recognizes the pace and depth of the work to be done and shows appropriate judgment in helping patients through this work.

Case Study 7.4

Letter to Parents from a Recovering Alcoholic and ACA about the Parents' Alcoholism

Dear Mom and Dad,

It's hard to write a letter like this, so I guess I'll just get right to the point. I'm writing because I'm concerned that you both continue to drink a lot despite the fact that you have both been in ill health recently. And I'm sure that you, Dad, have been warned more than once by doctors that to continue to drink threatens your health.

I've wanted to talk to you both about your drinking for years, but so far I have never been able to break the silence and tell you how truly worried I am about it.

Only you can make a decision to stop drinking. But I feel very strongly that I must tell you both, with love and compassion, how concerned I am, and how much it hurts me to see you continue to damage yourselves through drinking.

I am sure that in your hearts you know that you have a problem, for I have seen you both struggle with it; seen your efforts to control what and when you drink; seen your efforts to cut back. I know I rejoiced during that period when you sobered up entirely for a few months, and you found renewed health and happiness together.

I am also sure you are both aware that the stakes are high; that you are endangering your health as you mix alcohol and various prescription medication, and that drinking can only worsen your struggles with heart disease, diabetes, and the effects of aging.

You know what you have to do. It's so simple, and yet I know from experience how hard it can be. You both so desperately need to stop drinking now, throw out all the booze in the house (even the supply reserved for guests), and get some help staying sober, for you have proven by slipping back into drinking that you cannot do it by yourselves.

I suspect getting help will be the hardest part; it certainly was for me. But it's really the most necessary part of getting better and infinitely better than struggling alone.

Getting help could mean any of the following: Telling Dr. Green that you know you have a problem with alcohol and are tired of struggling with it; that you want to get some counseling or get into a treatment program. Calling AA and attending a meeting together; the nearest AA meeting is right down the street on Maple Rd. Calling the local drug/alcohol helpline and getting a referral to a counselor, social worker, or therapist experienced in working with alcoholics who want to recover.

This letter is not meant to blame or shame or accuse you; it is merely a plea for you to help yourselves for your own sakes, and for the sake of our family. It is an effort to tell the truth about the problem that our whole family has struggled with for so many years.

The truth hurts sometimes. The truth is that all of us have begun to insulate ourselves from your drinking, to control the time and length of our visits, and to arrange sober holidays in our own homes, as my sister did this Christmas. We have all shied away from confronting you because it is so painful to see you both caught in this awful disease.

I hope that this letter has not made you angry or resentful. If it has, so be it; but I want you to know that I love you both, and that I want to help you, if there is any way in the world that I can. If you want to talk about this letter, please call me; if not, if it makes you too upset or uncomfortable, we need never discuss it.

(continued on next page)

Case Study 7.4 (*continued*)

Letter to Parents from a Recovering Alcoholic and ACA about the Parents' Alcoholism

Ultimately, there may be an element of selfishness in this letter; because, in the end, I want to be able to look into my heart and say "I tried to help. I told them the truth and encouraged them to get help and save their own lives." For me, it's an important step in dealing with my past and working on my own sobriety.

Please, for your own sake and the sake of us all, share this letter with each other, and talk about it openly together. I pray that you both will find the strength to quit drinking and get some help together.

Your loving son,

Epilogue

The parents who were sent this letter both got sober. Unfortunately, the mother died shortly thereafter. The son spent some quality time with her during the months before she passed away. The father has been in recovery for a number of years now and has remarried. Father and son have quality time together when they visit.

Discussion Questions

1. Would you write a letter like this to one of your parents about a family issue?
2. Would you send a letter like this?
3. What are the "real" healing elements of this exercise?
4. Suggestion: Write a letter and then identify what the depth and breadth of the problem is.

Group Psychotherapy

Group psychotherapy is the next step once ACA have worked through some of the previously described core issues. Group psychotherapy is a dynamic process in which each group member gets feedback from other group members. Members share their perceptions, feelings, and insights into each other's behavior.

Irvin D. Yalom (1975) describes the following eleven curative factors that make group psychotherapy such an effective process. (See Case Study 7.5.)

1. *Instilling hope.* ACA group members see firsthand the growth of other group members. Continued contact with other group members who have improved while doing their work in the group gives ACA hope for their own recovery and confidence in the group process.
2. *Sharing universality.* ACA realize that they are not alone and that others share common problems. Group therapy reveals that ACA characteristics are universal to those who grew up in alcoholic/addict family systems, as well as imbalanced family systems. ACA no longer suffer in social or interpersonal isolation. There is the opportunity for affirmation by other group members, who understand them and identify with the issues they have in common.

Case Study 7.5

Interpersonal Relationships

Naomi

Naomi was a very attractive, young, and active director of marketing for a major retail clothing manufacturer. She grew up in an alcoholic family and compensated by being extremely successful in all endeavors. She described her mom's sense of self as being directly related to all of Naomi's accomplishments. Unfortunately, Naomi approached interpersonal relationships outside of the family in the same manner and tended to attract friends who mirrored her accomplishments back to her. In group therapy, Naomi began to use this same interpersonal dynamic of trying to control others so they reflected a positive mirror image of her success back to her. Initially, she was worried that the group would ask her to leave when they began to see her self-centeredness. Instead the group was able to make her aware of her imbalanced need for affirmation. The group gave her permission to explore her issues and be herself, while not having to look good all the time. In fact, they enjoyed the Naomi who wasn't always on and saw this aspect of her personality as more relaxed, fun loving, vulnerable, available, present, and worth getting to know.

Discussion Questions

1. In what ways do you take control in your relationships?
2. In what areas do you need to "let go of control"?
3. Would you rather be right or be happy?

3. *Imparting information.* Group therapy provides information, education, and training on ACA issues, including family systems, alcoholism/addiction, codependency, and boundary setting in relationships. Both the therapist and other group members offer suggestions, advice, and direct guidance about life problems.
4. *Fostering altruism.* Altruism is the act of giving to others and caring about others' life situations. The group is a place for support, reassurance, encouragement, insight, and sharing, all of which help both the giver and the receiver to grow.
5. *Recapitulating the primary family group.* Recapitulation offers an opportunity for the group to act as a functional family with positive corrective capabilities. Early familial conflicts can be acted out. With the help of the group, ACA can resolve these conflicts in a functional manner, rather than the previously dysfunctional and rigid manner of the family of origin.
6. *Developing socializing techniques.* Socializing is an obvious curative factor of group therapy. ACA can explore maladaptive social behavior through honest and caring feedback from group members. Alternative social choices and techniques can be developed with the feedback of the group. ACA are particularly vulnerable to choosing dysfunctional relationships and maintaining

codependent interactions in relationships. The group can alert ACA who try to return to codependent ways of interaction and dysfunctional choice making.

7. *Imitating behavior.* By seeing the reactions and behaviors of others, ACA have numerous new models of behavior.

8. *Sharing interpersonal learning.* The group is a social microcosm of the real world. ACA tend to duplicate the way they approach the real interpersonal world in their therapy group. Insights into adult children's interpersonal behavior and corrective emotional strategies can be explored in the safe environment of the group setting.

9. *Developing group cohesiveness.* The bonding that occurs in therapy groups results in a cohesive understanding, which makes the group a safe place to go with stressful problems, interpersonal conflicts, difficult decisions, and other issues. The group develops a functional interpersonal cohesiveness, allowing members to pull for and struggle with the difficult issues in their lives.

10. *Sharing catharsis.* The group is a place where ACA feel safe in expressing feelings not safely expressed in other settings. Fears, insecurities, destructive thoughts, suicidal ideation, rage, shame, and other emotions are safe to express in the group.

11. *Exploring existential factors.* The group helps its members explore meaning in their lives. Issues of attachment in relationships, congruency in work efforts, and spirituality are all safe for each group member to explore and develop. In other words, the functional therapy group explores the human condition.

In summary, group therapy is a dynamic process that has a tremendous potential for ACA recovery, especially after ACA have spent time exploring their issues in individual counseling.

✖ In Review

- In 1983, the NACOA developed some basic facts about children of alcoholics in its charter statement:
    - An estimated 28 million Americans have at least one alcoholic parent.
    - More than half of all alcoholics have an alcoholic parent.
    - Children of alcoholics are at the highest risk of developing alcoholism themselves or marrying someone who is alcoholic.
    - In up to 90 percent of child abuse cases, alcohol is a significant factor.
    - Children of alcoholics are frequently victims of incest, child neglect, and other forms of violence and exploitation.
- Alcoholism affects the children of alcoholics, not just the alcoholic and spouse. Adults who were children in alcoholic family systems (adult children of alcoholics) are vulnerable to having feelings and behaviors that are characteristic of post traumatic stress disorder.
- Children of alcoholics tend to distrust their own feelings and to deny reality.
- Following are some of the behavioral characteristics of ACA:
    - Fear of losing control
    - All-or-none, black-or-white thinking

- Fear of experiencing feelings
- Overdeveloped sense of responsibility or irresponsibility
- Difficulty with intimacy and with asking for what is wanted or needed
- Flashbacks of childhood but many memory gaps
- Feelings of being little, or like a child, when under stress
- Unreasonable loyalty
- Addiction to excitement
- Difficulty relaxing
- Feelings of guilt, abandonment, and/or depression
- Tendency to confuse love with self-pity
- Backlog of shock and grief
- Compulsive behaviors
- Living in a world of denial
- Guessing at what is normal
- Tendency toward physical symptoms (e.g., headaches, gastrointestinal problems)

- Howard Clinebell (1985) reported that the following factors produce damage in the lives of children of alcoholics:

  - *Role reversal:* Children may undertake parental duties because the parent is unable to be responsible or because the parent forces responsibilities on the children. The alcoholic may be treated as a child and, in return, act helpless. In incestuous families, the daughter and mother often switch roles.
  - *Unpredictability:* An inconsistent and unpredictable relationship with the alcoholic emotionally deprives the children.
  - *Unavailability:* The nonalcoholic, inadequate parent is struggling with major problems; because this parent's own needs are unmet, he or she is unable to attend to the needs of the children.
  - *Social isolation:* The damaging factor is the social isolation of the family, as protection from further pain and suffering, due to embarrassment.

- Codependency is defined in this chapter as continual investment of self-esteem in the ability to influence or control feelings and behaviors in the self and others in the face of obvious adverse consequences.
- Alcoholism is a family disease, where the family is centrally organized around the alcoholic's behavior and/or drinking. Codependency and enabling behavior, plus denial, end up perpetuating both the alcoholism and the alcohol-related problems. The marriage is also at risk, with sexual and intimacy problems.
- One of the results of growing up in an alcoholic system is that interpersonal relationships are often imbalanced in the form of overattachment, overseparation, and codependent dances.
- Grief is a feature of recovery from growing up in an alcoholic system. Second-order change is one technique to change family interaction.
- The eleven curative factors of group therapy (Yalom 1975) are outlined as a way for adult children of alcoholics to pursue recovery:

  - Instilling hope
  - Sharing universality

- Imparting information
- Fostering altruism
- Recapitulating the primary family group
- Developing socializing techniques
- Imitating behavior
- Sharing interpersonal learning
- Developing group cohesiveness
- Sharing catharsis
- Exploring existential factors

⋈ Discussion Questions

1. Rate your own level for each of the ACA behavioral characteristics below, from 1 (hardly ever an issue) to 10 (almost always an issue). Then discuss these in small group discussion.

   - Fear of losing control
   - All-or-none, black-or-white thinking
   - Fear of experiencing feelings
   - Overdeveloped sense of responsibility or irresponsibility
   - Difficulty with intimacy and with asking for what is wanted or needed
   - Flashbacks of childhood but many memory gaps
   - Feelings of being little, or like a child, when under stress
   - Unreasonable loyalty
   - Addiction to excitement
   - Difficulty relaxing
   - Feelings of guilt, abandonment, and/or depression
   - Tendency to confuse love with self-pity
   - Backlog of shock and grief
   - Compulsive behaviors
   - Living in a world of denial
   - Guessing at what is normal
   - Tendency toward physical symptoms (e.g., headaches, gastrointestinal problems)

2. Tim Cermak, M.D., defined codependency using the following diagnostic criteria. Give examples for each criterion and explain why you think it meets the codependency criteria.

   - Continual investment of self-esteem in the ability to influence or control feelings and behaviors in the self and others in the face of obvious adverse consequences
   - Assumption of responsibility for meeting others' needs to the exclusion of acknowledging one's own needs
   - Anxiety and boundary distortions in situations of intimacy and separation
   - Enmeshment in relationships with personality-disordered, drug-dependent, and impulse-disordered individuals

- Maintenance of a primary relationship with an active substance abuser for at least 2 years without seeking outside support and/or exhibiting three or more of the following characteristics:

  a. Constriction of emotions with or without dramatic outbursts
  b. Depression
  c. Hypervigilance
  d. Compulsions
  e. Anxiety
  f. Excessive reliance on denial
  g. Substance abuse
  h. Recurrent physical or sexual abuse
  i. Stress-related medical illnesses

3. Rank the 11 curative factors of group psychotherapy in order of most to least important and explain your rationale.

   - Instilling hope
   - Sharing universality
   - Imparting information
   - Fostering altruism
   - Recapitulating the primary family group
   - Developing socializing techniques
   - Imitating behavior
   - Sharing interpersonal learning
   - Developing group cohesiveness
   - Sharing catharsis
   - Exploring existential factors

❈ References

Ackerman, Robert J. 1978. *Children of alcoholics: A guidebook for educators, therapists, and parents.* Holmes Beach, Fla.: Learning.

After drug treatment: What happens to the marriage. 1999. *Springbrook Northwest Newsletter,* summer.

Black, Claudia. 1982. *It will never happen to me.* Denver, Colo.: M.A.C.

Brown, Stephanie. 1988. *Treating adult children of alcoholics: A developmental perspective.* New York: Wiley.

Cermak, Timmen. 1984. Children of alcoholics and the case for a new diagnostic category of co-dependency. *Alcohol, Health, and Research World* 8: 38–42.

Clinebell, Howard J., Jr. 1985. *Understanding and counseling the alcoholic through religion and psychology.* Nashville, Tenn.: Abingdon Press.

Coleman, Eli, and Philip Colgan. 1987. Chemical dependency and intimacy dysfunction. *Journal of Chemical Dependency Treatment* 1: 75–91.

Cork, M. 1969. *The forgotten children.* Toronto: Addiction Research Foundation.

Newell, Nancy. 1950. Alcoholism and the father image. *Quarterly Journal of Studies on Alcoholism* 11: 92–5.

Yalom, Irvin D. 1975. *The theory and practice of group psychotherapy.* New York: Basic Books.

Motivation, Intervention, Co-occurring Disorders, Prevention, Recovery, and Relapse Prevention

❖ **Chapter 8:**

Motivation and Change

❖ **Chapter 9:**

Intervention

❖ **Chapter 10:**

Prevention of Substance Abuse Problems

❖ **Chapter 11:**

Disorders Co-occurring with Substance Abuse

❖ **Chapter 12:**

Alcohol/Drug Recovery, Co-Occurring Disorders, Suicide, and Alcohol/Drugs

❖ **Chapter 13:**

The Problems of Relapse: Relapse Prevention (RP)

Motivation and Change

Outline of Chapter 8

Introduction

Change

Choice Making—Family of Origin

Motivational Interviewing
 Client-Centered Motivational Interviewing
 Effective Motivational Strategies
 Active Ingredients of Effective Brief Counseling

Objectives

1. Define and describe the stages of change—precontemplative, preparation, contemplation, action, maintenance, and relapse prevention.
2. Identify the key elements of "quantum change."
3. Explain the issues of denial and delusion.
4. Describe some common defense mechanisms against change.
5. List the six styles of procrastination.
6. Explain and describe second-order change.
7. List and explain the eight general motivational strategies of motivational interviewing (MI).
8. Define MI, and explain the five general principles of MI.

✴ Introduction

This chapter explores motivation and stages of change and the ways each relates to alcohol/drug recovery and relapse prevention. It is important to understand the kinds of change that can occur, the determinants of change, and the stages of change and what influences them. Motivation and drive as well as relapse prevention strategies are necessary to stop drinking and/or drugging.

These issues are worth our focus, and I believe they will be studied even more in the future, to better understand and treat individuals with substance abuse disorders.

⚡ Change

The whole subject of change is fascinating and complicated. People change for very personal and individual reasons. Many people can go for years, even a lifetime, wanting to change, intending to change, even verbalizing a desire to change, without taking the action necessary to change.

Why will any given person stop drinking or taking drugs, eat healthier, exercise regularly, commit to a task, pursue a passion, or get out of an imbalanced situation or relationship? The answer is different for each person. Some people will put up with a lot before being forced to make a change. Others will make difficult changes, despite tremendous obstacles, risks, and personal sacrifice, because they feel or know it is what they have to do. In the alcohol/drug recovery field, we often refer to the experience of "hitting bottom," reaching the point where the consequences of drinking or taking drugs are so bad that the individual decides to do something about their drug/alcohol use. The consequences of their addictive behavior have become so demeaning, so shaming, and so foreign to their perception of themselves that users are motivated to take action to do whatever it takes to stop using alcohol or other drugs.

Some people stop using because the negative cycle and negative consequences have gone on for too long. They decide that they are "sick and tired of being sick and tired."

Change can sometimes occur when others influence, directly or indirectly, the motivation to change. Friends, teachers, family members, mentors, or significant others can help the individual to see the need for change and help support change. Certainly, counselors play a pivotal role in helping these individuals explore their perception of their alcohol/drug use, and the need for change. For some users, hearing the same thing from different people, in a timely manner, causes them to consider making a change. What motivates one individual to change might be quite different for another. Others might make a change because their job is in jeopardy, or because they have been touched in a heartfelt way by someone they love. The counselor is challenged to push the right "button" for each individual.

Change may be gradual, or it can seem sudden and abrupt. William Miller, lead author of *Motivational Interviewing* (Miller and Rollnick, 1991), describes this process of collaboration and gradual influence to motivate the client to explore healthy change. In *Quantum Change* (2001), Miller and coauthor Janet C'de Baca describe a more sudden and immediate kind of change. A quantum change is a personal transformation that has some key elements:

- *Vivid*—identifiable, distinctive experiences during which the transformation occurred, or at least began
- *Surprising*—not comprehensible as ordinary responses to life events
- *Benevolent*—involves loving kindness
- *Enduring*—it is a permanent transformation
- *Involves conflict*—a rupture in the knowing context

Miller and C'de Baca (2001) quote Bill Wilson, the co-founder of Alcoholics Anonymous, as he describes his quantum change:

> Slowly the ecstasy subsided. I lay on the bed, but now for a time I was in another world, a new world of consciousness. All about me and through me there was a wonderful feeling of Presence. A great peace stole over me and I thought, "No matter how wrong things seem to be, they are all right."

Whether change occurs gradually or suddenly, the outcome is the same—personal transformation.

Resistance is a natural part of the change cycle. Whether it is an adolescent who resists cleaning up his or her room or an adult who delays paying his or her taxes, resistance is embedded in our nature. For some, it is laziness or procrastination, probably related to family-of-origin issues. But most people resist doing something that may bring discomfort or dysphoria or that is just downright uninteresting. Resistance comes out in the various defense mechanisms used by people to avoid taking action on a problem behavior (e.g., substance abuse).

Common Defense Components of Resistance to Change

1. *Denial*—most common
   Counselor tip: Look for the usefulness of the defense to person, what he or she is avoiding and why; wait to point out denial—premature disclosure can "turn off" the client (i.e., you are judging them).
2. *Minimization*—used to maintain self-esteem (e.g., "My drinking/drugging never had an impact on my children, since I drank outside of the house")
   Counselor tip: Suggest client get feedback from valued and reliable other sources, rather than getting into a tireless debate with client.
3. *Projection*—has important protective function, may cover deeper disturbance
   Counselor tip: Be sensitive to self-blame and guilt, and the client feeling shamed by any suggestion of criticism; preface feedback with "some people might think."
4. *Rationalization*—clever answers used to avoid responsibility and maintain frozen feelings
   Counselor tip: Avoid your own frustration and anger in trying to get through to a highly intellectualizing client.
5. *Compliance*—hidden form of resistance, may cover up magical expectations
   Counselor tip: Recognize the potential of provoking rebellion at some point.
6. *Conflict avoidance*—problems handling feelings of anger and disappointment, need to be liked and approved
   Counselor tip: Provoking client to deal with conflict too much may be a hazard.
7. *Obsessive focusing*—all-or-none thinking, may be overly self-critical or overly critical of others, may be perfectionistic
   Counselor tip: Understand the person's situation while suggesting that he or she "lighten up."
8. *Acting out*—lacks awareness of feelings, impulses communicated by behavior, most provocative of defenses

Counselor tip: Direct to needed change, stay out of harm's way (i.e., be careful not to put self in jeopardy).

Denial and Delusion: Blocks to Seeing the Need for Change

When someone is having problems related to substance abuse, they often are in "denial" as to the true dimensions of their abuse. They are in "delusion" about the consequences and negative impact their drug use has on themselves, their family, and others. They use rationalizations and other defenses to maintain the denial and delusion that there is no need for change. They may acknowledge a problem but they justify procrastination and, therefore, avoid the needed change. The person in denial and delusion doesn't want to see the real dimensions of the problem. Change involves a painful acceptance of one's denial and delusion. Procrastination often leads to more severe negative consequences until the individual suffers enough to acknowledge the need for change.

> The essence of bravery is to be without self-deception.
> (Pema Chodron, *When Things Fall Apart*)

Change—"Mindful Acceptance"

In Buddhist teachings (dharma), change is described as "mindful surrender." Sometimes it is only when we truly let go that things can change. Admitting that you have a problem is the first step toward change.

> Buddhism recognizes that the central issue of our lives, from falling in
> love to facing death, requires an ability to surrender that often eludes us.
> (Mark Epstein, *Going to Pieces Without Falling Apart*)

The serenity prayer of Alcoholics Anonymous is a good way to remind yourself that you are not in control.

Serenity Prayer
God grant me the serenity
To accept the things I cannot change,
The courage to change the things I can,
And the wisdom to know the difference.

Procrastination

Procrastination is another obstacle to healthy change. People will gladly put off dealing with difficult issues and problems that block healthy change. Procrastination is the number one reason why people do not implement change (See Chart 8.1.)

Exertion: An Essential Element of Change

Overcoming procrastination and obstacles to change requires effort, commitment, and perseverance, especially during difficult times. Exertion or effort is needed to overcome resistance and unpleasantness.

C H A R T   8 . 1

Six Styles of Procrastination

1. **The Perfectionist Procrastinator**
   The Perfectionist Procrastinator waits and waits for the perfect time and situation to take action, and misses out on the opportunities for growth.

2. **The Dreamer Procrastinator**
   The Dreamer Procrastinator (The Talker) has unrealistic expectations. They talk about what they are going to do, but take little action toward those dreams (i.e., "One day I am going to . . .").

3. **The Worrier Procrastinator**
   The Worrier Procrastinator comes up with fearful reasons for not taking action.

4. **The Defier Procrastinator**
   The Defier Procrastinator doesn't follow good advice, rejects help, and continues to have the same problems.

5. **The Crisis-Maker Procrastinator**
   The Crisis-Maker Procrastinator creates crises to distract from taking "right action." They are "drama" prone. They are so busy putting out fires that they avoid working on the real issues.

6. **The Overdoer Procrastinator**
   The Overdoer Procrastinator will focus on one part of the problem, at the expense of ignoring and not taking up the priority issues.

(Adapted from *It's About Time: The 6 Styles of Procrastination and How to Overcome Them* by Sapadin and McGuire).

> Like waking up on a cold, snowy day in a mountain cabin ready to go
> for a walk but know that you have to get out of bed and make a fire.
> You'd rather stay in bed but you jump out and make the fire because the
> brightness of the day is bigger than staying in bed.
>
> (Pema Chodron, *When Things Fall Apart*)

⊀ Choice Making—Family of Origin

Changing old, imbalanced patterns is possible only if individuals feel they have choices. Discouraging voices of doom and gloom need to be quieted for recovery efforts to be implemented. Self-pity, victim roles, and the poor-me syndrome prevent one from even entertaining a choice to change. The old familial belief system whispers in the ACA's ear: "Change is not possible, so why even try? You'll just waste time and energy and fail, anyway, just as you always have in the past."

Changes involve integration and congruency with feelings and choosing not to respond in dysfunctional, codependent ways. There is the acknowledgment that change is difficult, takes time, may involve pain, and requires support. Sometimes small changes and positive choices can establish the foundation for more significant growth-related choices later.

A variety of therapeutic issues must be explored before the ACA can improve interpersonal relationships. Some of the cognitive and affective therapeutic themes are as follows:

- Family-of-origin issues (beliefs, roles, rules, and thoughts about relationships)
- Sense of self, or self-concept, and interpersonal interaction, choosing relationships, and maintaining dysfunctional imbalanced relationships
- Boundary setting and decision making in interpersonal situations
- Self-sabotage or destructive behavior, poor impulse control, poor anger and frustration tolerance, and an inability to set and maintain healthy long-range goals

�֍ Motivational Interviewing

William Miller and Stephen Rollnick (1991) developed a form of intervention known as motivational interviewing. They recognized that formal and informal interventions are effective for many individuals who are in denial of having a problem with alcohol or drugs, but for some individuals the traditional form of intervention doesn't work. Despite the intervention, the individual is not motivated to seek abstinence or recovery from alcohol/drugs.

The same holds true for many individuals who, once in alcohol/drug treatment, either terminated treatment early against medical advice or didn't respond when confronted by counselors about their denial. Miller and Rollnick espouse a different approach with individuals who are resistant to traditional intervention methods. Some individuals respond negatively to interventions.

Motivational interviewing draws its strategies from a number of disciplines, including client-centered counseling, cognitive therapy, systems theory, and the social psychology of persuasion. The work of motivational interviewing comes from Miller and Rollnick's contention that there is no one kind of alcoholic or addict or, for that matter, an addictive personality. "This idea of a common alcoholic or addictive personality is supported neither in the original writings of Alcoholics Anonymous, nor by five decades of psychological research" (Miller and Rollnick 1991). It therefore makes sense that alcoholics/addicts need a variety of approaches to engage them into recovery. Perhaps a different approach might reach those alcoholics/addicts who resist traditional confrontive interventions. Motivational interviewing was therefore designed to help clients build commitment and reach a decision to change.

Miller and Rollnick described motivation as a state of readiness or eagerness to change, and they recognized that motivation may fluctuate over time, situation, and circumstance. They described the basic stages of change and the influences a therapist can make in influencing motivation to change. (See Figure 8.1.)

Their approach uses brief, individual counseling, which helps the clients explore and resolve their "ambivalence" about change. Ambivalence is defined as feeling two ways about something, being in conflict between the pros and cons of

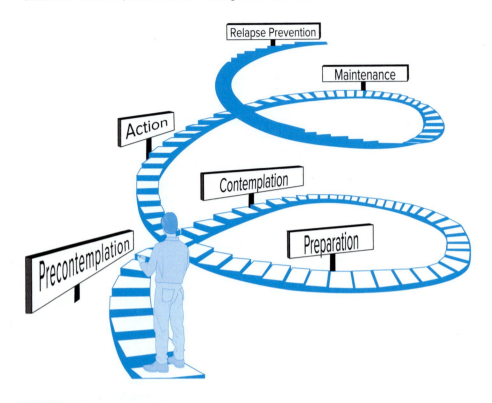

FIGURE 8.1   *The Spiral of Change*
SOURCE: Adapted from J. O. Prochaska, J. C. Norcross, and C. C. DiClemente, *Changing for Good,* Avon Books, New York, 1994 (First Avon Books Printing, Sept., 1995).

the status quo (or the pros and cons of changing). Ambivalence is a good description for the conflict many people have about changing, whether it is recovery from alcohol/drugs, unhealthy and self-destructive behaviors (e.g., smoking, overeating), a dysfunctional relationship, a bad work situation, or illegal activities. At the precontemplative stage of change, they are not considering change and may not see or admit problems with the self-destructive behavior (addiction). In the contemplative stage, they are considering change but are ambivalent about it. These are the individuals who waver from day to day and seem easily influenced to go in either direction. When it comes to alcohol/drug abuse and addiction, the alcoholic/addict wants to continue to use alcohol/drugs yet may recognize the risks and negative consequences of use. At the determination stage the individual decides to do something. The action stage is when there has been a recent change or an implemented plan of change. The maintenance stage involves a commitment to a long-term change, where the change has become habit, or part of the person's lifestyle. The relapse prevention stage explores strategies to not return to earlier stages.

Table 8.1 outlines an approach to a nondirective part of motivational interviewing.

T A B L E   8 . 1

The "Nondirective" Part of Motivational Interviewing (MI): OARS* (Tools for Rowing Along with Your Clients)

Open-Ended Questions

Can't be answered with "yes" or "no"
Keep resistance down
Build trust rapidly
Encourage client to talk about what's important to him or her
Reveal what's "delicious" to clients
Help therapist find the "carrot" for change

Affirmations

Very hard to use genuinely; requires much practice
Build self-esteem
Show respect
Reduce treatment dropout rates
Get a "winning streak" going for clients (clients who succeed come back for more success)

Reflecting

Takes practice; sounds phony at first
Is like throwing "empathy darts" while client holds up the target
Client will always let you know if you're accurate or not
Very satisfying for both to be accurate
More than just paraphrasing the client's message content; also reflects underlying feelings
Happens after every few sentences spoken by clients
About three of every four statements by MI therapist is a reflection (how do you get anything done?)

Summarizing

Gathers together what client said, so it can be heard again (especially the positive change talk)
Shows client what's been accomplished during the session
Can help therapist close one topic and move on to another
Can help end sessions on good terms

*"OARS" symbolizes the way motivational interviewing therapists act during a session. Whenever you are stuck, you can fall back on this style of being with your client, until you figure out what your directive strategy is going to be. Without adding the directive motivational interviewing techniques, OARS will only help you row about in circles (but at least you're not sinking . . .).

Client-Centered Motivational Interviewing

Motivational interviewing is "client centered," which means that it focuses on eliciting and understanding the client's view.

The motivational interviewing technique is quite different from the intervention model. It is controversial because the active alcoholic/addict wants to continue to drink and will often delay taking action despite significant negative consequences. Many counselors believe that not confronting denial, and giving control back to the alcoholic/addict, will only result in continued destructive, maybe even life-threatening, patterns of alcohol consumption. However, the motivational interviewing approach has the perspective that people follow through better and are more committed to recovery if they voluntarily make the decision to choose treatment for themselves. Another controversial aspect of motivational interviewing is the counselor eliciting the client's doubts about recovery, as well as the positive aspects. This helps the counselor reflect back to the client the positive and negative aspects of the decision. Case Study 8.1 presents an example of client-centered motivational interviewing.

Effective Motivational Strategies

There are eight general motivational strategies.

1. Giving *advice*. Well-timed and tempered advice to change can make a difference. Advice should (1) clearly identify the problem or risk area, (2) explain why change is important, and (3) advocate specific change.
2. *Removing barriers*. Address blocks to change, such as resistance to go to AA meetings.
3. Providing *choice*. Few people like to be told what to do. Intrinsic motivation is enhanced by the perception that one has freely chosen.
4. Decreasing *desirability*. Weigh the benefits and costs of change against the merits of continuing as before.
5. Practicing *empathy*. This kind of empathy is not an ability to identify with a person's experiences. Rather, it is a specifiable and learnable skill for understanding another's meaning through the use of reflective listening, whether or not you have had a similar experience yourself.
6. Providing *feedback*.
7. Clarifying *goals*. Help the client to restate the goal in realistic or attainable terms.
8. Helping *active*. Express actively and affirmatively your interest in your client's change process.

Motivational interviewing is a nondirective approach. Miller and Rollnick (1991) use the mnemonic OARS to describe nondirective counseling. You can "row along with your clients" if you O—ask *open-ended questions,* A—provide *affirmations,* R—*reflect* on client verbalizations, and S—*summarize* what the client says. (See Table 8.1.)

Active Ingredients of Effective Brief Counseling

Miller and Rollnick (1991) have developed the mnemonic FRAMES* to remind counselors of the effective ingredients for motivational interviewing and brief

Case Study 8.1

Contemplative and Action Stages

Don

Don knew he had a problem with alcohol/drugs. He took some action by attending AA meetings, yet he still didn't want to stop drinking. He would maintain abstinence for limited periods of time (30 to 100 days) but then would lapse into drinking. Despite negative consequences at home and at work, and having gone through two inpatient programs, he still was not committed to recovery. He tried to convince himself that he wasn't really an alcoholic, yet he soon found himself in alcoholic binges. Each time he relapsed, he seemed motivated to get sober and work at a program of recovery, yet, despite attending AA, attending outpatient counseling, even working with a sponsor, he was ambivalent about recovery. At the suggestion of his sponsor, he attended several different AA meetings. After attending an AA meeting at a local mission for the homeless, he wondered if he had to "hit bottom" by losing his job, family, and home to stop drinking. The very next day, he talked to an old-timer at another AA meeting who told him, "Maybe things have to get really bad before you get better." He was then convinced that he had to continue to drink until things got worse, before he would stop. In his ambivalence, he called his sponsor with this new idea and was told, "You'll come up with any excuse to continue drinking." His resolve to seek recovery was so ambivalent and such a struggle that he could easily be influenced to go either way—recovery or self-destruction.

Don talked to his outpatient counselor about this conflict during a one-on-one session, and the counselor effectively used motivational interviewing techniques to help Don resolve this ambivalence, so he could move closer to action. The counselor focused more on Don's ambivalence about committing to AA, rather than the global issue of ambivalence about recovery in general.

Counselor:	It's good to see you again, Don. Tell me how have you been doing for the past few weeks, so I can get caught up? [open question]
Don:	Not great, if you really want to know. I haven't drunk or used in over 4 weeks now. In fact, I'll be 30 days sober tomorrow. But, big deal, I'm more screwed up than ever. I don't mean to sound sorry for myself, but I just feel lousy. And I know I've got to do something, but I don't know which end is up.
Counselor:	Congratulations on making it to 1 month! You've been working hard and it hasn't been a picnic for you. [affirmation acknowledging client's progress and empathic statement]
Don:	[silent]
Counselor:	But things are tough, and you aren't getting the rewards of feeling better yet. [accurate reflection] Tell me what you mean when you say you're more screwed up now than ever? [open question]
Don:	I was talking with my sponsor yesterday, and he told me he's worried about me. He thinks I'm gonna go out and drink again. He says I'm subconsciously planning a relapse.
Counselor:	What do you think he means? [open question]

(continued on next page)

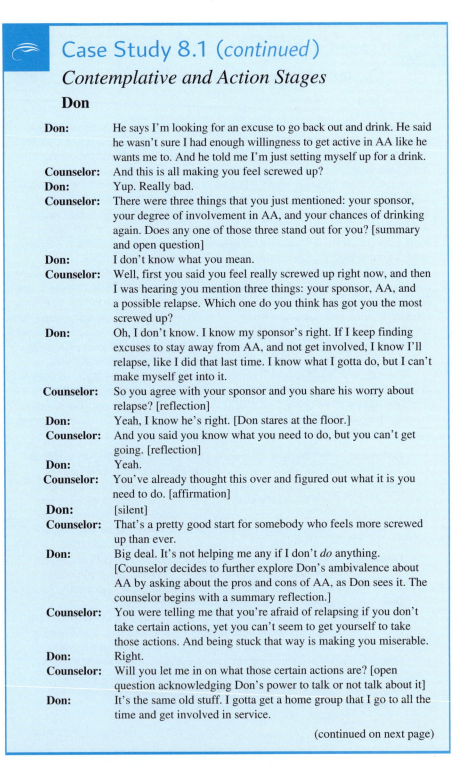

Case Study 8.1 (*continued*)

Contemplative and Action Stages

Don

Don:	He says I'm looking for an excuse to go back out and drink. He said he wasn't sure I had enough willingness to get active in AA like he wants me to. And he told me I'm just setting myself up for a drink.
Counselor:	And this is all making you feel screwed up?
Don:	Yup. Really bad.
Counselor:	There were three things that you just mentioned: your sponsor, your degree of involvement in AA, and your chances of drinking again. Does any one of those three stand out for you? [summary and open question]
Don:	I don't know what you mean.
Counselor:	Well, first you said you feel really screwed up right now, and then I was hearing you mention three things: your sponsor, AA, and a possible relapse. Which one do you think has got you the most screwed up?
Don:	Oh, I don't know. I know my sponsor's right. If I keep finding excuses to stay away from AA, and not get involved, I know I'll relapse, like I did that last time. I know what I gotta do, but I can't make myself get into it.
Counselor:	So you agree with your sponsor and you share his worry about relapse? [reflection]
Don:	Yeah, I know he's right. [Don stares at the floor.]
Counselor:	And you said you know what you need to do, but you can't get going. [reflection]
Don:	Yeah.
Counselor:	You've already thought this over and figured out what it is you need to do. [affirmation]
Don:	[silent]
Counselor:	That's a pretty good start for somebody who feels more screwed up than ever.
Don:	Big deal. It's not helping me any if I don't *do* anything. [Counselor decides to further explore Don's ambivalence about AA by asking about the pros and cons of AA, as Don sees it. The counselor begins with a summary reflection.]
Counselor:	You were telling me that you're afraid of relapsing if you don't take certain actions, yet you can't seem to get yourself to take those actions. And being stuck that way is making you miserable.
Don:	Right.
Counselor:	Will you let me in on what those certain actions are? [open question acknowledging Don's power to talk or not talk about it]
Don:	It's the same old stuff. I gotta get a home group that I go to all the time and get involved in service.

(continued on next page)

Case Study 8.1 (*continued*)

Contemplative and Action Stages

Don

Counselor: And you feel two ways about choosing a home group. First of all, what are some of your objections to getting one?

Don: I don't like joining groups because it's corny or something.

Counselor: Okay. What else?

Don: I don't want to have to go to the same group every week because I get tired of the people there.

Counselor: Okay, some groups seem corny to you and you get tired of some people. What else?

Don: I don't know; that's all I guess.

Counselor: O.K., what about the other side of the coin? What are the most positive things you might get from choosing a home group?

Don: Well, it might help me stay sober.

Counselor: How?

Don: Just by staying close to a group. They get to know you and, if you start to drop off meetings, somebody might ask you if you're okay.

Counselor: So people get to know you and care enough to say something to you to help you get back on track, and you might not mind hearing it because you know them, right?

Don: [Yes.]

Counselor: So people can help you stay on track. What else might be positive for you if you decided to get a home group?

Don: Well, they say people get to know your story and you get to know everybody there pretty good, because you hear their stories as well.

Counselor: So if you spend more time with your home group you could get to know them better than the people in other groups if you just "shop around" from group to group.

Don: Right.

Counselor: Almost as if each person in your home group were a separate TV show that you tune into each week to see how things are going with them. Kind of entertaining.

Don: Yeah, I never thought of it that way before.

Counselor: [summarizing] On one hand, you're not much of a joiner and you might get tired of seeing some people every week. But, on the other hand, you could get to know those people better and actually get some support, even enjoyment from being around them each week. Maybe even get so you look forward to going each week?

Don: I suppose so, although I don't think I'd ever feel really comfortable there. The way it is now, I just go to whatever meeting I feel like. But I never look forward to meetings, because I know I'm just gonna bolt right after it is over.

(continued on next page)

Case Study 8.1 (continued)

Contemplative and Action Stages

Don

Counselor:	[reflecting, then trying to tip the balance in favor of change] Sounds a little lonesome. As you look at the balance, pros and cons of getting a home group, Don, do any of those pros or cons stand out as more important to you?
Don:	[arguing for change] Yeah, making friends. It might be nice to get to know some people who don't drink. I never got that far last time I quit drinking. I stayed away from my old drinking buddies, but I also stayed away from people in AA.
Counselor:	People are a big deal to you. And you think you might find some that you like if you were to hang around one meeting long enough. Well, Don, the decision is totally in your hands. It's understandable that you haven't acted yet, considering that you basically feel two ways about getting a home group. But being stuck where you're at doesn't sound comfortable either. Based on what you've told me, it sounds like getting people in your life that you like and may even begin to trust might make your sobriety nicer. But what do you think?

Summary

Counselor tried to move client from contemplation into preparation and action, regarding the specific behavioral issue of getting a home AA group.

[Counselor turns over the responsibility for the decision to Don and then asks if he's ready for action—that is, getting a home group. If the answer is no, the counselor affirms the work that Don did in acknowledging both sides of the painful issue and lets the issue rest for now, closing the topic on good terms, to be returned to later. If the answer is yes, they proceed with discussing an action plan for getting a home group and removing barriers to doing so.]

---

counseling: FRAMES—feedback, responsibility, advice, menu (i.e., a list of choices), empathy, self-efficacy (i.e., you can do it). (See Figure 8.2.)

The general principles of motivational interviewing are the following:

1. *Express empathy.* Acceptance facilitates change; skillful reflective listening is fundamental; ambivalence is normal.
2. *Develop discrepancy.* Awareness of consequences is important; a discrepancy between present behavior and important goals will motivate change; the client should present the arguments for change.
3. *Avoid argumentation.* Arguments are counterproductive; defending breeds defensiveness; resistance is a signal to change strategies; labeling is unnecessary.

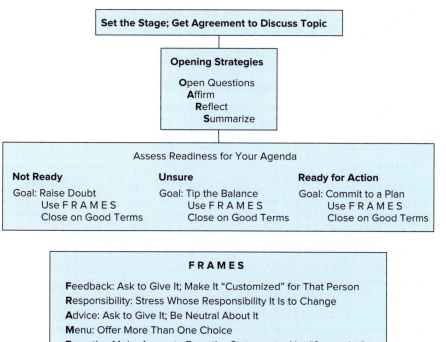

FIGURE 8.2   *One of Many Ways to Do a Brief Intervention*
SOURCE: William Miller and Stephen Rollnick. 1991. *Motivational Interviewing: Preparing People to Change Addictive Behavior.* New York: Guilford Press.

4. *Roll with resistance.* Momentum can be used to good advantage; perceptions can be shifted; new perspectives are invited but not imposed; the client is a valuable resource in finding solutions to problems.
5. *Support self-efficacy.* Belief in the possibility of change is an important motivator: the client is responsible for choosing and carrying out personal change; there is hope in the range of alternative approaches available.

In counseling, rolling with resistance is a valuable strategy, instead of "tireless debating" that only causes more resistance to change.

Since the publication of Miller and Rollnick's classic *Motivational Interviewing,* MI has become hugely popular as a tool for facilitating many different kinds of positive behavior change. (Naar-King and Suarez 2011)

Here are four books in the next era of motivational interviewing:

Motivational Interviewing in the Treatment of Psychological Problems
Hal Arkowitz, Henny A. Westra, William R. Miller, and Stephen Rollnick, Editors

Motivational Interviewing in Health Care: Helping Patients Change Behavior
Stephen Rollnick, William R. Miller, and Christopher C. Butler

Building Motivational Interviewing Skills: A Practitioner Workbook
David B. Rosengren

Motivational Interviewing with Adolescents and Young Adults
Sylvie Naar-King and Mariann Suarez

⋇ In Review

- Change may be gradual or it can seem sudden or abrupt (i.e., quantum change) and others can influence change.
- Miller and Rollnick (1991) describe motivational interviewing as a process of collaboration and gradual influence to motivate the client to explore healthy change.
- According to Miller and C'de Baca (2001) a quantum change (i.e., epiphany) has the following common elements—it is vivid, surprising, benevolent, enduring, and it usually involves conflict.
- Some common defense mechanisms against change are denial, delusion, minimization, projection, rationalization, passive-aggressive compliance, conflict avoidance, obsessive focusing, and acting out.
- Change is defined in Buddhist teachings (dharma) as "mindful surrender" and noted dharma teacher Pema Chodron says, "The essence of bravery is to be without self-deception."
- Sapadin and McGuire (1997) describe six types of procrastinators:
  - The perfectionist procrastinator
  - The dreamer procrastinator
  - The worrier procrastinator
  - The defier procrastinator
  - The crisis-maker procrastinator
  - The overdoer procrastinator
- Change requires exertion, perseverance, discipline, and self-compassion.
- Motivational interviewing (MI) is a client-centered approach that uses cognitive therapy, systems therapy, and social psychology.
- The stages of motivational interviewing are precontemplative, contemplative, determination (i.e., planning), action, maintenance, and relapse prevention.
- There are eight general motivational strategies:
  - Receiving well-timed advice
  - Removing barriers to change
  - Providing choices
  - Decreasing desirability (weighing costs and benefits of drug use)
  - Having empathy

- Providing feedback
- Clarifying goals, and
- Helping client to take action

- "Rolling with resistance" is a valuable strategy instead of entering into "tireless debates."
- The general principles of motivational interviewing are as follows:
  - Expressing empathy
  - Developing discrepancies
  - Avoiding argumentation
  - Rolling with resistance
  - Supporting self-efficacy

⚹ Discussion Questions

1. Discuss a change you are considering and/or have made; outline your beliefs, thinking, and actions for each of the stages of change as they apply:

   Precontemplative
   Contemplative
   Determination
   Action
   Maintenance
   Relapse prevention

2. Identify a healthy and growth-producing change you would like to make.

   List as many benefits as you can to *not* making the change.
   List as many benefits as you can to making the change.
   What did you discover?

3. Identify ways you procrastinate.

   Which of the following types of procrastinator are you—perfectionist, dreamer, worrier, defier, crisis-maker, overdoer? Explain.

⚹ References

Alcoholics Anonymous. 1976. *The history of how many thousands of men and women have recovered from alcoholism,* 3rd edition. World Services.

Chodron, Pema. 2000. *When things fall apart, heart advice for difficult times.* Boston: Shambhala.

Epstein, Mark. 1998. *Going to pieces without falling apart, lessons from meditation and psychotherapy.* New Jersey: Broadway Books.

Miller, William, and Janet C'de Baca. 2001. *Quantum change: When epiphanies and sudden insights transform ordinary lives.* New York: Guilford Press.

Miller, William, and Stephen Rollnick. 1991. *Motivational interviewing: Preparing people to change addictive behavior.* New York: Guilford Press.

Naar-King, Sylvie, and Mariann Suarez. 2011. *Motivational Interviewing with Adolescents and Young Adults.* New York: Guilford Press.

Sapadin, L., and J. Maguire. 1997. *It's about time: The 6 styles of procrastination and how to overcome them.* New York: Penguin.

Intervention

Outline of Chapter 9

Intervention
   Interventions at Various Stages of the Alcohol/Drug Use Continuum
   Obstacles to Interventions
   Intervention Services
   Intervention Approaches
   Professional Intervention Assistance
   Intervention as a Caring Response
   Goals of Intervention
   Family Interventions
   Candidates for Intervention
   Stages of Formal Intervention

Objectives

1. Define intervention; describe interventions at various stages of use.
2. Classify some common dos and don'ts for interventions.
3. Identify the tasks for each of the four stages of a formal intervention: assessment, preintervention, intervention, and postintervention.

❧ Intervention

Everything one does to create awareness of an alcohol/drug problem is an intervention. The slightest suggestion to a friend, colleague, or family member that he or she may be drinking/drugging too much is an intervention. Everyone is different. Those who are at early stages of substance abuse without a family history of alcoholism/addiction may very well pay attention to your observations. If enough people are bringing the drink/drug problem to the person's attention, he or she might decide to do something about it. On the other hand, there are individuals who, if they were hit over the head with a two-by-four, wouldn't recognize their substance-abuse problem.

Interventions at Various Stages of the Alcohol/Drug Use Continuum

Alcohol/drug intervention is any action taken by someone to interrupt the progression of problems with alcohol/drugs. This definition can be expanded to any attempt to help someone from further developing problems with alcohol/drugs. At each stage of alcohol/drug use (i.e., initial contact, experimentation, integrated use, excessive use, addiction), intervention attempts may prevent progression to the next, more damaging stage of alcohol/drug use. This may take the form of an employer expressing concern about an employee's job performance or a teacher talking with parents and letting them know their child is tired and falling asleep in class. There have been a variety of intervention programs in the school system. One such program helps teachers develop core teams (usually involving the school nurse, an administrator, a coach, a dean, etc.), which identify students with behaviors, attitudes, and problems that may indicate alcohol/drug problems. All of these approaches are interventions. Whether it is a conversation expressing concern about alcohol/drug use or a formal intervention, the common goal is to let the individual know that we are concerned about him or her.

In Chapter 4, the various stages of alcohol/drug use are described—nonuse, initial contact, experimentation (situational and circumstantial), integrated use, excessive use (periodic and continuous), and addiction. At each of these stages, there are opportunities for intervention. If one can effectively intervene at earlier stages and interrupt the progression to later stages of alcohol/drug use, the negative consequences may be avoided. Obviously, the later stages of alcohol/drug abuse require more concerted efforts, such as a formal intervention.

The following suggestions illustrate various interventions for children at each stage of the alcohol/drug use continuum.

Stage 1—Nonuse Interventions

- Parental, peer, and other support to maintain nonuse
- Emotional support during difficult times, conflicts, developmental tasks, and emotionally charged events that may make the at-risk individual try alcohol/drugs
- Affirmation and support in activities that promote a good sense of self and alternative activities to alcohol/drug use
- Focus on refusal skills and dealing with peer pressure
- Education and implementation of effective parenting, communication skills, and other alcohol/drug prevention skills

Stage 2—Initial Contact Interventions

Two common problems at this stage are overreaction and underreaction. As a parent, you don't want to be an alarmist and overact in rigid, shaming, and blaming ways to a child's initial contact with alcohol/drugs. You also don't want to ignore the use, disregard the significance, and minimize the impact on the child. As a result,

- Become more aware of the child's behavior and signs of alcohol/drug use.
- Talk with other parents about the child's behavior in their homes.
- Once aware of initial contact, talk with child (i.e., break the no-talk rule); don't ignore the fact that your child used or avoided the opportunity to discuss his or her use of alcohol/drugs.

- If your child has used, let him or her describe the situation, without being judgmental, blaming, or negative.
- Express concerns about safety (e.g., Was your child with friends that he or she could trust? Was it a safe place if problems occurred? Was your child in physical or psychological danger?).
- Without being negative and an alarmist, or lecturing, let the child describe his or her own perception of safety.
- Discuss at-risk factors of alcohol/drug dependence and addiction (especially if there is a family history of alcoholism and/or drug dependence).
- This may be an opportunity to reevaluate other aspects of the child's life (e.g., school, friends, activities).
- This may be an opportune time to explore other family problems and seek an assessment from a counselor who specializes in alcohol/drug recovery and family systems.

Stage 3—Experimentation Interventions

- Focusing on communication and exploration of values, attitudes, and feelings about alcohol/drugs
- Teaching and modeling skills in decision making, conflict resolution, goal setting, and so on
- Teaching and modeling skills in coping with conflicts, dealing with authority figures, and controlling destructive impulses
- Providing information about chemical dependency and addiction
- Providing information about at-risk factors if there is a family history of chemical dependency (e.g., if one parent has or had problems with alcohol/drugs, the child has a four times higher risk of developing problems with alcohol/drugs; if both parents have or had a problem, there is an eight times higher risk for the child to develop problems with alcohol/drugs)
- Identifying, assessing, and perhaps counseling for problems in the family, at school, and so on
- Educating about alcohol/drug prevention and family systems

Stage 4—Interventions at the Integrated Stage

- Identification and communication of concerns and negative consequences as a result of integrated alcohol/drug use
- Expression of concern—in a caring, nonjudgmental way—regarding the well-being of the individual using alcohol/drugs
- Pointing out the individual's denial of an alcohol/drug problem
- Assessment by a trained chemical dependency family counselor to assess alcohol/drug use and family dynamics
- If problems are identified, work on these issues in counseling (i.e., family members attend Al-Anon; take educational classes on chemical dependency, parenting, and family systems; and attend regular counseling).

Stages 5 and 6—Interventions at the Excessive Use and Addiction Stages

All of the previous strategies are appropriate at both the excessive and addictive stages. However, the longer and more pervasive the problems with alcohol/drugs, the more difficult and intense the level of intervention.

- Alcohol/drug assessment, including regular urinanalysis for drugs and blood alcohol tests
- Intensive outpatient counseling for chemical dependency and family issues
- Strong boundary setting and consequences for violation of family rules and alcohol/drug use
- Formal alcohol/drug intervention
- Inpatient/residential treatment for chemical dependency
- Involvement in AA and other self-help meetings, including active involvement in 12-step work with a sponsor

Table 9.1 describes the dos and don'ts of dealing with someone who has an alcohol/drug problem.

Obstacles to Interventions

There are many obstacles that prevent families from getting help for alcohol/drug problems. Getting the family member with the alcohol/drug problem into treatment may not be realistic unless these obstacles are first addressed. Some common obstacles to families getting help are listed in Table 9.2.

Intervention Services

The concept of alcohol/drug intervention began in the 1960s, when Vernon Johnson—at that time a pastor—felt frustrated when he was unable to help spouses of alcoholics. Deciding to abandon the traditional approach of waiting until the alcoholic/addict hit bottom, he tried a strategy that he later called intervention (Johnson 1986).

Merriam-Webster's Collegiate Dictionary, Eleventh Edition, defines *intervene** this way: "to occur, fall, or come between points of time or events." Alcohol/drug intervention is a process that prevents, alters, or interrupts the progression of the disease. The intervention is a process of getting involved or stepping into a situation in an attempt to interrupt the disease and to get the individual into alcohol/drug treatment. Persons who intervene choose to talk about the issue of alcohol/drug dependence that is destructive to the individuals, their families, and friends. Due to the alcoholic/addict's strong denial system, a trained interventionist with an expertise in chemical dependency treatment must lead or facilitate the intervention.

Intervention services are offered by most chemical dependency inpatient and residential treatment centers. Trained chemical dependency counselors also specialize

---

*By permission. From Merriam-Webster's Collegiate® Dictionary, 11th Edition ©2016 by Merriam-Webster, Inc. (www.Merriam-Webster.com)

TABLE 9.1

Dos and Don'ts of Dealing with Someone Who Has an Alcohol/Drug Problem

1. Deal with your emotions.

If possible, try to be calm, balanced, and caring. This may be difficult; however, remember that if you lose control, you lose.

Do Not

Try to talk with someone while he or she is under the influence of alcohol/drugs; if your child or spouse comes home late at night under the influence of alcohol/drugs, wait until the morning to discuss it.

Threaten to make ultimatums unless you have had time to think them through (e.g., Is it realistic? Can you follow through? What is the impact of the ultimatum on other family members?). Threats said in anger can be unrealistic, inflexible, and abusive. Idle threats or constant threats that are not followed through are meaningless in changing behavior. Threats only set up a lack of consistency, poor trust, and lack of credibility.

Lose your temper, rant and rave, or lose control. It might temporarily make you feel good to let out your frustration and anger, but it does not help the child or adult in addressing the alcohol/drug problem.

Do

Express a willingness to get help and resolve the problem. This is usually in the form of counseling.

Communicate your concern and feelings (e.g., fear, worry, love) without trying to control or lecture the alcohol/drug user.

Set boundaries that are reasonable (to promote appropriate behavior and consistent family rules).

Follow through with consequences for boundaries that were violated.

2. Communicate with behavior-specific examples, rather than generalizations and secondhand or speculative information.

Do Not

Ask why the person is using alcohol/drugs. "Why" questions are often blaming questions, as if asking, "How could you do this to your mother and me?"

Use words such as *drunk, loaded, wasted.* Instead, describe specific behaviors you observe (e.g., slurred speech, staggered gait, etc.).

Generalize about alcohol/drug use. Be specific about alcohol/drug use, if possible (e.g., "I saw you drink five glasses of wine and snort two lines of cocaine").

Use sarcasm, ridicule, and other behaviors that may shame or embarrass the alcohol/drug user. This only perpetuates resentments and often results in later passive-aggressive behavior.

Do

Seek professional counseling to help with family communication about alcohol/drug problems. Seek out a counselor experienced in alcohol/drug treatment and family systems.

3. Trust what you see (behaviors), not what the addict/alcoholic or problem user says.

Do Not

Expect that things will get better on their own. Often, the problem alcohol/drug user will decrease his or her use when he or she suspects that you may do something. Alcoholism and drug addiction are progressive diseases that only get worse over time unless the individual is motivated to change.

Expect that the problem alcohol/drug user will recognize his or her use as a problem. Denial is often the case.

Assume that the alcoholic/addict will be rational and logical. Instead, he or she may exhibit self-deception and delay getting help.

(continued on next page)

TABLE 9.1 (*continued*)

Dos and Don'ts of Dealing with Someone Who Has an Alcohol/Drug Problem

4. Avoid being distracted from the real issue—the individual's abuse of alcohol/drugs.

Do Not

Spend time or physical and emotional energy on distracting wild goose chases (e.g., finding out who gave the person alcohol/drugs or blaming the school system or other parents). These are all secondary issues. The primary issue is that your child or family member may have an alcohol/drug problem.

Compare the alcohol/drug problems of others that are more involved in alcohol/drug use. This is a form of rationalizing away the problem. Expressions such as "kids will be kids," "he or she will outgrow this," and "most people drink/drug this way" tend to discount the real dimensions of alcohol/drug dependence.

Get distracted by excuses for alcohol/drug abuse (e.g., "I'm experiencing a great deal of pressure right now" or "It's because my girlfriend just broke up with me"). The fact is the person has a problem with alcohol/drugs and is vulnerable to relapse when normal, stressful events happen again.

Take responsibility for the total problem. Avoid self-blaming statements (e.g., "I'm an awful parent" or "I should have_____ ; then he or she wouldn't have an alcohol/drug problem"). Self-blame serves only to distract from the issue at hand—the fact that your child or family member has an alcohol/drug problem and needs help. You cannot go back and change the past; you can only work on the future.

Do

Seek treatment for the addicted person and the entire family. The sooner you do this, the better is the prognosis.

5. Seek professional help for alcohol/drug assessment, education, prevention, intervention, and treatment.

Do Not

Isolate from others and hide the family alcohol/drug problem. The longer you hide the problem from others to avoid feelings of shame and embarrassment, the more damage occurs to your family system.

Get advice from people who may have an alcohol/drug problem themselves or individuals who deny the problem. This only reinforces denial.

Attempt to counsel the family member who has the alcohol/drug problem yourself. This will inadvertently end up being another form of enabling behavior.

Do

Attend Al-Anon, Codependency Anonymous, and other self-help meetings and develop a relationship with a sponsor. This will help you develop a support system necessary to make changes.

Attend educational presentations, classes, and conferences that focus on parenting, family systems, prevention, alcohol/drug recovery, intervention, codependency, and other personal growth issues.

Find a counselor who specializes in alcohol/drug treatment, family systems, and codependency. For more information on choosing a counselor, see Chapter 12.

Take care of yourself and continue with your own recovery, regardless of whether the family member who has the alcohol/drug problem gets help.

in conducting interventions. The choice of the interventionist is a critical element in determining the success of an intervention. Local, state, and national alcohol/drug help lines are excellent referral sources for finding trained and experienced interventionists.

TABLE 9.2

Obstacles to Reaching Parents and Families

- Denial of family dysfunction/imbalance and alcohol/drug problems
- Skepticism about alcohol/drug messages that don't fit parents' own experience
- Assumption by parents that children's alcohol/drug use will be O.K.
- Distorted, depressed view of life by dysfunctional families
- Fear of being stigmatized or labeled as dysfunctional
- Fear of loss of confidentiality
- Narcissism of parents
- Lack of insurance resources for parenting/counseling services
- Lack of energy/time by parents
- Distrust of the system
- Lack of credible message sources for cultural/racial minority groups
- Lack of concern/respect for experts' opinions about alcohol/drugs
- Lack of awareness of community resources, discomfort with middle-class settings
- Overwhelming need for services for basic survival
- Cultural mores

SOURCE: Office for Substance Abuse Prevention 1990.

Intervention Approaches

There are a variety of approaches to the alcohol/drug intervention, including formal and informal chemical dependency interventions, in which each interventionist has his or her own style of conducting the intervention. The principles described in this chapter form a basic framework within which most interventionists work.

Professional Intervention Assistance

Whatever the format or style, conducting an intervention without professional guidance is often doomed to failure, no matter how powerful the individual. Untrained, grandstanding individuals who coerce someone into chemical dependency treatment often cause further resistance by the individual needing help. Do not use this information to try to conduct an intervention on your own; consult a professional interventionist for help.

Intervention as a Caring Response

The most important aspect of an intervention is that it is a caring effort designed to interrupt the disease of alcoholism and drug addiction. Individuals involved in an intervention can be effective only if they maintain a caring, behavior-specific approach and support each other within the basic guidelines of their intervention group.

Goals of Intervention

The primary goal in developing an intervention is to get the addicted person to recognize that he or she has an alcohol/drug problem and to get that person into appropriate chemical dependency treatment. Treatment is usually a minimum 21- to 28-day inpatient or residential program.

Secondary goals of the intervention are to

1. provide an opportunity for those who care about the alcoholic/addict to express concern about the impact the alcoholic/addict's dysfunctional behavior has had on them.
2. provide information on alcohol/drug addiction and family patterns of interaction, such as enabling behavior, to the significant others (parents, spouses, family members, employers, and peers).
3. promote the development of a healthy family system and provide resource information for family members to continue working on their issues.

Family Interventions

Interventions are 100 percent effective in that, regardless of whether the alcoholic/addict decides to get help and go to treatment, family members go on with their recovery. The family has begun a process of change. The growth that the family members experience in developing an intervention can empower them to continue to be true to their feelings and to their own individual recovery, whether or not the alcoholic/addict decides to seek treatment. Via the intervention process, the family members learn about the disease of alcohol/drug addiction. They recognize their own enabling behavior and the role they play in the dynamics of the disease. The intervention may be the first time in a long time that the family members have interacted by functionally discussing their feelings. It may be the first time they have candidly discussed the impact that the alcoholic/addict's alcohol or drug use has had on each of them.

Candidates for Intervention

Using a formal intervention process on adolescents, or young adults who are developmentally still at the adolescent stage, is usually ineffective. Adolescents often feel violated by the process of intervention. Because they are still exploring their own issues of identity and boundaries, they feel that it is unfair for family members to be planning an intervention without their knowledge. Adolescents fail to recognize or acknowledge that all previous direct efforts have not been effective in getting them to listen and understand the true dimensions of their problems.

Interventions are far more effective in getting individuals into treatment when addicts recognize that their behavior has been a problem. The addict who still values and respects members of the intervention group is the best candidate. In some situations, addicts have alienated so many people that only job-related people are left. This relationship with an employer or business associates might be the integral element that makes some addicts good candidates for intervention.

Stages of Formal Intervention

The four basic stages of a formal intervention are assessment, preintervention, intervention, and postintervention. The rest of this chapter describes these stages with many examples and a case study.

Assessment

Families consider an alcohol/drug intervention because a family member recognizes that the family needs to do something about the person with the alcohol/drug problem. Likely, people have approached the addict about getting help on numerous occasions. Despite their efforts, the addict still chooses not to recognize the problem or get help. The alcoholic/addict's goal is to continue drinking or drugging.

A family member begins the intervention process by contacting a professional who conducts interventions. The interventionist schedules an appointment with family members to assess the alcohol/drug problem and to determine if an intervention is appropriate.

An experienced interventionist is trained to assess alcohol/drug problems. In the initial assessment sessions, several family members, friends, colleagues, and even the employer describe what they know about the alcohol/drug use of the person being assessed for the intervention. Individuals seeking to intervene on a family member with an alcohol/drug problem are often at a late stage of frustration with the alcoholic/addict's dysfunctional and destructive behavior. Many look at the intervention as a last-ditch alternative. Despite the family's urgency to conduct an intervention, the interventionist conducts a proper assessment to determine if the person really does have an alcohol/drug problem.

The key element of the assessment is eliciting *behavior-specific information* and avoiding hearsay and generalized information. The interventionist needs specific times, dates, and firsthand knowledge of the actual level of consumption of alcohol and drugs. Some assessment questions are "What makes you think the individual has a problem with alcohol/drugs?" "What have been the consequences of this individual's alcohol/drug use?" The interventionist asks family members to explain or clarify the

Frequency of use, amounts used (dose and routes of administration), and set and setting of use
Patterns of use—binges, periods of nonuse, and cycle of use
History of negative consequences—overdoses, medical complications, and physical and emotional harm
Periods of abstinence, if any, and methods used
Any medical conditions that affect alcohol/drug use
Use of coffee, cigarettes, and medications and other addictions
Difficulties with the criminal-justice system
Financial problems and interpersonal problems

Family members at the assessment sessions are asked to describe specifically what they know about the addict's use of alcohol and drugs and resulting dysfunctional and destructive behavior. The assessment clarifies the dimensions of the problem with alcohol/drugs. The family, and others present, usually recognize, confirm, and validate their own worst fears—the individual has an alcohol/drug problem.

Another extremely important aspect of the assessment is to determine whether the person you are going to intervene on is able to listen and understand. Someone who is going to physically attack, verbally explode, or rage at others at the intervention is not appropriate for an intervention. During the assessment stage, interventionists often ask the family members and others present, "How does the person you are planning to intervene on deal with anger?" "What do you think his or her reaction is going to be to the intervention?" These questions should elicit responses that determine if the individual is violent and if there have been some physical violations in the past. Sometimes individuals can be paranoid and/or delusional, especially if they have been using cocaine, crack, or freebase. Obviously, you do not want to do an intervention if there is a high risk that the individual will be violent or unable to listen and understand. One alternative is to videotape the intervention and give it to the addict.

Some people have a negative reaction to the concept of an alcohol/drug intervention. They believe that it is an invasion, or a violation, of the individual and his or her right to use alcohol/drugs. For the intervention to be effective, it must be planned without the knowledge of the person being intervened on. Some individuals have difficulty with this behind-the-scenes aspect. Once the interventionist has assessed that an intervention is warranted, members of the intervention group must decide whether they are comfortable proceeding with the intervention.

Case Study 9.1 illustrates the perils of initiating an intervention without first doing a proper assessment.

Preintervention

The preintervention stage consists of all the sessions necessary to prepare for the actual intervention to take place. The ingredients essential for a successful intervention include (1) the commitment and participation of meaningful and significant

Case Study 9.1

Intervention Without Proper Assessment

J. R.

J. R., an aspiring vice president in a developing company, contacted an interventionist and requested an intervention for another vice president in the same company. The family members of the person with the supposed alcohol problem believed that Roger had been drinking regularly but were not sure that he had an alcohol problem. Insisting that his co-worker's drinking was a problem, J. R. was unable to come up with any behavior-specific examples of increased alcohol use. Despite the limited information and secondhand generalizations, the interventionist decided to go ahead with the intervention. The result was disastrous. Roger did not have an alcohol problem and quickly identified sabotage by his colleague, who desired his sales territory. Needless to say, Roger was justified in proceeding with litigation against the interventionist for not conducting a proper assessment.

others (family members, friends, relatives, peers, and children); (2) a proper assessment by the interventionist; and (3) specific, nonjudgmental information about the individual's alcohol and drug behavior.

In preparation for the intervention, preintervention sessions develop a cohesive group of significant others—a group that has the goal of getting the alcoholic/addict into appropriate treatment.

The interventionist begins developing this group by educating the members, giving them information about the dynamics of chemical dependency. The education emphasizes the progressive nature of the disease of alcoholism/drug addiction, which affects the entire family.

The group members then develop their scripts and role-play the intervention. Role-playing allows the group to anticipate the reactions of the person they are going to intervene on. The group members can then redevelop their intervention to make it more effective.

The alcoholic/addict is a master in distracting the intervention group from the goals of the intervention. When each family member communicates generalizations and judgments, the alcoholic/addict picks at their statements and distracts the group, thus weakening their ability to get the alcoholic/addict to commit to treatment. Therefore, the members of the intervention group must develop and communicate behavior-specific examples of the alcoholic/addict's dysfunctional and self-destructive behavior.

The following examples illustrate generalized statements, followed by the alcoholic/addict's distracting statements. The appropriate behavior-specific statement follows each set of generalized and distracting responses.

Example 1

Generalized and blaming statements: "Boy, you were really wasted at the party picnic and got violent. You were drunk and loaded on cocaine."

Alcoholic/addict distracting statements: "What do you mean wasted? You were drinking just as much as I was. Weren't you? Boy, are you hypocritical. You use cocaine."

Behavior-specific statements: "John, I'm here because I care about you. On Saturday, July 4, 1991, at the company picnic, I saw you drink five beers from 1 to 3 p.m., then snort six lines of cocaine, which was followed by two more beers. You sat down in the outfield during the softball game and fell asleep. When I went over to wake you up, you threw a punch at me, right in front of the head of our company. You left the field. I found you a half hour later, with a six-pack in the back of your car. Two of the cans of beer were already empty. I am worried about you. I'm afraid you are going to lose your job. You've been like a brother to me. I pray that you will get help. I know it's the alcohol and drugs."

Example 2

Generalized and blaming statements: "You are an awful husband and father. You are always using drugs and drinking too much. Last night you were drinking and snorting cocaine all night. You scared the kids to death that night by yelling so loud at them, like a madman."

Alcoholic/addict distracting statements: "You think you are such a great mother? I remember the time you. . . ."

Behavior-specific statements: "John, I'm your wife and I'm here because I care about you. On Friday night, November 3, I went to the church meeting. When I came home at 10:15 p.m., I smelled alcohol on your breath and clothes. There was an empty gram bottle of cocaine on the kitchen table and three lines of cocaine still on the mirror. There were 12 empty beer cans on the living room floor and the kids were hiding in their closet upstairs. When I went into their room, they ran to me, shaking and out of control. That night I had to sleep with them because they were so frightened. The next day, they told me you threw beer cans at them and told them you would kill them if they didn't stop bothering you. I love you, John; I know it's the alcohol and drugs. I would like all of us to get help."

Each person involved in the intervention uses the following script format to avoid generalized, blaming statements:

"I'm here because I care about you. You are my _____. I *care* about you."
"I saw _____" (describe the behavior-specific incidents that occurred)
"I feel _____" (embarrassed, hurt, frightened, worried, ashamed, etc.)
"I know it's the drugs." (or the alcohol or cocaine)
"I want you [us] to get help."

Script Example

> "John, I'm here because *I care* about you. We've been friends a very long time. During Christmas, *I saw* you snort half a gram of cocaine. In the next hour, you drank four beers. *I felt embarrassed* when you were trying to kiss your niece. *I felt ashamed. I saw* the hurt on your wife's face. *I know it's the cocaine. I know it's the alcohol. I want you to get help.*"

Some interventionists prefer the words "I want you to get help." Others prefer "I want us to get help" because everyone in the family is going to get help to stop enabling the alcoholic/addict's use of alcohol/drugs.

During the preintervention, the intervention group members determine

1. When the intervention will take place
2. Where the intervention will take place—usually a neutral setting such as the interventionist's office is best
3. Who will bring the person to the intervention
4. Their scripts, role-play the intervention, and determine the most effective way of communicating their message
5. In which order each member will talk during the intervention
6. Who is going to ask for a commitment to listen from the person being intervened on
7. That arrangements have been made with the alcohol/drug treatment program; insurance and other details have been completed; and a bed is reserved at the treatment center starting on the day of the intervention
8. All contingencies, so that the individual can go directly to the treatment program; bags have been packed and are in the car; and a family member drives the addict directly to the treatment program.

Every detail is planned, even the seating arrangement. The actual intervention session will start and flow as planned. The family members will be prepared to continue their own recovery, regardless of the addict's decision. The session will not escalate into an uncontrollable situation. The family will approach the intervention as a process, rather than a static event. Bear in mind that if the preintervention sessions have gone well, the interventionist is available to help the family members during the intervention, but most often he or she plays a minimal, facilitating role.

Intervention

Each intervention is unique. However, they all have the same common ingredients for success, such as a nonjudgmental tone and behavior-specific caring responses by family and friends. The following is an example of an intervention.

Audrey is an attractive, energetic 33-year-old. She owns a very successful travel agency. She is the single parent of two children: Andy is 12 years old and Bridget is 7 years old. Audrey is dynamic, aggressive, and—the most critical feature—an alcoholic.

Audrey's sister, Mary, 39, is concerned enough to seek intervention for her sister. Both sisters grew up in an alcoholic family system. Their father died of alcoholism when Mary was 16 and Audrey was 9 years old. Those involved with the intervention are the following:

Mary—Audrey's older sister
Ann—Audrey and Mary's mother, a very successful businesswoman
Roger—Mary's son, Audrey's nephew, a 20-year-old student at the University of
    Washington
Andy—Audrey's 12-year-old son

Mary has taken Audrey to the interventionist's office under the pretense that they have been having some family counseling sessions for her son Roger. She said they wanted Audrey to participate in one session. All the family members are present at the office, waiting for Audrey and Mary to arrive.

Mary:	Audrey, this is Dr. Fields. [Shakes hands.] Just sit right here. Audrey, we are all here because we care about you. We are concerned about you and the children. We would like to be able to talk to you about our concerns. We would each like to say some things. We need your commitment to listen to us and not to respond until we are finished. You will have an opportunity to respond then. Will you promise to first listen to us and not talk until we are finished?
Audrey:	But, I thought we were here for Roger.
Mary:	We are here for you, Roger, and all the family members.
Audrey:	Yeah, but you didn't let me know what this was about.
Mary:	Audrey, we wanted you to come. Will you just hear us out? Then you can have your chance.
Audrey:	I, I . . . don't . . . yeah, I guess so. O.K., I'll listen to what you have to say. [Establishing ground rules allows each family member to talk without being distracted by the addict's ambiguous arguments. Having the addict agree to listen and not talk back is an essential

ingredient for the intervention to be successful. Even though Audrey has been deceived in getting her to the intervention, she knows or suspects what the meeting is about. She is curious and is even challenging the group to try to affect her.]

Roger: Thank you. You've been like a big sister to me, even though you are my aunt. You have provided a lot of opportunities to me. You've taken me on vacations and introduced me to all sorts of people, activities, and even jobs that I never would have had access to. I care about you a great deal. You've been a tremendous influence and I am very proud of you. I am here because I love you.

Lately, however, I find that I'm not so proud of you anymore. I'm worried about you. I'm worried about Andy. I'm worried about Bridget. At your birthday party on January 7, you came home smelling of alcohol. You had three margaritas within an hour. I saw you in the kitchen, downing two doubles, as if they were water. You stumbled out of the kitchen and fell and cut your lip.

Audrey: That was my birthday party. Don't you understand?

Roger: You promised you would listen. After you cut yourself, when Andy, Bridget, and I came into the kitchen to help, you screamed and yelled at us to get away. Andy was so frightened he hid in his room and Bridget couldn't stop crying. They said they were so frightened that you were going to hit them again.

This isn't the first time this has happened. The same thing happened when we went down to Mexico. You had four drinks at the airport bar and four drinks on the flight. I was so embarrassed when you were flirting with the man next to you. The kids were embarrassed when you were kissing him and when you yelled at me for interfering. When we got to our hotel, the first thing you did was to order more booze.

In February, I was at the travel agency and you went into the bathroom. You invited me in and you had some lines of cocaine that you offered me. I saw you do ten lines of cocaine and then come out and act as if everything was O.K. You made six trips to the bathroom in the hour that I was there.

Audrey: I didn't do that much. As if you are so innocent!

Roger: You promised that you would listen and not interrupt. I was with you the night you got arrested for driving under the influence of alcohol. The kids were frightened sitting in the back seat. Despite my arguing with you, you insisted on driving. I was so frightened that we all would be killed. I went along because I felt guilty that you would kill yourself and the kids. I tried to take the keys away from you, but you wouldn't let me. I was so angry with your boyfriend, Al, for insisting that you were O.K., when you couldn't even walk straight. I was so angry with you when the police arrested you in front of your children. But I was more upset with myself for allowing myself to get drawn into the whole situation.

Audrey, despite all of this I love you and the children and I want you to get help.

Audrey: What kind of help?

Roger: [No response, head tilted down to ground, feeling emotionally spent.]

Ann: Audrey, you were a beautiful child; I gave birth to you. I love you a great deal. You were always so fun loving, energetic, and interested in so many things. We went shopping the other day, last Wednesday, and you had four beers at lunch, after you said you would cut back. You told me that you were just wired. You were agitated, nervous, jittery. Audrey, I'm frightened for you. When we came home from the travel agency last Friday, you smelled of alcohol. You were driving erratically. I was afraid we would get pulled over and you'd be arrested again. When I told you that you were in no condition to drive, you yelled at me to stop nagging.

Audrey: You, you're always telling me what to do. You're always bothering me. You're always involved in my life, telling me how to parent my kids.

Ann: That day, I saw you drink three beers before we left the agency.

Audrey: You guys are in this together. I don't even know why I'm here.

Roger: You said you'd listen.

Audrey: How can I listen to you if you keep on getting together? How could you guys get together behind my back to do this?

Ann: We're here because we care about you. We love you. I know it's the drugs. I know it's the alcohol. I want us to get some help.

Mary: We've grown up together. We've always been close. I love you. I care about you. Last week, we went out to Morgan's restaurant. You drank five margaritas within an hour and a half. You were snorting cocaine in the bathroom. You left the restaurant with two men whom you didn't know. I am really frightened for you. The next day you called me and told me you had a problem with alcohol and wanted help. Two days later, on Sunday, when I asked you about getting help, you said that you were doing much better and were getting your act together.

It was only a week later, that Friday night, when you were back at Morgan's. I saw you drink three doubles in an hour. You insisted that I stay. It was too hard to stay and watch you order another drink. I'm afraid that you are hurting yourself. I worry about you. I want my younger sister back. I want you to get help.

Andy: [Tears rolling from his eyes] Mommy, I am afraid when you drink and use drugs that you will hurt me. I am afraid that you will hurt Bridget. I want you to go get help. Will you?

Audrey: [Hugs Andy] Yes, I'll get help. I love you and don't want you to be frightened.

Mary: We have reserved a bed at the treatment center and Roger will drive you there.

Audrey: You mean you want me to go right now?

Mary: Yes.

Audrey: But what about the appointments at the agency?

Mary: I've arranged for Natalie to come in and manage the agency while you are gone.

Audrey: But what about the meeting with the accountant on Thursday?

Ann: I can cover the meeting, since I know all about the new book-keeping system.

Audrey: What about clothes?

Mary: I packed some of your things in a suitcase. Anything else you want I can get to you tomorrow.

Audrey: Can the children come and visit?

Mary: After the first week, there are regular family visits and a family counseling program. We chose this program because it specializes in providing counseling for young children.

Audrey: I guess you thought of everything.

                 [In reality, the family did think of everything. Any potential form of denial was anticipated, so that Audrey and her family could get the help they needed.]

In the event that Audrey did not agree to go into treatment, the family had prepared another bottom-line script. The purpose of the bottom-line script is to let the addict know that if she refuses to go into treatment, the family is not going to continue to enable her alcohol/drug use, as they have in the past. In implementing the bottom-line script, family members have to be willing to follow through with their bottom lines. Otherwise, there is no point in stating them. For example, if Audrey had refused to go into treatment, the bottom-line stage of the intervention would have followed:

Roger: Audrey, I care about you. You've been a person that I greatly admire. I love you a great deal. I'm frightened about the alcohol and drugs. I'm fearful that you'll hurt yourself or the kids. If you don't go into treatment, I can no longer come over to the house. I won't see you until you get help. It's too difficult for me to see you killing yourself.

Ann: Audrey, I love you. You are a wonderful, caring mother. I see you teaching the kids to read and doing wonderful, creative things with them. You'll always be my daughter. If you don't get help I'm going to have my lawyer start the process of declaring you unfit. It hurts me to do this, but I can't allow the children to be abused the way they are. I know it's the alcohol and drugs, and I want us to get help. [Ann cries.]

Mary: We've been more than sisters. We've been best friends. If you don't get help, I'll help Mom get the children in a safe environment and away from the alcohol and drugs. I'm afraid for the children and their future. Please get help.

The bottom-line script is implemented only if the individual refuses to get treatment. If the individual still refuses treatment after the bottom line, the intervention is over, and the family members implement the bottom line.

Postintervention

The trauma and emotion of the intervention affects all of the family members and friends involved in the intervention. Immediately after a successful intervention, families are often relieved and hopeful. However, the road to family recovery has just begun. The family should get together with the interventionist within a month, prior to the end of the 30-day inpatient program attended by the person who was intervened on. This gives the family members an opportunity both to reflect on their original commitment to the intervention and on their own enabling behavior and to reiterate their commitment to recovery.

⚹ In Review

- Everything one does to create awareness of an alcohol/drug problem is an intervention.
- An intervention is any action taken by someone to interrupt the progression of problems with alcohol/drugs.
- The primary goal of an intervention is to have the person with an alcohol/drug problem to agree to get into treatment (i.e., usually in-patient treatment).
- The stages of a formal intervention are assessment, preintervention, intervention, and postintervention.
- The key element of the assessment is eliciting behavior-specific information and avoiding hearsay and generalized information.
- Interventions are non judgmental, behavior-specific, caring responses by family members, friends, employers, etc.

⚹ Discussion Questions

1. Discuss your opinion and concerns about a formal intervention. Organize a debate on the topic.
2. Plan a role play of a formal intervention: assign a counselor, family roles, and the person you are going to focus the intervention on; go through the stages from assessment, preintervention, intervention, and postintervention.
3. Discuss any interventions—informal or formal—in which you have been involved.

⚹ Reference

Johnson, Vernon E. 1986. *How to help someone who doesn't want help*. Minneapolis: Johnson Institute Books.

Prevention of Substance Abuse Problems

Outline of Chapter 10

Introduction

Early Prevention Approaches

Alternative Activities as a Prevention Approach
    Alternatives Are Actively Pursued by the Individual
    Alternatives Are Acceptable, Attractive, and Attainable
    Alternatives Use Mentors and Role Models
    Alternatives Integrate Self-Concepts

Prevention Approaches of the 1980s

School-Based Prevention Curricula
    Empowerment
    Goal Setting
    Capability Development

Key Components of a Prevention Program
    Address Community Needs
    Include Youth in Prevention Planning
    Promote Proactivity
    Develop a Long-Term Perspective

Programs Aimed at At-Risk Youth

Risk Factors for Substance Abuse

Resiliency

Emotional Intelligence

Domains of Prevention

Prevention Programs and Prevention Emphasis
    Developmental Assets Model

High-Risk Youth and CSAPs

Prevention and Special Populations
    People of Color and Other Minorities
    College Students
    Older Adults
    Prevention and the Family

Objectives

1.   Describe early prevention approaches (i.e., scare tactics, converting approaches, drug-specific approaches) and explain why they were ineffective.
2.   Describe "alternative activities" and explain why they need to be acceptable, attractive, and attainable.
3.   Explain the shift in prevention efforts in the 1980s and list the kinds of skills that were emphasized.
4.   Define primary, secondary, and tertiary prevention.
5.   Describe elements of various school-based prevention curricula.
6.   Explain the key components of prevention:
     • Addressing community needs
     • Including youth in the planning process
     • Promoting proactivity
     • Developing a long-term plan
7.   Describe the "social stress model," including the coping track and the abuse track.
8.   Explain the importance of targeting prevention efforts for at-risk youth.
9.   Identify and describe the at-risk factors for youth.
10. Define and describe resiliency and resilient factors.
11. Define and describe emotional intelligence and emotional intelligence factors.
12. Identify and describe the forty developmental assets.
13. Identify why there is a need for prevention efforts for special populations, including people of color and minorities, older adults, young older-adults, and the family.

✖ Introduction

Alcohol/drug prevention has often been a misunderstood and neglected aspect in addressing the American drug problem. This chapter provides a foundation so that you can apply prevention efforts at home, in school systems, and in the community. Prevention efforts have shifted from scare tactics (dangers and evils of drugs) to emphases on the worth of people and the coping skills needed to avoid a destructive pattern of alcohol/drug dependence. The goal of prevention, outlined in this chapter, is to develop active, involved, empowered, and capable young people.

✖ Early Prevention Approaches

For years, society has searched for easy ways to prevent drug dependence and addiction. Frightening movies and horror stories of drug abuse failed to make young people too scared to use drugs. Early efforts to prevent drug use focused primarily on providing the following:

   • Information on the dangers of specific drugs
   • Warnings of physical, social, and psychological harm
   • Punishments for sale, use, and possession

Scare tactics proved to be an ineffective prevention strategy. Much of the information was invalid, exaggerated, and overgeneralized, causing young people to question the credibility of the program.

Similar programs were developed and labeled by drug educator Walter M. Mathews (1975) as **converting programs.** These programs used the following tactics to attempt to dissuade young people from using drugs:

1. *Directing:* Teacher tells students what they must believe, value, and do.
2. *Preaching:* This was similar to directing, with an added appeal to the students' duty to a vague external authority.
3. *Convincing:* Teachers appealed to logic where lecturing was the method used.
4. *Scaring:* Teachers emphasized the dangers of drug use.

Additional converting approaches emphasized admonishment, indoctrination, persuasion, distortion, and fear.

Adolescence is a time of questioning and exploration. The information provided in these approaches was not geared to the sensitivity of young people; it insulted their individuality and ability to make decisions. Adults in authority told them what to do, rather than talking with them. These propaganda approaches did not emphasize communication and open discussion.

The failure of these approaches led to a new prevention strategy of providing factual information about drugs, or **drug-specific approaches.** These approaches emphasized each drug and its pharmacological properties and assumed young people would make responsible decisions about drug use if they knew the negative effects. Inadvertently, these drug-specific approaches heightened curiosity and caused the opposite, alleviating fears of drugs. Many students acquired the knowledge to better attain desired levels of intoxication.

As a result of the failure of scare tactics and drug-specific approaches, the government's Special Action Office on Drug Abuse Prevention (SAODAP) declared a 6-month moratorium in 1973 on all prevention materials development, prevention program implementation, and prevention activities. The moratorium allowed further review of research and determined that scare tactics and drug-specific information did not significantly deter drug use and were therefore ineffective. In 1974, Robert DuPont, then the director of the National Institute on Drug Abuse (NIDA), surveyed drug education programs and concluded that the educators and students believed that the majority of school-based drug education programs were ineffective and should be abolished. In a review of research on school-based drug education programs, Michael Goodstadt (1975) concluded that "there is an almost total lack of evidence indicating beneficial effects of drug education, very few educational programs have been evaluated and almost none have shown any significant improvement in anything other than levels of knowledge; attitudes and drug use have generally remained the same."

In 1974, the prevention branch of NIDA initiated a nationwide, 14-month planning process to develop a national strategy for primary prevention. This planning process involved over 400 prevention specialists in a series of nine planning conferences. In 1975, the institute published the resulting recommendations in *Toward a National Strategy for Primary Drug Abuse Prevention.* The report defined primary drug abuse prevention as "a constructive process designed to promote personal and social growth of the individual to full human potential and thereby inhibit or reduce physical, mental, emotional, or social impairment, which results in or from the abuse of chemical substances."

The report established three basic themes for primary prevention: (1) primary prevention must be understood as the development and reinforcement of positive behaviors; (2) primary prevention programs must be responsive in both design and operation to the needs of those they are intended to serve or support; and (3) primary prevention should, wherever possible, use collaborative efforts to utilize the already available capacities and resources of existing human service institutions.

The result of SAODAP's moratorium and prevention planning meetings was a major shift in focus from drugs to the young people and from pharmacological effects to healthy children.

In 1977, NIDA and other agencies developed an interagency report entitled *Recommendations for Future Federal Activities in Drug Abuse Prevention.* This report outlined three major goals for prevention activities:

1. Reducing the percentage of frequent use of the three gateway drugs (tobacco, alcohol, and marijuana) by 15 percent among 8- to 20-year-olds.
2. Reducing the destructive behavior associated with alcohol and other drug abuse by 20 percent among 14- to 20-year-olds, as evidenced by a reduction in overdose deaths, emergency room visits, drug arrests, and other alcohol/drug-related incidents.
3. Retraining attitudes concerning the use of psychoactive substances, especially the gateway drugs, by maintaining current levels of awareness regarding the addictive nature of heroin and alcohol and raising awareness of the addictive nature of tobacco by 50 percent.

✼ Alternative Activities as a Prevention Approach

In Chapter 1, we examined the primary function of alcohol/drugs as serving our natural innate drive to alter our sense of consciousness. Ronald Siegal, in his book *Intoxication,* describes altering one's consciousness as the fourth drive, after hunger, thirst, and sex. The primary goal of alternative activities is to teach people that they are capable of altering their consciousness in a meaningful, longer-lasting, life-enhancing, and satisfying way that is incompatible with alcohol/drug use.

The late 1970s saw a strong movement toward alternative activity programs for young people. The programs usually involved wilderness activities, requiring teamwork, challenge, and risk that developed feelings of competence, skill, and self-worth. Today, many adolescent and adult inpatient and residential chemical dependency treatment programs are including alternative activity program elements as a natural part of the clients' recovery program. This can include rope courses, climbing structures, and even what one program calls "equine therapy" (i.e., working with horses).

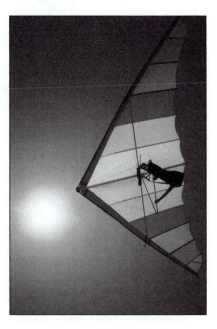

Hang glider against a blue sky.

© Elmer Frederick Fischer/ Corbis

Allan Cohen (1972), a strong advocate of alternative activities, defines alternatives as pursuits that are valued and truly preferred by individuals and seen as incompatible with drugs. Cohen emphasizes that alternatives are not just a substitution for drugs; they are an integrated and valued part of the person's life.

Alternatives Are Actively Pursued by the Individual

Cohen felt that for an alternative to be successful, the process of searching for the alternative should be a potent alternative in itself. Individuals are encouraged to find other activities they can develop, persevere through to mastery, and enjoy. The process of being able to choose ways to get high naturally through one's own interests is truly empowering. It follows that alternatives are more effective if they call for activity, assertion of will or will power, and effort and commitment. Alternatives are less successful if individuals are passive recipients of the activity. This is consistent with the function of drug dependence and alcoholism as a rather passive activity. All alcoholics/addicts have to do is sit back and passively wait for the alcohol/drug to take effect.

Cohen (1972) illustrates this in the example of listening to music: "Passively listening to music is not necessarily a promising alternative to drugs, since one could be passively stoned at the time. Training in active listening and deep study of music is more likely to be frustrating to drug use since the clarity of one's senses and cognition become important in successful completion of the task."

Alternatives Are Acceptable, Attractive, and Attainable

Alternatives must be acceptable and attractive. Any alternative offered must be realistic, attainable, and meaningful. Alternatives must also help people understand themselves and improve their self-image and personal awareness. Dohner (1972) outlined the following characteristics of positive alternatives:

1. They must contribute to the individual's identity and independence.
2. They must offer active participation and involvement.
3. They must offer a chance for commitment.
4. They must provide a feeling of identification with a larger body of experience.
5. Some of the alternatives must be in the realm of the noncognitive and the intuitive.

Alternatives Use Mentors and Role Models

Another essential feature of alternatives is a successful role model or mentor—someone who can guide, facilitate, and encourage the successful attainment of the alternative skill. This person could be a positive parent model, a coach, a teacher, a peer, or anyone else who understands and respects the boundaries in the development of the alternative skill.

Alternatives Integrate Self-Concepts

Alternative activities are effective as preventive tools if they enhance the development of skills associated with improving one's sense of self.

Use the worksheet shown in Table 10.1 to list your motives and preferred alternatives to alcohol/drug use. Also, identify the steps and resources necessary to implement each alternative.

TABLE 10.1		
Alternatives Worksheet		
Level of Experience	*Corresponding Motives*	*Steps and Resources to Implement Alternatives to Alcohol/Drugs*
Physical		
Sensory		
Emotional		
Interpersonal		
Social		
Political		
Intellectual		
Creative-aesthetic		
Philosophical		
Spiritual, mystical		
Miscellaneous		

⚹ Prevention Approaches of the 1980s

In the 1980s, the prevention strategy shifted from drugs to people, emphasizing the following:

- Educational information
- Coping skills
- Personal competence
- Decision making
- Refusal skills
- Alternative activities

The goal of these programs was to develop capable young people able to make responsible decisions about alcohol/drugs. The focus changed to understanding the impact of drugs on individuals, rather than understanding the pharmacological properties of alcohol/drugs. The affective aspect focused on the individual's needs, feelings, and emotions about alcohol/drugs.

These prevention programs worked toward developing the following skills:

- Clarifying personal values and ethics
- Improving self-concept
- Learning effective decision making
- Understanding and listening to each other's viewpoints
- Communicating about alcohol/drugs with peers, parents, and others
- Being involved in social and interpersonal activities
- Dealing effectively with feelings of anger, depression, and anxiety
- Having the ability to relax, play, and enjoy daily activities
- Developing and exploring ways to alter one's sense of consciousness through alternative activities

Agencies originally focused on prevention in secondary schools for adolescents 12 to 17 years of age. It quickly became apparent that in many cases it was already too late to provide preventive education to adolescents. This group required more intervention, skill building, and treatment-related approaches.

As a result, alcohol and drug curricula and primary prevention activities shifted to kindergarten through sixth grade. Agencies also developed secondary and tertiary prevention approaches for grades seven to twelve.

A definition of prevention covers three basic categories:

1. **Primary prevention** assumes that the individual has never tried drugs or alcohol and enforces a no-use norm by building positive self-esteem, developing good coping and refusal skills, and providing information on alcohol and drugs.
2. **Secondary prevention** assumes that the individual is in the early stages of use but does not regularly use drugs. Secondary prevention/intervention strategies try to stop drug use by providing drug information, developing decision-making and refusal skills, and improving family communication; it may also include individual counseling.
3. **Tertiary prevention** assumes that the individual is regularly using drugs but has not become a habitual user. Tertiary prevention/intervention includes counseling, drug education, and family therapy. There is a very fine line between the tertiary level of prevention and intervention and treatment services.

❧ School-Based Prevention Curricula

In 1983, the U.S. Department of Health and Human Services monograph *Drug Abuse Prevention Research* outlined four dimensions of prevention:

1. Course content centers on mental health, drug information, human development, nutrition, ethics, and chemical safety; these courses usually

fit into regular social studies, language arts, science, and other subject area
curricula

2. Courses on values clarification, problem-solving and decision-making skills,
    communication skills such as reflection and confrontation, alternative means
    for meeting needs, group process skills, role-playing, and dramatization
3. Courses that include competencies in human development, interpersonal
    relationships, personal autonomy, self-esteem, identity, decision-making skills,
    personal accountability, and accurate attributions of causality
4. Courses that also include general knowledge, conceptual frameworks, implicit
    assumptions and perspectives that define and describe the way each individual
    perceives the meaning of self, the nature of the world external to self, and the
    interrelatedness of things

Empowerment

A term often used in prevention programs is *empowerment.* Many prevention programs emphasize the empowering of the individual. The basic goal of prevention is
to empower individuals and prevent the destructive passive choice of alcohol/drug
dependence and addiction. Empowerment is a feeling that is developed by being
able to

- Say no when that is what one feels and wants.
- Establish the core aspects of a sense of self.
- Be aware of what one feels and integrate and communicate those feelings to
  others in establishing goals and making decisions.
- Establish and set boundaries, especially in interpersonal and intimate
  relationships.
- Establish integrity in relationships and a healthy, nondestructive,
  nonsabotaging approach to life.

These prevention programs are usually targeted at the general school population, rather than the high-risk students who have already exhibited problem behaviors in and outside of school.

Goal Setting

A model lesson for goal setting would include lessons on (1) setting goals, (2) ranking
priorities, (3) making decisions in relation to the goals, (4) persevering in the face
of difficult situations, and (5) maintaining effort (motivation) until goals are attained
or modified.

Capability Development

Other prevention lessons involve developing capabilities. I had the good fortune
many years ago to work with Stephen Glenn at the National Drug Abuse Center in
Washington, D.C. Today, Glenn lectures throughout the United States on the family

prevention theme of developing capable people. His model for developing capable children includes fostering the following in children:

1. Identification with viable role models
2. Identification with and responsibility for family process
3. Faith in personal resources to solve problems
4. Adequate development of intrapersonal skills (responsibility)
5. Adequate development of interpersonal skills (communication)
6. Well-developed situation skills (demand skills)
7. Adequately developed judgment skills (application)

ᕱ Key Components of a Prevention Program

Address Community Needs

Alcohol/drug prevention should address itself to the needs of the community and interface with community leaders, agencies, and the people. Edward M. Brecher knew community was important when he wrote the following in *Licit and Illicit Drugs* (1972): Stop viewing the drug problem as primarily a national problem to be solved on a national scale. In fact, as workers in the drug scene confirm, the drug problem is a collection of local problems. The predominant drugs differ from place to place and from time to time. Effective solutions to problems also vary; a plan that works now for New York City may not be applicable to upstate New York and vice versa. With respect to education, . . . the need for local wisdom and local control is particularly pressing. Warning children against drugs readily available to them is a risky business at best, requiring careful, truthful, unsensational approaches.

Include Youth in Prevention Planning

A prevention program must take into account the consumer of that program. To develop prevention programs in a vacuum, or from a strictly theoretical base, does not take into account the most important variable—the needs of youth.

Promote Proactivity

A core theme in prevention is to teach young people to move from being passive to being active, or proactive. Being proactive involves taking initiative, anticipating potential problems, and integrating your feelings. Too many young people spend excessive time in passive activities (e.g., watching television, playing computer games).

Parents can teach and model active behaviors and encourage activities that help young people develop a capable, positive sense of self. Proactive choices help develop the child's coping skills and ability to overcome setbacks.

Develop a Long-Term Perspective

Prevention is a long-term strategy. Longitudinal studies over 5 to 10 years are necessary to determine the effects of prevention. Unfortunately, most prevention programs have short-term funding, which limits the evaluation of their true effectiveness. Currently, we focus on the short-range perspective of drug enforcement and interdiction without the balance of a comprehensive prevention strategy to deal with the demand side of alcohol/drugs with youth. Our true hope is that the prevention and family approaches used with 3- to 10-year-olds—the next generation—may break this cycle of problems with dependence and addiction to alcohol/drugs.

In summary, an effective substance-abuse prevention strategy should do the following:

Emphasize cognitive and affective skills that help young people accept responsibility and motivate them to make wise decisions about alcohol and drugs.

Focus on people, not pharmacology, emphasizing educational information, coping skills, personal competence, decision making, refusal skills, and alternative activities.

Develop prevention programs that provide information plus communication, establish credibility, and meet community needs.

Take into account the needs of youth and develop prevention approaches cooperatively with young people in the community.

Develop primary efforts (those who have never used alcohol/drugs), secondary efforts (those in early stages of alcohol/drug use), and tertiary prevention efforts (those in regular stages of alcohol/drug use).

Develop longitudinal commitment to long-term prevention efforts.

Table 10.2 presents additional guidelines for making prevention programs more effective.

✖ Programs Aimed at At-Risk Youth

Clinicians and researchers have identified a variety of factors that are predictive of later substance abuse by young people. Antisocial behaviors and aggressiveness can predict, as early as the first grade, early alcohol/drug initiation and later substance abuse. Family imbalance, parental problems with alcohol/drugs, and parental dysfunction are also predictive of children having problems with alcohol/drugs.

At-risk youth require a more intensive and modified prevention program than students with no real social and interpersonal problems, who are supported by fairly functional family systems.

Often, teachers and parents cooperatively identify at-risk youth appropriate for the program. Sometimes, key school personnel—teachers, coaches, dean of students, school-nurse, counselor, psychologist—develop a team approach with parents in identifying students at risk for alcohol/drug problems.

The number of young people who are high risk for developing substance abuse problems is astounding.

High-risk youngsters are hard to reach because they resist traditional authority, often have a low literacy level, and may be on the streets instead of in school or in structured community settings.

T A B L E   1 0 . 2

Guidelines for Making Prevention Programs More Effective

- **Blend school-based and community prevention efforts to effect environmental change.** Community-wide approaches that involve broad participation of all sectors in the development of prevention efforts, including individually focused and environmental and policy focused, are needed.

- **Link prevention programs with the primary mission of schools: academics.** Prevention efforts at schools need to be more fully integrated with academic curricula. The case needs to be made that time spent in schools on prevention programs contributes to academic success.

- **Integrate prevention resource systems to support prevention efforts.** A more integrated approach that crosses disciplines and agencies is needed to maximize available resources. A less categorical approach to prevention is needed in order to address common risk factors. Prevention is about systems and strategies, not more discrete programs.

- **Forge agreement on what is to be prevented as a foundation for program design.** Standards for definitions and terms across prevention disciplines need to be developed in order to avoid contributing to confusion in those looking for guidance.

- **Employ new technologies to support prevention.** Technologies are now available to both reach individuals with prevention messages as well as disseminate information on evidence-based prevention to help communities develop prevention efforts.

- **Increase funding, training, and support for prevention researchers and practitioners.** Prevention works, but questions remain about both what works best in prevention and how communities can implement effective prevention activities.

- **Learn what practitioners, including teachers, are doing at ground level.** Because of the likelihood that practitioners consider program components to be fungible, it is important to know more about which components are essential and in what combinations.

SOURCE: Copyright 2001. Robert Wood Johnson Foundation. Used with permission from the Robert Wood Johnson Foundation.

Their self-efficacy makes them less likely to respond to appeals based on caring about self, such as "take care of your health" or "don't take unnecessary risks that may hurt you." Also, these youth are already drinking and, in some cases, using multiple drugs at early ages. It is too late for refusal skills (saying no). Other obstacles include the following (Office for Substance Abuse Prevention 1988):

- Rejection of help because of fear and lack of trust or perhaps bravado
- Feelings of ambivalence and confusion about alcohol as a result of the many conflicting messages about alcohol use in U.S. society
- Fear by children and youth of being rejected again
- Hopelessness by young people in inner cities about the possibility of ever having a worthwhile future with a decent job and a chance of achieving the American Dream

- The presence in some inner-city neighborhoods of an open, accessible drug culture without apparent social sanctions and of large sums of money for youth who deal in drugs

Often, the special relationship with a parent, a family member, a teacher, a minister, a coach, or others is what keeps some children on the road to a sober and successful life. Strong religious training is an example of a family ritual that also may save many young people from the streets.

One example of a school-based program for at-risk youth is *Interpersonal Problem Solving.* The program's major focus is on effective problem solving and effective interpersonal skills. Program topics include

- Dealing with authority figures
- Developing empathy
- Standing up for one's rights
- Resisting peer pressure
- Improving behavior in school
- Getting along better with family members

⋈ Risk Factors for Substance Abuse

In the early years of alcohol/drug prevention, efforts were primarily focused on generic prevention programs. The thinking was "this is a good thing to promote; maybe it will prevent substance abuse" (e.g., good health habits). These programs were global and aimed at the entire school population. Prevention in the new millennium is targeted at specific at-risk populations, communities of high risk, while focusing on specific risk factors.

J. David Hawkins, Richard E. Catalono, and Janet Y. Miller in their 1992 study "Risk and Protective Factors for Alcohol and Other Drug Problems in Adolescence and Early Adulthood: Implications for Substance Abuse Prevention" outline 17 risk factors for substance abuse and accompanying interventions:

1. Laws and norms
2. Availability
3. Extreme economic deprivation
4. Neighborhood disorganization
5. Physiological factors
6. Family drug behavior
7. Family management practices
8. Family conflict
9. Low bonding to family
10. Early and persistent problem behaviors
11. Academic failure
12. Low commitment to school
13. Peer rejection in elementary grades
14. Association with drug using peers

15. Alienation and rebelliousness
16. Attitudes favorable to drug use
17. Early onset of drug use

Table 10.3 presents factors associated with risk behaviors. Table 10.4 presents factors associated with healthy behaviors.

❧ Resiliency

Steven Wolin, M.D., a professor at George Washington University, and his wife, Sybil Wolin, Ph.D., a developmental psychologist, are co-authors of *The Resilient Self: How Survivors of Troubled Families Rise Above Adversity* (1994) and developers of Project Resilience, Washington, D.C.

The Wolins define resiliency as an internal protective factor and the ability to bounce back. In their research on adult children of alcoholics, they found that some children of alcoholics grow up free of drinking because they

---

T A B L E   1 0 . 3

Factors Associated with Risk Behaviors

Demographic

Less education
Low income
Unemployment

Psychosocial

High level of stressful life events
Poor social support[a]
Poor ethnic identity[b]

Ecological

Exposure to community and interpersonal violence[c]
Poor interactions with health care workers[d]

Individual

Psychological status (e.g., alienation,[e] powerlessness, depression,[f] or post traumatic stress disorder)
Perceptions of levels of stress
Experiences of racism

[a]Neighbors and Jackson 1984; Gombeski et al. 1982.
[b]Bullough 1967; Abrams, Allen, and Gray 1993; Carter 1991; Munford 1994.
[c]Sanders-Phillips 1994a, 1994b, 1996a; Cohen et al. 1991.
[d]Freimuth and Mettzger 1990; Harrison and Harrison 1971; James et al. 1984; Perez-Stable 1987; Webb 1984; Makuc, Fried, and Kleinman 1989; Sanders-Phillips 1996a; Balsheim 1991; Farris and Glenn 1976.
[e]Bullough 1972; Cohen et al. 1982; Hibbard 1985; Morris, Hatch, and Chipman 1966; Seeman and Evans 1962; Seeman and Seeman 1983.
[f]Cohen et al. 1991; Leftwich and Collins 1994.

T A B L E   1 0 . 4
Factors Associated with Healthy Behaviors
Demographic
High education level High income Employment Positive marital status[a]
Psychosocial

High level of social support[b]
   Emotional support
   Information sharing
   Provision of tangible goods and services
Church participation

Individual
Internal locus of control Greater self-efficacy regarding the prevention of disease Positive perceptions of health status Greater knowledge and positive attitudes about health-promoting behaviors

[a]Cohen et al. 1991; Gottlieb and Green 1984; Rakowski 1988.
[b]Gottlieb and Green 1984; Neighbors and Jackson 1984; Shumaker and Hill 1991.
SOURCE: Meyer D. Glantz and Christine R. Hartel. *Drug Abuse: Origins and Interventions*, 1999. Washington, D.C.: American Psychological Association.

- build on their own strengths
- develop their own lifestyle and values, which are an improvement over those of their parents
- establish healthy "rituals" in their own family

Applying this knowledge, the Wolins worked with adolescents and young adults from the inner city who grew up in dysfunctional and abusive, alcoholic/addict family systems. They applied their "challenge" model of resiliency, helping these young people realize their own resiliency in attaining healthy growth. They called this "survivor's pride"—a sense that you have been tested and that you have prevailed. (See Figures 10.1 and 10.2.)

Resiliency is described by the Wolins as not getting stuck in the "damage model" but, instead, challenging yourself and celebrating your survival and growth. Resiliency work is about reframing the damage, uncovering strength in a damage- or deficit-oriented story. In the damage model, the individual is seen as helpless, fragile, passive, and trapped. The Wolins emphasize that you need to help the individual understand the damage, express the anger, grieve the past, and move to resiliency.

RESILIENCY

Resiliency is defined as:

- Mastering your painful memories rather than compulsively rehashing the damage you have suffered

- Accepting that your troubled family has left its mark and give up the futile wish that your scars can ever disappear completely

- Getting revenge by living well instead of squandering your energy by blaming and fault-finding

- Breaking the cycle of your family's troubles and putting the past in its place

FIGURE 10.1
SOURCE: Wolin and Wolin 1994.

RESILIENT ACTIONS

Resilient actions:

- Find and build on your own strengths

- Improve deliberately and methodically on your parents' lifestyles

- Marry consciously into strong, healthy families

- Fight off memories of horrible family get-togethers in order to establish healthy family times, routines, vacations, celebrations, and rituals in your own generation

FIGURE 10.2
SOURCE: Wolin and Wolin 1994.

Resiliency involves deliberation (making a plan). In many abusive family situations, it is a "getaway plan," creating distance from unhealthy situations. Resiliency skills also involve eventually choosing a spouse who is healthy and is developing healthy rituals.

They also describe how, too frequently, therapists perpetuate the victim's trap by

- maintaining the myth that family problems will inevitably be perpetuated from one generation to the next
- having the patients deplete themselves by continually blaming their parents for hurting them

Instead, the Wolins describe a more positive therapeutic goal of helping patients get revenge by seeking resiliency: by living healthy, productive lives rather than blaming and finding fault.

They describe seven resiliency factors (Wolin and Wolin 1994):

1. Insight—the habit of asking tough questions that pierce the denial and confusion in troubled families

2. Independence—emotional and physical distancing from a troubled family, which keeps survivors out of harm's way
3. Relationships—fulfilling ties to others that provide the stability, nurturing, and love that troubled families do not give
4. Initiative—a push for mastery that combats the feelings of helplessness troubled families produce in their offspring
5. Creativity—representing one's inner pain and hurtful experiences in art forms; "building a new world on the ruins of the old"
6. Humor—the ability to minimize pain and troubles by laughing at oneself
7. Morality—an informed conscience, which imbues the survivor surrounded by "badness" with a sense of his or her own "goodness"

❧ Emotional Intelligence

In 1995, Daniel Goleman, in his book *Emotional Intelligence,* made a case for a new kind of intelligence, or IQ—an IQ that goes beyond the traditional verbal and performance scales of most IQ tests and redefines what skills make up a successful person. Goleman labels this new IQ *emotional intelligence* and defines it as abilities such as

- being able to motivate oneself and persist in the face of frustration
- being able to control impulse and delay gratification
- being able to regulate one's mood and keep distress from swamping the ability to think
- being able to empathize and hope

The characteristics of emotional intelligence make one more successful at work, at relationships, at parenting, at coupleship, and at life in general. As we see increases in domestic violence, abuse, physical violence, and alcohol/drug abuse in homes, schools, community, our nation, and throughout the world, we see the importance of emotional intelligence. Managing anger and other moods (depression, fear, worry, and anxiety) is one of the key components of emotional intelligence.

"Of all the moods . . . anger is the mood people are worst at controlling. . . . Anger is the most seductive of the negative emotions, the self-righteous inner monologue that propels along filling the mind with the most convincing arguments to vent rage" (Goleman 1995).

The goals of the emotionally intelligent individual are optimism, motivation, perseverance, and self-efficacy.

❧ Domains of Prevention

Schools, religious and voluntary organizations, the media, the private sector, law enforcement, and health care are the secondary line of defense against drug and alcohol abuse by young people (see Figure 10.3). Families can make a real difference. Secondary approaches have little effect if the home and family environment are not involved and supportive of prevention efforts.

In conducting alcohol/drug educational and skill activities for parents over the past 20 years, I have found that the parents who don't need the information and are

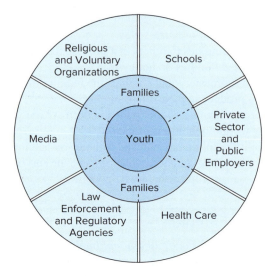

FIGURE 10.3   *A Conceptual Model for Preventive Approaches to Alcohol and Drug Abuse*
SOURCE: California Attorney General John Van De Kamp's Commission on the Prevention of Drug and Alcohol Abuse, 1986, Sacramento, CA. Used with permission from California Attorney General's Office.

already effective parents are the ones that come to every event. The parents who need help are either in denial, too embarrassed or ashamed, or too out of control to attend. Until we develop programs that can get these parents to participate, we are fighting an uphill battle.

✕ Prevention Programs and Prevention Emphasis Developmental Assets Model

The Search Institute of Minneapolis has developed a research-based framework of developmental assets, or factors that are critical for young people's successful growth and development. The institute's *Healthy Communities—Healthy Youth* programs are part of a national initiative to "motivate and equip individuals, organizations, and their leaders to join together in nurturing competent, caring, and responsible children and adolescents." The institute has identified and measured 40 developmental assets. These assets are the foundation that children and adolescents from many cultural backgrounds need to be responsible, successful, and caring human beings.

"These assets are more than just nice ideas. Research on youth in hundreds of communities finds that these assets are powerful influences on behavior [see Figure 10.4]. Yet, the average 6th- to 12th-grade student experiences only 18 of the 40 assets" (Search Institute 1999). The application of education and skill development of these developmental assets takes place in the schools, with parents and other adults, with young people, with youth serving organizations, in neighborhoods, in communities, in business and industry, in local government, in congregations, in the juvenile justice system, in community care systems, and in community organizations.

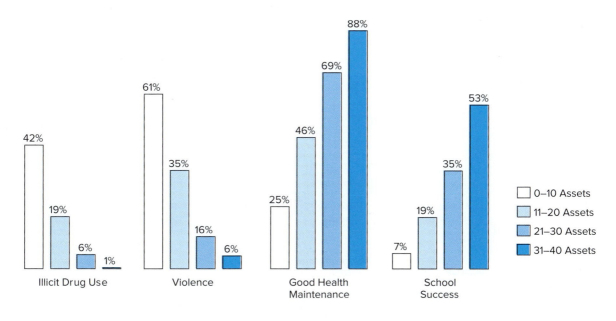

FIGURE 10.4   *The Power of Developmental Assets*   The more assets young people experience, the less likely they are to engage in a wide range of risky behaviors, and the more likely they are to engage in positive behaviors.
SOURCE: Based on Search Institute's study of almost 100,000 youth in 312 towns and cities across the United States during the 1996–1997 school year.

✖ High-Risk Youth and CSAPs

The National Cross-Site Evaluation of High-Risk Youth Program (NIDA 2002) found that the rate of substance use for high-risk youth participating in their CSAP (Community Substance Abuse Programs) was 12 percent lower at completion of the program than for comparison youth. They also found that this effect lasted—the rate of use for these youth was 6 percent below the rate for the comparison group 18 months later. These prevention programs work and produce lasting results despite the fact that these youth face multiple risk factors in their communities. Connections with positive social environments—schools, family, peers, community, and society— appeared to be important factors in preventing substance abuse. Figure 10.5 depicts this "Web of Influence."

✖ Prevention and Special Populations
People of Color and Other Minorities

A variety of factors put people of color and other minorities at risk for substance-abuse problems. Minorities as a group have more unemployment, have less prestigious occupations, and live in poverty and lower socioeconomic conditions. Thus, they experience more feelings of frustration, anger, resentment, and powerlessness. Inadequate education, housing, income, and other factors create additional stress and pressure, which may lead to problems with alcohol/drugs.

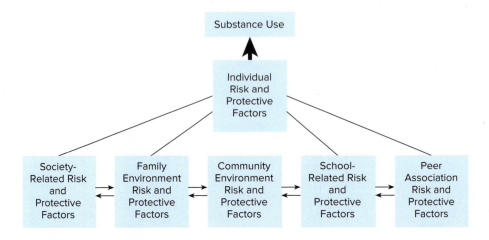

FIGURE 10.5   *The "Web of Influence" on Substance Use*
SOURCE: NIDA 2002.

For people of color, prevention must go beyond the approaches previously described. One of the biggest problems facing people of color is the crack epidemic in the inner cities, the increase in young cocaine and heroin addicts' giving birth to cocaine- and heroin-addicted babies, and the rise in methamphetamine use.

Prevention for people of color and other minorities must be community based. Residents must conceptualize the problem and jointly develop appropriate strategies.

Community-based prevention programs also must emphasize a systemic strategy to uproot the factors in the system that oppress people of color, such as prejudice and racism, and to implement training in diversity and methods of accessing the system.

College Students

During their first year of college, most students dramatically increase their alcohol/ drug use. The MTV spring break party illustrates the pervasive "let loose and get loaded" attitude of young college students.

Alcohol/drug use and abuse is a glamorized way of escape from the pressures of school. The newly acquired freedom of being away at college allows students more opportunities to use alcohol/drugs. The anxiety of adjusting to college and living away from home can result in escalated alcohol/drug use. The functions of alcohol/ drugs on college campuses are many—to party, to stay up late and study, to explore a personal sense of self and identity, to facilitate social and interpersonal relationships, and so forth.

Older Adults

Older adults are often forgotten or ignored when it comes to prevention efforts. The lack of any true role experienced by some elders leads to feelings of loneliness, boredom, frustration, rejection, abandonment, anxiety, fear, and depression. When elders complain about these feelings, sometimes the response is to prescribe medication.

Prevention efforts with elders frequently involve training and educational projects to assist them to keep accurate records of their medications or to develop methods to have someone monitor their medication. Elders need to be approached with individuality and dignity. They need to be empowered to develop their own advocacy. Pharmacists, physicians, and other health providers must act in cooperation and be sensitive to each individual case. Drug dosages and regimens must meet individual needs and be sensitive to the elders' ability to maintain their treatment plans.

Monitoring and educating the elder population are necessary prevention strategies. Advocacy for alternatives to medication are also essential, as well as the expansion of senior services. The more active and involved the lifestyles of elders, the healthier are the later years of their lives.

Prevention with elders also involves proactive approaches to healthy activities that promote physical movement (health permitting), interpersonal interaction, and a sense of value and worth. In the years to come, a majority of the population will be elders. Prevention programs and services need to be further developed now to meet the needs of this ever-expanding population.

Prevention and the Family

Unfortunately, prevention activities take place almost exclusively in school systems. We expect the school systems to prevent this epidemic of alcohol/drug use. The reality is that the families are the real first line of defense against alcohol/drug use by young people.

✐ In Review

- The early prevention approaches focused primarily on supplying information on the dangers of specific drugs; on warnings of physical, social, and psychological harm; and on punishment for sale, use, and possession. These scare tactics were ineffective, as were other converting programs, which tried to direct, preach, or convince young people not to use drugs. The information presented in these early prevention approaches was often invalid, exaggerated, and overgeneralized, causing young people to question the credibility of the prevention efforts.
- The next prevention efforts focused on drug-specific information in the hope that young people would make wise decisions about drugs. Unfortunately, these approaches heightened curiosity and alleviated fears, leading to an increase in drug experimentation, rather than the intended decrease.
- The ineffectiveness of scare tactics and drug-specific approaches led to a moratorium on prevention efforts by the government and a review of those features of a prevention program that were effective.
- In Chapter 1, we examined the primary function of alcohol/drugs as serving our natural innate drive to alter our sense of consciousness. Ronald Siegal, in his book *Intoxication,* describes altering one's consciousness as the fourth

drive, after hunger, thirst, and sex. The primary goal of alternative activities is to teach people that they are capable of altering their consciousness in a meaningful, longer-lasting, life-enhancing, and satisfying way that is incompatible with alcohol/drug use.

- Alternative activities are successful if they are acceptable, attractive, and attainable.
- In the 1980s, the thrust of these new prevention strategies shifted from drugs to people, emphasizing educational information, coping skills, personal competence, decision making, refusal skills, and alternative activities.
- Credibility is a basic premise for the effectiveness of any alcohol/drug prevention program.
- The key components of a prevention program are

  - Addressing community needs
  - Including youth in prevention planning
  - Promoting proactivity
  - Developing a long-term perspective

- Jean Rhodes and Leonard Jason (1988) developed a model that emphasizes the development of attachments, competence, and coping skills to minimize risk for substance abuse. The more stress the child experiences—without appropriate and strong bonding to parents, attachment to drug-free role models, access to models with a strong sense of self, and good coping skills and resources—the higher the risk of substance abuse.
- Current prevention programs should be aimed at at-risk youth and people of color and other minorities and should be community-based.
- Hawkins, Catalono, and Miller (1992) outlined 17 risk factors for substance abuse:

  Laws and norms
  Availability
  Extreme economic deprivation
  Neighborhood disorganization
  Physiological factors
  Family drug behavior
  Family management practices
  Family conflict
  Low bonding to family
  Early and persistent problem behaviors
  Academic failure
  Low commitment to school
  Peer rejection in elementary grades
  Association with drug using peers
  Alienation and rebelliousness
  Attitudes favorable to drug use
  Early onset of drug use

- Steven Wolin and Sybil Wolin developed a challenge model of resiliency. They define resiliency as an internal protective factor and the ability to bounce back.

In their research on adult children of alcoholics, they found that some children of alcoholics grow up free of drinking because they

- build on their own strengths
- develop their own lifestyle and values, which are an improvement over those of their parents
- establish healthy "rituals" in their own family

- The Wolins describe seven resiliency factors:
  - Insight—the habit of asking tough questions that pierce the denial and confusion in troubled families
  - Independence—emotional and physical distancing from a troubled family, which keeps survivors out of harm's way
  - Relationships—fulfilling ties to others that provide the stability, nurturing, and love that troubled families do not give
  - Initiative—a push for mastery that combats the feelings of helplessness troubled families produce in their offspring
  - Creativity—representing one's inner pain and hurtful experiences in art forms; "building a new world on the ruins of the old"
  - Humor—the ability to minimize pain and troubles by laughing at oneself
  - Morality—an informed conscience, which imbues the survivor surrounded by "badness" with a sense of his or her own "goodness"

- Daniel Goleman introduced the concept of emotional intelligence. Goleman labels this new IQ *emotional intelligence* and defines it as abilities such as
  - being able to motivate oneself and persist in the face of frustration
  - being able to control impulse and delay gratification
  - being able to regulate one's mood and keep distress from swamping the ability to think
  - being able to empathize and hope

- The Search Institute of Minneapolis has developed a research-based framework of developmental assets, or factors that are critical for young people's successful growth and development. The developmental assets model describes 40 developmental assets in the areas of support, empowerment, boundaries and expectations, constructive use of time, commitment to learning, positive values, social competence, and positive identity.

- The 40 developmental assets are

  Support

  1. family
  2. positive family communication
  3. other adults
  4. caring neighbors
  5. caring school climate
  6. parent involvement in school

Empowerment

   7. community values youth
   8. youth as resources
   9. service to others
10. safety

Boundaries and expectations

11. family
12. school
13. neighborhood
14. adult role models
15. positive peer
16. high expectations—parents and teachers

Constructive use of time

17. creative activities
18. youth programs
19. religious community
20. time at home

Commitment to learning

21. achievement motivation
22. school engagement
23. homework
24. bonding to school
25. reading for pleasure

Positive values

26. caring
27. equality and social justice
28. integrity
29. honesty
30. responsibility
31. restraint

Social competencies

32. planning and decision making
33. interpersonal competence
34. cultural competence
35. resistance skills
36. peaceful conflict resolution

Positive identity

37. personal power
38. self-esteem
39. sense of purpose
40. positive view of personal future

✄ Discussion Questions

1. The media ad that shows eggs frying in a pan, as a metaphor for how your brain looks on drugs, has been a controversial prevention approach. Do you think this is an effective prevention strategy? Why or why not?
2. Design a prevention advertising approach that you believe will be effective with young people, based on your reading of Chapter 10.
3. Discuss a prevention effort that had impact on you while you were growing up.

✄ References

Brecher, Edward M. 1972. *Licit and illicit drugs.* Boston: Little, Brown.

Cohen, A. Y. 1972. *Alternatives to drug abuse: Steps toward prevention.* Rockville, Md.: National Institute on Drug Abuse.

Dohner, V. A. 1972. Alternatives to drugs—A new approach to drug education. *Journal of Drug Education* 2(1): 3–22.

Drug abuse prevention research. 1983. Monograph No. 33. Washington, D.C.: U.S. Dept. of Health and Human Services.

Glantz, Meyer D., and Christine R. Hartel, eds. 1999. *Drug abuse: Origins and interventions.* Washington, D.C.: American Psychological Association.

Goleman, Daniel. 1995. *Emotional intelligence: Why it can matter more than IQ.* New York: Bantam Books.

Goodstadt, Michael. 1975. Evaluating drug prevention programs. In *Balancing head and heart: Sensible ideas for the prevention of drug and alcohol abuse,* edited by E. Schaps et al. Lafayette, Calif.: Prevention Materials Institute Press.

Hawkins, J. D., R. Catalano, and J. Miller. 1992. Risk and protective factors for alcohol and other drug problems in adolescence and early adulthood. *Psychological Bulletin* 112(1): 64–105.

Mathews, Walter M. 1975. A critique of traditional drug education programs. *Journal of Drug Education* 5(1): 57–64.

National Institute on Drug Abuse [NIDA]. 2002. *The National Cross-Site Evaluation of High-Risk Youth Program: Preventing substance abuse: Major findings.* Washington, D.C.: NIDA, Substance Abuse and Mental Health Services Administration.

Office for Substance Abuse Prevention. 1988. *Communicating about alcohol and other drugs: Strategies for reading populations at risk.* Monograph 5. Rockville, Md.: Author.

Rhodes, Jean E., and Leonard A. Jason. 1988. *Preventing substance abuse among children and adolescents.* New York: Pergamon Press.

Search Institute. 1999. *Ideas for asset building poster.* Search Institute, 700 South Third Street, Suite 210, Minneapolis, Minn. 55415.

Wolin, Steven, and Sybil Wolin. 1994. *The resilient self: How survivors of troubled families rise above adversity.* New York: Villard Books.

Disorders Co-occurring with Substance Abuse

Outline of Chapter 11

Introduction

Definition of a Co-occurring Disorder

Serious Mental Illness (SMI) and Substance Abuse

Affective (Feeling) Disorders and Substance Use Disorders

> The Difference Between a Depressive Mood and a Depressive Disorder
> Denial and Depression
> Categories of Mood Disorders

Affective Disorders and Suicide

Personality Disorders and Substance Use Disorders

> Personality Traits versus Personality Disorder
> Personality Disorder and Chemical Dependency Disorder
> Antisocial Personality Disorder
> Borderline Personality Disorder and Chemical Dependency
> Narcissistic Personality Disorder
> Trauma and Substance Abuse Disorder (SUD) in Adolescents

Treatment of Disorders Co-occurring with Substance Abuse

Objectives

1. Define co-occurring disorders.
2. Identify the number of people who suffer from serious mental illness (SMI) and SMI and substance abuse disorders.
3. Explain the differences between a depressive mood and an affective disorder.
4. Assess the depth of depression disorders using the criteria of severity, frequency, duration, and precipitating factors.
5. Describe in diagnostic criteria the differences between the following affective disorders:
   - Major depression
   - Dysthmia
   - Atypical depression
   - Bipolar disorder
   - Cyclothymic disorder
6. Describe and identify common characteristics of the manic phase of bipolar disorder.

7. Explain the difference between a personality trait and a personality disorder.
8. Explain the relationship between personality disorders and substance abuse disorders.
9. Identify diagnostic criteria and assessment questions you might ask in identifying antisocial personality disorder.
10. Identify the characteristics of borderline personality disorder and describe how alcohol/drugs complicate(s) the disorder.
11. List some assessment questions you might ask to help identify abandonment issues and abandonment depression.
12. Define narcissistic personality disorder and describe how alcohol/drug use complicates the disorder.
13. Explain the role of trauma in co-occurring disorders.
14. List the American Psychiatric Association's ten questions for the treatment of psychiatric disorders.

⚔ Introduction

A number of psychiatric disorders are prevalent with substance abuse disorders. We commonly call these "dual disorders" or disorders co-occurring with substance abuse. They include both affective (feeling) disorders and personality disorders. Affective disorders that often co-occur with substance abuse are depression and bipolar disorder; personality disorders are most frequently narcissistic disorder and borderline personality disorder.

This chapter explores the dimensions of these co-occurring disorders and how they interact with substance abuse.

⚔ Definition of a Co-occurring Disorder

The terms *dual disorders, comorbid disorders,* and *co-occurring disorders* have been used interchangeably to describe the condition of having both a psychiatric diagnosis and a chemical dependency diagnosis. The symptoms produced by psychiatric disorders and chemical dependency can overlap. The concept reminds us of this overlap in symptoms and highlights the need to make an accurate diagnosis, so that appropriate treatment can be provided.

Until recently, counselors in the mental health and chemical dependency fields took a somewhat provincial outlook. Each has accused the other of minimizing the importance of his or her own perspective. In many ways, the situation has become like the story of the blind men asked to describe an elephant. Each described it according to the body part he could touch but without regard to the remaining, unseen portions of the beast. Recent years have witnessed the emergence of a greater understanding and acceptance of the dual disorders or co-occurring disorder concept. Increasingly, members of both fields are educating themselves about each other's areas of specialty.

Clinically, we think of patients as existing on a continuum between purely psychiatric disorders at one end and purely chemical dependency problems on the other. Most patients lie somewhere between the extremes. An evaluation would take into account the relative position on the continuum. Today, it is rare to find a patient who has purely one condition, either psychiatric or chemical dependency. Many psychiatric patients are affected by alcohol/drugs, and many patients with alcohol/drug problems have psychiatric symptoms.

It is common to see prevalence rates of substance abuse ranging between 40 and 60 percent of any psychiatric population. A report of a commission of mental health providers in New York State estimated that, of the 75,000 individuals hospitalized in New York each year for psychiatric conditions, close to 40,000 admissions "involve persons with dual disabilities or a serious psychiatric illness and an alcohol and/or drug abuse condition" (Bauer 1987).

A more recent, community-based survey of 20,291 people found that 53 percent of the surveyed drug abusers and 39 percent of the alcohol abusers had at least one mental illness, and 29 percent of the mentally ill in the survey abused either alcohol or drugs (Regier et al. 1990). National surveys report co-occurring disorders (COD) as common in the adult population. The National Survey on Drug Use and Health (NSDUH) estimated that in 2002, 4 million adults met the criteria for both serious mental illness (SMI) and substance dependence and abuse. According to the survey, among adults with SMI, 23.2 percent were dependent on or abused alcohol or illicit drugs, while the rate among adults without SMI was only 8.2 percent (Sacks and Ries 2004).

The evolution of the co-occurring disorders concept has paralleled our expanded understanding of the biological nature of both alcoholism and certain mental disorders. The 1990s was labeled the "decade of the brain," as we learned more about brain functions and their relation to affect. Research suggests that the causes of mental illness such as schizophrenia, depression, anxiety disorders, and affective disorders are substantially, if not primarily, biological. Genetic research of families with a history of alcoholism has supported the biological nature of alcoholism. There is a higher rate of alcoholism and other drug abuse in the families of patients with affect and mood disorders and vice versa. Quite possibly the genetic traits that predispose one to depression or other mental illness may be the same or similar genetic traits for chemical dependency.

The two major co-occurring disorders covered in this chapter are (1) affective (feeling) disorders and chemical dependency and (2) personality disorders and chemical dependency.

⚔ Serious Mental Illness (SMI) and Substance Abuse

The number of people who have serious mental illness seems astounding in our American culture, considering our high standard of living. In 2002, there were 33.2 million adults aged 18 or older with SMI (SAMHSA June 2004) (see Figure 11.1).

Of the adults who had SMI, 13.4 million had only SMI, and 4 million had SMI and a substance abuse disorder. SMI and a substance abuse disorder is a co-occurring disorder that has gained much needed attention over the last few years. The substance abuse tends to complicate an already complicated situation for the severely mentally ill person. These patients are very challenging and require a more organized effort to stabilize (see Figure 11.2).

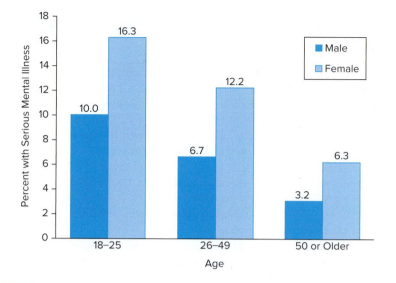

FIGURE 11.1 *Serious Mental Illness among Adults Aged 18 or Older, by Age and Gender: 2002*

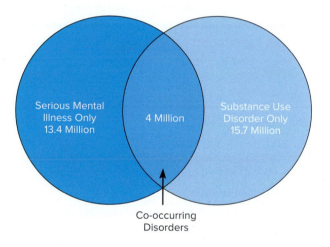

FIGURE 11.2 *Co-occurrence of Serious Mental Illness and Substance Use Disorders among Adults Aged 18 or Older: 2002*
Note: Circles are not drawn to scale.
SOURCE: SAMHSA, Office of Applied Studies. National Survey on Drug Use and Health 2002.

Of those, 12.2 percent, or 4 million, had a co-occurring disorder of both serious mental illness and a substance use disorder. Only 12 percent of this population received treatment for both mental health and substance abuse disorders, indicating the limited extent of adequate assessment and treatment approaches. Many of these co-occurring disorder patients (52 percent) received no treatment at all, or treatment for only one disorder (34 percent for mental disorder; only 2 percent for substance abuse disorder) (SAMHSA Sept/Oct 2004) (see Table 11.1 for further discussion).

T A B L E   1 1 . 1
Facts about Serious Mental Illness (SMI)
<ul><li>In 2002, there were 17.5 million adults aged 18 or older with SMI during the 12 months prior to being interviewed. This represents 8.3 percent of all adults in the United States. On average, adults with SMI were younger, less educated, and more likely to be female than adults without SMI.</li><li>Adults with SMI were more likely to be either unemployed or not in the labor force (36.4 percent) than were persons without SMI (31.2 percent).</li><li>Of the three age groups considered in this report, *adults aged 18 to 25 had the highest rate of SMI (13.2 percent), followed by adults aged 26 to 49 (9.5 percent) and adults aged 50 or older (4.9 percent).*</li><li>Overall, the rate of SMI was almost twice as high among females (10.5 percent) as it was among males (6.0 percent).</li><li>The two racial/ethnic groups with the highest prevalence of SMI were those reporting more than one race (13.6 percent) and American Indians and Alaska Natives (12.5 percent).</li><li>In 2002, there were 5 million adults aged 18 or older who had SMI and used an illicit drug in the past year. This represented 28.9 percent of all persons with SMI.</li></ul>
SOURCE: SAMHSA 2004.

⚹ Affective (Feeling) Disorders and Substance Use Disorders

The Difference Between a Depressive Mood and a Depressive Disorder

It is common to feel down, sad, or even depressed after experiencing disappointment, frustration (blocked goal), setback, or trauma. Feelings of sadness, melancholia, grief, and loss are normal aspects of life. Working through the grief or loss is an essential feature of growth. However, when these depressive feelings persist beyond the common period of time to work through them, an affective disorder may be developing.

It is also normal to feel bad or low in early recovery from abusing alcohol and other drugs. Some of this is due to withdrawal from the chemicals, but problems in mood may persist even after withdrawal. Chemical dependency causes financial, civil, criminal, interpersonal, and family problems in the lives of many alcoholics/addicts—all of which can cause lasting pain. However, what is going on if the depression continues beyond normal alcohol/drug recovery?

Everyone experiences symptoms of depression from time to time. When symptoms become severe and persistent, however, diagnosis of an affective (feeling) disorder could be warranted. As researchers and clinicians have used various systems of classifying depression over the years, they have increasingly recognized the different types and subtypes of depression. What differentiates various types from one another is their **severity, frequency, duration,** and **precipitating factors.**

Affective disorders are different from the normal emotions of feeling down or sad. The following questions may help distinguish common depressive feelings from an affective disorder:

Severity: How deep is your depression? How low do you feel? Are you suicidal or self-destructive?

Frequency: How often do you feel depressed?

Duration: How long does the depression last? Are there periods when you are not depressed?

Precipitating factors: What triggers your depression? Do you know what is causing your depression?

Regardless of what causes depression initially, once it has been present for long enough it locks in and takes on a life of its own. This is another way of saying that the brain changes physiologically in response to internal or external events that have persisted for a sufficient time. After the physiological changes have taken place, a number of biological, or physical, signs of depression emerge. These *vegetative signs* include disturbances in the basic biological functions that the brain regulates. Vegetative signs of depression include the following:

- Disrupted sleep patterns
- Difficulty with appetite and weight regulation
- Decreased cognitive functioning (including problems with concentration, memory, and problem solving)
- Decreased libido, or sex drive
- Lack of motivation, decreased energy (anergia)
- Difficulty experiencing pleasure (anhedonia)

Denial and Depression

The psychological aspects of depression bring with it feelings of shame, as outlined in Chapter 6. Many individuals are extremely frightened to be labeled depressed, labeled manic-depressive (with bipolar disorder), or labeled with other affective and mood-cycling disorders. The denial of these feeling disorders is often self-medicated with the use of alcohol/drugs in an attempt to avoid the shame. Despite the fact that a vast majority (99 percent) of individuals suffering from affective disorders can be helped, only one in three depressed individuals seeks help. It is estimated that over 10 million people suffer from depressive illness, and 2 million people suffer from bipolar disorder. Serious depressions are "whole body" disorders affecting body, feelings, thoughts, and behaviors (U.S. Department of Health and Human Services 1987). "Substance use disorders and mood and anxiety disorders that develop independently of intoxication and withdrawal are among the most prevalent psychiatric disorders in the United States" (Grant et al. 2004).

Most people view themselves as weak and inferior in not having the will power to overcome depressive illness. This is much like the denial of the disease of alcoholism and drug addiction. In fact, depressive disorder is a disease much like

Case Study 11.1

Major Depression and Addiction

Elaine

Elaine is a 53-year-old divorced woman with two previous psychiatric hospitalizations for severe depression. These were treated successfully with antidepressant medication. She returned to her psychiatrist after a 10-year absence due to progressively worsening depression for 2 months. Further questioning revealed that she had experienced anxiety symptoms last year and her gynecologist had prescribed diazepam (Valium). She took the medication in low doses as prescribed until sustaining a neck injury in an automobile accident 5 months ago. At that time, the doctor prescribed narcotic pain medication. Initially, she took the pain medication as prescribed but later took the medication in increasing doses. She found that her pain and anxiety symptoms were manageable with the higher doses and she simultaneously increased her daily dose of Valium, taking a moderate to heavy dose at night to help her overcome her physical discomfort and to improve sleep. Her escalating use of the medication surprises her, since she had never used similar drugs in the past and had avoided alcohol and street drugs because of religious beliefs. She is troubled by a growing preoccupation with suicide and fears that she may commit suicide, as her mother and maternal grandmother did. A physical exam by her internist later in the day revealed slightly elevated blood pressure, sweaty palms, and slightly dilated pupils.

Discussion Questions

1. What are the signs of depression?
2. What role do you think age played in this case?
3. Can you describe a case that is similar to this and identify signs?
4. Give some examples of maladaptive behaviors as a result of depression.

alcohol/drug addiction in that it has a known etiology, gets progressively worse over time, and has significant negative consequences if untreated. Case Study 11.1 presents an example of an individual who suffers from both depression and substance addiction.

Categories of Mood Disorders

Common affective disorders include the following:

- Major depression
- Dysthymic disorder (a low-grade depression)
- Atypical depression (depression related to sudden loss)
- Organic depression
- Bipolar disorder, formerly referred to as manic-depressive illness (severe mood swings)
- Cyclothymic (mood-cycling) disorder (a less severe form of mood swings)

Case studies in this section give you an understanding of the dynamics of the affective disorder and chemical dependency. In some case studies, chemical dependency is the primary diagnosis. Other case studies demonstrate that, even after sobriety, the underlying affective disorder still persists and requires treatment.

Many mood disorders are treated with antidepressant medications.

Major Depression

This depressive syndrome may occur as a single episode or as repeated episodes over the years. This diagnosis generally connotes a severe depressive episode with fairly clear onset and accompanying vegetative signs. Individuals suffering from major depression exhibit difficulty in the most basic of tasks (e.g., getting out of bed, brushing their teeth).

Episodes of major depression typically last from 6 to 12 months and then clear sometimes even without treatment. However, an episode can last significantly longer. Episodes of depression that are longer in duration require adequate and careful attentiveness and sensitivity to potential suicide attempts. (For the Diagnostic Criteria of Major Depressive Disorders please see *Diagnostic and Statistical Manual of Mental Disorders, Fifth Edition, pp 160–161.* Copyright © 2013. American Psychiatric Association.)

Case Study 11.2 takes a look at a familiar storybook character who suffers from depression.

Case Study 11.2

Eeyore Syndrome

The donkey, Eeyore, in the children's story *Winnie-the-Pooh,* could be clinically described as suffering from major depression or dysthymic disorder.

When Eeyore is asked by Pooh and other characters in the story, "Would you like to go swimming today?" Eeyore answers, in his low, depressed voice in a number of negative statements, "No, I'm so tired today and it's too far to walk to the swimming hole," or "I might get sun burned on a sunny day like today," or "It's too hot and I might get overheated."

Eeyore worries about everything. Instead of enjoying being with his friends, he isolates himself. Instead of enjoying the activity (swimming) and a beautiful summer day, he can't see anything positive. He is constantly in the black cloud of depression, even though it is a bright, sunny day.

Discussion Questions

1. Is dysphoria a natural part of life, or is it something that is genetically determined? Give rationals and site information from this chapter.
2. What activities help with overcoming "eeyore syndrome" (e.g., exercise)?
3. Explain the difference between "situational dysphoria" and clinical depression?
4. Do you think the term "depression" is overused and inaccurate in describing mood? Explain why.

Persistent Depressive Disorder (Dysthymia)

Persistent depressive disorder, or dysthymia, is a mood disorder of longer term than major depression but is a lower-grade depression. Patients with dysthymia frequently comment that they have never felt completely happy, or that if they do achieve a period of feeling well, it is relatively short-lived. Anxiety symptoms, headaches, and muscle tension are frequent, in addition to symptoms of depression. (For Diagnostic Criteria of Persistent Depressive Disorder (Dysthymia) please see *Diagnostic and Statistical Manual of Mental Disorders, Fifth Edition, pp 168–169*. Copyright © 2013. American Psychiatric Association.) Patients with dysthymia come to assume that their own baseline mood is normal; they are frequently surprised that they actually do experience improvement with treatment. Only 25 percent of patients with major depression receive adequate diagnosis and treatment; it is very likely that the percentage is even lower for dysthymic disorder, given the less intense and less notable degree of symptoms. Case Study 11.3 presents an example of dysthymia.

Atypical Depression

Atypical depression is not a common condition, as the symptoms and duration of symptoms are different from those of major depression or dysthymic disorder.

Case Study 11.3
Persistent Depressive Disorder (Dysthymia)
Duane

Duane is a 39-year-old married male who completed inpatient treatment for alcoholism and cocaine dependence nearly 3 years ago. Since then he has maintained sobriety while regularly attending his aftercare counseling sessions and cocaine and Alcoholics Anonymous meetings. He has also been involved in individual and group counseling to deal with the effects of growing up in an alcoholic and emotionally abusive family system. Despite these efforts, he continues to experience symptoms of low energy, periods of irritability, and an inability to have fun without a great deal of effort. His therapist has referred him for a psychiatric evaluation.

Most notable in Duane's history is that earlier he was abstinent from alcohol and drugs for approximately 4 to 5 months. During that time, he experienced the same depressive symptoms. Besides alcoholism, his family history includes several relatives with depression. A recent physical exam was unremarkable.

Discussion Questions

1. Explain why his relapses might occur after 4 to 5 months.
2. As his counselor, what would you recommend to cope with the depression?
3. What kinds of physical, emotional, and interpersonal activities might help this client?
4. What kind of cognitive-behavioral approaches might be taken?

Atypical depression is frequently the diagnosis for many adult children of alcoholics. Usually, a patient with atypical depression experiences intense and sudden depressions in response to interpersonal loss or threatened interpersonal loss. We may, in fact, be talking about a condition similar to that described by James Masterson (1976) as abandonment depression.

This condition is common in patients who may also have severe personality disturbances, such as borderline personality disorder. Psychodynamically, a sudden severe depression in response to feelings of loss, rejection, and/or abandonment may be related to a childhood loss so traumatic that it triggers this depression when feelings of loss are activated in present-day situations.

Atypical depression is also different because these patients may not report a loss of appetite and insomnia but, instead, experience an increase in appetite and sleep. Perhaps this is also indicative of the frequent problems in body image, binge patterns of eating, and other eating disorders that these clients exhibit. Patients with atypical depression may increase alcohol/drug use in a similar manner.

Case Study 11.4 presents an example of atypical depression.

Organic Depression

Depression may also occur as a result of organic factors, such as brain tumors, head injuries, nutritional deficiencies, physical illness, or alcohol/drug use. Many chemically dependent patients have nutritional deficiencies as a result of decreased intake,

Case Study 11.4
Atypical Depression
Gail

Gail is 28 years old, single, and an accountant. She is extremely shy and often feels uncomfortable in social situations. She is 7 years sober and attends AA meetings regularly. Gail cries easily whenever she is involved in conflict. She suffered a number of losses in her childhood, including the loss of her father, who was reported missing in action in the Vietnam War. Around the same time, Gail's maternal grandmother, to whom Gail was extremely close, died while sleeping in the same bed with Gail. Gail has also had to deal with the issue of having been sexually abused at 12 years of age.

After Gail began counseling, her self-confidence improved. But she still felt sad, so she got an evaluation from a psychiatrist experienced in alcohol and drug recovery. The psychiatrist recommended an antidepressant. After 2 weeks, Gail felt tremendous relief and realized that she had been struggling with depression for quite some time.

Discussion Questions

1. Can you describe the stages of grief (DABDA)?
2. How does grief get complicated by an "atypical" depression?
3. What would you recommend for Gail's shyness?

malabsorption, and poor eating habits. Alcohol is especially high in calories with poor nutritional value. Other drugs disrupt the appetite (e.g., cocaine reduces appetite) and create problems in nutrition. After initial recovery from alcohol/drug use, depression may continue for a while due to nutritional causes. However, once a normal diet and vitamin therapy have been reimplemented, organic (nutritional) depression should improve.

Head injuries are fairly common, especially in end stage alcoholics, and may contribute to cognitive deficits as well as mood disturbances. Pancreatic cancer is also more common in the alcoholic population and can look identical to major depression clinically.

Prolonged use of opiates, benzodiazepines, alcohol, sedative hypnotics, and especially stimulant drugs can produce depression. Users of cocaine and amphetamines typically experience a crash at the end of a binge pattern of cocaine use. This occurs because of the depletion of the neurotransmitter that the stimulant drug causes to be released in greater than normal quantities.

Bipolar Disorder

Bipolar disorder is the highest affective (feeling) disorder associated with co-occurring disorders. In other words, of all the affective disorders (e.g., major depression, dysthymia, etc.), bipolar disorder is found more often with co-occuring substance abuse disorders. Some common themes found with clients who have bipolar disorder and substance abuse are

- A strong emphasis on depression, as opposed to mania
- Predominance of hopelessness
- Specific pattern of medication noncompliance
- Patients labeling of their substance abuse as self-medication (Weiss 2004)

The first bipolar disorder described and understood was the classic manic-depressive illness. Manic-depressive illness consists of repeated depressive episodes over the years; these episodes are typically briefer than those in a major depression. In addition, a manic-depressive has less frequent but equally intense highs, or manic episodes. Characteristics of the manic phase of the disorder include the following:

- Euphoria
- Irritability
- Racing thoughts
- Decreased need for sleep
- Excessive spending
- Grandiosity
- Pressured speech
- An increased preoccupation with sexuality, religious, and/or philosophical themes

A manic episode may also include delusional beliefs and disorganization of thinking. Highs may not always involve euphoria; many patients simply become much more irritable, bizarre, and erratic in their behavior. Case Study 11.5 presents an example of bipolar disorder.

Descriptions offered by people with bipolar disorder give valuable insights into the various mood states associated with the illness (NIMH 2001):

Severe Mania

Hypomania (Mild to Moderate Mania)

Normal/Balanced Mood

Mild to Moderate Depression

Severe Depression

Case Study 11.5
Bipolar Disorder
Gustav

Gustav is a 45-year-old salesman with a history of binge drinking and erratic job performance. He goes on 2- to 3-week binges every spring and uses alcohol only socially at other times. He feels remorseful about these binges. In the weeks preceding a binge, he typically is quite productive, energetic, and successful in making sales. Gustav comments that his springtime burst in earnings helps compensate for his lackluster winter performance, when he typically feels lethargic and moody. In the past, he has used cocaine intermittently during the winter months to help brighten his mood. His finances have not allowed him to do cocaine in recent years. His occupational history is notable for multiple sales jobs across the country. He has made a number of impulsive springtime moves to pursue hot job possibilities. He does not find this unusual because his father, uncle, and brother all have similar histories. Closer questioning reveals that during the springtime bursts of increased sales activity, he has less need for sleep, a feeling of euphoria, and an increased philosophical preoccupation. Co-workers have commented on his high energy level and rapid speech. He has no history of previous psychiatric treatment.

Gustav's history reveals a patient with a bipolar disorder who binge drinks when he is high. There is a seasonal component to his mood swings, as he experiences manic symptoms in the springtime and symptoms of depression in the winter. Notably, he has a family history of similar mood swings and a personal history of minimal alcohol or drug use when he is not high. He is a good candidate for treatment with a mood-cycling agent, such as lithium, and would benefit from counseling on how to manage his impulses to drink. He should use available resources for support, such as AA.

Discussion Questions

1. Why is this client/patient so difficult to treat?
2. What would you recommend for treatment?
3. How would you "engage" this client in counseling?
4. Would you get permission and talk to family members for counseling with Gustav?
5. What problems and sabotaging do you anticipate in counseling Gustav?

Depression: I doubt completely my ability to do anything well. It seems as though my mind has slowed down and burned out to the point of being virtually useless. . . . (I am) haunt(ed) . . . with the total, the desperate hopelessness of it all. . . . Others say, "It's only temporary, it will pass, you will get over it," but of course they haven't any idea of how I feel, although they are certain they do. If I can't feel, move, think or care, then what on earth is the point?

Hypomania: At first when I'm high, it's tremendous . . . ideas are fast . . . like shooting stars you follow until brighter ones appear. . . . All shyness disappears, the right words and gestures are suddenly there . . . uninteresting people, things become intensely interesting. Sensuality is pervasive, the desire to seduce and be seduced is irresistible. Your marrow is infused with unbelievable feelings of ease, power, well-being, omnipotence, euphoria . . . you can do anything . . . but somewhere this changes.

Mania: The fast ideas become too fast and there are far too many . . . overwhelming confusion replaces clarity . . . you stop keeping up with it—memory goes. Infectious humor ceases to amuse. Your friends become frightened . . . everything is now against the grain . . . you are irritable, angry, frightened, uncontrollable, and trapped.

A variety of bipolar disorders have somewhat different patterns. Some patients experience recurrent depressive episodes with smaller and less intense manic episodes (hypomania) in between. During a hypomanic episode, a patient might typically experience all of the preceding symptoms except for the psychotic symptoms, such as disorganization of thinking, delusional material, and bizarre behavior.

Patients with bipolar disorder are typically plagued by mood instability; they may experience mood swings as frequently as daily. Patients who have significant mood swings, more than four times per year, are said to have a rapid cycling bipolar disorder. A growing accumulation of evidence suggests that some of these rapid cycling bipolar disorders may actually be a variation of epilepsy. Some of these patients may respond favorably to the medication that had previously been used only for epilepsy.

Mood-Cycling Disorder

The frequency of the cycling and the amplitude of the highs and lows are aggravated by alcohol/drug use. A relatively low-grade mood-cycling pattern may become much more aggravated with the use of alcohol/drugs, and the symptoms may become more clinically apparent.

Patients who otherwise have no psychotic symptoms, such as delusions, hallucinations, or disorganization of thinking, and have a mood-cycling disorder may develop psychotic symptoms, given the extra push from alcohol/drug use. (This is especially apparent with cocaine, amphetamines, hallucinogens, and even marijuana use.) Again, this stresses the importance of taking a thorough alcohol/drug history with each patient.

⚹ Affective Disorders and Suicide

One can clearly understand why depressive disorders may lead to suicidal ideation and suicide. The combination of depression and alcohol/drug use places patients at an even higher risk for suicide. Self-destructive acts that otherwise might be contemplated and dismissed are frequently acted on impulsively by those who are intoxicated and disinhibited. In earlier chapters, we discussed alcoholism and drug addiction as a kind of death wish. Disaster might also occur when a depressed, forgetful patient is drinking and inadvertently takes an overdose of antidepressant medication. The antidepressants, especially the tricyclic antidepressants, are lethal when mixed with alcohol.

The vicious psychological pattern of affect (feelings) plus shame can also contribute to suicidal ideation and actions—for example,

$$\text{depressive feelings} + \text{shame} = \text{feelings of despair}$$

Shame is exemplified as "I shouldn't feel depressed; I'm weak to have these feelings. I feel unable to control my feelings and there must be something inferior about me."

This cycle continues to the next stage of

$$\text{feelings of despair} + \text{shame} = \text{suicidal ideation}$$

The shame takes the form of thoughts such as "I'm not worthy. There is no hope; things won't change; I don't have any choices. Things are so painful and never change; they only get worse. There is nothing to get any pleasure or joy from life."

The next and often fatal stage is

$$\text{suicidal ideation} + \text{shame} = \text{suicide}$$

It is no wonder that initial or normal feelings of sadness, or melancholia from unresolved trauma from childhood, is avoided and not grieved. The individual suffering from depressive illness is fearful that any negative experience will start in motion this cycle of depression to self-destruction. As a result, feelings of sadness and emotional pain are often self-medicated with alcohol/drugs. One can see the importance of supportive counseling for depressed patients in addition to the appropriate use of antidepressant medication.

⚹ Personality Disorders and Substance Use Disorders
Personality Traits versus Personality Disorder

In describing people's personalities, we may think of traits that describe the way people behave, experience life, and interact in relationships. Personality is an important dimension that defines who we are. "Each of us is known not only by his or her physical features, occupation, and family background, but especially by what is called personality" (Nace 1990).

The American Psychiatric Association (APA) defines personality as "the ingrained pattern of behavior that each person evolves, both consciously and unconsciously, as the style of life or way of being in adapting to the environment" (APA 1984).

Most personality traits have both adaptive and maladaptive qualities or features. For example, being logical and organized are valuable traits in a computer programmer. But always being ruled by logic and being compulsively organized can also be maladaptive, since these traits may limit one's capacity to be emotionally expressive. On the other hand, a creative and artistic person might not be as suited to a situation or an occupation that requires logical, politically correct, and decisive action. We all have a mix of personality traits, which define us as individuals. When personality traits are persistently maladaptive and lead to chronic difficulty in interpersonal, occupational, and social functioning, there is a personality disorder.

The *DSM-V* recognizes eleven personality disorders and divides them into three clusters:

> **Cluster A** is characterized by odd and eccentric traits and may lead to psychiatric conditions, such as delusional disorder or schizophrenia.
> **Cluster B** is characterized by behavior that is erratic, emotional, or dramatic. This cluster has the strongest association with substance abuse, particularly antisocial and borderline personality disorder.
> **Cluster C** is characterized by feelings of fear and anxiety. Substance abuse occurs in this group, but not as frequently as in Cluster B.

For a list of the personality disorders in each cluster, please refer to the *Diagnostic and Statistical Manual of Mental Disorders, Fifth Edition, pp xxxii–xxxiii.* Copyright © 2013. American Psychiatric Association.

Personality Disorder and Chemical Dependency Disorder

The difficulties in differentiating between a personality disorder and an alcohol/drug disorder are often confounded by a common overlap in behaviors associated with each disorder. "Some behaviors that are symptomatic of particular Axis II disorders (manipulativeness, exploitativeness, dishonesty) may be integral or sometimes even adaptive aspects of addicted behavior, particularly among individuals who use illicit drugs" (Weiss 1996).

Personality-disordered individuals may be attracted to alcohol/drugs to self-medicate feelings of discomfort, anxiety, depression, anger, grief, and even shyness. V. M. Hesselbrook and associates (1983) reported that 52 percent of a sample of male alcoholics had a current or lifetime diagnosis of antisocial personality disorder.

Kleinman and colleagues (1990) found that, of 76 lower- social-class cocaine abusers, 71 percent had at least one personality disorder and 40 percent had two or more. The four most common personality disorders identified were

- Antisocial personality disorder—21 percent
- Passive-aggressive personality disorder—21 percent

- Borderline personality disorder—18 percent
- Self-defeating personality disorder—18 percent

Weiss and Mirin (1986), in their study of an upper-middle-class addict population, found borderline personality disorder and narcissistic personality disorder to be the most common diagnoses.

Craig (1988) used the very sensitive Millon Clinical Multiaxial Inventory and found that, of 121 opiate addicts from the Chicago area, all of them (100 percent) had at least one personality disorder and 27 percent had more than one. The most common diagnoses were

- Antisocial personality disorder—22 percent
- Narcissistic personality disorder—18 percent
- Borderline personality disorder—16 percent
- Dependent personality disorder—16 percent

This surprising result brings up the question of whether drug abuse and addiction lead to behaviors that are characteristic of personality disorders. Edward Kaufman, author of *Psychotherapy of Addicted Persons* (1995), points out that the characteristics inherent in substance abusers—such as unstable and intense interpersonal relationships; inappropriate, intense, out-of-control anger; affective instability; and physically self-damaging acts—can all meet the diagnostic criteria for borderline personality disorder and other personality disorders. Widiger et al. (1986) state that there is good evidence that many substance abusers who are diagnosed as having borderline personality disorder are really "pseudoborderline."

It is clear from the research that personality traits and personality disorders play a major role in substance abuse. The extent and depth of the role personality plays in substance abuse is confounded by the old "chicken or egg" question. Did the personality disorder cause substance abuse, or did substance abuse lead to behaviors that resemble the criteria for a diagnosis of a personality disorder? Case Study 11.6 presents an example of an individual who suffers from depression when withdrawing from an addictive substance. Case Study 11.7 describes personality problems for an individual who is addicted to alcohol.

Antisocial Personality Disorder

Antisocial Personality Disorder and Chemical Dependency

Antisocial personality disorder (ASPD) is estimated to be found in 2 to 3 percent of the male population. Of all the personality disorders, the strongest relationship with substance abuse is with antisocial personality disorder. ASPD has been found in 15 percent of alcoholic men, as compared with a 4 percent lifetime prevalence in nonalcoholic men (Helzer and Pryzbeck 1988). Hesselbrook, Meyer, and Kenner (1985) found ASPD to be the most common additional diagnosis in criteria for ASPD. The diagnosis is predominantly attributed to men, whereas borderline personality disorder is primarily found in women. The ratio of men to women with antisocial personality is approximately 8 to 1. In contrast, the ratio of women to men is 8 to 1 for borderline personality disorder.

Case Study 11.6
Depression and Withdrawal Symptoms
Evan

Evan is a 27-year-old male who is receiving inpatient treatment for his cocaine dependency. He was referred for a psychiatric evaluation because of his current severe depression symptoms. He had been freebasing cocaine for 2 to 3 months prior to admission to the treatment unit 3 days ago. Now he is feeling severely depressed and experiencing cocaine cravings.

Evan has no history of depression and no family history of psychiatric disorders. During childhood, he experienced hyperactivity and had mild learning disabilities. He notes that since beginning drug use in his midteens, he has preferred stimulant drugs ("they calm me down"). He has received inpatient treatment for cocaine dependence once previously and had 2 years of complete abstinence before relapsing several months ago. During his clean time, he experienced no mood difficulties but continued to feel somewhat hyper.

Evan is a patient who experiences severe depression as part of cocaine withdrawal. There is no reason to suspect an underlying problem with depression, given his personal and family history. He would benefit from a short course of treatment with desipramine, an antidepressant that is particularly effective for treating acute depression and cocaine cravings during cocaine withdrawal. Such treatment typically lasts for 2 to 4 weeks.

Discussion Questions

1. What relapse prevention strategies might you suggest for Evan? (See Chapter 13 for relapse-prone behaviors.)
2. Could Evan be diagnosed with ADHD? What symptoms indicate this?
3. What do you think Evan's prognosis is for recovery?
4. What would he need to do to increase the probability that he would sustain recovery and sobriety?

Childhood Precursors of Antisocial Personality Disorder

Conduct disorders and attention-deficit hyperactive disorder (ADHD) in children are precursors of both substance abuse and antisocial personality disorder. Early assessment, intervention, and counseling with these young people and their families are recommended to address current problems and to prevent future problems.

Denial, Alcohol/Drugs, and Antisocial Personality Disorder

The shame attached to identifying one's personality traits as causing problems in life and in relationships often results in denial. It is easier to blame others for conflicts, problems, and personality issues than to take responsibility. A major feature of a personality disorder is that the individual may not consider the personality trait that is causing conflict as undesirable. The individual might attribute others' complaints about them as the fault of others—"The hell with them if they can't take a joke."

Case Study 11.7

Alcoholism

Charlie

Charlie is a 53-year-old married engineer at a local aerospace company. He has a long-standing, but progressively worsening, history of irritability, nervousness, and difficulty sleeping. Charlie is under the care of Dr. Greenhorn, a physician just out of his internal medicine residency. Dr. Greenhorn assumed the practice of Charlie's previous physician and golfing buddy, Dr. Barleycorn.

Dr. Greenhorn reviews the previous medical record and notes difficulties with stomach irritation and ulcers, elevated triglyceride and cholesterol levels, and persistent complaints of decreased libido, or sex drive. Charlie requests some of the sleeping pills that Dr. Barleycorn had prescribed. Further questioning reveals a history of regular heavy drinking, which began when Charlie and Dr. Barleycorn were fraternity brothers. This heavy drinking behavior persisted over the years. Charlie typically drinks three or four mixed drinks or glasses of beer per weeknight and six or seven drinks per night on the weekends. He can recall going 2 to 3 days without alcohol during a church retreat several years ago. At that time, he felt very shaky and irritable. Physical examination reveals a moderately enlarged liver, and laboratory studies reveal elevated liver enzyme levels and mild anemia.

Discussion Questions

1. Do you think his personal relationship with his previous physician has been a problem? If so, explain why.
2. Why do you think Charlie has sleeping problems?
3. What would you recommend?

The traditional denial defense mechanisms of rationalization and minimization are used to deny the true dimensions of a personality disorder. Integrity, honesty, and responsibility are discounted in the self-centered behavior of the ASPD.

Difficulty *regulating behaviors* (poor impulse control, recklessness, and a failure to anticipate consequences) and *affect intolerance* (the inability to recognize, regulate, and tolerate emotions) lead to substance abuse (Khantzian 1981).

Nace and associates (1983) described alcohol/drugs as providing immediate gratification followed by regressive behaviors. These regressive behaviors include the following:

- *Impulsivity*—cannot delay gratification; has stimulus-bound decreased frustration tolerance; is impatient; overreacts to situations; is inconsistent
- *Self-centeredness*—is stubborn and defiant; lacks empathy; exhibits grandiosity; either overvalues or undervalues self; sees things in either/or, rather than shades of gray; can't compromise; exhibits perfectionism, sees self as unique

- *Passivity*—is withdrawn; is isolated; feels helpless; is "mentally lazy"; avoids self-revelation
- *Affect intolerance*—has difficulty in recognizing feelings; fears feelings; has decreased ability to endure or regulate painful emotional states

Some questions that may identify antisocial personality traits are the following:

- Do you exaggerate your achievements and talents?
- Are you preoccupied with thoughts of great success, power, brilliance, beauty, achievement, or idealized love?
- Do you often want a great deal of attention and admiration?
- Do you have a tendency to dominate conversations and activities (perhaps "showing off")?
- Do you expect special favors but feel you don't have to return them?
- Do you sometimes feel surprised and angry that people do not do what you want them to?
- Do you ever take advantage of others so that you can get what you want?
- Do you sometimes disregard the rights or personal boundaries of others?
- Do you alternate between thinking too much and too little of a person?
- Do you sometimes feel you don't care enough about other people's pain and feelings?
- Do you change jobs frequently? Have you changed jobs three or more times in the past 5 years, but not because of the kind of job or because of economic or seasonal fluctuations?
- Have you been unemployed for 6 months or more during a period of 5 years, when you might have been able to work?
- Have you walked off jobs at various times without having another job already lined up?
- If you have children, do you feel you adequately provide food, safety, and shelter for them?
- Have you spent money on drugs, alcohol, or personal items that probably should have been spent on *necessities?*
- Have you committed repeated thefts or engaged in illegal occupations (fencing, selling drugs, prostitution, pimping, etc.)?
- Have you had multiple arrests or been convicted of a felony?

Extreme difficulties in relationships with your spouse or partner could also indicate antisocial personality traits. The following are some further questions to consider.

- Have you been separated (whether legally married or not) or divorced several times?
- Have you had ten or more sexual partners in 1 year?
- Do you sometimes feel that you are overly irritable and aggressive?
- Have you frequently been involved in physical fights or assaults?
- Have you ever physically abused your spouse or children?
- Have you failed to plan ahead for the future or have you been extremely impulsive?

- Have you lied repeatedly, used aliases, or "conned" others to get what you wanted?
- Have you frequently driven while drunk?

Case Study 11.8 presents an example of the problems an individual with ASPD can create for himself and others. For the diagnostic criteria for antisocial personality disorder, please refer to the *Diagnostic and Statistical Manual of Mental Disorders, Fifth Edition, pp 476.* Copyright © 2013. American Psychiatric Association.

Borderline Personality Disorder and Chemical Dependency

The second most common personality disorder that has a high incidence of substance abuse is borderline personality disorder. A number of studies have reported

---

Case Study 11.8
Antisocial Personality Traits
Tony

Tony is a 24-year-old construction worker. He says he began working after leaving high school at the age of 15. As a child, he was hyperactive, and his behavior problems caused him to perform poorly in school. Thus, school was frustrating for Tony and his teachers.

Tony told lies, stole, and fought with other children. His family took him to a counselor (a behavioral specialist) after Tony repeatedly set fires. During one school year, Tony was treated with Ritalin, a medication that helps children calm down and stay focused, and he did better in school. But during summer vacation he stopped taking the medication and refused to resume taking it the next fall.

Since dropping out of high school, Tony has held a number of jobs. Usually he gets fired because he fights with his co-workers or doesn't show up for work; this irritates Tony, who feels victimized. Although his employment—or lack of it—has caused financial problems, Tony admits that he has lied and not paid his bills. He tells friends, creditors, and bill collectors, "The check is in the mail," or "I'll send the payment as soon as. . . . " Although he has a relationship with a woman, he has also had several one-night stands with other women he has met at bars. He has snorted and smoked cocaine, often squandering his money while partying with friends and women he picks up. His parents have bailed him out financially several times. Tony's attitude was "They have the money, so they should be able to help me out."

After two DUIs, Tony was referred to a chemical dependency program as part of a deferred prosecution. He is now slowly working on both his chemical dependency and his personality problems.

Discussion Questions

1. What is your prediction for Tony's sobriety?
2. What would help Tony stay sober?
3. Do you think Tony could be "rigorously honest"?

co-occurring substance abuse and borderline personality disorder—43 percent (Koenigsberg et al. 1985), 28 percent (Johnson and Connelly 1981), and 13 percent (Nace, Saxon, and Shore 1983).

In Chapter 6, we described abandonment depression as the common factor in borderline personality disorder. As previously mentioned, the term *abandonment depression* was coined by James Masterson to describe a personality disorder that has six key elements: (1) feelings of emptiness and void; (2) hopelessness and help-lessness; (3) panic; (4) guilt; (5) suicidal depression; and (6) homicidal rage.

Someone suffering from abandonment depression probably had a highly stressful separation from parent(s) or a primary caregiver early in life (18 months to 2 years of age). The separation could have been caused by natural events (death, separation, divorce, health, etc.), or the parent(s) might not have been emotionally available.

Some common questions that may help identify abandonment follow. Did you have parents or guardians who

- Were not open or available to you physically and emotionally?
- Attacked you verbally or physically or blamed you for many of their problems?
- Gave mixed messages, called *double binds,* saying one thing but meaning something else?
- Had unreasonably high expectations or standards for you or had ambiguous expectations of how you should behave, what you should do, and how you should feel?
- Did not show you warmth or sensitivity, did not make you feel secure or safe, or did not pay much attention to your feelings, concerns, and conflicts?
- Discounted your sense of self or violated your physical and psychological boundaries, such as by committing physical, emotional, or sexual violations?
- Disparaged, blamed, or rejected you if you had any difficulty with developmental tasks?
- Disregarded, ridiculed, blamed, or teased you?
- Jokingly or seriously threatened to abandon or leave you?
- Made you feel that your fears were unwarranted or inappropriate?
- Did not understand you or were insensitive to your needs and desires?

Patients with borderline personality disorder have a marked instability of mood and often form intense interpersonal attachments. They typically feel abandoned and rejected during instances of real or perceived interpersonal loss. Many border-line patients engage in repeated self-destructive or suicidal acts during episodes of intense depression and despair. Theoretical explanations of the origin of this person-ality disorder range from developmental to biochemical explanations. In all probabil-ity, the condition is a result of both nature and nurture (i.e., inadequate bonding and parenting during early years and a genetic predisposition). Most clinicians agree that borderline patients have a great deal of difficulty regulating their degree of attach-ment to others. They want the closeness and trust that intimacy brings but fear the dependency, vulnerability, and possible rejection that may occur. Not surprisingly, these patients have a high incidence of chemical dependency as they attempt to blunt the intensity of their emotions by using alcohol/drugs. They are especially prone to becoming dependent on addicting prescription drugs, such as benzodiazepines. Their impulsivity, frequent thoughts of suicide, and substance abuse make them especially at risk when prescribed psychiatric medication. Many psychiatric medications are lethal when taken in amounts only 5 to 10 times the usual dosage, especially if the individual is already toxic with alcohol or drugs.

Abstinence from alcohol/drugs is essential in treating borderline patients, as their already fragile mood stability is quite sensitive to alcohol/drugs. Such patients generally need psychotherapy. When medication management is indicated, doctors commonly prescribe antidepressant or mood-cycling agents. Which medication the patient receives depends on the clinical symptoms that are most troublesome (more on treatment of dual disorders appears in Chapter 12).

Do you have a pattern of unstable and intense personal relationships? For instance, does your attitude about your relationships keep changing? Do you idealize or romanticize your friends? Do you put them down, manipulate them, or often use them to meet your own needs? Do you find yourself treating some friends very well and some very poorly? Do you have intense anger that is not really justified? Or do you lack control of your anger? Are you concerned about your self-image, your gender identity, your long-term goals or career choice, your friendship patterns, your values, or your loyalties? (If you are concerned, you might have thoughts like these: "*Who am I?*" or "*I feel just like my sister when I'm good.*") Do you have deep mood swings? Are you depressed when alone? Do you try very hard to avoid being alone? Do you feel empty or bored most of the time?

Case Study 11.9 illustrates the dual disorder of borderline personality disorder and substance addiction. For a list of diagnostic criteria for borderline personality disorder, please see the *Diagnostic and Statistical Manual of Mental Disorders, Fifth Edition, pp 663*. Copyright © 2013. American Psychiatric Association.

Narcissistic Personality Disorder

The *DSM-V* definition of narcissistic personality disorder is "a pervasive pattern of grandiosity, need for admiration, and lack of empathy." (For the diagnostic criteria for narcissistic personality disorder, please see the *Diagnostic and Statistical Manual of Mental Disorders, Fifth Edition, pp 669–670*. Copyright © 2013. American Psychiatric Association.) The narcissist can have several of the following qualities:

- A grandiose sense of self-importance
- A preoccupation with fantasies of unlimited success, power, brilliance, beauty, or ideal love
- Trouble in interpersonal relationships
- Requires excessive admiration
- Unreasonable expectations of others
- Interpersonally exploitive of others
- Lacks empathy
- Envious of others
- Arrogant attitude

Case Study 11.9

Borderline Personality Disorder

Francine

Francine is 26 years old and single. Her alcoholic parents divorced when she was 3 years old. She lived with her mother, who drank heavily and had a series of live-in boy-friends. Her mother was physically and emotionally unavailable and spent a great deal of time at bars. Her mother's boyfriends physically and sexually abused Francine. To try to cope, Francine began using alcohol in midadolescence. She was also sexually promiscuous. She was involved in shoplifting and occasionally went on eating binges. Today, she acknowledges that she drinks to blunt emotional pain.

As an adult, she has had intense relationships with men. When a relationship breaks up, her rage and anger have been equally intense. Francine cannot cope with rejection in relationships and says she feels "empty inside" when she thinks she has been abandoned. Her sudden shifts in mood and her occasional threats of suicide have alienated boyfriends and other friends.

Although she drinks alcohol to lessen the intensity of her feelings, it ultimately causes deeper depression and leads to impulsive, self-destructive behavior. Several times, when her relationships have broken up, Francine has taken overdoses and cut her wrists.

Francine ended a previous therapy after three or four sessions—she said the therapist was getting "too close" and she felt too vulnerable. But she is once again in counseling and is making progress in dealing with her addiction and the personality traits that have caused problems.

Discussion Questions

1. What is the prognosis for Francine?
2. What would help her to maintain recovery and sobriety?
3. Do you think her problems in relationships are important? Explain.
4. Do you think she would benefit from all-women AA meetings and/or a women's therapy group? Why? Explain.

Combine these qualities with the abuse of alcohol and/or other drugs, such as cocaine, and you have the potential for real problems. (See Case Study 11.10.)

Trauma and Substance Abuse Disorder (SUD) in Adolescents

It is interesting to consider the diverse and multiple pathways that explain the high incidence of trauma and substance abuse disorders (SUD) in adolescents.

These possible pathways are

1. Substance abuse disorders preceding trauma because substance abuse by the adolescent increased the likelihood for the adolescent to engage in risky behaviors that cause trauma.

Case Study 11.10

Narcissism and Cocaine

Aaron

Aaron is 38 years old and a partner in a marketing and advertising firm. He is the tall, handsome, dark, and not-so-silent type. He epitomizes the singer Carly Simon's line "You're so vain, you probably think this song is about you." He is good looking and well educated, but his self-centeredness pervades his conversation. The first half-hour of the therapy session he talked about his success, his six-figure income, and his "trophy" wife. He then began to describe some business problems and his anxiety about some unethical and illegal business he was doing and the possibility of legal and criminal action. As he went on, he soon talked about a conflict with the Internal Revenue Service over some deductions he took and the unpaid and overdue interest on those deductions. This threatened his financial situation, which was already compromised by his cocaine binges. Upon further discussion, he revealed that his partners were upset with him because his cocaine use was interfering with business. His partners had become aware of Aaron forging their signatures, without their approval, in order to withdraw funds from the company. Aaron admitted he did this because he needed the money to repay a cocaine debt.

He was in his second marriage. He had one child by the first marriage and two young children by the second marriage. His current wife had filed for divorce and moved with the two children back east to her family.

In subsequent sessions, Aaron was able to realize that his own behavior and personality had caused his downfall. The more successful he got, the more entitled he felt. The more demanding he got, the more angry and disrespectful were his interactions with others. He blamed others and held them responsible for his unhappiness. This vicious cycle continued in a self-sabotaging criticism and contempt of others that led to even more dissatisfaction, shame, and isolation. The cocaine binges would then further the downward cycle. Aaron's inability to modulate his own emotions (especially anger), combined with his cocaine binges, led to further distrust of others and, eventually, to paranoia. His periods of abstinence with cocaine (a few months at a time) became shorter and shorter, as his world became more and more chaotic.

His arrogance caused him to reject AA and other self-help methods, and he still maintained resentment about his 30-day stay in a residential drug treatment program that he had completed a year ago. He was obsessed with childhood incidents related to his parents, describing a narcissistic mother and distant father, and his constant feelings "that no matter whatever I did, it was not good enough."

Aaron tried to stay sober, but he refused to go to any self-help meetings. He tried to reestablish his relationship with his partners, but they were done with him. He went on one last cocaine binge, borrowing some money from an old friend who also used cocaine. With his business relationships destroyed, the IRS after him, and his marriage coming to an end, he had nowhere to turn. He considered suicide as an option, but ironically he was so self-absorbed that he really didn't see that as a way out. He considered a "geographical relocation" and then flew back east to try to reunite with his wife and children. That was short-lived, as he relapsed while on the East Coast, getting drunk and then using cocaine.

(continued on next page)

Case Study 11.10 (*continued*)

Narcissism and Cocaine

Aaron

Tired and depressed, emotionally bankrupt, he surrendered and entered a 90-day residential treatment program. It took him a few years to stabilize. He is currently sober for 2 years, participating in AA and a recovery therapy group, has reached an agreement with the IRS, is working in the counseling field, sees his children when he can, and is a lot more humble. Fortunately, Aaron has achieved a relatively "happy ending." Many others have been less fortunate, suffering worse outcomes, and some have died.

2. Substance abuse disorders interfere with the adolescent's ability to cope effectively with the trauma.
3. Substance abuse disorders occur when adolescents try to self-medicate the stress symptoms of trauma (Giaconia et al. 2003).

✕ Treatment of Disorders Co-occurring with Substance Abuse

Treatment of co-occurring disorders means addressing both the mental illness and the substance abuse. Treating one and ignoring the other will only result in relapse. American Psychiatric Association (1994) Practice Guidelines for the Treatment of Psychiatric Disorders include these:

1. Establish and maintain a therapeutic alliance with the client.
2. Manage the client's psychiatric (or substance use) symptoms and monitor the status of these over time.
3. Provide education regarding the disorder(s) and treatment.
4. Determine the need for medications and other specific treatments.
5. Develop an overall treatment plan.
6. Enhance adherence to the treatment plan.
7. Help the client and family adapt to the psychosocial effects of the disorder(s).
8. Promote early recognition of new episodes and help identify factors that precipitate or perpetuate these episodes.
9. Initiate efforts to relieve and improve family functioning.
10. Facilitate access to services and coordinate resources among different service providers.

Working with co-occurring disorders requires a strong team approach and good communication among mental health caregivers (case counselor, psychologist, psychiatrist, group counselor, etc.) so that the client doesn't "fall between the service gaps." This supportive team approach also can counter recurrent sabotaging by client and family members, treatment and medication noncompliance, and inconsistency in care and messages to the client and his or her family (i.e., it avoids triangulation).

Adolescent Co-occurring Disorders Complicates Treatment

Co-occurring disorders in adolescents complicates the treatment for substance abuse. Many more issues need to be addressed in coordination with the treatment for substance use disorder (SUD). Estimates of rates of co-occurring conduct disorder with substance use disorder are 50 to 80 percent.

The disorders that co-occur with substance abuse can be classified as

- internalizing problems—depression, anxiety, or trauma disorders, suicidal thoughts
- externalizing problems—conduct disorders, ADHD, victimization, physical violence toward others, illegal activity (see Chart 11.1)

For more information on the treatment of co-occurring disorders and difficult clients, see Chapter 12.

CHART 11.1   *Co-occurring Disorders at Intake: CSAT*
The chart represents the rates of co-occurring disorders drawn from GAIN assessments (N = 4,421) administered in CSAT-funded adolescent programs from 1998 to 2004. The chart clearly illustrates the high prevalence of co-occurring disorders for adolescents. The development tasks of adolescence include issues of identity, self-concept, social skills, academic skills, and many other issues. No wonder it is difficult for young people to work through these developmental issues when they have both psychiatric and substance problems to address.

✷ In Review

- The term *co-occurring disorder* refers to the condition of having both a psychiatric diagnosis and a chemical dependency diagnosis.
- Four million adults in the United States had serious mental illness (SMI) co-occurring with substance abuse disorder. Only 12 percent of this population received treatment for both disorders.
- This chapter describes the problems related to mood disorders and chemical dependency, with specific emphasis on major depression, dysthymia, atypical depression, bipolar disorder, and mood-cycling disorder.
- What differentiates these various types of affective (feeling) disorders are their severity, duration, frequency, and precipitating factors. Common vegetative signs of a mood disorder are disrupted sleep, difficulty with appetite and weight regulation, decreased cognitive functioning (including problems with concentration, memory, and problem solving), decreased libido or sex drive, lack of motivation, decreased energy (anergia), and difficulty experiencing pleasure (anhedonia).
- Bipolar disorder is the highest affective (feeling) disorder associated with co-occurring disorders.
- Some common themes found with clients who have bipolar disorder and substance abuse are
  - A strong emphasis on depression, as opposed to mania
  - Predominance of hopelessness
  - Specific pattern of medication noncompliance
  - Patients labeling of their substance abuse as self-medication (Weiss 2004)
- This chapter also explores the co-occurring disorder of personality disorders and chemical dependency. Most personality traits have both adaptive and maladaptive qualities or features. When personality traits are persistently maladaptive and lead to chronic difficulty in interpersonal, occupational, and social functioning, there is a personality disorder. The major personality disorders most frequently associated with chemical dependency are antisocial personality disorder, borderline personality disorder, and narcissistic personality disorder.
- There is a high incidence of trauma and substance abuse disorders in adolescents.
- The possible pathways of trauma are
  - Substance abuse disorders preceding trauma because the substance abuse by adolescents increased the likelihood for the adolescent to engage in risky behaviors that cause trauma.
  - Substance abuse disorders interfere with the adolescent's ability to cope effectively with the trauma.
  - Substance abuse disorders occur when adolescents try to self-medicate the stress symptoms of trauma (Giaconia et al. 2003).

✖ Discussion Questions

1. Which do you think occurs more often—depression and then substance abuse, or substance abuse and then depression? State your reasons for your position.
2. Discuss the differences and give examples of the differences between major depression, dysthymia, atypical depression, bipolar disorder, and cyclothymic disorder.
3. Explain and describe the differences between a personality disorder and a personality trait.
4. Describe treatment approaches to co-occurring disorders. Illustrate each approach with case examples.

✖ References

American Psychiatric Association [APA]. 1984. *Psychiatric glossary.* Washington, D.C.: American Psychiatric Press.

American Psychiatric Association [APA]. 1994. *Diagnostic and statistical manual of mental disorders.* 4th ed. Washington, D.C.: Author.

Bauer, Anne. 1987. Dual diagnosis patients: The state of the problem. *Information Exchange (TIEUNES)* 9(3, July): 1–4, 8.

Craig, R. J. 1988. A psychometric study of the prevalence of DSM-III personality disorders among treated opiate addicts. *International Journal of the Addictions* 23(2): 115–24.

Daley, Dennis C., and Howard B. Moss. 2002. *Dual disorders: Counseling clients with chemical dependency and mental illness.* 3d ed. Center City, Minn.: Hazeldon Foundation.

Fields, Richard, and Russell Vandenbelt. 1992a. *Understanding mood disorders and addictions* [pamphlet]. Center City, Minn.: Hazeldon Educational Materials.

Fields, Richard, and Russell Vandenbelt. 1992b. *Understanding personality problems and addiction* [pamphlet]. Center City, Minn.: Hazeldon Educational Materials.

Giaconia, Rose M., et al. 2003. Comorbidity of substance use disorders and posttraumatic stress disorder in adolescents. In *Trauma and substance abuse: Causes, consequences, and treatment of comorbid disorders,* edited by Paige Ouimette and Pamela J. Brown. Washington, D.C.: American Psychological Association, pp. 227–42.

Grant, Bridget F., et al. 2004. Prevalence and co-occurrence of substance use disorders and independent mood and anxiety disorders: Results from the National Epidemiologic Survey on Alcohol and Related Conditions. *Archives of General Psychiatry* 61: 807–16.

Helzer, J. E., and T. R. Pryzbeck. 1988. The co-occurrence of alcoholism with other psychiatric disorders in the general population and its impact on treatment. *Journal of Studies on Alcohol* 49: 219–24.

Hesselbrook, M. N., R. E. Meyer, and J. J. Kenner. 1985. Psychopathology in hospitalized alcoholics. *Archives of General Psychiatry* 42: 1050–55.

Hesselbrook, V. M., E. G. Shaskan, and R. E. Meyer. 1983. Summary of bio/genetic factors in alcoholism. *NIAAA Research Monograph Series* 9: 159–66.

Johnson, R. P., and J. C. Connelly. 1981. Addicted physicians take a closer look. *Journal of the American Medical Association* 245: 253–57.

Kaufman, Edward. 1995. *Psychotherapy of addicted persons.* New York: Guilford Press.

Khantzian, E. J. 1981. Some treatment implications of the ego and self-disturbance in alcoholism. In *Dynamic approaches to the understanding and treatment of alcoholism,* edited by M. H. Bean and N. E. Zinberg. New York: Free Press.

Kleinman, P. H., A. B. Miller, and R. B. Millman. 1990. Psychopathology among cocaine abusers entering treatment. *Journal of Nervous and Mental Disease* 178: 442–47.

Koenigsberg, H. E., et al. 1985. The relationship between syndrome and personality disorder in DSM-III: Experience with 2,462 patients. *American Journal of Psychiatry* 142(2): 207–12.

Masterson, James. 1976. *Psychotherapy of the borderline adult: A developmental approach.* New York: Brunner/Mazel.

Nace, E. P. 1990. Substance abuse and personality disorder. In *Managing the dually diagnosed patients: Current issues and clinical approaches,* edited by D. F. O'Connell [Special issue]. *Journal of Chemical Dependency Treatment* 3(2): 183–98.

Nace, E. P., J. J. Saxon, and N. A. Shore. 1983. A comparison of borderline and nonborderline alcoholic patients. *Archives of General Psychiatry* 40: 54–56.

National Institute of Mental Health [NIMH]. 2001. *Bipolar disorder.* NIMH Publication No. 01-3679, Washington, D.C.: Dept. of Health and Human Services.

Regier, Darrel A., et al. 1990. Comorbidity of mental disorders and alcohol and other drug abuse: Results from the Epidemiologic Catchment Area (ECA) Study. *Journal of the American Medical Association* 19: 2511–18.

Sacks, Stanley, and Richard K. Ries. 2004. Substance abuse treatment for persons with co-occurring disorders. A Treatment Improvement Protocol 42. Rockville, Md.: U.S. Dept. of Health and Human Services, SAMHSA/CSAT.

SAMHSA. June 2004. Serious mental illness and its co-occurrence with substance use disorders, 2002. Analytic Series A-24. Rockville, Md.: U.S. Dept. of Health and Human Services.

SAMHSA. Sept./Oct. 2004. 4 Million have co-occurring serious mental illness, substance abuse. *SAMHSA News* 12(5): 15–18.

U.S. Department of Health and Human Services. 1987. *Helpful facts about depressive illnesses* [DART pamphlet]. Rockville, Md.: National Institute of Mental Health.

Weiss, R. D., and S. M. Mirin. 1986. Subtypes of cocaine abusers. *Psychiatric Clinics of North America* 9: 491–501.

Weiss, Roger. 1996. Personality parallels. *Professional Counselor Magazine,* January/February, pp. 15–16, 40–41.

Weiss, Roger. 2004. Treating patients with bipolar disorder and substance dependence: Lessons learned. *Journal of Substance Abuse Treatment* 27: 307–12.

Widiger, T., et al. 1986. Diagnostic criteria for the borderline and schizotypal personality disorders. *Journal of Abnormal Psychology* 95: 43–51.

Alcohol/Drug Recovery, Co-Occurring Disorders, Suicide and Alcohol/Drugs

Outline of Chapter 12

Introduction

Need for Support
> Self-Help Meetings/Alcoholics Anonymous
> Social Support Empowers Recovery—Voluntary Mutual Help Association
> Online Social Support Networks (OSSN)
> Rational Recovery

Stages of Alcohol/Drug Recovery
> Withdrawal Stage (0–15 days)
> Honeymoon Stage (15–45 days)
> The Wall Stage (45–120 days)
> Adjustment Stage (120–180 days)
> Resolution Stage (180–360 days)

Counseling and Chemical Dependency
> Early Phases: Safety and Stabilization
> Breaking Through Denial
> Affect (Feeling), Recognition, and Modulation
> Group Therapy
> Family Treatment
> An Effective Alcohol/Drug Recovery Strategy
> Boundaries with Difficult Patients

Treatment of Co-occurring Disorders
> Counseling for Co-occurring Disorders
> Treatment Compliance—Medications
> The Family of the Client Who Has Co-occurring Disorders

Suicide and Alcohol/Drugs
> Clues to Suicidal Intentions

Objectives

1. List the benefits and advantages of Alcoholics Anonymous in addressing an alcohol/drug problem.
2. Outline the benefits and importance of a social support system for recovery.
3. List the advantages of online social support networks (OSSN).
4. Identify and describe the stages of recovery, from the withdrawal to the resolution stages.

5. Describe the public self, the private self, the blind self, and the discovery self—the four windows of the Johari window.
6. List the key elements of an effective recovery strategy.
7. Describe some counseling approaches used with difficult clients/patients.
8. Describe the challenges of working with clients/patients with co-occurring disorders.
9. List some warning signs of suicide and some approaches used with suicide and alcohol/drug abuse.

❧ Introduction

Approximately 1 million people in the United States currently receive treatment for drug or alcohol addiction. This final chapter gives an overview of alcohol/drug treatment and relapse prevention. Sobriety from alcohol/drugs is an ongoing process. Recovery and relapse prevention is a lifelong process involving not only the recovering addict/alcoholic but also his or her entire family system.

This chapter highlights treatment issues and approaches for specific alcohol/drug and co-occurring disorders. You are encouraged to explore referenced material, take counseling courses specific to alcohol/drugs, and pursue supervised internships for more in-depth counseling skill development.

❧ Need for Support

Self-Help Meetings/Alcoholics Anonymous

The most widely used approach for recovery from alcoholism and drug addiction is self-help groups. Alcoholics Anonymous (AA) was founded in the early 1930s by Bill W., a stockbroker, and Dr. Bob, a surgeon. Both of these men found that willpower alone was not enough to keep them from using alcohol. After admitting to each other their common disease and shared frustration with alcohol recovery, and failed attempts at sobriety, they discovered that they could help each other remain sober through mutual support. They soon discovered that others had the same experiences in struggling with recovery from alcoholism, and the movement was begun. Small groups of alcoholics met on a regular basis to share their experience, strength, hope, and support for one another. In 1938, the basic principles of AA were first outlined as the now famous Twelve Steps. (See Table 2.1.)

There are AA meetings every day in almost every city and town in the United States. Throughout other parts of the world, more than ninety countries have AA meetings. The fellowship crosses all religious and racial barriers; the only requirement for membership is a desire to stop drinking.

"There are no dues or fees for AA membership; they are self-supporting through their own contributions. AA is not allied with any sect, denomination, politics, organization, or institution; does not wish to engage in any controversy; neither endorses nor opposes any causes. Our primary purpose is to stay sober and help other alcoholics to achieve sobriety" (Alcoholics Anonymous 1978).

Advantages of AA as a Recovery Model

Lawson, Peterson, and Lawson (1983) identified the following key factors that contribute to the success of AA in helping addicts/alcoholics stay sober:

1. Mutual sharing by members, which provides solutions to alcohol-related problems and helps alleviate guilt by showing members that others have acted irrationally also
2. Provision of a regular support group of individuals working toward the goal of abstinence
3. Frequent and regular meetings to help members structure their time
4. Availability of AA as an adjunct to other treatments, such as counseling and psychotherapy
5. Absence of membership fees and nondiscrimination by race, sex, or socioeconomic status
6. Establishment of comprehensive goals covering the emotional, behavioral, and spiritual life of the members

A number of studies have found favorable treatment outcomes from participation in AA (e.g., Armor, Polich, and Stambul 1978; Bateman and Peterson 1971; Browne-Mayers, Seeley, and Brown 1973; Kish and Herman 1971). In 1965, a study by Robson, Paulus, and Clark found that 71 percent of regular AA attendees improved and 57 percent improved from attending no more than ten meetings.

Despite these figures, treatment programs that are exclusively AA-oriented without the incorporation of other treatment methods and modalities have been less effective. Costello (1975) found that the effectiveness of intermediate care was doubled (18 to 36 percent) when the unit converted from an exclusively AA-oriented model to a program with many treatment methods, AA being one of them.

Resistance to Attending AA and Other Self-Help Groups

For a variety of reasons, individuals in early alcohol/drug recovery often resist attending self-help meetings. Some of the reasons they give are the following:

1. Difficulty with the concept of a higher power, or references to God
2. Lack of tolerance by self-help members, at times, to
   a. Use medication for affective or feeling disorders and other psychological conditions
   b. Help understand that there are different types of alcoholism
   c. Reject treatment (therapy and other treatment modalities)
3. People are uncomfortable in group settings and are concerned with the group's maintaining strict confidentiality
4. The disruptive influence of people (especially court-referred) who don't have a true desire to be sober

Despite these drawbacks, which can be overcome, AA and other self-help meetings have been a positive and extremely beneficial source of inspiration and hope for millions of recovering alcoholics/addicts.

Social Support Empowers Recovery—Voluntary Mutual Help Association

One of the major strengths of AA and other self-help meetings is the social support, which empowers people. Social support is a strong factor in recovery, especially because addicts/alcoholics have trouble with asking for help in the first place.

It makes us feel good when we are supportive of others, and—if we give them the opportunity—it also feels good when others are supportive of us. Social support empowers people to cope more effectively, both with difficulties and during difficult times.

There is an old AA proverb: "Silence is the enemy of recovery." Not letting others in your social support system know that you are in a state of vulnerability to relapse, makes it more likely that you will relapse.

Borkman (2008) describes AA as a "voluntary mutual help association." That is a pretty good definition of a support system. AA can be a source for social support, prescribed healthy lifestyle practices, social contacts, community, cohesion of common purpose and meaning, and psychosocial resources.

Online Social Support Networks (OSSN)

The Internet, smart phones, electronic tablets, and technology in general revolutionized the way we communicate and get information. The advent of online social support networks is a natural and efficacious new way of helping with alcohol/drug recovery and relapse prevention.

> Where contact with social support used to be limited to letters, phone calls and face to face visits, the advent of the internet and smart phones has revolutionized the ways with which people can connect with one another, creating increasingly sophisticated and expansive support groups. (Spelman 2011)

For example, a new OSSN, SUPPORTbuddy.org, offers a color-coded mood (feeling) self-rating scale that goes out to the person's personally developed online support network. This allows those individuals in the support network to interact and lend support during difficult emotional and vulnerable times.

Rational Recovery

Rational Recovery (RR) was started by Jack Trimpey in 1986 as an alternative to Alcoholics Anonymous and other self-help meetings. The principles of RR are based on the rational-emotive approach developed by Albert Ellis, Ph.D. The major focus of rational recovery is on changing the way people think and feel about themselves and their use of alcohol/drugs. "In RR, we learn to take control of our emotions so that we are not compelled to reach for an anesthetic when we are feeling bad" (Trimpey 1996). Trimpey, a clinical social worker in California, wrote *The Small Book* (1985), which attacked the principles of the AA *Big Book*. Unfortunately

Trimpey's book is too intent on bashing AA, rather than outlining another alternative for people who have problems with AA meetings or principles.

F. Michler Bishop's article "Rational-Emotive Behavior Therapy and Two Self-Help Alternatives to the 12-Step Model" (1995) describes some of the common tenets of these approaches as the following:

1. People are largely responsible for their behaviors, including addictive behaviors.
2. A person can recover; that is, a person can gain control over his or her addictive behaviors.
3. Lifetime membership is not required; many people can recover in a year or two.
4. Labeling of all kinds is discouraged; a person does not have to call himself or herself an alcoholic to begin to recover.
5. Alcoholism may or may not be a disease; however, a person has to find a way to cope and take responsibility for his or her life in any case.
6. The value of a person is not linked to his or her behavior, addictive or otherwise. A person will not be a better person if he or she gives up alcohol or some other addictive behavior; he or she may be a happier person, a person who has better relationships and can keep a job, but behavioral change does not affect the "goodness" of the self.
7. A person is not necessarily, ipso facto, "in denial" if he or she does not accept the basic AA tenets.
8. A person is not doomed to a life of alcoholism if he or she does not accept help from AA, a rehabilitation clinic, a hospital, and so on. People can recover on their own with or without the help of professionals and/or self-help groups.

Regardless of your own viewpoint about Alcoholics Anonymous, the Rational Recovery movement provides another alternative that may help a specific population. However, the approach may also cause others to continue to deny their alcoholism and drug addiction and continue to suffer the negative consequences of their alcohol/drug use.

✖ Stages of Alcohol/Drug Recovery

Richard Rawson and associates (1988) outlined five basic stages of cocaine recovery, which also apply to alcohol/drug recovery. The time periods for each stage vary from individual to individual and are based on the kinds of drugs used. The stages are

0–15 days—withdrawal
15–45 days—honeymoon
45–120 days—the wall
120–180 days—adjustment
180–360 days—resolution
1 year—after resolution and beyond

Withdrawal Stage (0–15 days)

Most of the physical aspects of withdrawal clear up after 3 to 7 days. Emotional feelings of anxiety, fatigue, pain, and depression persist throughout the first 15 days. Patients require education and direction during the withdrawal phase. Once patients go through the initial physical withdrawal, they want to leave treatment to avoid the emotional issues.

Honeymoon Stage (15–45 days)

The honeymoon stage is the opposite of the withdrawal stage. The neophyte to recovery has gone through the difficult withdrawal stage and now feels energetic, confident, and optimistic. Cravings for alcohol/drugs are usually reduced and moods improve. This may lead clients to believe that recovery is easier than they thought it would be. Unwittingly, they begin to stray from the elements of their recovery program that helped them stay sober. Their behavior becomes more unstructured, inconsistent, and at times frenetic. They may go through a manic cycle, doing many things and overextending themselves. These behaviors then disrupt their recovery. This is the time when patients are most at risk to return to alcohol use, marijuana use, or other drug use. They may convince themselves that they had a problem with a particular drug, not that they are at risk with all alcohol/drugs.

The Wall Stage (45–120 days)

After 45 days of sobriety, the largest percentage of relapses to alcohol/drugs occur. Personal and interpersonal issues are emotionally experienced more fully during this stage. Relapse vulnerability increases as patients start feeling these emotional issues and begin to further sort out some of the problems in their lives and in their relationships. Patients often get discouraged and may verbalize that they "feel this will go on indefinitely." Patients may lose hope, strength, and motivation to continue in their process of recovery. This is a time when the supportive elements of their recovery program need to be strengthened, even though patients may attempt to alienate those who can help. Group counseling can be especially helpful at this stage. Others in the group who have gone through this difficult stage can share their struggle and ultimate success and lend support.

Adjustment Stage (120–180 days)

The achievement of working through the intense feelings of the wall stage gives patients new hope and energy for recovery. Patients begin to accept that this is a life-long struggle. The achievement of being sober for 120 or more days affirms the addicts' ability to be sober for a long time. This is the longest time that most patients have ever been sober.

Resolution Stage (180–360 days)

Completion of an intensive 6-month program signals a shift from learning new skills to monitoring for relapse signs, maintaining a balanced lifestyle, and developing new areas of interest. Some clients may need individual psychotherapy or relationship work.

❈ Counseling and Chemical Dependency

Early Phases: Safety and Stabilization

In the early phases of counseling with substance abusers, the therapist must be concerned with *safety* and *stabilization.*

Safety and stabilization focus on a variety of factors that help the recovering alcoholic/addict maintain sobriety and a basic sense of balance in his or her life. Mistakenly, in their zealousness to uncover traumatic content, therapists may open up wounds without first determining if the individual has the emotional strength, resources, and support network to help him or her heal these wounds. Opening up these wounds may exacerbate already fragile relationships with family members and the spouse or partner. The result inevitably is a relapse to alcohol/drug use. (See Table 12.1.)

Breaking Through Denial

At early stages of recovery there is denial of the extent of the impact of alcoholism/ drug addiction. There is denial as to the extent and consequences of the drug use and behaviors on the individual and family members.

Common Denial Defenses

> Minimization
> Projection
> Rationalization
> Compliance
> Conflict avoidance
> Obsessive-compulsive behavior
> Acting out

TABLE 12.1

Stages of Drug Alcohol Treatment

Stage of Treatment	Patient Status	Treatment
1	"I can't drink." (need for external control)	Alcohol detoxification, directive psychotherapy, AA, Al-Anon, family therapy, Antabuse
2	"I won't drink." (internalized control)	Directive psychotherapy, supportive psychotherapy, AA, consider discontinuing Antabuse
3	"I don't have to drink." (conflict resolution)	Psychoanalytically oriented psychotherapy

SOURCE: S. Zimburg, "Principles of Alcoholism Psychotherapy" in *Practical Approaches to Alcoholism Psychotherapy*, 2d ed, edited by S. Zimberg, J. Wallace, and S. B. Blume, Human Science Press, 1985

Affect (Feeling), Recognition, and Modulation

Once stabilization and safety needs are addressed, the next stage of counseling may focus on affect, recognition, and modulation. The therapist slowly works with the client in labeling and tolerating feelings. The counseling can then take many forms, exploring a variety of issues relevant to the chemical dependency. Throughout this process, regular review of relapse dynamics and support for a stable and secure recovery from alcohol/drugs are maintained.

Counseling approaches explore both the conscious and the unconscious levels of feelings. The Johari window (Table 12.2) is a training model that describes the domain of counseling. Counseling focuses on all four of these areas of self:

1. *Public self:* The public self includes all the aspects about the individual that are known by the individual and others close to the individual (e.g., age, marital status, hobbies, job, interests, basic personality type).
2. *Private self:* The private self involves information that the individual is aware of but others don't know (e.g., sexual practices, mistakes in the past or present, private feelings or thoughts, family of origin issues).
3. *Blind self:* The blind self includes things the individual is not consciously aware of that others are aware of about the individual (e.g., personality characteristics; denial about others' behavior or own behavior; lack of awareness of interpersonal, occupational, social, and marital issues).
4. *Discovery self:* Discovery self is the category of the future. These things are not in the conscious awareness of the individual or of others and will be discovered in the future (e.g., the natural changes that occur in life's unexpected journey).

By placing a major emphasis in counseling on Category 2, the private self, and Category 3, the blind self, individuals can see changes in Category 1, the public self, and Category 4, the discovery self. When individuals are defensive or unwilling to deal with their feelings about their private selves and blind selves, there are limitations to progress and personal change. Clients would do well to follow Louise Hay's (1984) advice: "If you think of the hardest thing for you to do and how much you resist it, then you're looking at your greatest lesson at the moment. Surrendering,

---

T A B L E   1 2 . 2

Johari Window

Others	Self	
	Things You Know About Self	**Things You Don't Know About Self**
Things They Know About You	1. Public	3. Blind
Things They Do Not Know About You	2. Private	4. Discovery

SOURCE: Adapted from *Group Processes: An Introduction to Group Dynamics* by Joseph Luft. Mayfield Publishing Company, Copyright © 1984, 1970, and 1963 by Joseph Luft.

giving up the resistance, and allowing yourself to learn what you need to learn, will make the next step easier."

Other techniques that are often included as part of the counseling approach to chemical dependency recovery include relaxation training (e.g., biofeedback), stress reduction, anger management, problem-solving/coping skills, communication skills, exercise, nutrition, life management (i.e., balance in activities), relationships, and work.

The common goals of all counseling approaches are education; the provision of information and resources; catharsis (patients' release of emotion and feelings); connectedness and trust, which facilitates disclosure of feelings and concerns; support for positive growth; awareness and insight; and personality change (reorganization).

Group Therapy

Therapy groups have the same guidelines as individual counseling. Members adhere to strict confidentiality and do not socialize outside of the group. The group's purpose is to provide a safe environment to explore individual and interpersonal issues.

Most therapy groups are led by professional counselors trained in group therapy and experienced in the dynamics of chemical dependency recovery, family systems, and related areas of expertise. Some therapy groups have co-therapists, usually male–female counseling teams that co-lead and clarify issues in the group.

Therapy groups can take many forms. I have found more success leading all-male recovery groups, and female therapists have seen a benefit to all-female therapy groups. This avoids some of the sexual and gender-specific issues that may distract from the focus on alcohol/drug recovery. Most groups have from four to eight members to allow adequate opportunity for interaction by all group members.

As discussed in Chapter 7, Yalom outlined eleven curative factors of group psychotherapy:

1. Instilling hope
2. Sharing universality
3. Imparting information
4. Fostering altruism
5. Recapitulating the primary family group
6. Developing socializing techniques
7. Imitating behavior
8. Sharing interpersonal learning
9. Developing group cohesiveness
10. Sharing catharsis
11. Exploring existential factors

Family Treatment

Peter Steinglass (1979) outlined five major family modalities for alcohol/drug treatment:

1. Pure family therapy is based on a family systems mode, in which all family members are present at the same time in therapy sessions.

2. Individual or group treatment approaches fulfill specific criteria suggested by a family therapy theory of alcoholism, such as the concept of homeostasis.
3. Therapies involving concurrent therapeutic work with both the alcoholic and family members rely on a more traditional, individual, psychodynamic theoretical base.
4. Specific therapies designed for the spouses or partners of alcoholics
5. Supportive treatments assist nonalcoholic family members in dealing with common problems related to having an alcoholic family member.

Following are some of the goals of the family treatment modality:

1. Develop family commitment for recovery.
2. Identify enabling behaviors and counter them.
3. Encourage leveling or open communication.
4. Validate members' reality and feelings regarding the chemical abusing member and the negative consequences of chemical abuse.
5. Educate the family to the family disease concept.
6. Elaborate on concrete rules and consequences.
7. Plan and define family leisure activities.
8. Solidify the parental coalition.
9. Specify attitudinal and behavioral changes for each member.
10. Prepare relapse prevention guidelines and family response.

According to Steinglass (1979), the advantages of a family systems approach are the following:

1. It bridges the disparity between psychodynamic and stress-reduction explanations of drinking.
2. It explains diversity in alcoholic families by redirecting the focus from common etiological characteristics in alcoholic families to the common function of alcohol to maintain imbalanced family systems.
3. It gives therapists an understanding of alcoholism as a total system's behavior.

An Effective Alcohol/Drug Recovery Strategy

The following steps can help those in recovery achieve their goal:

1. *Break the bonds of denial.* Recovery is an ongoing process often facilitated by the support of others—friends, others in recovery from alcohol/drugs, family, or a counselor. All of these people can help alcoholics/addicts work through their denial and maintain sobriety.
2. *Actively work and apply the 12 steps and other AA principles in recovery.* This provides guidelines, structure, and support for recovery efforts. Developing a relationship with an AA or NA sponsor is a key element in effectively helping the newly recovering person understand and implement the principles of AA.
3. *Seek nonchemical altered states of consciousness.* The innate human drive to alter one's sense of consciousness can be attained through healthy and

balanced activities, not the use of alcohol/drugs. These activities enhance the individual's sense of self and well-being.

4. *Work through negative emotional states and control destructive impulses.* Negative life experiences commonly result in emotions that get out of control and cause additional problems. The individual in recovery can learn new coping skills and gain support in working through impulses that may lead to destructive decisions and interactions.

5. *Move from passive to active decision making in all aspects of life.* Most addictive behaviors are passive, automatic, ritualistic, and habitual. This includes workaholism, gambling, eating disorders, and many other behaviors that fit our behavioral definition of addiction. Recovering individuals need to be involved and active in their recovery. Most learning comes from doing.

6. *Resist social or peer pressure.* When it endangers welfare or inhibits growth, peer pressure can cause those in recovery to make the wrong choices. Recovery is maintained by being and talking with others in recovery, rather than isolating. Associating with people who don't understand or, more important, don't respect the individual's recovery could require changing relationships. Recovering alcoholics/addicts should develop and maintain relationships that support a healthy alcohol/drug-free lifestyle.

7. *Improve and continue to work on the sense of self.* Those in recovery need to be involved in activities and relationships that promote a positive sense of self. To develop a sense of self, they must believe they are unique, worthwhile individuals with emerging talents and skills; individuals who can accomplish things; individuals who can trust and be trusted while setting appropriate boundaries in relationships and avoiding codependency and dysfunctionality.

8. *Deal more effectively with stress.* Recovering addicts/alcoholics must develop awareness in recognizing stressful situations and the need for support (attachments), coping skills, and resources to deal with or adapt to the stress.

9. *Maintain the structure of the recovery program.* Recovering alcoholics and addicts should consistently attend self-help meetings, aftercare, counseling sessions, and other elements of the recovery program.

10. *Have patience and direction.* Those in recovery must have a road map, while maintaining a day-at-a-time perspective in recovery.

11. *Learn how to enjoy life and others.* By developing the capacity to relax, enjoy, and have fun with others, recovering persons can establish leisure activities, hobbies, and personal interests.

12. *Maintain a sense of humor.* Those in recovery very much need to keep things in perspective, and remember, "I'm not O.K. You're not O.K. But that's O.K."

13. *Take responsibility for self.* No matter what the event is, those in recovery have the freedom to choose their response to it. Taking responsibility for self leads to awareness, which in turn helps the individual make effective choices.

14. *Maintain physical, emotional, and spiritual well-being.* Recovering alcoholics/addicts need regular exercise, balanced nutrition, and adequate sleep and rest. Recovery also involves effective communication in relationships, especially intimate relationships. One must work on spiritual

values in life and strive to experience the joy and creativity of life, while exploring one's own sense of spirituality.

15. *Avoid shame.* Mistakes may occur, but alcoholics/addicts can return to recovery without a burden of shame. Shame generated by others or themselves inhibits personal recovery and growth from situations that may be painful.

16. *Work on relapse-prevention strategies.* Those in recovery need to deal with urges and cravings to use alcohol/drugs, imbalanced lifestyles, negative emotional states, social pressures, high-risk situations, and other factors that may make them vulnerable to relapse.

17. *Adapt to changes in life.* Alcoholics/addicts can remind themselves that they are human and subject to human feelings and emotions. Life is not perfect and always involves change. Recovery is facilitated by the individual's ability to adapt to change and integrate feelings related to change. Striving for progress rather than perfection is a healthy goal.

Boundaries with Difficult Patients

Groves (1978) identified some of the troublesome behavior patterns in describing four categories of patients who arouse negative feelings in the counselor.

1. Dependent Clingers
   - Need a great deal of "attention."
   - Perceive the therapist as "inexhaustible."
   - Express gratitude to therapist, causing feelings of specialness and power in therapist (set up to continue giving to client).
   Guidelines for counselor:
   - Establish boundaries (limits of time, knowledge, skill, and stamina).
   - Avoid promises that can't be kept.
   - Avoid supporting illusions that will be shattered.

2. Demanders
   - Intimidate, devalue, and try to instill guilt in the counselor.
   - Are unaware of their deep dependency needs and terror of abandonment.
   Guidelines for counselor:
   - Resist the temptation to make a devastating response.
   - Support entitlement but direct it to needed treatment ("You are entitled to the best help we can give you, but we can't give good treatment unless you help").
   - Avoid tireless debates.
   - Repeat theme or acceptance that they deserve good treatment.

3. Manipulative Help-Rejectors
   - Try your recommendations but nothing works.
   - Seek an undivorcible marriage with an inexhaustible caregiver who will maintain the relationship as long as symptoms/problems exist.
   - Intense dependency needs but fear closeness.
   Guidelines for counselor:
   - You are putting out "fires"—band-aid treatment.
   - Use gentle, simple reasoning rather than complicated explanations.

- Establish clear boundaries.
- Agree that progress is slow.

4. Self-Destructive Deniers
   - Continue drinking/drugging, despite significant negative consequences.
   - Have given up hope to have needs met.
   - Seem to enjoy defeating recovery attempts.
   Guidelines for counselor:
   - Fight the impulse to abandon these clients.
   - Recognize your own limitations, get help through consultation.
   - Intervene to try to "raise their bottom."

Many clients with co-occurring disorders present these kinds of troublesome behaviors, which make treatment difficult. However, the counselor skilled in setting appropriate boundaries and having clear expectations for these clients can be more effective.

✖ Treatment of Co-occurring Disorders

As outlined in Chapter 11, a person who has *co-occurring disorders* is chemically dependent and has a psychiatric disorder. Affective (feeling) or mood disorders and personality disorders were the major focus in Chapter 10. However, any psychiatric disorder classified in the fourth edition of the *Diagnostic and Statistical Manual of Mental Disorders (DSM-IV)* combined with a chemical dependency is considered a co-occurring disorder.

Traditionally, patients with co-occurring disorders are viewed as difficult, distracting, and disorganized in treatment. Many patients with co-occurring disorders are multiple users of psychiatric, medical, and chemical dependency treatment facilities and are often described as "revolving door" treatment users, moving from agency to agency. Such patients are reported to be difficult, noncompliant, and resistant to treatment. They tend to become crisis users of the emergency room and of inpatient and medical detoxification services (Hellerstein and Meehan 1987).

Counseling for Co-occurring Disorders
Breaking Denial—Educating and Empowering Patients

These patients tend to have strong denial that can be difficult to break through. The client may focus on one co-occurring disorder as the primary cause for his or her problems while ignoring the impact of the other disorder. The family may also focus on one cause of the problem (i.e., his or her drinking/drugging or manic-depressive behavior) to avoid recognizing the painful dimensions of the co-occurring disorder.

Education and intervention are needed to help the client and family members recognize that they are dealing with not one but two interrelated disorders. The counselor can establish rapport by educating clients with co-occurring disorders and helping them recognize the dimensions and impact of their disorder. The primary treater is the patient. Once educated, patients become experts on their diagnosis. They are then empowered to take personal responsibility for their recovery.

Developing Skills in Patients Who Have Co-occurring Disorders

Feelings and Emotional Buildup Like most counseling approaches with individuals who have an alcohol/drug problem, counseling for co-occurring disorders involves helping the client identify feelings, especially feelings of anger, guilt, and shame. It is important to help these clients also identify how these feelings may build up and eventually result in psychiatric relapse.

Methods to reduce stress and deal with these feelings are an integral aspect of the counseling (e.g., redirection to recreational activities, exercise and relaxation, stress-reduction techniques).

Cognitive-Behavioral Approaches Cognitive-behavioral techniques help in the recovery from co-occurring disorders. One major focus is to instill hope and to change depressive thinking.

The way a person thinks plays a major role in feelings of depression, mood disturbances, and personality problems. The individual's perception of events in life colors his or her emotional reaction dramatically. This can be described as depressive thinking. Although one should not ignore one's feelings, overreacting to situations may develop into a pattern or habit of depressive thinking, or thinking the worst. If the individual is already depressed, it may significantly deepen his or her depression.

Some of these negative and depressive ways of thinking may have their roots in childhood. Parents may have modeled depressive thinking and depressive patterns of behavior. Parents who shame their children with negative statements (e.g., "You are stupid") teach them to internalize these depressive messages, which are then carried into adulthood. Cognitive-behavioral approaches can teach the individual to change these unhealthy ways of thinking and of reacting to life situations by countering these negative thoughts.

Alcoholics Anonymous has a number of slogans that trigger cognitive-behavioral change from depressive thinking:

Shame statement: "No matter what I do, it's never good enough."
AA slogan: "Progress not perfection" reminds us that we don't have to see ourselves as either successes or failures, or be perfect all the time.

Shame statement: "I am aggressively argumentative, and always have to be right. I feel especially bad when I behave this way with those close to me."
AA slogan: "Would you rather be right or happy?" reminds us that always having to be right or prove another wrong is often alienating, and isolating, behavior.

The following are some examples of common depressive thinking patterns:

- Black-and-white or right-wrong thinking: "If you're recovering, you can't take any medication, because all medications are drugs."
- "Awfulizing," or making things seem worse than they really are: "I'm probably going to get fired because I missed that deadline."
- Overgeneralizing: "Boy, I'm really stupid because I made that mistake."
- Catastrophizing: "What if they tell me I've got cancer?"
- Disqualifying the positive: "Oh, anybody could've done it."
- Jumping to conclusions: "He looked upset when I walked past his office. He probably saw me come in late."

- Feeling that temporary situations are permanent: "I'm never going to find a job."
- Shaming ourselves with "should" and "why" statements: "Why didn't I study harder?" or "I should have known the answer to that."
- Negative labeling: "I'm stupid." "I'm hopeless." "I'm a failure."
- Personalizing, or taking responsibility for things we're not responsible for: "We probably lost the account because I wasn't aggressive enough."

Depression feeds on inactivity and depressive thinking. Clients can interrupt the depressive inactivity and depressive thinking by taking action. Physical activity is the remedy prescribed most often for mood disorders. I will joke with my patients by telling them to use "LSD"—*l*ong, *s*low, *d*istance, walking for clients recovering from alcohol/drugs and/or depression. The first step is to make *taking action* as easy as possible by eliminating the obstacles. For example, to be successful, an exercise program needs to be realistic and allow little room for procrastination.

Taking action can also mean eating in a healthy manner, taking a class, working on relationships at work and home, taking a vacation, playing with friends, and so forth. All of these things help clients recover from the co-occurring disorders of chemical dependency and mood disorder.

Both chemical dependency and affective disorders are diseases that grow with isolation and withdrawal. The metaphor of the dragon in the corner, eating its own tail, describes their crippling effects. The AA motto "Silence is the enemy of recovery" applies here. Clients must develop relationships with others in recovery. They can find friends and support by being active in 12-step recovery programs, educational groups, counseling (both individual and group), and community and church groups.

Treatment Compliance—Medications

Frequently, antidepressant medication is an integral part of the recovery from co-occurring disorders. The selective serotonin reuptake inhibitors (SSRIs) category of antidepressants are most frequently used with patients who have co-occurring disorders. As their name implies, these drugs work in the brain by blocking the reuptake of serotonin into nonactive storage areas, thus increasing its availability, which has an antidepressant effect. (See Table 12.3.)

Interestingly, in double-blind studies, with nondepressed alcoholics who were given an SSRI antidepressant, approximately 20 percent reported a decrease in alcohol craving and were therefore aided in maintaining abstinence (Jancin 1994).

Unfortunately, many patients with co-occurring disorders do not comply with the directions given by their psychiatrist regarding medication. The counselor who may have more ongoing contact can help monitor medication compliance.

The common noncompliance behaviors include stopping medications abruptly, reducing dosage, and stopping and starting or forgetting to take medication on schedule. Some patients will discontinue medication before they have given the medication time to begin working (usually 2 or more weeks). Working closely with the psychiatrist prescribing medication can assure the proper dosage, and the type of medication can be adjusted to best serve the patient with co-occurring disorders.

TABLE 12.3

Generic and Proprietary Names of Psychiatric Medications*

Antidepressants	Antianxiety (continued)
Imipramine (Tofranil, Presamine)	Oxazepam (Serax)
Doxepin (Sinequan, Apapin, Sinequan)	Alprazolam (Xanax)
Desipramine (Norpramin, Pertrofrone)	Clonazepam (Clonopin)
Amitriptyline (Elavil)	Buspirone (BuSpar)
Nortriptyline (Pamelor, Aventyl)	Hydroxyzine (Vistaril, Atarax)
Protriptyline (Vivactil)	
Chlomipramine (Anafranil)	**Antipsychotic**
Fluoxetine (Prozac)	Haloperidol (Haldol)
Trazodone (Desyrel)	Chlorpromazine (Thorazine)
Maprotiline (Ludiomil)	Fluphenazine hydrochloride (Prolixin)
Amoxapine (Asendin)	Trifluoperazine (Stelazine)
Bupropion (Wellbutrin)	Perphenazine (Trilafon)
Tranylcypromine (Parnate)	Thioridazine (Mellaril)
Phenelzine (Nardil)	Thiothixene (Navane)
Antianxiety	**Mood Cycling**
Diazepam (Valium)	Lithium
Chlordiazepoxide (Librium)	Carbamazepine (Tegretol)
Chorazepate dipotassium (Tranxene)	Valproic acid (Depakote)
Lorazepam (Ativan)	Clonazepam (Clonopin)

*Not all medications in each group are listed.

Suboxone (Buprenorphine and Naltrexone) to Reduce Opioid Cravings

Buprenorphine (subutex) and suboxone are both schedule III drugs used for maintenance treatment of opioid dependence. Subutex contains bupenorphine while suboxone contains buprenorphine and naltrexone. Suboxone effectively addresses the abuse potential of buprenorphine—by using naltrexone in combination with bupenorphine alone.

Suboxone is an opioid itself, so dependence on suboxone can develop. Various opioids require different periods of abstinence and objectively measurable withdrawal symptoms before introduction of bupenorphine, or suboxone. Due to its lower potential for abuse and overdose, suboxoner seems to be a promising pharmacological intervention for opioid dependence. Additional counseling is recommended as an integrated approach to treatment.

The Family of the Client Who Has Co-occurring Disorders

The behavior (e.g., suicide attempts, psychotic episodes, grossly disturbed behavior, feeling disorders) of the patient with co-occurring disorders may expose other family members to tremendous stress and trauma. The severity and length of the problem may emotionally, physically, financially, and spiritually exhaust family members. Some family members (e.g., brothers, sisters) may have felt that their needs were not being met. Family members can benefit from supportive counseling.

Often, family members have unique perceptions of the family member who has co-occurring disorders. This causes tremendous conflict and tension between parents and other family members.

Frequently, the mother sees her son as ill and needing acceptance and understanding (e.g., "If only we could get him the right help he will be O.K."). The father, on the other hand, sees the son as lazy and irresponsible and that the problem stems mainly from the son's drinking/drugging too much. (e.g., "If he only would stop using alcohol/drugs, things would get better.") Unfortunately, they are both wrong—the problem involves both alcohol/drugs and psychological problems, and both need to be addressed.

Educating the family and engaging them in treatment early often positively affects treatment outcome. Families are more likely to cooperate if approached in a supportive manner by clinicians. Clinicians can be viewed as people who understand their experience and don't blame them. The counselors' ability to demonstrate their expertise regarding co-occurring disorders (both the psychiatric and alcohol/drug aspects of recovery) can help in establishing trust and rapport with the family.

The goals of family treatment are these:

1. Acquiring knowledge about co-occurring disorders
2. Increasing self-awareness, especially each family member's role in the family
3. Helping individual members make changes in the family system
4. Maintaining family members' involvement in ongoing recovery efforts (e.g., Al-Anon, individual and family counseling, groups)

⚹ Suicide and Alcohol/Drugs

Suicide is the second leading cause of death for youth ages 15–24 years of age. More people are killed by suicide each year than by car accidents. We are seeing an increase in suicides. Previous estimates indicated that 29,000 Americans commit suicide each year. In 2014 that increased to 42,773 suicides in the United States, and we expect this to increase. The top three groups that commit suicide in 2014 are white males (24.1%), Native Americans (10.8%) and Nonwhite Males (9.6%).

Studies reveal that between 7 and 27 percent of all deaths of alcoholics are by suicide. We know that affective disorders (depression), and alcohol and drug abuse significantly contribute to suicide.

Frequently, alcohol or drugs impair judgment and influence suicidal ideation and behavior. The right combination of trauma, stress, loss, depression, isolation, health problems, interpersonal/spouse conflict, financial/occupational problems, and alcohol/drug use may lead to feelings of hopelessness, helplessness, and shame, making the individual vulnerable to suicide.

The following facts have been drawn from the research literature to help you understand and possibly help someone thinking of suicide.* (See Table 12.4.)

- Most people who die by suicide give some clue or warning of their intent; therefore, talk of suicide, suicide threats, gestures, or attempts should always be treated seriously.
- Having fallen out of love with life, most suicidal people remain ambivalent about dying. Thus, most can be talked back into living.
- Some depressed people appear to be "suddenly" happy after they decide to "resolve" all their problems at the same time.
- Alcohol/drug abuse greatly enhances the short- and long-term risk of suicide even in people who are not alcoholic.
- If the person in a suicide crisis receives the proper assistance and support, he or she will probably never be suicidal again. Only about 10 percent of suicide attempters go on to complete a suicide.

TABLE 12.4

Counseling a Suicidal Client

- Screen for suicidal thoughts or plans with anyone who makes suicidal references, appears seriously depressed, or who has a history of suicide attempts. Treat all suicide threats with seriousness.
- Assess the client's risk of self-harm by asking about what is wrong, why now, whether specific plans have been made to commit suicide, past attempts, current feelings, and protective factors.
- Develop a safety and risk management process with the client that involves a commitment on the client's part to follow advice, remove the means to commit suicide (e.g., a gun), and agree to seek help and treatment. Avoid sole reliance on "no suicide contracts."
- Assess the client's risk of harm to others.
- Provide availability of contact 24 hours per day until psychiatric referral can be realized. Refer those clients with a serious plan, previous attempt, or serious mental illness for psychiatric intervention or obtain the assistance of a psychiatric consultant for the management of these clients.
- Monitor and develop strategies to ensure medication adherence.
- Develop long-term recovery plans to treat substance abuse.
- Review all such situations with the supervisor and/or treatment team members.
- Document thoroughly all client reports and counselor suggestions.

SOURCE: Sacks and Ries 2004.

---

*This section was developed by, and permission was granted by, Paul Quinnett, Ph.D., President and CEO of the QPR Institute, Spokane, Washington. www.qprinstitute.com. The QPR Institute offers basic and advanced training in suicide prevention, both in classroom and online. Dr. Quinnett is the author of *Suicide: The Forever Decision, Counseling Suicidal People, A Theory of Hope*, and the past editor of *Preventing Suicide: the National Journal*.

- Asking someone directly about suicidal intent does not increase the risk of suicide. Rather, the question lowers anxiety, opens up communication about the problems worth dying for, and lowers the risk of an impulsive act.
- Many suicidal people will visit a physician within 3 months of an attempt to kill themselves. Too often, their thoughts of suicide are neither expressed to the doctor, nor asked for.
- Twenty to 40 percent of patients with affective disorder (depression) exhibit nonfatal suicidal behavior, including thoughts of suicide.
- Sudden unemployment is associated with increased risk of suicide.
- Suicide occurs more often in midweek.
- Suicide rates decline during major holidays, such as Thanksgiving and Christmas.
- Drinking alcoholics have a lifetime suicide rate much higher than the general population and are 5 to 10 times more likely to die by suicide.
- Suicide increases with age, reaching a peak among older white males. Older people are at greater risk for suicide than teenagers.
- Most suicidal people plan their self-destruction in advance and leave clues indicating they have become suicidal.
- Of those who die by their own hand, men outnumber women 4 to 1.
- Women make gestures or attempts on their lives three times more often than men.
- As age increases, so does the risk that a first attempt at suicide will end in death.
- Contrary to popular myth, those who talk about suicide often do make an attempt on their own lives.
- The most common emotional states of the suicidal person are ambivalence and hopelessness.
- People are not acutely suicidal forever; rather, the actual crisis during which the person may act typically lasts only a few days, or a few hours.

Clues to Suicidal Intentions

People thinking of suicide often give clues to their thoughts and feelings and plans to deal with their growing sense of hopelessness. One clue may or may not mean a great deal, but *any* clue is worth asking about. (See Table 12.5.)

There are many motivations for suicide and suicidal behavior. Some of them include the following:

- Wanting to end psychological pain
- Wanting to escape an unacceptable situation
- Wanting to join a deceased loved one
- Wanting to gain attention
- Wanting to control others
- Wanting to avoid punishment for a crime
- Wanting to control when death occurs
- Wanting to become a martyr
- Wanting to punish the survivors
- Wanting to avoid loss of face

TABLE 12.5

Clues to Suicide

Direct Verbal Clues*	Behavioral Clues (continued)
• "I've decided to kill myself." • "I wish I were dead." • "I'm going to commit suicide." • "I'm going to end it all." • "If [such and such] doesn't happen, I'll kill myself."	• Putting personal and business affairs in order • Making or changing a will • Taking out insurance or changing beneficiaries • Making funeral plans • Giving away money and/or possessions • Making changes in behavior, especially episodes of screaming, hitting, or throwing things or failure to get along with family, friends, or peers • Acting suspiciously, such as going out at odd times of the day or night and waving or kissing goodbye (if not characteristic) • Showing sudden interest or disinterest in church or religion • Scheduling appointments with a doctor for no apparent physical causes or very shortly after the last routine visit • Losing physical skills; general confusion; or losing understanding, judgment, or memory • Relapsing into drug or alcohol use after a period of recovery
Indirect or Coded Verbal Clues*	
• "I'm tired of life." • "What's the point of going on?" • "My family would be better off without me." • "Who cares if I'm dead, anyway?" • "I can't go on anymore." • "I just want out." • "I'm so tired of it all." • "You would be better off without me." • "I'm not the person I used to be." • "I'm calling it quits—living is useless." • "Soon I won't be around." • "You shouldn't have to take care of me any longer." • "Soon you won't have to worry about me anymore." • "Goodbye. I won't be here when you return." • "It was good at times, but we must all say goodbye." • "You're going to regret how you've treated me." • "You know, son, I'm going home soon." • "Here, take this [cherished possession]; I won't be needing it." • "Nobody needs me anymore." • "How do they preserve your kidneys for transplantation if you die suddenly?"	
	Situational Clues
	• Sudden rejection by a loved one (e.g., girlfriend or boyfriend) or an unwanted separation or divorce • Recent move—especially if unwanted • Death of a spouse, child, friend (especially if by suicide or accident) • Diagnosis of terminal illness • Flare up with friend or relative for no apparent reason • Sudden, unexpected loss of freedom (e.g., about to be arrested) • Anticipated loss of financial security • Loss of cherished counselor or therapist
Behavioral Clues	
• Donating body to a medical school • Purchasing a gun • Stockpiling pills	

*Many of the following statements were made by people who subsequently went on to kill themselves.

SOURCES: Marv Miller, *Suicide After Sixty,* Springer, New York, 1979; Edwin Schneidman and Norman Farberow, *Clues to Suicide,* McGraw-Hill, New York, 1957; David Spain, *Post-Mortem,* Doubleday, New York, 1974; Louis Wekstein, *Handbook of Suicidology,* Brunner/Mazel, New York, 1979.

- Wanting to avoid becoming a burden to others
- Wanting to take revenge
- Wanting to avoid social ridicule
- Wanting to please a cult leader

It is good to remember that the risk of acting on a suicidal thought or feeling shifts over time and that, although persons who have been considering death believe they are no longer at-risk, something terrible or unexpected can hit them from "out of the blue." Whatever this new source of stress is, it is essential that suicidal persons know there is someone whom they can call, someone who will listen, someone who will care enough to help. If you happen to be that person, Table 12.6 lists some things you can do.

Remember, if you feel that any persons you know may be thinking about suicide, go ahead and ask. If they weren't thinking of suicide, the worst they can do is

---

T A B L E   1 2 . 6

Dos and Don'ts with Suicidal Individuals

Dos
<ul><li>Get involved. If in doubt, ask questions. Don't wait for a call from someone in trouble; make the call yourself. Examples of how to ask the question: Are your problems so big you are thinking of harming yourself? Do you wish you could end it all? Have you been thinking of suicide?</li><li>Be accepting and nonjudgmental. Don't offer simple solutions (they sound like brush-offs). Be realistic about the problems, but offer reassurance (hope).</li><li>Be confident and bold. As a solution, suicide can wait. What needs fixing may take a little time, but, at least for today, suicide can wait. Buy time—any way you can.</li><li>Remove the means of suicide. Get rid of guns, pills, razors, whatever. Suicidal people are running red lights without a seat belt; buckle them up.</li><li>Always take a positive, hopeful approach. Suicidal people feel hopeless. Fortunately, hope is infectious, so assure them things will get better because, in fact, they usually do.</li></ul>

Don'ts
<ul><li>Don't act shocked, dismayed, or frightened. Suicide is drastic, but it's only a solution to a problem. What's the problem worth dying for? Try to understand this and you can save a life.</li><li>Don't ignore the person's threats. Even if he or she doesn't really intend to die, can either of you afford to ignore this cry for help?</li><li>Don't point out the shock, embarrassment, or suffering the family or loved one will endure if the person dies, unless you are sure that isn't exactly what the person wants.</li><li>Don't get into a debate on the merits of living or dying. You might lose the argument.</li><li>Never put yourself at risk of injury (taking a gun or knife away) unless you are highly trained in this area.</li></ul>

be a little offended that you would think them capable of such an act; however, if they were thinking of suicide, they may be forever grateful.

⚹ In Review

- Some of the elements many alcohol/drug treatment programs now focus on include:
    - Treatment for co-occurring disorders
    - Adjunct tracks for eating disorders
    - Specialized treatment for sexual addiction and sexual disorders
    - Cognitive behavioral therapies
    - EMDR and other techniques for trauma treatment
    - Dialectical behavior therapy (DBT) for borderline personality disorders
    - More emphasis on family members and family systems
    - Medications to deal with anxiety and depression
    - Specialized tracks for gambling disorders
    - Residential halfway houses, intensive outpatient programs, and treatment planning upon discharge
    - Relapse prevention
    - Mindfulness training
    - Equine therapy, challenge courses, and alternative wilderness experiences

- Suicide and Alcohol/Drugs. Suicide is the eighth leading cause of death in the general population and the third among adolescents. Less than 1 percent of the general population commits suicide, yet studies reveal that between 7 and 27 percent of all deaths of alcoholics are by suicide.
- Self-help meetings are the most widely used and successful approach to alcohol and drug recovery.
- Advantages of AA as a Recovery Model:
    - Mutual sharing by members
    - Provision of a regular support group
    - Frequent and regular meetings
    - Availability of AA as an adjunct to other treatments
    - Absence of membership fees and nondiscrimination by race, sex, or socioeconomic status
    - Establishment of comprehensive goals covering the emotional, behavioral, and spiritual life of the members

- Resistance to attending AA and other self-help groups includes the following reasons:

    1. Difficulty with the concept of a higher power, or references to God
    2. Lack of tolerance by self-help members, at times, to
        - Use medication for affective or feeling disorders and other psychological conditions

- Help understand that there are different types of alcoholism
- Reject treatment (therapy and other treatment modalities)
3. People are uncomfortable in group settings and are concerned with the group's maintaining strict confidentiality
4. The disruptive influence of people (especially court-referred) who don't have a true desire to be sober

- Richard Rawson's model describes the five stages of alcohol/drug recovery:

   0–15 days—withdrawal

   16–45 days—honeymoon

   46–120 days—the wall

   121–180 days—adjustment

   181+ days—resolution

Each of these stages has its own behavioral, cognitive, emotional, and relational symptoms.

- Early phases of alcohol/drug recovery focus on issues of stabilization and safety.

⚹ Discussion Questions

1. Pick the stage of alcohol/drug recovery that you might find the most difficult and explain why.
   - Withdrawal
   - Honeymoon
   - The Wall
   - Adjustment
   - Resolution

2. Group therapy or group counseling is a good way to work on issues. Explain why one would use the curative factors of group counseling. The curative factors are:
   - Instilling hope
   - Sharing universality
   - Imparting information
   - Fostering altruism
   - Recapitulating the primary family group
   - Developing socializing techniques
   - Imitating behavior
   - Sharing interpersonal learning
   - Developing group cohesiveness
   - Sharing catharsis
   - Exploring existential factors

⚹ References

Aharonovich, Efrat, et al. 2002. Suicide attempts in substance abusers: Effects of major depression in relation to substance use disorders. *American Journal of Psychiatry* 159: 1600–1602.

Armor, D. J., J. M. Polich, and H. B. Stambul. 1978. *Alcohol and treatment.* New York: Wiley.

Bateman, N. I., and D. M. Peterson. 1971. Variables related to outcome of treatment for hospitalized alcoholics. *International Journal of Addictions* 6: 215–24.

Bishop, F. Michler. 1995. Rational-emotive behavior therapy and two self-help alternatives to the 12-step model. In *Psychotherapy and substance abuse,* edited by Arnold Washton. New York: Guilford Press.

Borkman, Thomasina. 2008. The 12-step recovery model of AA: A voluntary mutual help association. In *Recent Developments in Alcoholism,* 18, *Research on Alcoholics Anonymous and spirituality in addiction recovery,* 9–33, Eds. Marc Gallenter and Lee Ann Kaskutas.

Bowen, Sarah, Neha Chawla, and G. Alan Marlatt. 2010. *Mindfulness-based relapse prevention for addictive behaviors: A clinician's guide.* University of Washington, Dept. of Psychology.

Brewer, Judson A., Sarah Bowen, Joseph T. Smith, G. Alan Marlatt, and Marc N. Potenza. 2010. Mindfulness-based treatment for co-occurring depression and substance use disorders: Who can learn from the brain? *Society for the Study of Addiction* 105: 1698-1706.

Browne-Mayers, A. N., E. E. Seeley, and D. E. Brown. 1973. Reorganized alcoholism services: Two years after. *Journal of the American Medical Association* 224: 233–235.

Costello, Raymond M. 1975. Alcoholism treatment and evaluation: In search of methods. II. Collation of two-year follow-up studies. *International Journal of the Addictions* 10(5): 857–67.

Groves. 1978. Troublesome behavior patterns. *New England Journal of Medicine* 4.

Hay, Louise L. 1984. *You can heal your life.* Santa Monica, Calif.: Hay House.

Hayes, Steven, Victoria Follette, and Marsha Linehan, eds. 2004. *Mindfulness and acceptance: Expanding the cognitive behavioral tradition.* New York: Guilford Press.

Hellerstein, D., and B. Meehan. 1987. Outpatient group therapy for schizophrenic substance abusers. *American Journal of Psychiatry* 144: 1337–39.

Inciardi, James A., and Lana D. Harrison, eds. 2000. *Harm reduction: National and international perspective.* Thousand Oaks, Calif.: Sage.

Jancin, Bruce. 1994. SSRIs help drinkers reduce, but not eliminate, alcohol consumption. *Clinical Psychiatry News* (April).

Kish, G. B., and H. T. Herman. 1971. The Fort Meade Alcoholism Treatment Program: A follow up study. *Quarterly Journal of Studies on Alcohol* 32: 628–35.

Lawson, Gary, James S. Peterson, and Ann Lawson. 1983. *Alcoholism and the family: A guide to treatment and prevention.* Rockville, Md.: Aspen.

Rawson, Richard, J. Obert, M. McCann, and David Smith. 1988. *Treatment of cocaine dependence: A neurobehavioral approach.* Beverly Hills, Calif.: Matrix Institute on Addictions.

Robson, R. A., H. I. Paulus, and G. G. Clark. 1965. An evaluation of the effect of a clinic treatment program on the rehabilitation of alcoholic patients. *Quarterly Journal of Studies on Alcohol* 26: 264–78.

Sacks, Stanley, and Richard K. Ries. 2004. *Substance abuse treatment for persons with co-occurring disorders.* A Treatment Improvement Protocol 42. Rockville, Md.: U.S. Dept. of Health and Human Services, SAMHSA/CSAT.

Steinglass, Peter. 1979. An experimental treatment program for alcoholic couples. *Journal of Studies on Alcohol* 40: 159–82.

Trimpey, Jack. 1985. *The small book: A revolutionary alternative for overcoming alcohol and drug dependence.* New York: Delacorte Press.

Trimpey, Jack. 1996. *Rational recovery: The new cure for substance addiction.* New York: Pocket Books.

The Problem of Relapse: Relapse Prevention (RP)

Outline of Chapter 13

Introduction

Causes of Relapse
> Treatment Causes

Definition of Relapse

Definition of Relapse Prevention (RP)

Recognizing the Signs of Relapse—Relapse Prone and Recovery Prone Behaviors

Vulnerability to Relapse
> Applying Halts
> Cravings and Urges

Relapse Prevention Strategies
> AA Serenity Prayer as a Relapse-Prevention Technique

Mindfulness: A Tool for Relapse Prevention
> Addiction—"Land of the Hungry Ghosts"
> Definition of Mindfulness
> Mindfulness-Based Relapse Prevention (MBRP)
> Mindfulness and Relapse Prevention—Shifting from Reacting to Skillful Responding

Objectives

1. Describe some major causes of relapse.
2. Define relapse and relapse prevention.
3. Describe the differences between relapse-prone and recovery-prone behaviors.
4. Explain what "HALTS" stands for in relation to relapse.
5. List some ways that mindfulness can be used to enhance alcohol/drug recovery and relapse prevention.
6. Define mindfulness; then briefly explain the role of compassion, self-delusion, and surrender, from a mindfulness perspective.
7. Outline the eight sessions of Mindfulness-Based Relapse Prevention (MBRP).

❧ Introduction

The high relapse rates for alcohol/drug addiction is indicative of the depth of the challenge to maintain abstinence and sobriety and the need for more skillful relapse-prevention strategies. It also challenges treatment programs to do a better job preparing their clients for the rigors of early sobriety.

A majority of relapses occur in the first 30 to 180 days of recovery. Ironically, this is the time when most people have left alcohol/drug treatment and are taking their first, tentative steps in maintaining sobriety outside the treatment environment. It is a time when the recovery person is back home and among their former friends and associates and experiencing the same stressors that existed before they entered treatment, and possibly new ones. It is a time when the newly recovering person needs the most support. They are subject to high expectations from family, employers, and friends and may feel strong pressure to stay abstinent. This environment becomes one in which relapse may be more likely.

Unfortunately, relapse prevention is an often neglected, misunderstood, and mismanaged set of skills. This chapter focuses on relapse and relapse prevention and highlights an innovative more progressive way of viewing, understanding, and responding to relapse.

Relapse is best viewed from a preventive, neurobiological, and affect management approach. Relapse can alert us to issues that need to be addressed.

This chapter will provide a better understanding of relapse, relapse-prevention (RP), and RP tools, including the use of mindfulness and compassion in reducing both the number and severity of relapse.

⚹ Causes of Relapse

Marlatt and Gordon (1985) identified three major categories that cause recovering alcoholics to be vulnerable to relapse (see Table 13.1):

1. *Negative emotional states* cause 35 percent of all relapses. In these situations, individuals experience negative emotional states, moods, or feelings, such as frustration, anger, anxiety, depression, or boredom. (See Table 13.2.)
2. *Interpersonal conflict* causes 16 percent of all relapses. These situations involve an ongoing or a relatively recent conflict associated with any interpersonal relationship, such as marriage, friendship, relationships with family members, and employer-employee relations. Arguments and interpersonal confrontation occur frequently in this category. (See Table 13.3.)

TABLE 13.1	
Causes of Relapse	
Negative Emotional States	35%
Interpersonal Conflict	36%
Social Pressure	20%
Other	9%
SOURCE: Marlatt and Gordon (1985)	

TABLE 13.2

Negative Emotional States

Difficulty Managing Negative Emotional States	Difficulty Managing Stress Effectively	Difficulty Dealing with Feelings from Family of Origin	Difficulty with Blocked Goal-Directed Activities	Physical States That Contribute to Negative Emotional States
Feelings of depression, anxiety, rage, and distress exacerbated by feelings of shame and a poor sense of self	Feelings of confusion and overreaction to problems and conflicts	Feelings of emotional pain, loss, grief, separation, abandonment, violation, rejection, and isolation	Feelings of aggressiveness and rage Feelings of being hassled by normal daily living Feelings of boredom, loneliness, isolation, uselessness, helplessness, or hopelessness; lack of purpose in life	Physical health problems, pain, illness, injury, fatigue, specific physical disorders (e.g., chronic or recurrent pain caused by headaches, menstrual cramps, back pain) Physical states associated with prior substance abuse

TABLE 13.3

Interpersonal Conflicts

Conflicts with Partner/Spouse	Conflicts with Family	Other Stressful Interpersonal Conflicts
Once sober, the recovering person begins to see dysfunctional aspects of the relationship. Different stages of recovery: one person is working on her recovery program and the other is not actively working on his issues. New adjustment in relationship due to recovery Fear that the relationship will not be maintained or improve	Recognition of family dysfunction may lead to unresolved feelings of loss, abandonment, violation, and rejection; then these issues are stuffed and not worked out. Family system does not change or adapt to alcoholic/addict's recovery but maintains some dysfunctional patterns of communication and interaction.	Separation; divorce; or continued physical, sexual, or emotional violations Conflicts with employer, employees, friends, and other social situations Pattern of excessive fighting, arguments, and conflicts that go unresolved and are a repetitive cycle Pleasing people, avoiding conflicts, not telling others how one feels, acquiescing, and avoiding anger and other feelings associated with conflict

TABLE 13.4	
Social Pressure	
Peer Group	**Isolating**
Return to old alcohol/ drug—using peer group Hang out with alcohol/drug users	Withdrawing from friends who support recovery; nonattendance or passive involvement with support group, such as AA or NA Not maintaining contact with sponsor, counselor, or aftercare program Emotionally shutting down, not sharing feelings with others who are trusted and supportive of recovery; AA's motto is "Silence is the enemy of recovery"

3. *Social pressure* causes 20 percent of all relapses. In these situations, individuals respond to the influence of another person or group of people exerting pressure on them to engage in the taboo behavior. (See Table 13.4.)

Sometimes recovering alcoholics/addicts do not develop or maintain all aspects of their recovery program. Table 13.5 lists some of the reasons certain persons are more prone to relapse. These factors may lead people to make impulsive decisions to test their recovery by using alcohol/drugs. In effect, this testing of their willpower to go back to controlled alcohol/drug use frequently leads to relapse.

There are many causes for relapse. These causes can act at the same time, as they interact with each other. Stress, conflicts in relationships, and reactivity make for a combustible interaction that often leads to relapse. (See Table 13.6.)

Stress

Excessive stress is a major cause for relapse.

Interpersonal Conflict

Conflicts, loses, and changes in relationships are major causes for relapse.

Reactivity

Escalating and overreacting to issues, conflicts, and situations clearly makes things worse and is a major contributor to relapse. (Later in this chapter mindfulness and compassion tools are described in reducing reactivity.)

Physiological Causes

Illness, and physical problems can make one vulnerable to relapse.

Cognitive Causes

Much suffering and relapses are caused by a lack of awareness, unwise decisions, and clouded thinking.

Behavioral Causes

Relapsing behaviorally back to unhealthy habits and relationships.

TABLE 13.5
Other Risk Factors for Relapse
Miscellaneous Factors
High-stress personality type   Mood swings, temper, and rage   Shutting down, withdrawing emotionally   Overseparation and overattachment   Difficulty establishing intimacy and maintaining appropriate boundaries in relationships   Personality disorders: narcissism, bipolar disorder, borderline personality, codependent personality, depression (affective disorder), anxiety disorders, obsessive-compulsive disorders, and others   High-risk lifestyle: constant changes, high-stress job (i.e., always wheeling and dealing), financial and employment roller coaster, partner/spouse relationship changes and/or conflicts, always around others who use alcohol/drugs (entertainment industry, business-related drinking, bars, nightclubs, etc.)   Financial: problems in managing finances, inability to control spending, making inappropriate financial commitments, and taking on inappropriate financial obligations   Problems in employment, career change with poor planning   Trouble with back taxes and the Internal Revenue Service or other previous debt
Thinking and Perceptual Factors
Self-defeating or self-sabotaging thoughts   Painful memories and/or euphoric recall of alcohol/drug use   Return of denial and inability to consciously recognize loss of control over alcohol/drugs   Poor judgment and negative or grandiose thinking, which leads to impulsive self-destructive decisions   Overreacting, crisis building, and creating problems when things are beginning to go better
Spiritual Factors
Feeling at a loss, not feeling that life has meaning   Difficulty maintaining sobriety or having a reason for staying sober   Existential despair: not seeing a function of or reason for living

Affective Causes

Sadness, depression, anxiety, and shifts in mood lead to vulnerability to relapse.

Psychological Causes

Personality issues that cause problems, conflicts.

Environmental Causes

Socioeconomic conditions, imbalanced lifestyle, availability, etc.

Spiritual Causes

Diminished hope and disconnection.

C H A R T   1 3 . 1

Relapse
A complex, nonlinear process in which various factors act jointly to affect relapse timing and severity.

Treatment-Related Causes

Receiving poor treatment will cause relapse.

Treatment Causes

Anne Fletcher, author of Inside Rehab, visited and interviewed patients in a number of residential treatment programs. She describes the following sentiment "I heard sad tales of repeated visits to rehab with the implication that the client had somehow failed, when it seemed apparent that something about the treatment had very likely failed the individual."

Flethcher described residential treatment programs as being Cookie-Cutter approaches and having a My Way or the Highway attitudes. She says residential treatment can be counterproductive (removal from home), and she suggests doing away with it. She says "For most individuals, outpatient treatment is as good as or better than residential."

⚹ Definition of Relapse

Relapse is also defined as a return to a problematic behavior. Alcoholism and drug addiction can be described as "chronic relapsing."

T A B L E   1 3 . 6

Relapse Factors and Situations Factors

Interpersonal/Environment Relapse
Coping with negative emotional states
Coping with negative physical physiological
Enhancement of positive emotional states
Testing personal control
Giving in to temptations or urges

Relapse Situations
Interpersonal determinants (interpersonal events)
Coping with interpersonal conflicts
Social pressure
Enhancement of positive emotional states

High Relapse Rate

Estimates of relapse rates are widespread. A fair estimate would be in the 60 to 80 percent range. Whatever the range of relapse rates, all would agree that it is high.

As stated earlier, 2/3 of relapses involve negative emotional states, interpersonal conflict, and social pressure (Cummings et al. 1980).

⍟ Definition of Relapse Prevention (RP)

Alan Marlatt defined relapse prevention as "A congitive-behavioral approach to help individuals anticipate and cope with setbacks during the behavior change process."

Another definition of RP is "a tertiary intervention strategy for reducing the likelihood and severity of relapse following the cessation or reduction of problematic behavior." (Christian Hendershot et al. 2011)

The overall goal of RP is to reduce the incidence and severity of relapse.

Of course the primary goal of RP is to prevent relapse. A more expanded view sees the actual relapse and the falling back to unhealthy habits as the problem. Other goals include awareness and building coping skills, and limiting relapse proneness by promoting a healthy and balanced lifestyle.

⍟ Recognizing the Signs of Relapse—Relapse Prone and Recovery Prone Behaviors

One must be trained to recognize the signs and problems that may cause relapse. (See Table 13.7.) The defense mechanisms of denial (rationalization and minimization) may be invoked to avoid looking at the potential for relapse. Many alcoholics/addicts tend to discount the stressful situations and distressful lifestyles and behaviors that contribute to relapse. The alcoholic/addict trained in relapse prevention can recognize these problem areas and avoid being blindsided by high-risk relapse situations. (See Table 13.8 and Figure 13.1.)

TABLE 13.7

Relapse-Prone versus Recovery-Prone

Denial and Evasion	Recognition and Problem Solving
Relapse-Prone	**Recovery-Prone**
Evade or deny the sticking point	Recognize a problem exists
Stress	Accept that it is O.K. to have problems
Compulsive behavior	Detach to gain perspective
Avoid others	Ask for help
Problems	Respond with action when prepared
Evade/deny new problems	

SOURCE: © Terence T. Gorski, The Cenaps Corporation, Homewood, Ill., 708-799-5000. Published by Herald House Press, Independence, Mo., 1-800-767-8181.

TABLE 13.8

Analysis of Situations for Relapse

Situations	Example	Sample Number	Percent (%)
Frustration/anger	Patient tried to call his wife (they were separated); she hung up on him; he became angry and took a drink.	14	29
Social pressure	Patient went with friends to a bar after work. They put pressure on him to join the crowd, and he was unable to resist.	11	23
Intrapersonal temptation	Patient walked by a bar and just unconsciously walked in for no real reason; could not resist the temptation to take a drink.	10	21
Negative emotional state	Patient living alone, no job, complained of feeling bored and useless; could see no reason he should not take a drink.	5	10
Miscellaneous other situations	Patient reported that everything was going so well for him that he wanted to celebrate by having a drink.	5	10
No situation given or unable to remember		3	7

SOURCE: From *Relapse Prevention* by Alan Marlatt and Judith Gordon. © 1985 by the Guilford Press.

✷ Vulnerability to Relapse

Applying HALTS

HALTS is a valuable alcohol/drug relapse prevention tool. HALTS reminds the recovery person that when they are **H**ungry, **A**ngry, **L**onely, **T**ired, and/or **S**ick, they are vulnerable to relapse.

Over the past 30 years counseling clients, I have often heard them say, *"It seemed like a good idea at the time,"* when talking about a relapse. Clients will remember invoking the "screw it" attitude. At the time they metaphorically said to themselves, "Oh well, I know this is a bad decision, but I am going to do it anyway."

FIGURE 13.1   *Caution: Relapse Ahead*
SOURCE: Drawing by Ed Arno; © 1980 The New Yorker Magazine, Inc. Reprinted with permission.

Hungry

Addressing Hunger Be mindful to:

- Understand the relationship of "mood to food"
- Identify when you are hungry and when you are not hungry
- Take the time to eat
- Eat "gently" and slowly—tasting each bite
- Enjoy meals with others
- Practice "mindful" eating
- Stop eating when you begin to feel full

Angry

Would You Rather Be Right or Happy? People argue about who is right instead of respecting each other. They argue about things that don't really matter in the long run.

I was counseling a couple recently who spent most of a session arguing about which bananas were cheaper. They were arguing whether the bunch at Costo (factoring in the spoilage factor since it is a lot of bananas in the bundle) or the sale on a small bunch of bananas at the local grocery store was cheaper.

When you are in the throws of anger, calm down and take the time to ask yourself these reflective questions:

- Is this an effective approach to solve the problem?
- Is this approach likely to make things worse and hurt others' feelings?
- I am catastrophizing this; what is the real harm and damage?
- Am I being respectful of others?

Of course, the ultimate question is Would you rather be right or happy?

"If you get angry easily, it may be because the seed of anger in you has been watered frequently over many years, and unfortunately you have allowed it to be watered." (*Taming the Tiger Within*, Riverhead Books, by Thich Nhat Hanh 2004.)

Addressing Anger Be mindful to:

- Own what you say and do
- Take responsibility for your actions and decisions
- Avoid trying to convince others that they are wrong
- Avoid "tireless" debates
- Develop anger awareness
- Be "happy" rather than "right"
- Be gentle and patient rather than angry and aggressive

Lonely

Cool Loneliness Pema Chodron, in her book *When Things Fall Apart* (2000), describes cool loneliness:

> Usually we regard loneliness as an enemy. Heartache is not something we choose to invite in. It's restless and pregnant and hot with the desire to escape and find something or someone to keep us company.
>
> When we can rest in the middle, we begin to have a non-threatening relationship with loneliness, a relaxing and cooling loneliness that completely turns our usual fearful patterns upside down.

Addressing Loneliness Be mindful to:

- Work through feelings of loneliness
- Develop cool loneliness
- Accept our own separateness
- Counter loneliness with connection
- Realize that loneliness will pass with time

Tired

Addressing Tiredness Be mindful to:

- Evaluate when you might be overdoing it
- Balance your work and home life
- Balance work with fun
- Make time to do things you enjoy
- Take regular breaks (rest and renewal)
- Not be so hard on yourself

Sick

Keep health and wellness as a mindful priority. A good strategy is to value, seek, and do everything possible to be in good health.

Addressing Being Sick Be mindful to:

- Make physical and emotional health your top priority
- Take better care of yourself
- Value, celebrate, and have gratitude for good health
- Commit to preventive, maintenance, and restorative health practices

Cravings and Urges

Thoughts, desires, and even dreams about using alcohol/drugs are very common in chemical dependency recovery. A variety of things can trigger this craving for alcohol/drugs, and cravings acted on can lead to relapse. The most effective way of coping with cravings and urges is to detach from the craving. "Instead of identifying with the urge (e.g., I really want a cigarette right now) the client can be trained to monitor the urge or desire from the point of view of a detached observer (I am now experiencing the craving/urge to smoke). By externalizing and labeling the craving/urge and watching it come and go through the eyes of the observer, there will be a decreased tendency to identify with the urge and feel overwhelmed by its power" (Marlatt and Gordon 1985).

Recovering alcoholics/addicts can identify triggers leading to cravings for alcohol/drugs and develop an awareness as to why cravings occur. Then the alcoholics/addicts can structure their lives either to avoid these triggers or to desensitize themselves to the trigger.

A trigger is "a stimulus which has been repeatedly associated with the preparation for, anticipation of, or the actual use of alcohol/drugs. These stimuli include people, places, things, times of day, emotional states, and alcohol/drugs" (Rawson 1989). The following lists of time, place, thing, and people triggers show how diverse triggers are.

Time

- Periods of idle or leisure time
- Periods of extended stress
- Payday, holidays, Fridays, and Saturdays
- Birthdays and anniversaries
- Specific times of the day or evening
- Vacation
- Periods of unemployment

Place

- Drug dealers' home, bars, and parties
- Neighborhoods where drugs are dealt
- Clubs, concerts, and social events
- Places where alcohol/drugs have been used before

Things

- Drug dealers' car, telephone number, or name
- Large amounts of cash, $100 bills, and bank machines
- Paraphernalia: pipes, syringe, and rolling papers
- Movies, films, and television shows about alcohol/drugs and alcohol/drug lifestyle
- Particular music
- Alcohol and tobacco advertisements
- Conferences or seminars on alcohol/drugs
- Sexually explicit movies or magazines

People

- Alcohol/drug using friends
- Drug dealers and bartenders
- Partner/spouse, relatives, and family members who use alcohol/drugs
- Sexual encounters
- Groups of people talking about or using alcohol/drugs

✴ Relapse Prevention Strategies

Interpersonal and Social Recovery Support System

- Drug-free friends who understand and support recovery from alcohol/drugs
- Self-help groups, such as Alcoholics Anonymous, Narcotics Anonymous, Adult Children of Alcoholics, and Co-Dependents Anonymous
- Spouse/partner and family members who understand recovery and are involved in their own recovery and counseling
- Support of an AA or NA sponsor; someone who has strong personal recovery is available and active in pointing out relapse vulnerability
- Support from an aftercare program, group, or individual and family counseling on a regular basis

Health and Physical Well-Being

- A regular program of exercise: athletic activities, slow long-distance walking, or jogging/running, minimum three to five times per week
- Balanced, nutritionally sound, and structured diet
- Adequate sleep, functional stress level, appropriate balance between work and play and activity and rest

Cognitive, Emotional, and Spiritual Self

- Good sense of self, as a person (1) who is unique and worthwhile with emerging talents and skills; (2) who can accomplish things and has good decision-making and problem-solving skills—no self-sabotaging; (3) who can trust and be trusted while setting appropriate boundaries in relationships; and (4) who has the ability to resolve conflict and communicate feelings

- Ability to be aware of feelings and thoughts and to integrate feelings and thoughts in taking appropriate action
- Ability to adapt to life changes and stresses and to choose to grow emotionally, intellectually, occupationally, and interpersonally
- Ability to achieve at work, at school, at home, and in the community
- Spiritual orientation and growth with others and to spiritual life in general

AA Serenity Prayer as a Relapse-Prevention Technique

The serenity prayer of AA is an extremely valuable relapse-prevention technique that is easily invoked:

> God grant me the serenity
> To accept the things I cannot change,
> Courage to change the things I can,
> And wisdom to know the difference.

Accepting the things I cannot change means accepting what can't be controlled. Those in recovery need the skills to let go, to not control others or project their wishes on others. As a result, recovering alcoholics/addicts avoid the negative emotional feelings of anger, rage, anxiety, depression, and intolerable frustration.

> **Self-serenity prayer**
> Grant me the serenity
> To accept the PEOPLE I cannot change,
> Courage to change the ONE I can,
> And the wisdom to know it's ME.
> (Anonymous)

TABLE 13.9

Relapse Prevention—Reducing the Severity

What To Do If Relapse Occurs?

1. Use the relapse as a learning experience
2. See the relapse as a specific, unique event
3. Examine the relapse openly (to reduce guilt, shame, feelings of hopelessness)
4. Analyze the triggers for the relapse
5. Expectations—What would drinking/using accomplish?
6. Plan for dealing with the altermath/consequences of the relapse
7. Tell yourself—"Control is only a moment away"
8. Renew your commitment to abstinence
9. Make immediate plans for recovery—don't hesitate—do it now!
10. Contact your support system and discuss slips

SOURCE: Substance Abuse Treatment & the Stages of Change, Connors, DiClimente Velasquez, Donovan, 2013

Courage to change the things I can means controlling what can be controlled. Those in recovery need the skills to focus on today, to take action, and to work on themselves. As a result, recovering alcoholics/addicts develop positive affirmations, progress toward long-term goals, and develop a stronger sense of self.

Wisdom to know the difference means learning to discriminate between the impossible and the possible. Those in recovery need the skills to talk about feelings, accept limits, and ask "Can I change this?" As a result, recovering alcoholics/addicts can achieve a balanced lifestyle, can develop the ability to deal with urges and cravings, and can learn to avoid impulsive, destructive decisions, and interactions.

> Recovery is facilitated by the individual's ability to adapt to change and integrate feelings related to change. Striving for progress rather than perfection is a healthy goal.

❧ Mindfulness: A Tool for Relapse Prevention Addiction: "Land of the Hungry Ghosts"

Buddhist cosmology describes addiction as the "Land of Hungry Ghosts," where people have huge appetites that are unable to be satisfied. Buddhism describes addiction as a being a "false refuge," a delusional place to try and hide and escape from being present in life with the good and bad. Addiction is viewed as the inability to see the abundance and joy in our everyday lives. Developing a "calm awareness" can help in not distracting from life, and instead being more present and mindful "in the now."

The foundation of all mindfulness practices is compassion. In Western culture, we are prone to be hard on others and even harder on ourselves. But as the Dalai Lama stated: "I am the source of my own suffering, because of the habits of my mind."

I have worked for more than 25 years as a counselor, specializing in outpatient alcohol/drug recovery. For the past 3 years, I have used mindfulness practices in my outpatient recovery groups and my clients have found it very helpful, especially because it is not so "reactive." I see mindfulness as enhancing recovery, improving relapse prevention skills, and as being complementary to the 12-step process. (See Table 13.10.)

Often during counseling sessions, we sit and smile together as we see how we trick ourselves. We smile at the self-delusion, recognizing how easily it can be evoked. It starts by recognizing how "the fire of the ego" will blind us to our own self-delusion.

> "Because of mindfulness, we see our desires,
> And our aggression, our jealousy and
> Our ignorance. We don't act on them;
> We just see them. Without mindfulness,
> We don't see them and they proliferate."
> (Pema Chodron, *Comfortable with Uncertainty*)

T A B L E   1 3 . 1 0

Common AA and Dharma Teachings

AA	Dharma
Denial	Delusion
One Day at a Time	Being in the Now
The Serenity Prayer	Issues of Control, Surrender, Acceptance
Progress not Perfection	Letting go of Attachment to Outcome
Shit Happens	Life includes Suffering
Let Go & Let God	Forgiveness & Loving Kindness

Fields, 2014

Definitions of Mindfulness

To get a better sense of mindfulness, here are some definitions by various practitioners:

- "The awareness that emerges through paying attention on purpose, in the present moment, and nonjudgmentally to the unfolding of experience, moment by moment." (Kabet-Zinn 2003)
- "Mindfulness has to do with the quality of both awareness and participation that a person brings to everyday life." (Hayes, Follette, and Linehan 2004)
- "Broadly conceptualized mindfulness has been described as a nonelaborative, nonjudgmental, present-centered awareness in which each thought, feeling, or sensation that arises in the attentional field is acknowledged and accepted as it is." (Lau and Segal 2007)

Meditation, mindfulness practices, and Buddhist teachings (dharma) have proven to be effective in helping treat many physical and psychological problems from headaches and back pain to anxiety and depression. John Kabat-Zinn (1990) is well known for using mindfulness-based stress reduction (MBSR) to help patients with pain and anxiety disorders. Marsha Linehan (1993) integrated mindfulness practices in her dialectical behavior therapy (DBT) for borderline personality disorders. Steven Hayes, Strosahl, and Wilson (1999) developed a mindfulness model called acceptance and commitment therapy (ACT). Zindel Segal (2002) used mindfulness-based cognitive therapy (MBCT) as a relapse prevention approach to depression.

Alan Marlatt at the University of Washington explored the application of mindfulness and meditation in reducing relapse to alcohol. Marlatt et al. found that "the heightened state of present-focused awareness that is encouraged by meditation may directly counteract the conditioned automatic response to use alcohol in response to cravings and urges" (Marlatt and Chawla 2007).

TABLE 13.11

Mindfulness-Based Relapse Prevention

Session 1: Automatic Pilot and Craving

Participants discuss:

"Automatic pilot," or the tendency to behave mechanically or unconsciously, without a full awareness of what is happening

Automatic pilot in relation to alcohol/drug cravings and urges

Patterns of the mind, and how we react to cravings or to triggers in the environment

Participants learn a technique called the body scan that helps them practice purposely paying attention to the body.

Session 2: Triggers, Thoughts, Emotions, and Cravings

It is explained that you can experience cravings and thoughts of using without reacting. There is a focus on what cravings feel like in the body (i.e., what sensations, thoughts, and emotions go with temptations).

Session 3: Mindfulness in Everyday Life

Participants learn "breathing spaces" from formal sitting or lying down practice to the daily situations we encounter—"being with" the various physical sensations that arise, including cravings and urges.

Session 4: Staying Present and Aware in High-Risk Situations

Using mindfulness to relate to pressures/urges to use without automatically reaching for substances. Each participant identifies individual relapse risks and ways to cope with the intensity of feelings to use.

Session 5: Balancing Acceptance and Skillful Action

Establishing balance between accepting thoughts, feelings, and sensations that arise and also taking action when necessary. Practicing techniques such as the "breathing space," and focusing on using the breathing space in challenging situations.

Session 6: Seeing Thoughts as Just Thoughts

Exploring awareness of and relationship to thoughts, focusing on experiencing them as merely thoughts, even when they feel like the truth. Explore what role thoughts play in the relapse cycle.

(continued on next page)

T A B L E   1 3 . 1 1 *(c o n t i n u e d)*
Session 7: How Can I Best Take Care of Myself? Creating a More Balanced Life
Specific skills and resources we can use when we experience cravings and urges to use. Discuss personal warning signs of relapse. Discussion of lifestyle balance and the importance of nourishing activities in daily life.
Session 8: Building Support Networks and Using What Has Been Learned
Focus on the importance of a recovery support system. Individual plans incorporate mindfulness practices into daily life.

Mindfulness-Based Behavioral Relapse Prevention (MBRP)

The overall goal of MBRP is "to develop awareness and nonjudgmental acceptance of thoughts, sensations, and emotional states through the practice of mindfulness and meditation." Marlatt (1992) described "urge surfing" as an example of a MBRP technique. The recovering person is asked to visualize the urge/craving as an ocean wave. The wave has a beginning, a crest, and a smooth cycle until it turns and crashes on the shore. The breath is used as a "surfboard" to ride out the wave of the urge/ craving without giving into it. (See Table 13.11.)

Mindfulness and Relapse Prevention—Shifting from Reacting to Skillful Responding

Different mindfulness relapse prevention programs can help reduce incidences of relapse and the severity of relapse.

Since reactivity is a major cause of relapse, especially in interpersonal relation-ships and conflicts, the question is what can help reduce reactivity.

Mindfulness, self-compassion, and compassion for others are three tools that can help reduce reactivity, and in turn reduce relapse.

Three reactive emotions, anger, criticism (blame), and impatience, can be reduced with mindfulness, mediation, and compassion. Many Buddhist teachings (dharma) help the individual to make wiser and healthier decisions.
Here are some examples:

Delusion—Being unaware of unhealthy behaviors and habits, and deluding yourself that it is not a problem, creates a lack of awareness.

> "The essence of bravery is being without self-deception."
>
> *Pema Chodron*

Self-Compassion—We are often too hard on ourselves, shaming and blam-ing behaviors or traits that we don't like about ourselves. We must first be self-compassionate, and then be able to be truly compassionate to others.

"The curious paradox is that when I accept myself just as I am, then I can change."

Carl Rogers 1961

Love and Compassion—Connection through compassion and love is an essential element for a healthy life.

"Love and compassion are necessities, not luxuries, without them humanity cannot survive."

His Holiness the Dalai Lama

Open-Heartedness and Loving Kindness—Many Buddist teachings focus on the importance of open-heartedness and loving kindness for all.

We end this chapter on the topic of relapse and relapse prevention with this wish:

"May all beings omitting none, feel safe, and content, and happy, and live with ease."

Metta Suttra

�֎ In Review

- Relapse Prevention. The most common causes of relapse are as follows:
    - Negative emotional states
    - Social pressure and relationship problems
    - Abstinence violation effect
    - Financial and work-related problems
    - Boredom, lack of purpose, and meaning
    - High-risk lifestyle
    - Difficulty with personality traits, stress, and intimacy

- Urges and Cravings. Recognizing that specific times, places, things, and people can trigger alcohol/drug cravings is an important component of chemical dependency relapse training. It has been demonstrated that drug relapse is induced by a return to alcohol use.
- HALTS is a mnemonic device that reminds individuals in recovery that they are prone to relapse when they are hungry, angry, lonely, tired, and sick.
- Mindfulness (i.e., meditation, mindfulness practices, and dharma) is being used to enhance alcohol/drug recovery.
- Mindfulness-based behavioral relapse prevention (MBRP) is a relapse prevention model that develops awareness and nonjudgmental acceptance of thoughts, sensations, and emotional states, through the practice of mindfulness and meditation.
- Mindfulness practices help with recovery by improving compassion for self and others, awareness of self-delusion, while understanding the role of surrender and control.
- There is a very high relapse rate following alcohol/drug treatment. Most relapses occur after 30 to 180 days of sobriety.

- Causes of relapse are
  - Negative emotional states
  - Interpersonal conflict
  - Social pressure

❧ Discussion Questions

1. Negative emotional states and interpersonal conflicts are two major relapse factors. Explain why and list some others.
2. Define "mindfulness" in your own words or use your favorite definition. Discuss the benefits of mindfulness for alcohol/drug recovery and for relapse prevention.

❧ References

Chodron, Pema. 2000. *When things fall apart, heart advice for difficult times.* Boston, Mass.: Shambhala.

Hayes, S. C., K. D. Strosahl, and K. G. Wilson. 1999. *Acceptance and commitment therapy: An experiential approach to behavior change.* New York: Guilford Press.

Hayes, Steven, Victoria Follette, and Marsha Linehan, eds. 2004. *Mindfulness and acceptance: Expanding the cognitive behavioral tradition.* New York: Guilford Press.

Kabet-Zinn, John. 2003. Mindfulness-based interventions in context: Past, present and future. *Clinical Psychology: Science and Practice:* 145–46.

Lau, Mark A., and Zindel V. Segal. 2007. Mindfulness-based cogntive therapy as a relapse prevention approach to depression. In K. A. Witklewitz and G. A. Marlatt (eds.), *Therapist's guide to evidence-based relapse prevention.* Burlington, Mass.: Academic Press.

Linehan, M. M. 1993. *Cognitive-behavioral treatment of borderline personality disorder.* New York: Guilford.

Marlatt, G. Alan, and Neharika Chawla. 2007. Meditation and alcohol use. *Southern Medical Journal* 100(4).

Marlatt, Alan, and Judith Gordon. 1985. *Relapse prevention.* New York: Guilford Press.

Rawson, Richard. 1989. *Cocaine recovery issues: The neurobehavioral model.* Beverly Hills, Calif.: Matrix Institute on Addictions.

Segal, Z., et al. 2002. *Mindfulness-based cognitive therapy for depression: A new approach to preventing relapse.* New York: Guilford Press.

Index

Note: Page references followed by "f" or "t" refer to figures or tables, respectively

A

AA. *See* Alcoholics Anonymous (AA)
Abandonment and interpersonal
  relationships, 161–62
Abandonment depression, 161, 284
Abstinence, 285, 287
ACA. *See* Adult children of
  alcoholics (ACA)
Academic failure, 47
Acceptance and commitment
  therapy (ACT), 331
Acceptance stage (family recovery),
  155
Acetaldehyde, 82
Achievement, anxiety and addiction,
  52
Ackerman, Nathan, 141
Ackerman, Robert, 181
ACT (Acceptance and commitment
  therapy), 331
Acting out, 208
Addiction
  cognitive-behavioral points, 42
  definitions, 70–73, 122–23
  final stage of progressive
    disease, 124–25
  "land of hungry ghosts", 330
  3Cs, 71, 123
Addiction to pleasure, 52
Addictive personality, 31–32
ADHD, 280, 289
Adjustment stage (of recovery), 298
Administration of drugs. *See* Routes
  of administration
Adolescence
  case study, 37, 38
  college students, 258 (*See also*
    Colleges/universities)
  converting approaches, 242

co-occurring disorders, 289
CSAPs, 257
disorders, 286
functional hypothesis, 160
future orientation and hope, 47
identifying a problem, 127–29
interventions, 230
methamphetamine, 63
overinvolvement hypothesis, 160
PEACE, 36
self-concept, 36–37
sense of self, 37–39
sexual identity, 168
trauma and substance abuse
  disorders, 286, 288
Adoptees, 163
Adoption studies, 31
Adult children of alcoholics (ACA)
  atypical depression, 190
  behavioral characteristics,
    182–83
  boundary inadequacy, 191
  case study, 184–85, 195, 196,
    198–99
  codependency, 190–91
  core belief system, 193
  disengaged ACA, 190
  feeling awareness, 194–97
  grief work, 197
  group psychotherapy, 199–201
  NACOA, 182
  overattachment/overseparation,
    191–92
  powerlessness, 194
  PTSD, 183–85
  recovery, 193–201
  sense of identity, 189
  See also Children of alcoholic
    families

Aerosol cans, 106
Affect-shame binds, 168t
Affect tolerance, 281
Affective disorders. *See* Mood and
  affective disorders
Alcohol, 77–82
  absorption of, in the body, 69f
  Antabuse, 81–82
  FAS, 81
  historical overview, 77–78
  integrated into fabric of
    American lifestyle, 3
  major effects, 79–80
  most problematic drug, 5
  related illnesses, 81
  sobering up, 80
  tolerance, 80
  usage, 79
  withdrawal, 67, 80, 80t, 81
Alcohol/drug abuse
  early and late stages, 126t
  failed approaches, 3–4
  hopelessness, 47–48
  job/financial problems, 132t
  lack of understanding, 3
  legal problems, 132t
  marriage, 189
  myth of simple solution, 5
  perspectives, 18–21
  pessimism, 49–50
  physical problems, 132t
  physical signs, 129
  psychological problems, 132t
  relationship/social problems, 132t
  sexual problems, 132t
  stages (*See* Stages of alcohol/
    drug abuse)
  systemic problems, 10–15
  See also Drug abuse

Alcohol/drug assessment, 129–31
Alcohol/drug prevention. *See*
        Prevention activities
Alcohol/drug recovery, 297
    AA (*See* Alcoholics Anonymous
        (AA))
    adult children of alcoholics
        (ACA), 193–201
    counseling, 299–305
    cravings and urges, 327–28
    denial, 305
    family treatment, 301–2
    group therapy, 301
    guidelines/pointers, 302–4
    OSSN, 296
    RR, 296–97
    stages of recovery, 297–99
    triggers, 327–28
    See also Relapse prevention
Alcoholics Anonymous (AA),
        294–95
    disease model, 28
    reasons for success, 295
    resistance to attendance, 295
    serenity prayer, 209
    silence, 133
    slogans (cognitive-behavioral
        change), 306–7
    social support, 296
    twelve steps, 30t
Alcoholism
    AMA declaration, 27
    biological nature, 266
    case study, 281
    family disease, as, 181
    genetic model, 31
Alcoholism, disease model,
        27–30
Alcohol relapse. *See* Relapse
        prevention
Alcohol-related problems
    binge drinking, 6–15
    drinking and driving, 8–9
    high-risk behaviors, 6
    injury/death, 10
    scholastic difficulties, 6, 8
    violence, 10
Alcohol withdrawal symptoms, 80,
        80t, 81
Alexander, Charles, 190

Alpert, Richard, 97
Altered states of consciousness, 24,
        41, 46, 302–3
Alternative activity program,
        243–46, 245t
Altruism, 200
Ambiguous boundary inadequacy,
        171
Ambiguous family systems, 142
Ambivalence, 211
American Dream, 13
Amnesia, 79
Amobarbital, 82, 82t
Amphetamines, 89–91, 112–13
Amytal, 82, 82t
Anabolic-androgenic steroids
        (A-AS), 111
Anabolic steroids, 111, 112
Androgenic steroids, 111
Anger, 246, 253, 255, 257, 306
Anger stage (imbalanced family
        system), 152–53, 153t
Anslinger, Henry J., 4
Antabuse, 81–82
Antagonism, 68
Antianxiety agents, 87t
Antianxiety drugs, 308t
Antifreeze, 106
Antipsychotic agents, 87t
Antipsychotic drugs, 308t
Anti-Semitism, 12
Antisocial personality disorder
        (ASPD), 279–83
    case study, 283
    childhood precursors, 280
    diagnostic criteria, 283
    questions to ask, 282
Anxiety, 148t
Artane, 86
ASPD. *See* Antisocial personality
        disorder (ASPD)
Aspirin, 74
Associated factors
    healthy behaviors, 253t
    risk behaviors, 252t
Athletes and drugs, 110–14
    amphetamines, 112–13
    chewing tobacco, 113–14
    other drugs, 114
    steroids, 110–12

At-risk factors, 158–77
    abandonment depression, 161
    abandonment–impact on
        adult interpersonal
        relationships, 161–62
    adoptees, 163
    boundary ambiguity, 171–72
    boundary inadequacy, 171
    compassion, 175–76
    criticism, anger, and blame,
        173–72
    early parent-child attachment,
        159–60
    obstacles to reaching parents,
        174–75, 175t
    parental imbalance and boundary
        setting, 169–71
    parental support and control,
        163–64
    parents' use/abuse of drugs,
        173–74
    shame and feelings, 168–69
    shame and imbalanced
        parenting, 164–67
    traits and temperament, 162–63
    triangulation, 172–73
Attempting to control, 150t
Attention-deficit hyperactive disorder
        (ADHD), 280, 289
Atypical depression, 190
Ausubel, David P., 50
Availability-proneness theory, 51
Avoiding and shielding, 150t
Awfulizing, 306

B

Barbiturate overdose, 84
Barbiturates, 82–85
    classification, 82t
    major effects, 83
    medical uses, 82
    other drugs, and, 85
    overdose, 84
    pregnancy, 83
    routes of administration, 83
    sleep, 83
    street names, 82t
    tolerance, 83–84
    usage, 83
    withdrawal, 84, 84t

Barbiturate withdrawal, 84, 84t

Bargaining stage (imbalanced family system), 153–55

Behavior-specific information, 231

Behavior-specific statement, 233

Bejerot, Nils, 52

Belushi, John, 59

Benadryl, 86

Benzodiazepines, 87t, 285

"Beyond Drug Education" (Robinson), 38

Bias, Len, 59

Bibliotherapy, 197

Binge drinking
  age groups, 7–8
  driving, 8–9
  drug problem, 10–15
  injuries and deaths, 10
  intimate partner violence, 10
  sexual assault and rape, 8

Bishop, F. Michler, 297

Black-and-white thinking, 306

Black, Claudia, 141, 181

Blackouts, 79

Blame, 173

Blamers, 143, 148t

Blind self, 300

Bonds, Barry, 110

Bootlegged amphetamines, 91

Borderline personality disorder, 32, 265, 273, 278, 279, 283–85

Boredom, 39–41

Boundaries, 170

Boundary ambiguity, 171–72

Boundary inadequacy, 171, 191

Brain, 52

Breaking the Patterns of Depression (Yapko), 47

Brecher, Edward M., 12, 19, 248

Brief counseling, 214–20

Brown, Stephanie, 181, 182

Buddhism, 209

Building Motivational Interviewing Skills: A Practitioner Workbook (Rosengren), 220

Buprenorphine, 308

Bush, George W., 5

Butabarbital, 82, 82t

Butisol, 82, 82t

Butyrophenones, 87t

C

Cannabis resin, 101

Cannabis sativa, 99–104
  See also Marijuana

Capability development, 247–48

CAP theory, 50–51

Carnes, Patrick, 160

Case studies/vignettes
  ACA–decision making, 196
  ACA–interpersonal relationships, 200
  ACA–letter to parents, 198
  ACA–PTSD, 184–85
  adolescence, 37, 38
  alcoholism, 281
  alcohol problem, 38
  antisocial personality traits, 283
  atypical depression, 273
  bargaining, 153
  bipolar disorder, 275
  borderline personality disorder, 286
  depression and addiction, 270
  depression and withdrawal symptoms, 280
  dysthymic disorder, 272
  Eeyore syndrome, 271
  enabling behavior, 149
  future orientation, 47
  intervention-ineffective assessment, 232
  intervention-vignette, 235–38
  lost child, 146
  marijuana and seduction, 46
  marijuana search, 130
  motivational interviewing, 215–18
  narcissism and cocaine, 287–88
  personality disorders, 33
  rejection sensitivity, 195
  sexual violation and addiction, 29
  suicide, 134
  symptoms, 280
  trauma and addiction, 28

Casey Jones reaction, 94

Catalono, Richard E., 251

Catastrophizing, 306

Catecholamines, 94

Catharsis, 201

C'de Baca, Janet, 207

Central nervous system (CNS) depressants, 77
  alcohol (*See* Alcohol)
  barbiturates, 82–85
  tranquilizers, 86–89

Central nervous system (CNS) stimulants
  amphetamines, 89–91
  cocaine (*See* Cocaine)
  tobacco, 95

Cermak, Timmen, 181, 182, 190

Change, 207–10
  See also Motivation and change

Chewing tobacco, 113–14

Chief enabler, 145

Children
  ACA (*See* Adult children of alcoholics (ACA))
  conduct disorders/ADHD, 280

Children of alcoholic families, 186
  behavioral characteristics, 186
  common reactions, 187–88
  denial of feelings, 187
  role reversal, 187
  social isolation, 187
  unavailability, 187
  unpredictability, 187
  See also Adult children of alcoholics (ACA)

Chinese question (California), 11

Chloral hydrate, 85t

Cigarette smoking, 15, 68t, 95

Clear boundaries, 171

Clemens, Roger, 110

Client-centered motivational interviewing, 213–14

Clinebell, Howard, 187

Clinton, Bill, 5

Club des Hachichias, 100

Clustering, 172

CNS depressants. *See* Central nervous system (CNS) depressants

CNS stimulants. *See* Central nervous system (CNS) stimulants

Coca-Cola, 92
Cocaine, 91–95
    additives, 95
    adverse effects, 93–94
    African Americans, 12
    case study, 287–88
    celebrity mishaps/deaths, 59
    crack, 59, 93
    depression, 35
    effects of, 44
    freebase, 59, 93
    historical overview, 91–92
    major effects, 93
    power drug, as, 44
    progressive disease, 125t
    routes of administration, 92–93
    street names, 92
    tolerance, 94
    usage, 72
    withdrawal, 68t, 94
Cocaine additives, 95
Cocaine clinical syndromes, 93t
Cocaine dysphoria, 93t
Cocaine euphoria, 93t
Cocaine schizophreniform
        psychosis, 93t
Codependency, 190–91
Codependent dance, 193
Codependent personality disorder,
        190
Cogentin, 86
Cognitive-affective-pharmacogenic
        (CAP) theory, 50–51
Cognitive-behavioral therapy, 49,
        306–7
Cohen, Allan, 243, 244
Cohesion, 174
Coleman, Eli, 171, 172, 191
Colgan, Phillip, 171, 191
College Alcohol Study (CAS), 6
Colleges/universities
    alcohol-related problems, 6, 8
    binge drinking, 6–15
    high-risk behaviors, 6
    prevention activities, 259
    sexual assault/rape, 8
    See also Adolescence
Comfortable with Uncertainty
        (Chodron), 330
Communication clarity, 174

Community substance abuse
        program (CSAP), 257
Compassion, 175
Compliance, 208
Conduct disorders, 280, 289
Conflict avoidance, 208
Conjoint Family Therapy (Satir), 143
Consequences of alcohol/drug use,
        132t
Converting programs, 242
Co-occurring disorders
    adolescents, 289
    ASPD (See Antisocial
        personality disorder
        (ASPD))
    atypical depression, 272–73
    bipolar disorder, 274–76
    borderline personality disorder,
        283–85
    counseling, 305–7
    difficult patients, 304–5
    dsythymic disorder, 272
    family treatment, 308–9
    GAIN assessments, 289f
    mood-cycling disorder, 276
    narcissistic personality disorder,
        279, 285–286
    organic depression, 273–74
    statistics, 266–67
    treatment, 288–89, 290, 305–9
    treatment compliance
        (medications), 307–8
Cork, M., 187
Counseling, 300, 301, 303, 305–7,
        309, 310
Crack cocaine, 59, 93
Creativity, 255
Criminal justice problems, 128
Crisis-maker procrastinator, 210
Cross-tolerance, 68
Crystal methamphetamine, 62–63
CSAP (community substance abuse
        program), 257

D

Dalmane, 85t
Danaher, Brian G., 126
Darvon, 74
DBT (Dialectical behavior therapy),
        331

Defier procrastinator, 210
Delusion, 209
Delusionogen, 108
Demanders, 304
Demerol, 74
Denial
    antisocial personality disorder,
        280
    assessment, 126–27
    depression, 269–70
    families, and, 15
    recovery, 299
    resistance to change, 208–9
Dependent clingers, 304
Depressants. See Central nervous
        system (CNS) depressants
Depression, 271
    abandonment, 161
    ACA, 190
    atypical, 272–73
    case study, 271, 273
    denial, 269–70
    drugs, and, 34, 35
    organic, 273–74
    SAD, 35
    vegetative signs, 269
Depressive feelings, 268, 269
Depressive thinking patterns, 306–7
Designer drugs, 59–60
Developmental assets model,
        256–57, 257f
Developmental-genetic model of
        alcoholism, 31
Dharma, 209
Diagnostic criteria, 122
Dialectical behavior therapy (DBT),
        331
Difficult patients, 304–5
Dilaudid, 74
Discovery self, 300
Disease model of alcoholism, 27–30
Disengaged ACA, 190
Disengaged boundaries, 171
Disinhibition, 41
Disorders co-occurring with drug
        abuse. See Co-occurring
        disorders
Disqualifying the positive, 306
Distancers, 148t
Distorted family systems, 142

Distorted thoughts, 49
Distracters, 144
Distracting statements, 233
Disulfiram, 81
Donovan, James, 44
"Don't talk. Don't trust. Don't feel", 141
Doriden, 85t
Double binds, 284
Dreamer procrastinator, 210
Drinking and driving, 8–9
Driving
  alcohol, and, 8–9
  marijuana, and, 104
Drug absorption, 69f, 71, 72t, 73t
Drug abuse, 128–29, 136
Drug Abuse Prevention Research, 246
Drug distribution, 71–73
Drug elimination, 71–73
Drug problem
  academic failure, 14
  denial and minimization, alcohol/drug, 15
  racist approaches, 11–13
  socioeconomic inequities, 13
  U.S. federal government role, 11
Drugs and Drinking (Strack), 36
Drugs Demystified (Nowlis), 18
Drug-specific approaches, 242
Drug subculture theories, 51
Drug trafficking, 5, 11
Drug use
  athletes, 110–14
  boredom, 39–41
  effects of, 39, 39t
  impaired performance, 169
  impulsivity/disinhibition, 41
  medications (anti-psychotic drugs), 307–8
  power, 44–45
  seduction and sexuality, 46–47
  self-destruction, 45
  See also Alcohol/drug abuse
Drug withdrawal. *See* Withdrawal
Dry drunk, 140, 172
Dual disorders. *See* Co-occurring disorders
DuPont, Robert, 242
Dysfunctional family, 141, 143, 145
DZ twins, 31

E

Early parent-child attachment, 159–60
Ecstasy (MDMA), 64, 65t
ED (energy drinks), 61
Edgewalkers, 41
Educational system, 14
Eeyore syndrome, 271
Ego-self theory of substance dependence, 51
Ellis, Albert, 296
Embarrassment, 166
Emotional intelligence, 255
Emotional Intelligence (Goleman), 255
Empathy, 214
Empowerment, 247, 262
Enabling behavior, 147, 149
Energy drinks (ED), 61–62
Enger, Daniel, 61
Enmeshed boundaries, 171
Entitled family systems, 143
Erikson, Erik, 165
Eskabarb, 82t
Ethchlorvynol, 85t
Examples. *See* Case studies/vignettes
Excessive use, 125t
Existential boredom, 40
Existential theory, 46–47, 51
Experimentation, 124, 125t
Experimentation intervention, 225
Externalizing problems, 289

F

Family, 35–36
  adjustment to problem/stages of recovery, 149–51
  at-risk factors (*See* At-risk factors)
  denial, 15
  patterns of communication, 143–44
  prevention activities, 259
  risk factors, 39
  survival roles, 144–46
  system, as, 139–41, 146
Family cohesion, 174
Family disease, 36
Family disease model, 188
Family hero, 145

Family intervention, 230
Family mascot, 145
Family model, 35–36, 51
Family of origin, 210–11
Family, prevention activities, 259
Family Reconstruction Therapy: The Living Model (Wegscheider-Cruse), 144
Family rules, 141
Family scapegoat, 145
Family system
  alcoholic (*See* Adult children of alcoholics (ACA); Children of alcoholic families)
  ambiguous, 142
  distorted, 142–43
  dysfunctional *vs.* imbalance, 141
  entitled, 143
  overextended, 142
  rigid, 142
Family system roles, 144–49
Family Therapy of Drug Abuse and Addiction (Stanton), 45
Family Trap, The (Wegscheider-Cruse), 144
Family treatment, 301–2
FAS (fetal alcohol syndrome), 81
Fear of and Craving for Cocaine (Freud), 92
Feeling awareness, 194–97
Feeling diary, 197
Feeling stage (family recovery), 155
Fenichel, Otto, 43
Fetal alcohol syndrome (FAS), 81
Fifth perspective worksheet, 19
Fingernail polish removers, 106
Flashbacks, 98
Flexibility, 174–75
Flurazepam, 85t
Fossum, Merle, 164–66
FRAMES mnemonic, 214, 219f
Framo, James, 146
Fraternal twins, 31
Fraternity parties, 8
Freebase cocaine, 59, 93
Freud, Sigmund, 92, 165
Functional hypothesis, 160
Functional therapy group, 199–201
Future orientation, 47

G

GAIN assessments, 289
Gasoline, 67, 106
Gender
    inhalants, 67
    SMI, 268t
Generalized and blaming
        statements, 233
Genetic influence disease model, 29
Genetic model of alcoholism, 31
Gitlow, Stanley, 26
Glenn, Stephen, 247
Glue, 67
Glue sniffing, 104
Glutethimide, 85t
Goal setting, 247
*Going to Peaces Without Falling
        Apart* (Epstein), 209
Gold, Steven R., 50–51
Goleman, Daniel, 255
Goodstadt, Michael, 242
Goodwin, Donald W., 31
Gottman, John, 189
Greaves, George B., 51
Greenleaf, Jael, 194
Grief work, 197
Group psychotherapy, 199–201
Group therapy, 301
Guilt, 166, 167t

H

Habituation, 67–68
Haley, Jay, 146, 172
Half-truths, 127
Hallucinogens, 95–99
    adverse effects, 98–99
    classification, 97t
    defined, 95
    historical overview, 97–98
    major effects, 98
    routes of administration, 98
    set, setting, 69
    tolerance and dependence, 99
    usage, 98
HALTS mnemonic, 324–27
Harrison Narcotics Act, 75
Harvard School of Public Health
        Alcohol Survey, 8
Hashish, 99, 101

Hawkins, J. David, 251
Hayes, Steven, 331
Hay, Louise, 300
Health and physical well-being, 328
Healthy behaviors, associated
        factors, 252, 253t
*Healthy Communities-Healthy
        Youth programs,* 256
Helping Families to Change
        (Satir), 143
Hendin, Herbert, 52
Hennecke, Lynne, 26
Heroin
    cost, 66
    pregnancy, 77
    street names, 74
    usage, 66, 75
    See also Narcotic analgesics
Hesselbrook, V. M., 278, 279
Hicks, Thomas, 110
High school drug use trends,
        15–17
High traumatic stress (HTS), 27
Historical overview
    alcohol, 77–78
    cocaine, 91–92
    hallucinogens, 97–98
    inhalants, 105
    marijuana, 99–100
    narcotic analgesics, 74–75
Homeostasis, 25
Honeymoon stage, 298
Hopelessness, 47–48
HTS (high traumatic stress), 27
Humboldt County, 102
Humor, 255
Hunger, 325
Hypervigilance, 185
Hypomania, 276

I

Ice, 63
Identical twins, 31
Illusion of normalcy, 187
Illustrated examples. *See* Case
        studies/vignettes
Imbalance, 147
Impulsivity, 41, 281
impulsivity/disinhibition, 41
Independence, 244, 255

Inhalants, 67, 104–7
    adverse effects, 107
    available forms, 106
    classification, 105t
    gender, 67
    historical overview, 105
    long-term effects, 107
    major effects, 106, 106t
    route of administration, 105–6
    tolerance and dependence, 106–7
Inhalation of drugs, 72t
Initial contact, 124, 124t
Initial contact intervention, 224–25
Initiative, 255
Injection of drugs, 72t, 73t
Insight, 254
Intellectualizers, 144
Internalizing problems, 289
Interpersonal and social recovery
        support system, 328
Interpersonal boredom, 40
Interpersonal conflicts, 318, 319t
Interpersonal Problem Solving, 249
Intervention, 223–39
    adolescents, 230
    assessment, 231–32
    caring response as, 229
    case study, 232
    defined, 226
    dos/don'ts, 227–28t
    example, 235–38
    excessive use/addiction stage,
        226
    experimentation stage, 225
    family, 230
    goals, 230
    initial contact stage, 224–25
    integrated stage, 225
    nonuse stage, 224
    obstacles to, 226, 229t
    postintervention stage, 239
    preintervention stage, 232–35
    professional guidance, 229
    when to do it, 230
Intervention approaches, 229
Intervention services, 226
Intimate partner violence (IPV), 10
Intoxication (Siegal), 243
Intramuscular injection, 72t, 73t
Intravenous injection, 72t, 73t

Invasive boundary inadequacy, 171
IPV (intimate partner violence), 10

J

Jackson, Ron, 146
Jessor, Richard, 51
Johari window, 300, 300t
Johnson, Ben, 111
Johnson, Bruce D., 51
Johnson, Vernon, 226
Jones, Marion, 110
Journaling, 197
Jumping to conclusion, 306
"Just Say No" approach, 5

K

Kabat-Zinn, John, 331
Kaplan, Howard B, 51
Kaufman, Edward, 279
Kemadrin, 86
Kempher, Carol L., 169
Khantzian, Edward, 32, 34, 51
Kindling effect, 94
Korsakoff's psychosis, 81
Krystal, H., 44

L

Learned Optimism (Seligman), 49, 50t
Leary, Timothy, 96–97
Leisure time boredom, 40
Lerner, Harriet, 147
Leveling, 144
Lichtenstein, Edward, 126
Licit and Illicit Drugs (Brecher), 248
Licit and Illicit Drugs (Brecher), 12
Lidz, Theodore, 146
Life boredom, 40
Lifestyle imbalance, 304
Lighter fluids, 106
Liver disease, 81
Loney, Jan, 51
Lost child, 145, 147
LSD, 95–99
    See also Hallucinogens
Lukoff, Irving F., 52
Luminal, 82t

M

Major depression. *See* Depression
Major tranquilizers, 87t
Maladaptive motivational
        structure, 32
Mania, 276
Manic-depressive illness, 274
Manipulative help-rejectors, 304
Marijuana, 99–104
    adverse effects, 103
    case study, 46, 130
    driving, 104
    effects of, 39, 39t, 101–4
    historical overview, 99–100
    ingestion without smoking, 60
    legalization, 17f
    major effects, 101–2, 102t
    medical usage, 17, 60–61, 101
    potency, 102–3
    resurgence, 61
    routes of administration, 101
    street names, 99
    usage, 16, 101
Marijuana scare story, 3
Marlatt, Alan, 311, 312, 331, 332
Marriage, 189
Martin, William R., 52
Mason, Marilyn, 164–66
Masterson, James, 161, 162, 273, 284
Mathews, Walter M., 242
MBCT (Mindfulness-based
        cognitive therapy), 331
MBRP (Mindfulness-based relapse
        prevention), 332–33t
MBSR (Mindfulness-based stress
        reduction), 331
MDMA (Ecstasy), 64, 65t
Medical-health perspective, 18
Medical marijuana, 16–17, 60–61,
        101
Medications (anti-psychotic drugs),
        306–7
Meditation, 331
Mencken, H. L., 5
Mentor, 244
Meperidine, 74
Meprobamate, 87t
Mescaline, 96
Methadone, 74
Methamphetamine, 62–63, 90

Methaqualone, 85–86
Methyprylon, 85t
MI. *See* Motivational interviewing
        (MI)
Miller, Janet Y., 251
Miller, William, 207, 211
Mindful acceptance, 209
Mindfulness, 175–76
    addiction, 330
    definitions, 331
    MBRP, 332–33t, 333
    relapse prevention programs,
        333, 334
    12-step process, 330
Mindfulness-based cognitive
        therapy (MBCT), 331
Mindfulness-based relapse
        prevention (MBRP),
        332–33t
Mindfulness-based stress reduction
        (MBSR), 331
Minimization, 127, 208
Minor tranquilizers, 87t
Minuchin, Salvador, 146
Misra, Rajendra K., 52
Models and theories, 24–50
    achievement, anxiety
        andaddiction, 52
    addiction to pleasure, 52
    availability-pronenesstheory, 51
    CAP theory, 50–51
    disease model of alcoholism,
        27–30
    drug subculture theories, 51
    ego-self theory of
        substancedependence, 51
    existential theory, 46–47, 51
    family model, 35–36, 51
    genetic model of alcoholism, 31
    miscellaneous theories, 50–52
    personality-deficiency theory, 50
    problem-behavior theory, 51
    psychoanalytic meaning, 43–44
    psychoanalytic models, 43–44
    psychosocial theory, 52
    self-esteem and self-derogation
        theory, 51
    social learning theory, 41–42
    sociocultural models, 43
    tension-reduction theory, 25–26

Monitoring the Future (MTF) study, 15–17
Mood and affective disorders, 34–35, 268
  atypical depression, 272–73
  bipolar disorder, 274–76
  categories, 270–71
  depression (*See* Depression)
  depressive feelings, distinguished, 277
  dysthymic disorder, 271
  mood-cycling disorder, 276
  organic depression, 273–74
  suicide, 277
Mood cycling drugs, 308t
Morality, 244
Moral-legal perspective, 18
Motivational interviewing (MI), 211–20
  case study, 217–18
  client centered, 213–14
  defined, 207
  FRAMES, 214, 219f
  general principles, 214–15
  motivational strategies, 214
  OARS, 213t, 214
  reference books, 220–21
Motivational Interviewing (Miller/ Rollnick), 207
Motivational Interviewing with Adolescents and Young Adults (Naar-King/ Suarez), 220
Motivational strategies, 214
Motivation and change, 206–21
  ambivalence, 211
  cognitive/affective therapeutic themes, 211
  denial and delusion, 209
  exertion/effort, 209
  MI (*See* Motivational interviewing (MI))
  mindful acceptance, 209
  motivation, defined, 211
  procrastination, 209, 210
  resistance to change, 208–9
  spiral of change, 212f
Motrin, 74
Mourning, 197
MTF study, 15–17
MZ twins, 31

N

NACOA, 182
Naltrexone, 308
Naprosyn, 74
Narcissistic personality disorder, 33, 279, 285–86
Narcotic analgesics, 73–77
  hazards, 76
  heroin (*See* Heroin)
  historical overview, 74–75
  major effects, 75–76
  pregnancy, 77
  routes of administration, 75
  tolerance, 76
  withdrawal, 76–77
National Association for Children of Alcoholics (NACOA), 182
National Institute of Justice Survey on Sexual Assault on Campus, 8
National Institute on Drug Abuse (NIDA), 242, 243, 257
Negative emotional states, 303, 304
Negative labeling, 307
Negative parenting, 161t
Negative worldview, 50
Nembutal, 82, 82t
Neurotransmitters, 52
Nicotine withdrawal, 68t
NIDA, 242, 243, 257
Nixon, Richard, 4
Noctec, 85t
Noludar, 85t
Nonbarbiturates with barbiturate like action, 85t
Nonnarcotic analgesics, 74
Nonpsychoactive drugs, 73
Nonsteroidal anti-inflammatory drugs (NSAIDs), 74
Nonuse intervention, 224
Nowlis, Helen, 18
NSAIDs, 74

O

OARS mnemonic, 213t, 214
Obsessive focusing, 208
Obstacles to interventions, 226, 227t
Obstacles to reaching parents, 174

Older adults, 258–59
Online social support network (OSSN), 296
Opioids, 68t, 74t
Optimism, 49–50, 50t
Oral administration, 72t
OSSN (online social support network), 296
Overattachment, 191–92
Overdoer procrastinator, 210
Overextended family systems, 142
Overgeneralizing, 306
Overinvolvement hypothesis, 160
Overly rigid boundary inadequacy, 171
Overseparation, 191–92
Oxidation, 69
Oxycodone, 66
OxyContin, 66

P

Paint/paint thinners, 106
Panther mushroom, 96f
Papaver somniferum, 74
Paraldehyde, 85t
Parental competence, 174
Parental guidelines, 166, 167
Parental imbalance, 169–71
Parenting
  abandonment, 161–62
  at-risk behaviors (*See* At-risk factors)
  early parent-child attachment, 159–60
  influencing offspring's behavior, 173–74
  negative, 161t
  shame, 175
Passive-aggressive compliance, 208
Passivity, 282
Patterns of communication, 143–44
PCP, 107–10
  See also Phencyclidine (PCP)
PEACE mnemonic, 36
Peer pressure, 303
Pentobarbital, 82, 82t
Pento-secobarbital, 82t
Peoplemaking (Satir), 142
Percodan, 74
Perfectionist procrastinator, 210

Periodic excessive use, 125f
Peripheral neuritis, 81
Personality
    addictive, 31–32
    Cloninger's three dimensional
        model, 32
    defined, 277
    disorders, 31–32
Personality-deficiency theory, 50
Personality disorder, 277–88
    antisocial, 279–83
    borderline, 283–85
    case study, 33
    codependent, 190
    DSM-IV clusters, 278
    major feature, 280
    narcissistic, 285–86
    personality traits, distinguished,
        277–78
Personality traits, 277–78
Personalizing, 307
Perspective of hope, 20
Perspectives on drug use
    medical-health perspective, 18
    moral-legal perspective, 17–18
    psychological perspective, 18
    reader's personal perspective,
        19–20
    socio-cultural perspective, 19
Pessimism, 49–50, 50t
Peyote, 96
Phenacetin, 74
Phencyclidine (PCP), 107–10
    accidents, 109
    adverse effects, 109
    major effects, 108
    pregnancy, 109
    routes of administration, 108
    street names, 108
    tolerance and dependence, 110
    usage, 108
    violence, 109–10
Phenothiazines, 87t
Physical dependence, 67
Placaters, 143–44
Placidyl, 85t
Poor future orientation, 47
Poor self-concept, 36–39
Poppy plant, 74
Postintervention, 230

Post-traumatic stress disorder
        (PTSD), 27, 183–85
Power, 44–45
Powerlessness, 194
Pregnancy
    barbiturates, 83
    opiates, 77
    PCP, 109
Preintervention, 232–35
Prevention activities, 241–62
    adolescents, 243
    at-risk youth, 249–51
    capability development, 247–48
    college students, 258
    community needs, 248
    conceptual model, 256f
    consumer participation, 248
    converting programs, 242
    CSAPs, 257, 257f
    developmental assets model,
        256–57, 256f
    domains of prevention, 255, 256
    drug-specific approaches, 242
    early prevention approaches,
        241–43
    effectiveness, 249, 250t
    emotional intelligence, 255
    empowerment, 247
    family, and, 259
    goals, 243
    goal setting, 247
    long-term perspective, 248–49,
        250t
    older adults, 258–59
    people of color/minorities,
        257–59
    prevention approaches (1980s),
        245–46
    primary prevention, 243, 246
    promote proactivity, 248
    resiliency, 252–55
    SAODAP moratorium, 242, 243
    school-based prevention
        curricula, 246–47
    secondary prevention, 246
    tertiary prevention, 246
Primary drives, 24
Primary prevention, 243, 246
Private self, 300
Proactivity, 248

Problem-behavior theory, 51
Procrastination, 209, 210
Proctor, Dwayne, 6
Professional intervention assistance,
        229
Projection, 208
Pryor, Richard, 59
Psilocybe mushroom, 96f
Psychiatric medications, 308t
Psychic numbing, 183, 185
Psychoactive drugs, 73
    cannabis sativa, 99–104 (*See
        also* Marijuana)
    CNS depressants (*See* Central
        nervous system (CNS)
        depressants)
    CNS stimulants (*See* Central
        nervous system (CNS)
        stimulants)
    hallucinogens, 95–99
    inhalants, 67, 104–7
    narcotic analgesics, 73–77
    PCP, 107–10
Psychoanalytic meaning, 43–46
Psychoanalytic models. *See*
        Psychoanalytic meaning
Psychological dependence, 67, 68
Psychological perspective, 18
Psychological vulnerability, 32
Psychosocial theory, 52
Psychotherapy of Addicted Persons
        (Kaufman), 279
PTSD (post-traumatic stress
        disorder), 27
Public self, 300
Pursuers, 148t

Q

QPR Institute, 310n
Quaalude, 85t
Quantum change, 207
Quantum Change (Miller/C'de
        Baca), 207

R

Race and ethnicity
    drug problem, 11–13
    inhalants, 105
    prevention activities, 257–59

Raging and ragging, 152
Raleigh, Walter, 100
Rape, 8
Raskin, H. A., 44
"Rational-Emotive Behavior
        Therapy and Two Self-
        Help Alternatives to the
        12-Step Model"(Bishop),
        297
Rationalization, 127, 208
Rationalizing and accepting,
        150–51t
Rational recovery (RR), 296–97
Rawson, Richard, 124, 297
Reagan, Nancy, 5
Recapitulation, 200
Recommendations for Future
        Federal Activities in Drug
        Abuse Prevention, 243
Rectal administration, 72t
Reefer Madness, 4
Regressive behaviors, 281
Rejection sensitivity, 195
Relapse, 323
    analysis, 323, 324
    causes, 318
    definition, 322
    factors, 322t
    high rates, 317, 323
    interpersonal conflicts, 318, 319t
    negative emotional states, 318,
        319t
    recognition, signs and
        problems, 323
    recovery, 318
    risk factors, 318, 321t
    RP (*See* Relapse prevention
        (RP))
    social pressure, 318, 320t
    timing and severity, 321
    treatment causes, 321
    vulnerability (*See* Vulnerability
        to relapse)
Relapse prevention
    cravings and urges, 327–28
    HALTS, 324–27
    risk factors for relapse, 321t
    triggers, 327–28
Relapse prevention (RP), 126
    causes, 334

cognitive, emotional, and
        spiritual self, 328–29
    definition, 321–23
    health and physical well-being,
        328
    interpersonal and social recovery
        support system, 328
    mindfulness (*See* Mindfulness)
    reducing the severity, 329t
    serenity prayer of AA, 329–30
    See also Alcohol/drug recovery
REM sleep, 83
Resiliency, 50, 252–55
Resiliency factors, 254–55
Resilient actions, 254, 254f
*Resilient Self: How Survivors of
        Troubled Families Rise
        Above Adversity, The*
        (Wolin/Wolin), 252
Resistance to change, 208
Resolution stage (of recovery),
        297–99
Revolving-door relapse, 305
Right-wrong thinking, 306
Rigid family systems, 142
"Risk and Protective Factors
        for Alcohol and Other
        Drug Problems in
        Adolescence and Early
        Adulthood: Implications
        for Substance Abuse
        Prevention" (Hawkins
        et al.), 251
Risk behaviors, associated factors,
        251, 252t
Risk factors (substance abuse),
        251–52
Robinson, Paul, 38
Role model, 244
Role-playing, 233
Rolling with resistance, 219
Rollnick, Stephen, 211
Routes of administration, 69
    amphetamines, 90
    barbiturates, 83
    cocaine, 92–93
    hallucinogens, 98
    inhalants, 104–5
    injection, 73t
    marijuana, 101

methods of absorption, 72t
    narcotic analgesics, 75
    PCP, 108
    tranquilizers, 87
RR (rational recovery), 296–97
Rush, Benjamin, 78

S

SAD (seasonal affective disorder),
        35
SAODAP moratorium, 243
Satir's family patterns of
        communication, 143–44
Satir, Virginia, 139, 141
Scare tactics, 3, 241, 242
School-based prevention curricula,
        246–48
Schorr, Lizbeth, 13
Seasonal affective disorder (SAD),
        35
Secobarbital, 82, 82t
Seconal, 82, 82t
Secondary prevention, 246
Sedating antihistamines, 87t
Segal, Zindel, 331
Selective serotonin reuptake
        inhibitors (SSRIs), 307
Self, 305
    See also Sense of self
Self-centeredness, 281
Self-compassion, 175–76
Self-concept, 37
Self-criticism, 175–76
Self-destructive deniers, 305
Self-destructiveness, 45
Self-esteem and self-derogation
        theory, 51
Self-help meetings, 294–95, 303
    See also Alcoholics Anonymous
        (AA)
Seligman, Martin, 49, 50t
Sense of humor, 303
Sense of self, 37–39, 303
Separation stress, 160
Serenity prayer (AA), 209
Serious mental illness (SMI),
        266–68, 268t
    See also Co-occurring disorders
Set, 69, 123–24
Setting, 69, 123–24

Sexual assault, 8
Shame, 164–69
    affect-shame binds, 168t
    drugs/sex, and, 169
    embarrassment, contrasted, 166
    feelings, and, 168–69
    Freud, 165
    guilt, compared, 166–67, 167t
    overview, 167t
    recovery, and, 304
    sexual identity, 168–69
    sexual violation, 169
Shame-based system, 165t
Shameful experiences, 164t
Shoe polish, 67
Siegal, Ronald, 243
Silence, 133, 296, 307
Skin patches, 72t
Skin popping, 75
Sleep, 83
Small Book, The (Trimpey), 296
Smart, Reginald G., 51
SMI, 266–68, 268t
    See also Co-occurring disorders
Smith, David, 70, 89, 122
Smokeless tobacco, 114
Sobering up, 80
Social competencies, 262
Socializing, 200
Social learning theory, 41–42
Social pressure, 304
Sociocultural models, 43
Socio-cultural perspective, 19
Socioeconomic inequities, 13
Sopor, 85t
Special Action Office on Drug Abuse
        Prevention (SAODAP)
        moratorium, 243
SSD (sudden sniffing death
        syndrome), 107
SSRIs (selective serotonin reuptake
        inhibitors), 307
Stages of alcohol/drug abuse,
        123–26
    addiction, 124–25
    excessive use, 125t
    experimentation, 124
    initial contact, 124, 125t
    integrated use, 125f
    overview, 125f

Stages of grieving (family recovery)
    acceptance, 155
    anger, 152–53
    bargaining, 153–55
    denial, 151–52
    feeling, 155
Stanton, M. Duncan, 45, 51
Steffenhagen, R. A., 51
Steinglass, Peter, 301, 302
Steroids, 110–12
Stimulants. See Central nervous
        system (CNS) stimulants
Stimulus augmenters, 26
Stimulus moderators, 26
Stimulus reducers, 26
Strack, Jay, 36
Street names
    amphetamines, 89–90
    barbiturates, 82t
    cocaine, 92
    crystal meth, 62
    heroin, 74
    LSD, 96–97
    marijuana, 99
    MDMA, 64
    mescaline, 96
    methaqualone, 85
    PCP, 108
    peyote, 96
Stress, 26, 303
Structure, 302
Struggle for Intimacy (Woititz), 193
Subcutaneous injection, 72t, 73t
Suboxone, 308
Substance abuse, 122
Substance abuse prevention. See
        Prevention activities
Substance dependence, 123
Substance-induced disorders, 122
Substance intoxication, 122
Substance-related disorders, 122
Substance-use disorders, 122
Success, 49
Sudden sniffing death syndrome
        (SSD), 107
Suicide
    affective disorders, 277, 309
    assessment questions, 131
    behavioral clues, 311, 312–13t
    case study, 134

    counseling, 310t
    dos/dont's, 311, 313
    factoids, 133t, 310
    motivation for, 311
    situational clues, 312t
    verbal clues, 312t
Sunday syndrome of amphetamine
        use, 113
Support, 261
SUPPORTbuddy.org, 296
Survival roles, 144–46
Survivor guilt, 185
Survivor's pride, 253
Synergism, 68
Synthetically produced drugs, 59

T

Taking over responsibilities, 150t
Temperament, 162–63
Tension, 26
Tension-reduction theory (TRT),
        25–26
Tertiary prevention, 246
Tetrahydrocannabinol (THC), 99,
        101
THC, 99, 101
Theories. See Models and
        theories
Therapy groups, 301
Thinking small, 20
Thioxanthenes, 87t
3Cs of addiction, 71, 122
Three-dimensional model of
        personality, 32
Three Ps of pessimism, 49
"Time to Purge Binge Drinking
        Is Now, The" (Proctor), 6
Tiredness, 326
Tobacco, 68t, 95
Todman, McWelling, 40
Tolerance
    barbiturates, 83–84
    cocaine, 94
    defined, 68
    hallucinogens, 99
    inhalants, 106–7
    narcotic analgesics, 76
    PCP, 110
    tranquilizers, 88
Tour de France, 110

Toward a National Strategy for Primary Drug Abuse Prevention, 242
Traits and temperament, 162–63
Tranquilizers, 86–89
    alcoholics/addicts, 88–89
    classification, 87t
    dependence, 88
    major effects, 88
    medical uses, 87
    routes of administration, 87
    tolerance, 88
    usage, 87
    withdrawals, 88
Trauma
    adolescents, 286, 288
    case study, 28
    defined, 26
    substance abuse disorders, 26–27
Traumatic stressors, 27
Trial-and-error approach, 152
Triangulation, 172
Triggers, 327–28
Trimpey, Jack, 296
TRT (tension-reduction theory), 25–26
Tuinal, 82t
Twelve steps (AA), 30t

U

Underfunctioners, 148t
Universality, 199

Universities. *See* Colleges/universities
Urge surfing, 333

V

Verbalizing and communicating, 197
Vignettes. *See* Case studies/ vignettes
Violence
    alcohol-related, 10f
    IPV, 10
    PCP, 110
    sexual assault/rape, 8
Vulnerability to relapse
    cravings and urges, 327–28
    HALTS, 334–36

W

Wall stage, 298
War on drugs, 4, 5
Washington, George, 100
Washton, Arnold, 131
Wegscheider-Cruse's family system survival roles, 144–47
Wernicke's encephalopathy, 81
Wesson, Donald, 59, 89
When Things Fall Apart (Chodron), 174, 209
Whippets, 67
Whitaker, Carl, 139
White, Burton, 174
Why Marriages Fail (Gottman), 189

Wilson, Bill, 208
Withdrawal
    alcohol, 68t
    amphetamines, 91
    barbiturates, 85, 85t
    cocaine, 68t, 94
    defined, 67
    diagnostic criteria, 123
    narcotic analgesics, 76–77
    nicotine, 68t
    opioids, 68t
    tranquilizers, 88
Withdrawal stage (of recovery), 298
Within Our Reach: Breaking the Cycle of Disadvantage (Schorr), 13
Woititz, Janet Geringer, 193
Wolin, Steven, 262–65
Wolin, Sybil, 262–65
Woolsey, Conrad, 61
Words of My Perfect Teacher, The (Rinpoche), 173
Workaholism, 303
Worrier procrastinator, 210
Wright, Hamilton, 12
Wurmser, Leon, 44, 51
Wynne, Lieman, 145

Y

Yalom, Irvin D., 199
Yapko, Michael, 47
"Yellow peril", 12